OPEC AND THE THIRD WORLD

OPEC and the Third World

THE POLITICS OF AID

SHIREEN HUNTER

INDIANA UNIVERSITY PRESS
Bloomington

Manufactured in Great Britain

Library of Congress Cataloging in Publication Data

Hunter, Shireen T.
OPEC and the Third World.
Bibliography: p. 294.
1. Economic assistance – Political aspects. 2. Developing countries – Foreign economic relations. 3. Organization of Petroleum Exporting Countries. I. Title.
II. Title: O.P.E.C. and the Third World.
HC60.H868 1984 338.91'09172'4 84-47812
ISBN 0-253-34249-X
1 2 3 4 5 88 87 86 85 84

CONTENTS

To the memory of my parents, Reza and Azra

TABLES

ABBREVIATIONS

ADB	African Development Bank
ADFAED	Abu Dhabi Fund for Arab Economic Development
AFESD	Arab Fund for Economic and Social Development
AMF	Arab Monetary Fund
BADEA	Arab Bank for Economic Development in Africa (French acronym)
CDB	Caribbean Development Bank
CIEC	Conference on International Economic Cooperation
CMEA	Council for Mutual Economic Assistance
DAC	Development Assistance Committee
ECDC	Economic Cooperation Among Developing Countries
IBRD	International Bank for Reconstruction and Development
IDA	International Development Association
IDB	Inter-American Development Bank
IFAD	International Fund for Agricultural Development
IFED	Iraqi Fund for External Development
IMF	International Monetary Fund
IsDB	Islamic Development Bank
KFAED	Kuwait Fund for Arab Economic Development
MEED	Middle East Economic Digest
MEES	Middle East Economic Survey
NIEO	New International Economic Order
OAPEC	Organisation of Arab Petroleum Exporting Countries
ODA	Official Development Assistance
OECD	Organisation for Economic Cooperation and Development
OPEC	Organisation of Petroleum Exporting Countries
PDRY	Peoples Democratic Republic of Yemen
RCD	Regional Cooperation for Development
SAMA	Saudi Arabian Monetary Agency
SFD	Saudi Fund for Development
TCDC	Technical Cooperation Among Developing Countries
UAE	United Arab Emirates
UNCDF	United Nations Capital Development Fund
UNCTAD	United Nations Conference on Trade and Development
UNDP	United Nations Development Programme
UNRWA	United Nations Relief and Works Agency
UNSF	United Nations Special Fund
YAR	Yemen Arab Republic

PREFACE

The phenomenon of OPEC aid has been one of the most important developments in the history both of the Third World and of development assistance.

The OPEC states have been the only group of developing countries – suffering from severe economic, technological, social, and political deficiencies – which have subsequently acquired financial resources of such size that they could assist other less-fortunate developing countries. They have stood out among the few developing countries that have managed to increase their impact on international economic, financial, and political relations.

This development acquired special significance because it occurred at a time of growing Third World questioning about the nature, functioning and justice of the international economic system. It was a time of increasing Third World demands for the reform and restructuring of the international system in order to eliminate or reduce its discriminatory aspects. Likewise, this was a time of profound questioning about the old development theories, the role of foreign aid, the structure and performance of the principal international development and financial institutions, and their overall contributions to Third World development. Meanwhile, new development theories were being advanced that, among other things, emphasised the importance both of closer cooperation among Third World countries and of collective self-reliance.

Against this background, the OPEC countries declared their support for Third World efforts to begin a process of structural reform of the international economic system. They also committed themselves to use their financial assets, especially in the form of foreign aid, to achieve Third World development aims.

Because of this unique development in the Third World, an analysis of the OPEC countries' experience with foreign aid is important as a study in developing-country behaviour. Among other objectives, it can help to determine the degree to which common Third World goals affected the behaviour of OPEC members in practice; it can establish both the similarities and the differences in their behaviour as compared with that of the developed countries; and it can illustrate the difficulties faced by developing countries in trying to act upon the international system and to achieve their own national objectives.

This study was originally undertaken in partial fulfilment of the requirements of the PhD programme (Doctorat Des Sciences Politiques) at the Institut Universitaire Des Hautes Etudes Internationales in Geneva.

I am deeply indebted to Professor Harish Kapur for his valuable advice, overall guidance and wise counsel during the course of my research and writing.

In preparing this study, I interviewed many people and drew on their expertise, firsthand experience, and insight. I also benefited from the resources of many national and international aid organisations. To try thanking them all by name would be an imposing task. I thus wish to express my gratitude, in general, to everyone who was helpful; they will recognise their contributions in many pages of this work.

However, I especially want to thank Ms Parvaneh Khosropour of the Joint Library of the IBRD and IMF in Washington, DC, for her invaluable assistance in identifying and locating vital and hard-to-find research materials. I also wish to thank the Information Service of the OECD in Paris and the Secretariat of the OPEC Fund in Vienna for providing me with a regular supply of their published materials. Last but not least, I want to thank my husband, Robert Hunter, for his patience, moral support, and valuable critique of this study throughout its preparation.

Of course, responsibility for facts presented and judgements made in this study is mine alone.

INTRODUCTION

On 6 October 1973, during the Arab-Israeli war, a group of Arab countries – members of the Organisation of Petroleum Exporting Countries (OPEC) – imposed an embargo on the shipment of oil to Western industrialised countries as part of an Arab strategy of confrontation with their long-standing enemy, Israel.* Then, taking advantage of the situation created by the war, the ministers of six Persian Gulf countries, meeting in Kuwait on 16 October, decided henceforth to set oil prices unilaterally, thus in practice substituting legislation for the prior practice of negotiating these prices with oil companies. The two events were not coincidental. Both reflected awareness within OPEC states of their new power on the global scene – power both political and economic.

Following these actions, average global oil prices (based on the benchmark price of Arabian light crude) jumped from $3.01 per barrel in October 1973 to $11.65 that December, followed by further price increases in 1974. As a result of these price increases, there was a considerable transfer of financial resources from both developed and Third World countries to the members of OPEC. In turn, these new financial resources provided OPEC members with the means to embark simultaneously on rapid economic development and military build-up. Moreover, the accumulation of large monetary assets in the hands of a number of OPEC countries made them potentially capable of having a significant impact on international financial markets through the use of these assets.

At the same time, the Arab oil embargo of 1973 graphically illustrated the vulnerability of the developed world's sources of energy supplies to disruptive political action, creating great stress and even panic among energy-deficient industrialised countries, including West European states, Japan, and – to a lesser extent – the United States. The combined effect of these developments was a tremendous increase in the OPEC countries' economic and political influence on the international scene. Thus countries that had so far largely been at the periphery of the international scene became active participants and

* This decision was technically taken by the Organisation of Arab Petroleum Exporting Countries (OAPEC).

sometimes even occupied centre stage.

However, OPEC's gains were not without associated costs. In fact, higher oil prices prompted by OPEC's action contributed considerably to a global economic slowdown. As is so often the case, the Third World countries – particularly the poorest among them – were the principal victims of this slowdown, since they not only had to pay higher oil prices, but also saw their export earnings suffer because of the economic slump in the industrialised world that was caused partly by OPEC's price increases.

Yet despite these hardships, among Third World countries there was an acute sense of new possibilities created by OPEC's actions – possibilities for positive and strong actions to improve their long-term prospects. Thus, for example, for a period of time these countries were hopeful that the Third World, strengthened by OPEC's new wealth and influence, would be able to take good advantage of the developed countries' new sense of vulnerability and would successfully pressure them to make significant concessions on a whole range of issues vital to the Third World's future well-being. Third World countries were also hopeful that a new type of partnership – different from traditional relationships between donors and recipients of aid – would develop between themselves and OPEC. They hoped that this partnership would ultimately lead to a large influx of OPEC capital into their economies, followed by increased trade and closer economic interaction, culminating in more development and prosperity for all.

Therefore, as a result both of hardships suffered by the Third World countries and of expectations aroused among them by OPEC's action, OPEC countries gained – though inadvertently – new responsibilities towards Third World countries, and particularly towards the poorest among them.

However, OPEC's responsibilities towards the Third World had deeper roots, stemming principally from the fact that OPEC members were themselves developing countries facing many of the problems of underdevelopment. Moreover, since its inception OPEC had justified its actions on oil pricing and ownership within the context of global efforts to improve conditions in the developing countries, by – among other measures – changing and reforming the negative and damaging aspects of the existing international economic system. In sum, OPEC's responsibilities towards the Third World derived not just from injury caused or expectations aroused, but also from a sense of shared interests and of solidarity with it – proclaimed or real.

In more specific terms, these responsibilities were widely characterised as existing in two forms:

(1) the need to help bring about a deep structural reform in the international economic system; and
(2) the need to help developing countries cope with new problems caused by oil price increases, and to assist them in their development efforts through massive financial aid and other forms of economic cooperation.

Indeed, OPEC countries did help in both regards. Partly as a result of OPEC's efforts, a global debate opened on the reform of the international economic order – debate both within the context of the United Nations and in smaller gatherings like the Conference on International Economic Cooperation (CIEC) and semi-governmental/academic groups like the Brandt Commission.

OPEC countries also began to provide considerable sums of money in foreign aid and created a whole range of new national, regional and international development institutions. In addition, trade and other economic relations were expanded between OPEC members and a number of developing countries, resulting – for example – in a higher level of mobility for capital and labour.

Yet after ten years, OPEC's performance in all these respects has fallen short of the expectations generated by its early declarations and behaviour. In fact, in all respects the OPEC countries have failed to act in ways that could have helped it achieve at least some of their stated goals. As a result, global negotiations on reform of the international economic system are at a standstill with no prospects for their early revitalisation, and the present international economic order is still heavily biased against the interests of the Third World, again with no signs of an early change. Quite the contrary, with persisting economic problems in the developed world, there are signs (for example, growing protectionism among the industrialised states and the falling level of economic aid) that these biases could become even more pronounced in the future, and the level of foreign aid provided by OPEC countries has hardly begun to offset the impact of higher oil prices on poorer developing countries.

Moreover, the kind of new and close partnership between OPEC and the Third World initially hoped for by the latter has also not materialised. Thus, although trade and economic cooperation between the OPEC countries and the Third World have expanded, they have been limited to a few countries and to a few areas of economic activity.

Likewise, OPEC's performance in the fields of development aid and transfer of capital have fallen short of Third World expectations. In this respect, too, the future does not hold much promise. In fact, OPEC's future seems uncertain in view of changed oil markets and conflict within the organisation. Thus, not only do OPEC surpluses no longer exist, but also many OPEC countries are scrambling to sell oil at concessionary prices in order to survive economically. Consequently, they are no longer able or willing to focus on the problems of the Third World.

It is very difficult to predict the future outlook for OPEC's position in the global energy market or for its monetary assets, and thus for the level of its international influence. Yet in view of the changes that have occurred in the last several years, including efforts in energy production and conservation by the industrial states, it seems unlikely that OPEC will regain the influential position it held during the early and mid-1970s.

Thus while the future is unpredictable, the historical record is there to be examined. Using this record, it is the aim of this study to find an answer to the question why the OPEC countries failed to achieve the goals that they – in conjunction with other Third World countries – set for themselves, by focusing on the use of foreign aid by the members of OPEC.

Organisational Framework

In order to substantiate the thesis outlined above, this study will focus on the use of aid by OPEC members. By describing and analysing *how*, *for what purposes*, and *why* the OPEC countries have used aid, this study will try to provide at least a partial answer to the broader question of why the OPEC countries have failed to advance Third World objectives. In so doing, this study will concentrate on describing and analysing five distinct areas, leading to significant conclusions about the overall phenomenon of OPEC aid. The areas chosen have been put in a logical order so as to lead to the central thesis of this study.

The first chapter proposes to set the scene, by discussing both OPEC's own history and the history of the developing countries' efforts to reform the international economic system in order to make it more responsive to their own needs. This chapter will focus particularly on OPEC's composition and development to determine whether it was capable as an institution of unified action on a continuing basis to achieve its goals. If the result of this analysis is not an unqualified 'yes', then what did that situation imply for OPEC's capacity for unified action on behalf of Third World countries? Should not the answer to OPEC's failure to some extent be found in the fragmented nature of the organisation itself? This chapter will also explore the assumption that there was indeed a community of interest between OPEC and the Third World countries. And if this assumption was incorrect, what were the implications in terms of OPEC's actions?

Chapter 2 will provide the framework for OPEC actions: the *why* of aid programmes, set within a broad context of foreign, security, and economic policies. It will include discussion of the following questions, among others: How consistent were OPEC-country motives with the organisation's declared objectives in granting aid? To what extent were these motives influenced by the needs – security, political, and economic – of the OPEC countries? To what extent did the internal political structure of these countries, their resource bases beyond oil, and the geo-strategic contexts within which they had to operate affect their aid performance? In addition, did the OPEC countries use aid as an instrument of security and foreign policy and – if so – how effective was it? What was the impact of OPEC aid on recipient countries in terms of their political or economic dependence on OPEC and their capacity for independent action? In sum, what were the *politics* of OPEC's aid?

Chapter 3 will focus on case studies of two countries – Iran and Saudi Arabia – analysing in greater detail the impact of the above-mentioned factors in determining their respective aid policies. Saudi Arabia and Iran were logical choices for this detailed analysis, since they have been representative of two different types of OPEC members: those with high absorptive capacity, relatively low oil reserves, and little or no monetary surpluses; and those with low absorptive capacity, large oil reserves, and large monetary surpluses.

Moreover, Saudi Arabia and Iran reflect other intra-OPEC conflicts, particularly those emanating from divergent ethnic and national aspirations and competition for regional superiority. In addition, differences between Saudi Arabia and Iran regarding the respective mixes of their available instruments of national policy – and the place of aid within these instruments – make for an interesting and enlightening comparative study of the use of aid by OPEC members.

Chapter 4 will explore a range of elements, in order to provide a means for understanding the *what* of OPEC aid programmes in terms of the basic questions underlying this study. Key issues will include the following: the volume of OPEC aid, its geographic distribution and level of concessionality; the composition of aid (financial, commodity, and technical); and the balance between tied and untied aid. What were the criteria used by OPEC countries to choose principal recipients of their aid? Was OPEC aid given on an *ad hoc* basis or through long-term aid relationships, taking into account the long-term developmental needs of recipients? Did OPEC countries promote any particular development philosophies? Were they receptive to alternative theories of development? How far – if at all – did OPEC countries try to fashion their aid to help achieve developing-country goals such as reform of the international economic order? And if OPEC countries failed to do so, why was that true? In sum, what was the *nature* of OPEC aid?

Chapter 5 is important in assessing particular means of dispersing aid which had an impact on basic questions of its orientation and effectiveness. It will explore the following key questions, among others: What were the factors that affected OPEC's choice of channels for aid? Did all OPEC countries prefer the same channels or were there differences among them and – if so – what were the reasons for the differences? What were the implication's of OPEC's choices here for achieving developing-country goals, including that of reforming the international economic order?

The sixth and concluding chapter will synthesise different factors that have made OPEC aid what it is. This chapter will also demonstrate how the interaction of these factors tended to strengthen the divisive elements both within OPEC and between OPEC and the rest of the Third World, thus preventing OPEC from using aid principally to advance Third World objectives. Further, this chapter will make some general comparative remarks regarding OPEC aid and that of the developed countries that belong to the Development Assistance Committee (DAC) of the Organisation for Economic Cooperation and Development (OECD) – and where appropriate with that of CMEA. Finally, this chapter will draw some general conclusions from OPEC's aid experience for the future pattern of OPEC-Third World relations.

Methodology

The methodological tools used in this study are essentially historical, analytical, and to some extent comparative. The methodology used in this study is also relatively simple and consists of the following three stages:

(a) conceptualisation of traditional patterns of aid, including the relationship between aid and development;
(b) investigation, through the use of a wide range of information and data, of whether the OPEC countries followed the same pattern; and
(c) the drawing of some general conclusions, including a brief comparative analysis of OPEC aid and that extended by the developed countries belonging to the DAC.

Sources

The extensive research underlying this study has been based on a wide variety of source material. Apart from the general literature that is available on the subject, the documents published by OPEC and by the OPEC Special Fund – now the OPEC Fund for International Development – were the main documentary sources for this study.

Among the documents published by OPEC, in addition to periodical OPEC publications such as the OPEC Bulletin and OPEC Review, particularly useful were the annual reports of the OPEC Fund and the occasional papers and studies published by the Fund on aid and other issues related to OPEC-Third World relations.

The second most important documentary source was the annual reports of the development institutions created by the OPEC members.

Also of considerable use were certain publications of the United Nations Conference on Trade and Development, the World Bank – including annual reports and the World Development Report – and the annual reports of the International Monetary Fund and the regional development banks.

Concerning the statistical data used in this study, in so far as aid figures are concerned, the annual reports of the Development Assistance Committee of the OECD were principally relied upon, in view of the fact that reliable data from Third World sources were relatively unavailable, and also to facilitate comparative study of aid figures. However, whenever possible these data were complemented by those available from other sources – including the OPEC Fund and UNCTAD. Also, such statistical sources as the United Nations Yearbook of International Trade Statistics and certain publications of the International Labor Office were used when necessary.

In addition to the foregoing sources, in view of the contemporary nature of this study and the paucity of available published data on certain vital aspects of the subject, extensive use was made of personal interviews – many on a not-for-attribution basis – with officials of international and OPEC organisations directly involved with the aid issue, as well as interviews with academics and other experts having long experience in the OPEC countries.

These interviews were particularly important in clarifying critical aspects of vital questions where available published data are inadequate. They have also been invaluable in helping to make sense of discrepancies between declaratory policies of OPEC states and their actions.

1 HISTORICAL FRAMEWORK

I The Genesis of OPEC

As is so often the case with a major historical event, the creation of the Organisation of Petroleum Exporting Countries was prompted by two sets of factors: those related to events occurring in the immediate past, and those connected with more deeply rooted forces that had shaped the pattern of international relations since the end of the Second World War.

The immediate factors were the two unilateral and arbitrary reductions of oil prices by the international oil companies in February 1959 and August 1960. These price reductions had a determining effect on the creation of OPEC by galvanising the oil producers to take action to counter the erosion of their economic position. Yet at the same time, the establishment of an association of oil producers would not have been possible if certain developments had not taken place within both these and other developing countries. Likewise, the emergence of new ideas and concepts regarding international economic relations, the relationship between developing and industrialised countries, and factors stimulating cooperation among developing countries all contributed to OPEC's establishment.

International Factors

In the world that developed following the end of the Second World War, nationalism emerged as the main force animating Afro-Asian and Latin American countries. This rising nationalism – as developed over the years – has had diverse manifestations, of which the political and economic aspects have had the most far-reaching effect on the development of international political and economic relations. On the political level, the objectives of emerging Third World nationalism were to end colonial domination, to take charge of their own destinies, and to play a more effective role in global affairs – particularly in those matters that directly affected their vital interests.

On the economic level, their goals were to generate and encourage international cooperation in the field of development assistance, and to establish their sovereign rights over their natural resources. For several reasons, the oil producing countries in time came to play a major role in advancing these objectives, particularly in economics.

First, a number of major oil producing countries – such as Iran and Venezuela – had been independent countries even at the beginning of the post-war era of rapid decolonisation, although they continued to be subjected to varying degrees of foreign influence and manipulation. Yet this relative independence meant that these countries could shift their focus from political liberation and the struggle for independence to economic independence. Second, the visibility of their oil industries – as the only developed sectors of their economies – inevitably made them the focus of their emerging nationalism, and thus gave rise to the phenomenon of oil nationalism. Third, a growing number of oil experts in these countries – or oil technocrats, as they were called – used their expertise to advance the nationalistic aims of their respective countries – a process that finally led to the setting up of OPEC.

The potential role of the oil producing countries as a harbinger of broader economic developments in the Third World was graphically illustrated by Iran's decision in 1951 to nationalise its oil industry – though the importance of this act was imperfectly understood at the time. This was indeed a dramatic crystalisation of a trend which had been gradually gathering strength and was to gain even more. A year later, the UN General Assembly began to take cognisance of this trend in a broader sphere. In its seventh session, the United Nations General Assembly passed the first resolution recognising the right of the developing nations to exploit freely their natural wealth and resources. The language of the resolution was tame compared to later UN documents, such as *The Charter of the Economic Rights and Duties of States*, but this fact did not reduce its significance. Of course, it is not possible to prove a cause and effect relationship between Iranian oil nationalisation and the passage of this resolution, yet the fact remains that both acts were manifestations of the same trend.

In the years that followed, the oil producers and other Third World countries became more interactive, and thus their efforts gradually came to reinforce one another. For instance, when in the early 1950s the terms of trade of the Third World countries started to deteriorate, this development generated a debate among these states on the need to find remedial measures. The oil producing countries were among the first victims of this trend, although their situation was somewhat different from that of other developing countries, given the special characteristics of the international oil market. It was natural, therefore, that the oil producers were in the forefront of efforts by raw material producers to gain some real influence over market forces, and also that after the founding of OPEC its members should use the argument of deteriorating terms of trade as justification for their actions.[1]

OPEC was created in 1960 and – in a development analogous to what had happened a decade earlier with Iran's nationalisation of oil industries – the UN again took a significant step forward on behalf of developing countries in general. In 1962, the UN General Assembly passed Resolution 1803 (XVII), recognising permanent sovereignty of states over their natural resources. Then in 1964, the first United Nations Conference on Trade and Development (UNCTAD) was held in Geneva. Again, although it is not easy to establish a cause and effect relationship between the creation of OPEC and these succeeding developments, the trend was evident.

It was also clear that the creation of OPEC did much to intensify the need felt among Third World countries for closer cooperation in order to achieve their political and economic objectives. Yet at the same time, OPEC to a certain extent owed its own existence to the cooperative trends that had emerged in the Third World and were manifested in such events as the Bandung Conference of Afro-Asian Countries in 1955.

The focus of these early efforts was mainly political – aimed at mitigating the effects of the polarisation of the world political system and the Cold War. But during the 1960s, as the Cold War subsided and the world started to move towards a more diffuse system of power relations – and as the process of decolonisation neared completion – the focus of Third World cooperation shifted towards economic issues. Already in 1962, a large number of developing countries held a conference in Cairo on the problems of development. Later, with the establishment of UNCTAD (1964) and the emergence of the so-called Group of 77, Third World cooperative efforts became more focused and semi-institutionalised.

Since then, the OPEC countries have continued to interact with other Third World countries and, although economic changes within the developing countries have introduced more complexity into OPEC-developing country relations, they continue to do so. In fact, some OPEC members have at times seen their membership as a way of contributing to general Third World efforts to affect the evolution of international economic relations in directions most responsive to their needs.[2]

In addition to general international factors, developments in the countries of the Arab Middle East – particularly the re-emergence after the Second World War of ideas regarding Arab unity and the role assigned to oil in its achievement – also played a part in speeding up the process that finally led to the creation of OPEC. It is interesting to note, however, that as the goal of Arab unity proved to be elusive, so – despite early intra-Arab efforts at cooperation in oil matters – the creation of OPEC was only made possible by the Arab oil producers' moving *away* from such ideals. Intra-Arab divergences and the existence at the time of two major non-Arab oil producers – namely Iran and Venezuela – made this inevitable as oil politics and Arab politics failed to mesh sufficiently.

Conflicting Views of Oil

Early attempts at cooperation among oil producing countries had begun as early as 1945. Given the fact that some Arab countries were major oil producers, 'The Arab League entertained the idea of creating a petroleum association of Arab countries . . .'; but it soon became clear that 'to be efficacious, the association envisaged had to include the non-Arab large exporters of petroleum, notably Iran and Venezuela'.[3]

Furthermore, divergences among Arab countries regarding their economic, political, and ideological priorities made very difficult the reaching of a consensus on the form, scope, and objectives of such an association. The most fundamental division among the League's members was that between the oil producers and the other Arab countries.

The League's major concern since its creation, and in particular since the 1948 Arab defeat in Palestine, has been the defence of the sovereignty and territorial integrity of Arab states. Therefore, it has tried to organise and coordinate defence efforts of the Arab states. Even economic cooperation was designed first and foremost to strengthen the Arabs' defensive capabilities by harnessing all their natural and human resources.

Given this frame of mind, it was thus natural for the Arab League to view oil – the most important natural resource in the Arab world – as 'essentially a strategic instrument of defence', and to see the coordination of Arab oil policies as a means for countering and, if possible, of frustrating Israeli expansion into neighbouring Arab territories.[4]

Also, despite the fact that the League's objectives fell short of the ideal of Arab unity, Pan-Arabist feelings were strong among its members. According to Pan-Arabist philosophy, oil was a wealth that belonged to the whole of the Arab nation and thus should serve its needs. On the economic level, this meant that oil wealth should be distributed among all Arab peoples and that a coordinated Arab oil policy was the most efficient way of achieving this goal. In fact, some advocates of this approach went as far as to make the achievement of Arab unity contingent upon the more equitable distribution of oil wealth among the Arab peoples. For example, Emile Bustani, the well-known Lebanese statesman who was one of the most ardent and outspoken defendants of this approach, said that:

> Until the non-oil producing states are allowed to benefit proportionately from the wealth accruing from Arab oil, there could be no settled progress in the Arab world, and Arab unity, even though inevitable, will remain far distant. The well-being of the Arabs tomorrow depends almost entirely upon some sensible re-allocation of oil wealth today.[5]

The non-producers – the so-called 'transit countries' through whose territories or ports part of the Arab oil was exported – had special grievances against the oil producers. To quote Bustani again, they considered that: 'The transit countries, without whose cooperation Arab oil could never reach the Western market in its present abundance, should be enabled to profit from the ever-expanding business to a much greater extent than they do today.'[6] Likewise, the Syrian position on what should constitute a unified Arab oil policy reflected its own particular interest as a transit country.[7]

Neither was the attitude of Egypt – the leading power in the Arab world – clear towards the issue of oil and its place in Arab politics. On the contrary, Egypt's attitude was both ambivalent and ambiguous. According to one expert writing about Egyptian oil policy during the 1950s and the 1960s:

> Two tendencies have vied with each other in Egyptian oil thinking. On the one hand the Egyptian government has sought to give the impression that it is not interested in benefitting from the oil revenues of the major Arab oil producers, and to that extent it has refrained from setting itself as a pioneer of oil policies in the Arab world. On the other hand, in the course of its general propaganda campaigns against the traditional regimes, it has inveighed against deplorable squandering of oil revenues by the privileged classes. This has led Egypt, in accordance with its cult of the masses, to preach the ill-defined gospel of some kind of people's takeover bid.[8]

By contrast, however, attitudes toward oil matters were developing in totally different directions within the oil producing countries. The new generation of indigenous oil experts that had emerged in these countries played a vital role in proposing alternative philosophies. They believed that, ultimately, the oil producers' success in obtaining better terms from their concessionaires depended on their full understanding of the workings of the intricate oil industry, and upon the adoption of a pragmatic rather than emotional approach to oil matters. In order to develop such an attitude, they argued in favour both of keeping oil affairs divorced from politics and of informing and educating the public in oil matters.

Prevalence of National Interest

The point of view of the Arab oil technocrats finally prevailed. First, it echoed the national interest of oil producing countries that were hardly willing to share their as yet limited revenues with those Arab countries that did not have it. This reluctance was further strengthened by the fact that some of these 'have-not' Arabs – notably Egypt – were establishing radical political systems and were bent on changing the regimes of the Arab oil producers, as well. Second, the injection of overly-political and ideological dimensions into issues that needed a pragmatic and apolitical approach was viewed as counterproductive by these technocrats. However, by far the most important reason was that the first view would have clearly excluded the non-Arab oil producing countries from any eventual cooperative arrangements, thereby undermining all attempts to establish a large, united front of all oil producers – obviously an important precondition for achieving an effective voice in all decisions pertaining to oil.

The unity of the oil producing countries was also viewed as vital by non-Arab nations. In fact, one non-Arab oil producer, Venezuela, as early as the mid-1940s, had been actively promoting the idea of cooperation among oil producers.[9]

Moreover, the ill-fated experience of Iran – the other major non-Arab oil producer – in nationalising its oil industry in 1951 had also demonstrated the necessity of cooperation among all oil producers if they were to be successful in their dealings with the oil companies. Yet in view of deep strains in Iran's relations with a number of Arab countries – including Egypt – as long as oil remained an issue closely linked to intra-Arab politics, Iran found it difficult to cooperate with Arab oil producers.

But when by 1959 the pragmatic point of view finally prevailed among the Arab oil producers, and when the satisfaction of national needs and aspirations rather than the achievement of some elusive goal of Arab unity was given priority, more favourable conditions were also created for the start of closer cooperation among oil producers, including Iran and the Arabs.

Formation of OPEC: Start of Cooperation

The first major manifestation of the new trend among the oil producers was the participation of Iran and Venezuela in the first Arab Oil Congress convened in Cairo in April 1959. The Oil Congress served a double purpose: (1) since it took place after the 1959 price reductions, it 'offered a handy forum for expressing oil exporting countries' dissatisfaction and apprehension over these (price) reductions . . .';[10] and (2) it created an opportunity for oil producers to 'exchange views informally and outside the regular meetings of the Congress – which were devoted to solely intra-Arab questions – concerning the possibility of creating an organisation in which all oil producing countries will participate'.[11]

The Congress yielded two important results: (1) the signing of a secret gentlemen's agreement among oil producers in regard to coordination of their oil policies; and (2) the creation of an Oil Consultation Committee that included Arab oil exporting countries, the members of the Arab League, and both Iran and Venezuela. This committee, which in a sense was the forerunner of OPEC, was very short-lived. That result was to be expected, however, given the extended membership of the committee and the political and ideological differences among its members. According to the Venezuelans, among factors contributing to the demise of the Oil Consultation Committee was opposition to the UAR (Egypt) on the part of the interested parties – particularly Iran and certain Arab leaders, notably General Kassem of Iraq. Important though these factors were, however, the real reason for the failure of the Oil Consultation Committee can be found in the deeply-rooted differences among Arab states. This failure, in fact, vindicated those technocrats who had maintained that the mixing of oil-related issues and Arab politics was a recipe for failure.

The Accelerator: 1960 Price Reductions

If left to themselves, the oil producers might not have agreed to cooperation as soon as they did. But in August 1960, the oil companies again unilaterally reduced the price of oil. This proved to be a determining factor in OPEC's creation.[12] Following these price reductions, five major oil exporters – namely, Iran, Iraq, Saudi Arabia, Kuwait and Venezuela – put aside their differences and met in Baghdad in September 1960. At the end of a four-day conference, they reached agreement on the creation of a permanent Organisation of Petroleum Exporting Countries, with a view to coordinating and unifying members' policies.

Thus, the unilateral price reductions – plus the emergence of a consensus among the oil producers that, to be workable, any association among them should be limited in membership and objectives and should adopt a non-political approach to oil – made the establishment of OPEC possible.

This consensus laid the foundation of OPEC's philosophy that, until recently, has been basically non-political in nature, functional in approach, and flexible in method. For a long time, this philosophy gave OPEC a flexibility of action that maintained its fundamental cohesion despite internal and external challenges.

II OPEC and Intra-Arab Politics of Oil

The creation of OPEC did not end intra-Arab debate on oil. With its pragmatic and non-political approach, from its very start OPEC was looked upon with scorn by more emotional, nationalist Arab forces whose champion was Egypt. Egyptian antagonism towards OPEC was intensified by the fact that OPEC came into being in Baghdad, and it was difficult for Egypt to give its blessing to any initiative that reflected credit on General Kassem's regime. Egyptians accused OPEC of diverting attention from the Arab Oil Congress, thus harming the interests of the Arab nation. OPEC members tried to answer these charges, explaining that OPEC and the Arab Petroleum Congress were entirely different in scope and conception, with OPEC being strictly confined to economic matters. Some even gave credit to the first Arab Oil Congress for having made OPEC possible.[13]

Despite efforts to assuage Arab fears and animosities towards OPEC, its members did not entertain the idea of abandoning cooperation among themselves. Yet the Arab members of OPEC could not remain oblivious to accusations that they had betrayed the cause of Arab unity. They therefore tried to portray OPEC as the governmental and international arm of the Arab Oil Congress, which was also at the service of the Arab nation. What this meant in fact was that, from then on, Arab oil policies were dealt with at two levels: intra-Arab and intra-oil producers.

Even among Arabs, however, the trend was towards limiting the circle of countries directly involved with oil matters to the oil producers. This trend in turn led to the founding of the Organisation of *Arab* Petroleum Exporting Countries (OAPEC) by Saudi Arabia, Libya and Kuwait on 9 January 1968. The immediate concern of the founding members of OAPEC was to move discussions relating to oil out of the Arab League and into another forum, thus excluding the more revolutionary Arab regimes from decisions regarding oil and particularly its use to achieve the Arabs' strategic and political objectives. The event that prompted the three major Arab producers to establish this organisation was the 1967 Arab oil embargo, which imposed heavy financial losses on them.[14] To achieve these purposes, they restricted the membership of the organisation to those Arab countries in which petroleum constituted the principal and basic source of national income.[15] The degree of restriction was not defined in the statute, but it was interpreted to mean that only those Arab countries were eligible in which the petroleum sector constituted the number one source of national income. According to this criterion, only one more country – Iraq – was qualified to join, and it was invited to do so. Algeria was excluded from membership, since at the time wine was still the number one source of Algeria's income.

As could be expected, the revolutionary Arab regimes reacted negatively to the creation of OAPEC. Iraq refused to join. Explaining the reason for its refusal and commenting on OAPEC's restrictive membership rules, the chairman of the Iraqi National Oil Company said:

> We think this wrong and unreasonable. According to the present rules, Algeria, which is by any standards a substantial exporter of oil, would be excluded from membership; so would the UAR, which is also expected to become a significant oil exporter within the next few years. We are not against the establishment of an organization for Arab oil exporting countries as such, provided the conditions are reasonable. But we would apply the same membership rules to the Arab petroleum organization as are applicable in OPEC.[16]

The revolutionary Arab regimes even went beyond denouncing OAPEC and made their own arrangements for cooperation. On 1 February 1968, the two state-owned oil companies of Iraq and Algeria signed an agreement calling for the utmost mutual cooperation in oil affairs in order to achieve 'an independent revolutionary oil policy for the benefit of Arab nations'.[17]

However, the situation was changed drastically by the overthrow of the Libyan monarchy in September 1969 and the establishment of a revolutionary regime. Without Libyan participation, OAPEC would have been nothing but a bilateral agreement between Kuwait and Saudi Arabia. But these two countries showed considerable flexibility and relaxed the eligibility rules, thus making possible the incorporation of other Arab oil producers within the organisation.

This meant a fundamental change in the nature of the organisation. The enlargement of its membership defeated the original purpose of its founders – namely, the exclusion of the revolutionary Arab governments from decisions related to oil. Yet OAPEC did serve one major purpose in that it provided a framework for the conduct of a purely Arab dialogue in oil and oil's different uses to achieve Arab economic and political goals.

The explanation given by the Saudi minister of oil for the exclusion of Iran from OAPEC clarifies the purposes OAPEC was intended to serve. He said:

> Insofar as our OAPEC is concerned, we have to recognise that the Arab countries have a number of political obligations – including the Palestine problem, for example – regarding which the degree of Arab commitment is considerably heavier than that which Iran could reasonably be expected to bear . . . Moreover, we regard OAPEC as to some extent a substitute for the various oil activities of the Arab League. And since Iran is not a member of the League, it would hardly be appropriate to have a non-Arab member in an organisation which is a substitute for certain activities of the Arab League.[18]

At its beginning, the main impetus behind the creation of OAPEC was the desire of three traditional Arab states to gain total control over decisions related to the use of oil in Arab politics. But the change in Libyan leadership defeated this purpose, and the later enlargement of the organisation's membership introduced to it some of the problems with which the Arab League also had to grapple.

In theory, the OAPEC charter had aimed at some kind of supranationality, but the way the organisation functioned in practice did not move it in this direction. Individual Arab countries still determine their oil policies independently and only cooperate to the extent that they consider such cooperation to be in their national interest. Nor did the establishment of OAPEC diminish the importance of OPEC as the sole framework for policy coordination of major oil exporting countries. From the very beginning, in fact, care was taken to prevent any rivalry between the two organisations. For instance, the OAPEC charter provides that OPEC decisions are binding on all members of the Arab organisation 'even if they are not members of OPEC' (Article 3). Also, the statement by Saudi Arabia's Sheikh Yamani to the effect that OPEC is the mother and our Arab OAPEC the child demonstrated that the desire for a more economically and politically integrated Arab region led to the creation of a purely Arab organisation, but not at the expense of the broader purposes of OPEC.[19]

III Operational Framework of OPEC

A recitation here of OPEC's formal organisation is not necessary. However, a number of characteristics of OPEC members, plus some aspects of the institution's working methods, need to be introduced since they have had a direct bearing on the development of OPEC's aid policies.[20]

OPEC's members differ widely in size, population, petroleum reserves, development needs, and political and ideological orientation. These fundamental differences have affected the outlook and approach of OPEC members towards oil matters, which in turn have deeply affected OPEC's operation and evolution. Of course, one major source of difference within OPEC is the division of its members between Arab and non-Arab countries. As noted earlier, the particular needs of Arab countries – as well as the imperatives of intra-Arab politics – have led them to establish a purely intra-Arab organisation in the form of OAPEC. Yet the Arab members of OPEC do not form a homogeneous group, but rather are divided along ideological lines between the so-called progressive and conservative regimes. In addition, there are significant differences among them in terms of size, population, economic needs, and petroleum reserves. At the same time, the three major non-Arab members of OPEC (Iran, Venezuela, and Nigeria) are each located in a different continent and each have their own specific security, political, and economic objectives. In the past, these needs and objectives sharply conflicted with one another – the best example of which is the Iran-Iraq dispute over border problems – and later their war – in addition to a whole range of other issues.

As mentioned earlier, however, political differences have not been the only source of division among OPEC members: widely disparate economic needs and conditions have also contributed to these divisions. Of all the non-political factors of divergence among OPEC members, the size of their petroleum reserves – and particularly the ratio of these reserves to their populations and development needs – has had the biggest impact in determining their attitudes towards a whole range of issues, in particular OPEC's pricing policy. Among OPEC countries, those with large petroleum reserves have generally favoured moderate increases in the price of oil – particularly since the sharp oil price increases of 1973 – whereas those with smaller reserves have advocated higher prices. This is logical, since the main concern of the low-reserve countries is to maximise their per-unit revenues before their oil runs out, whereas the high-reserve countries are more concerned with the security of future markets for their oil. The disparity in OPEC members' oil reserves has also prevented the organisation from agreeing on and successfully implementing a mandatory production programming scheme.

As noted earlier, OPEC's creation was made possible in part by the adoption by the interested parties of a basically non-political philosophy. Questions relating to oil were to be kept totally separate from politics, although in the past few years politics have been increasingly intruding in intra-OPEC relations and the approach of OPEC members towards oil matters. The Founding Members were also aware that, in order to achieve any measure of success, they had to keep these objectives limited to achieving specific goals where they either had a community of interest or could reach a consensus. Thus, from the very beginning they did not hold the ambition of making OPEC into a 'supra-national' organisation. This attitude in turn enabled them to introduce enough flexibility into OPEC's working methods, which in turn did much to prevent the above-mentioned divergences from putting unbearable pressure on the organisation. This situation has had important consequences for OPEC, of which the following have been particularly significant: the vulnerablity of OPEC to developments outside its member countries, which has meant that – more often than not – OPEC's policies have been reactive rather than initiative; and the premium placed on the action of individual OPEC members. In fact, often OPEC has followed a new course initiated by one of its members. Sometimes this process has worked for OPEC's benefit.

Decision-Making Methods

OPEC's working methods are principally influenced by two sets of factors: statutary rules and regulations; and informal habits of negotiation and consultation among its members.

According to OPEC's statute, the organisation's supreme authority – namely its Conference – operates on the basis of unanimity.[21] The smooth functioning of the Conference under such a rule requires a high degree of identity of views among members. Of course, the absence of such identity and the rule of unanimity do raise the real danger of paralysing the organisation and preventing it from taking important decisions. Yet at the same time, this rule makes give-and-take and mutual concessions among members imperative if paralysis is to be averted. The rule of unanimity also encourages informal consultation and behind-the-scenes contacts, which in turn make the ironing-out of differences much easier. In fact, in an indirect way this principle has contributed to OPEC's flexibility in handling issues and problems.

In discussing OPEC's methods of work, it is necessary to distinguish between the methods its members apply to intra-OPEC issues, and those that they have used when confronting the oil companies or consuming nations.

Concerning intra-OPEC relations, the unanimity rules make consensus-building through informal consultations, pre-conference negotiations, and the use of mediation imperative. This approach prevents confrontation among members, and by precluding formal defeat or victory, makes conciliation of conflicting views easier and enhances the organisation's flexibility. Furthermore, the fact that the organisation has never demanded the strict application of OPEC's resolutions – even the ones unanimously adopted – has helped keep it together.

With regard to methods of dealing with the oil companies, more often than not OPEC members have acted individually, although OPEC has given them support. However, the kind and degree of support has differed on occasions. In some cases, it has amounted to nothing more than lip-service, which has generated complaints from some members.[22] On other occasions, however, OPEC has presented a strong united front, thus exerting considerable influence.[23]

On one occasion, OPEC resorted to collective bargaining: the financial negotiations of January-February 1971, which led to the conclusion of the Teheran Agreement, were carried out by a Ministerial Committee appointed by the OPEC Conference.

The underlying principles of OPEC's decision-making methods have been flexibility and mutual compromise. The advocates of this approach argue that – by not imposing any strict criteria of co-operation on the member countries – they have prevented differences of opinion and interest from coming to the fore, and thus have helped preserve the underlying unity and solidarity of the organisation. But not all who are interested in OPEC-related issues consider this flexibility a virtue. Critics of OPEC – and in some cases some of its members – argue that this 'flexibility' is nothing but inability on the part of OPEC members to look beyond their immediate self-interest and to agree on policies that will lead to success irrespective of outside factors. They further stress that OPEC's success has resulted from developments in the energy market, rather than from any concerted action by the organisation.

Despite these criticisms, however, the former approach has prevailed, and has also been applied to decisions related to the specific issue of aid and its methods of disbursement.

Objectives

OPEC's principal objectives have been stated in Article 2 of its statute which reads:

> A. The principal aim of the organization shall be the coordination and unification of the petroleum policies of member countries, and the determination of the best means for safeguarding their interests individually and collectively.
> B. The organization shall devise ways and means of ensuring the stabilization of prices in international oil markets with a view to eliminating harmful and unnecessary fluctuations.
> C. Due regard shall be given at all times to the interests of the producing nations and to the necessity of receiving a steady income to the producing countries; an efficient, economical and regular supply of petroleum to consuming nations, and a fair return on their capital to those investing in the petroleum industry.[24]

The language of Article 2 clearly demonstrates the initial position of weakness from which the OPEC countries had to operate. This was the time of the so-called 'buyer's market' when the world had an oversupply of oil. That is why OPEC set as its overriding objective the stabilisation of oil prices rather than their increase, or even their restoration to the pre-1960 levels. Furthermore, the OPEC countries were still extremely dependent on the oil companies for the exploitation of their oil, and even more so for its marketing. Also, given the record of intervention by outside powers in the Middle East, OPEC members were extremely cautious not to generate any fears or misgivings on the part of the major consuming nations. Thus basic OPEC documents included ideas such as the need to secure an efficient and regular supply of oil to the consuming countries. This factor also prompted OPEC, since its creation, to try to project the image of an instrument of moderation. How far this helped OPEC in achieving its aims is a subject of controversy. What is certain, however, is that the desire to project such an image has greatly influenced OPEC's actions. Even after the sharp price increases of the last few years, OPEC countries maintain that their organisation has been, and still is, an instrument of moderation. For instance, in 1980 the President of Venezuela was reported to have said that: 'OPEC has been a moderating factor in the world energy market while oil multi-nationals speculated on the spot market.'[25] The Kuwaiti minister of oil also made a similar statement, saying that: 'OPEC countries pursued a moderate price policy and if oil producers really wanted to take what they could the price of oil would be three or four times higher.'[26]

As OPEC members gradually managed to secure higher revenues – principally through bringing about changes in the system of calculating the oil companies' tax and royalty payments rather than through increasing the price of oil – they developed other aims that were probably not part of the thinking of the Founding Members. These aims, however, were very much in line with the evolving trend of thought among Third World countries in regard to the need to assert full sovereignty over their natural resources.

In June 1968, OPEC spelled out these new objectives in the form of a Declaratory Statement of Petroleum Policy in the Member Countries, which was incorporated in Resolution XVI.90.

These new policy guidelines, which were not mandatory, were as follows:

(i) Direct exploration for and development of hydrocarbon resources, as far as possible. If that is not feasible, then contracts, as distinct from the traditional concessions, should be entered into. In the latter case, contracts should be open to revision, as justified by changing circumstances.

(ii) Participation in the equity of existing concessions.

(iii) Progressive and accelerated relinquishing of acreage of present contract areas.

(iv) Posted or tax reference prices should be adopted. These prices should be determined by the government and should move in such a manner as to prevent any deterioration in its relationship to the price of manufactured goods traded internationally.
(v) Conservation rules to be followed by operating companies.[27]

This Declaratory Statement is one of OPEC's most important documents. Its importance stems from the fact that it is not merely concerned with limited objectives of reforming producing country/oil company relationships and securing higher income for its members. In addition, it sets long-term, far-reaching goals aimed at the eventual economic emancipation of its members.

After having set the basic framework for its actions, and having established its main long-term goals, OPEC again concentrated its efforts on securing more financial gains for its members. Thus, in its meeting in Caracas in December 1970, OPEC agreed upon a third set of objectives and spelled them out in stronger language. This time the Conference resolved:

That all member countries adopt the following objectives:
(a) to establish 55 per cent as the minimum income tax rate;
(b) to eliminate existing disparities in posted or tax reference prices;
(c) to establish a uniform increase in the posted or tax reference prices;
(d) to adopt a new system for the adjustment of gravity differentials of posted or tax reference prices; and
(e) to eliminate completely the allowances granted to oil companies as from 1 January 1978.[28]

OPEC has had considerable success in achieving most of its aims. Since 1973, the posted prices of oil have been determined unilaterally by OPEC. Also, either through complete nationalisation or different kinds of participation arrangements, OPEC members have established control over their petroleum resources.

IV The Evolution of OPEC-Third World Relations

As alluded to earlier in terms of the circumstances attending OPEC's creation, its philosophy and aid have to a very large extent reflected the basic trend of thought among Third World countries concerning their needs, the obstacles in the way of satisfying these needs, and the means most likely to remove these obstacles. To cite one of many examples, when OPEC was setting as its objective the securing of its members' ultimate control over their petroleum resources and related industries, it was both responding to and influencing forces working in this direction within the developing countries. Moreover, OPEC's use of the deteriorating terms of trade argument, as well as its emphasis on the right of nations to use their natural resources for the advancement of their countries, reflected the general developing-country thinking.[29]

The creation of OPEC, which does qualify for the title of an instrument of collective self-help, was a major event in the history of developing-country efforts to rectify systemic inequalities detrimental to their interests. OPEC has served as a model for cooperation among other raw material exporting countries. Although its success was not duplicated in the case of other associations, it has been a source of inspiration to other raw material exporting countries.

Moreover, after the oil price increases of 1973-4, OPEC became the principal champion of Third World objectives, including those of systemic reform. However, OPEC-Third World relations have not always been harmonious. In fact, since 1971 there have been serious undercurrents of strain and conflict of interest in OPEC-Third World relations, despite their common rhetoric of solidarity.

Beginnings of Strain

The first sign of strain in OPEC-Third World relations appeared in 1971. This was triggered by the first significant oil price increase – after the Teheran and Tripoli agreements – which caused serious hardships for most Third World countries. Thus, the question arose as to how OPEC could help developing countries. OPEC's initial response was that developing countries should try to get better prices for their own raw materials, by following similar policies as OPEC. For instance, OPEC's then Secretary General, Nadim Pachachi, said in an interview that OPEC would readily support developing countries in their attempts to obtain better prices for their primary products from the industrialised countries:

> *Question*: Some press commentators have made much of the possible adverse consequences of the (1971) Teheran settlement on the underdeveloped oil consuming countries with acute foreign exchange problems. What do the OPEC countries feel about this?
> *Answer*: Yes, we do realise that the developing countries, as well as

> the industrialised nations, will have to pay more for their oil exports. *We, as developing countries, sympathise with them. We, like them, are raw material producers, trying to get an equitable price for the primary product on which our economies depend.* They too should use our example in getting the industrialised countries to pay a better price for their raw materials and primary commodities in general. And, we in OPEC are always ready to cooperate with other developing countries, and/or commodity price stabilisation organisations, and to put our experience at their disposal.[30]

Some OPEC countries had different ideas about the best means of helping Third World countries. For instance, the Shah of Iran thought that joint oil ventures between OPEC and developing oil-importing countries would be the best way of helping them.[31]

In general, OPEC members sensed early the need for a more conscious effort to assist other developing countries in a more concrete form. The interesting point to be noted here is the existence of a direct relationship between the economic emancipation of OPEC countries – at least as far as petroleum is concerned; their overall chances of development and their level of income; and their willingness to assist other developing countries.

The Arab members of OPEC took the lead in granting aid, but this initiative was at first prompted by the imperatives of intra-Arab politics rather than by strains in OPEC-Third World relations. Consequently, their early aid effort was limited to other Arab countries.

Events of 1973

The events of 1973 had a significant impact on OPEC-Third World relations. First, the oil embargo of 1973 and the ensuing oil price increases demonstrated for the first time the new vulnerability of industrialised countries to OPEC actions, and at the same time resulted in a considerable transfer of financial assets from the industrialised countries to OPEC members, ultimately leading to a relative shift of the balance of bargaining power in favour of OPEC. Second, these developments, by causing great hardships for the Third World, created new responsibilities for OPEC towards these countries. The combined effect of increased OPEC responsibility towards the Third World, and increases in its power, was a closer interaction between OPEC and the Third World countries, focused principally on the reform of the international economic system, to make it more responsive to Third World needs.

However, it took OPEC and the Third World countries some time before they could agree on an operational and conceptual framework for their cooperation. This was so because not all OPEC countries were equally interested in this matter. Their differences in outlook and interests were made manifest in their individual approaches. For instance, the Arab countries, constituting the majority of OPEC members, were more concerned with the Arab-Israeli conflict. The preoccupation of the industrialised countries with the security of their oil supplies, and their efforts to reach some sort of agreement with OPEC on this issue, also meant that the question of Arab-Israeli conflict, energy shortages in the West, and the link between these two questions – and not the broader problems of the Third World – would dominate early international negotiations. The widening of the scope of vital issues to be discussed in international forums, and the addition of the problems of development and raw materials, thus occurred later. This was also partly due to the fact that the Arab members of OPEC came to realise the value of Third World support for the advancement of their cause. However, despite these delays and differences in the order of priority of OPEC and Third World countries, these events were extremely important since they led to the most ambitious joint OPEC-Third World efforts to reform the international economic system to their own advantage.

The Western Response

The initial Western response to the crisis of 1973 was far from uniform. On the one hand, the United States adopted a policy almost of confrontation with the oil producers and tried to organise a common front of consuming nations to face OPEC. For instance, on 9 January 1974 President Nixon wrote to eight major oil consuming countries (Canada, Britain, West Germany, France, Italy, Japan, The Netherlands, and Norway), inviting them to a conference in Washington that February to work towards a 'consumer action program' to deal with the worldwide energy problem. To reassure the oil producers, Nixon also wrote to OPEC's heads of state, stressing that: 'The United States is undertaking this initiative as a constructive and positive step, consistent with the publicly stated views of a number of oil producing nations which have called for a consultative relationship between producers and consumers.[32]

On the other hand, America's European allies were more vulnerable to production cuts and oil embargoes, and thus they tried to establish bilateral contacts with the oil producers, for the purpose of striking mutually-acceptable deals that would guarantee continuation of their oil supplies. The United States looked unfavourably on these contacts and hoped at the Washington conference to put an end to such independent European actions.

Among European countries, France played an important role in resisting American efforts to create a common front of consuming nations. The French attitude was, of course, in accord with France's long-established policy of resisting a US-dominated international system and its generally favourable and friendly attitude towards the Arab countries. Thus, in order to prevent a confrontation between the oil producing and consuming nations, the French Foreign Minister toured several Arab countries and suggested the 'creation of a committee representing the Arab oil producing countries and the members of the European Community to help deal with the world energy crisis'. He added, however, that this would be a first step towards wider international consultations.[33] In a letter to the United Nations Secretary General on 18 January 1974, the President of France proposed the convening of a World Energy Conference under the auspices of the UN.

The rest of the major European countries vacillated between French and American policies and somehow tried to reconcile these two contradictory approaches. Thus, for instance, eight members of the European Community took part in the Washington Energy Conference and agreed to establish an International Energy Agency (IEA). Yet at their Brussels meeting of 5 February 1974, the European Community Foreign Ministers also agreed that:

> Their representatives would expect the Washington conference to explore the best form of dialogue to bring together all categories of consumer and producer nations; and to avoid all confrontation between 'certain consumer countries' and producer countries; and to pay particular attention to developing countries.[34]

OPEC's Reaction to the Western Response

A divergence of view about the best way to deal with the problems of the post-October 1973 era was not confined to the Western countries. OPEC members were also far from united in their approach to these problems. Irrespective of their political views and objectives, however, OPEC members were none the less united in their opposition to any consumers' organisation. For instance, President Boumedienne of Algeria criticised the US proposal for holding a conference of oil consumers, saying that the US 'was trying to impose a protectorate on oil producers and consumers through the conference'.[35] The Shah of Iran warned the consuming nations against confrontation. He said: 'I have a warning to give. I do not know what the reactions of the other OPEC members will be, but you can quote me loud and clear that if the consumer nations would like to put pressure on us, they would get much less oil.'[36] Even Sheikh Yamani of Saudi Arabia – which among OPEC members was most sympathetic to the industrialised countries – spoke against the Washington conference. While visiting Japan, he warned that 'very serious trouble could result if the oil consuming nations attempted in Washington to form a common front against oil producers'.[37]

Beyond this general opposition to a confrontational approach by the consuming nations, the fundamental differences among OPEC members were still manifest in the members' attitudes toward the post-October 1973 issues. Here again, the main sources of divisions were political differences between Arab and non-Arab members of the organisation, and between the radical and conservative Arab regimes – differences which were further compounded by disparate economic conditions and needs. The major preoccupation of Arab members of OPEC was to obtain a change in the Middle Eastern policies of European countries and the United States, and thus to increase the chances for resolving the Arab-Israeli conflict in a way favourable to the Arabs. However, substantial differences existed among Arab OPEC members on the best means for provoking such a change.

The radical Arab oil producers favoured exerting pressure on the industrialised countries, in order to gain concessions on the Arab-Israeli question. They were, however, prepared to give preferential treatment to those Western countries that supported the Arab cause, thus hoping to split the front of the industrialised countries. By contrast, the more conservative Arab regimes were more prepared to find common ground with the industrialised countries and to try obtaining concessions through persuasion.

In addition to traditional political considerations, economic factors also contributed to the division among Arab oil producers. Conservative Arab countries were also the low absorptive, high surplus countries with large oil reserves, and thus were accumulating large monetary assets. These assets were held in the currencies of the industrialised countries and were deposited in their banks, thus making them vulnerable to serious economic disturbances in these industrialised countries. Therefore, at least in the short term, conservative Arab interests coincided to a significant degree with the interests of the industrialised countries.

Short-term economic considerations were not, however, the only factors affecting these countries' policies. Some OPEC members had overriding national objectives which they were determined to pursue. Consequently, a number of key OPEC countries adopted different approaches to this issue.

The Role of Saudi Arabia

Since 1968, increased financial resources had already enhanced Saudi Arabia's impact on Arab politics and their evolution. For example, after the death of President Nasser, Saudi Arabia contributed to the evolution of Egypt's foreign policy in a more pro-Western direction.[38] It wanted to consolidate these gains, and at the same time recognised the importance of a satisfactory resolution to the Arab-Israeli conflict, if it were to succeed. However, the Saudis also knew that they could not achieve this objective without the United States' help. To obtain this US assistance, the Saudis were prepared to make concessions on other issues – such as the price of oil, the early lifting of the (1973-4) oil embargo, and the recycling of surplus funds in ways that would ease the balance of payment problems of the industrialised countries.

Moreover, even from a long-term perspective, the interests of Saudi Arabia – and to a lesser extent those of Kuwait and the UAE – regarding the price of oil were more in line with the interests of the industrialised countries than with those of other OPEC members. Given their huge oil reserves, the Saudis were concerned that high oil prices could make their oil non-competitive with other sources of energy. By contrast, other OPEC countries, with low reserves but more potential for economic development, wanted to sell their oil at the highest price and industrialise.

However, the Saudis could not be oblivious to Third World demands, if only to prevent the more radical Arabs from presenting themselves as the sole defenders of Third World interests. They also at times used the threat of closer cooperation with developing countries to obtain concessions from the West.

Consequently, Saudi Arabia behaved in a contradictory manner, on the one hand pressing in the mid-1970s for reduced oil prices and for the early lifting of the 1973-4 oil embargo and, on the other, was making the continuation of these efforts conditional on the West's favourable and cooperative response to Third World demands. However, ultimately the former considerations determined Saudi behaviour and led to its rather tepid support for Third World objectives.

The Role of Algeria

Like Saudi Arabia, one of Algeria's main objectives was to obtain a favourable resolution of the Arab-Israeli conflict. But unlike Saudi Arabia, the Algerians were more sincerely committed to realising Third World aspirations.

Algeria has long been a member of the Non-Aligned Movement and was very active within it during the early and mid-1970s. Since 1972, the Non-Aligned Movement has paid increasing attention to economic issues and the necessity of the structural reforms in the international economic system. Its 1973 conference in Algiers was very significant, in that it produced a document incorporating the most important principles on the basis of which its members believed the international economic system should be reformed. Following that conference, Algeria took the initiative in requesting the convening of a special session of the UN General Assembly to deal with the question of reforming the international economic system. Later, the Algerians continued their effort to strengthen ties between OPEC members and the Third World. They also played an important role in developing a common OPEC approach towards global economic issues, which was finally embodied in the Solemn Declaration of OPEC Heads of States and Governments, gathered in Algiers in March 1975. Moreover, Algeria was one of those OPEC members whose interests would best be served by maximisation of oil revenues as long as reserves lasted, with the transformation of these revenues into a viable industrial base.

Iran and Venezuela

Given the absence of any overriding objective, such as the question of the Arab-Israeli conflict (which affected Arab OPEC members), the attitude of Iran and Venezuela towards the above-mentioned issues was determined principally by their political preferences and other national objectives and ambitions. As far as Iran was concerned, its pro-Western orientation at the time, as well as its close political and economic links with Western countries, argued against its championing radical approaches to these issues. At the same time, however, Iran's ambitions to play an increasingly important role on the international scene, plus its desire to enhance its influence and prestige in the Third World made it a supporter of the latter's goals. Thus, whenever possible, Iran tried to make proposals which in its view would answer the needs of both industrialised and Third World countries. But whenever it was forced to choose, Iran supported the position of developing countries without, however, going too far in pressuring the industrialised countries. However, it is important to note that, given Iran's economic and financial needs, its capacity for such action was also limited.

Venezuela's position on these issues bears considerable resemblance to that of Iran, and emanated from its special needs and aspirations, including its desire to increase its influence among the Central American and Caribbean nations.

What the foregoing discussion demonstrates is that divergences of view, interest, and objectives within both OPEC and industrialised countries prevented the emerging of any single comprehensive policy towards global economic issues, either by OPEC or by the industrialised countries. Instead, contacts were established at different levels – among OPEC and as between industrialised and developing countries – and initiatives of diverse forms were taken. These tendencies were particularly intensified after the failure of the UN General Assembly's Sixth Special Session, which was held at Algeria's request (1974).

This session was significant in that it produced a declaration and programme of action on the New International Economic Order (NIEO), and set guidelines for the conduct of future negotiations. But it also made clear that the industrialised countries would not easily accept the demands of the developing countries. During this session, OPEC members – along with the rest of the Third World – demonstrated a high degree of solidarity, perhaps the highest level that they have ever reached. Yet even then, significant differences of objectives and in their order of priority were evident between OPEC and the Third World.

OPEC's Aid Initiatives

At the Sixth Special Session of the UN General Assembly, Iran first suggested the creation of a fund to assist Third World countries – a fund to which both OPEC and industrialised countries would contribute. The Iranian proposal, however, met with a cool reception from a number of influential members of OPEC – with the strongest opposition coming from Saudi Arabia and some of the other Persian Gulf countries. The main reason for their opposition was not aversion to the idea of a fund, but rather that Iran had made the proposal.[39] It seems that the Iranian sale of oil to the West during the 1973 embargo had not been forgotten. Moreover, Saudi Arabia and other Gulf countries were apprehensive about Iran's growing power and its ambitions for the leadership of the Persian Gulf. However, these disagreements were essentially reflective of one type – ethnic – of intra-OPEC divisions, which as long as OPEC was weak and struggling against the oil companies had been kept somewhat dormant, yet suddenly came to the fore after 1973. Furthermore, the Arab countries wanted to channel their aid through their own organisations, to achieve their own particular objectives and to enhance their own prestige. For instance, the Kuwaiti Minister of Oil said that 'Kuwait will deploy its oil wealth mainly through channels under Arab control.'[40]

While sharing these concerns, Saudi Arabia had another reason to oppose the idea of the fund. The Saudis were having problems with Iran concerning OPEC's pricing policies, and Iran was opposed to Saudi efforts designed to lower the price of oil. The Saudis argued that the creation of a fund 'will not solve the problem of the damage caused to the economies of the developing countries by the huge price increases of last January, and should not be regarded as a substitute for positive actions towards lowering these prices'.[41]

Other members of OPEC, including Venezuela, Algeria, and Libya, reacted favourably to the idea of a fund, and declared their readiness to join one should it be established. The interesting point is the favourable reaction of Algeria and Libya. But there was a logic to it, particularly in Algeria's case. Its reserves would not have permitted it to embark on any significant aid programme of its own, whereas contributing to the fund could further enhance its prestige and influence in developing countries.

Eventually, a fund was created in 1976 to which only OPEC countries contributed. But this fund (the OPEC Special Fund) had much less capital and a reduced scope of operations than had been envisaged.[42]

Once the idea was rejected of creating a large OPEC fund through which all aid to developing countries could be channelled, OPEC countries responded in different ways to the demands of developing as opposed to industrialised countries. For instance, even by November 1973, Arab leaders had declared at their summit meeting that they would give financial assistance to African members of the Organisation of African Unity (OAU) in appreciation of their support. Then, on 21-2 January 1974, member states of the OAU met with representatives of Arab oil-producing states to discuss possible price concessions to African countries. This event was followed by meetings between the representatives of Botswana, Cameroon, Ghana, Mali, Sudan, Tanzania, and Zaîre (members of the oil committee of the OAU) and oil ministers of ten Arab countries. Finally, the Arab members of OPEC decided to establish both a special fund to finance part of the oil purchases of African countries and an African Development Fund with Arab capital.

The Islamic Conference also turned its attention to economic matters and particularly to problems of the less-developed Islamic countries. For example, in its final communique, the Islamic Summit Conference held in Lahore from 22-4 February 1974 recognised the need for:

(a) the eradication of poverty, ill health, and ignorance in the Islamic states;
(b) the ending of the exploitation of developing states by the developed states;
(c) the reorganisation of the terms of trade between developed and developing states in raw materials in exchange for imported finished goods and technical knowledge;
(d) guaranteeing the complete sovereignty of the developing states and their absolute control over their natural resources;
(e) *the ending of economic difficulties forced on the developing states as a result of the recent rises in petroleum prices*; and
(f) economic solidarity and cooperation among Islamic countries.[43]

The summit conference also set up a committee of representatives of Algeria, Egypt, Kuwait, Libya, Pakistan, Saudi Arabia, Senegal, and the United Arab Emirates, and empowered it to seek help from other Islamic states in order to find ways and means of realising the communique's objectives. In addition, the committee was entrusted with the task of studying the possibility of creating an Islamic Development Bank.[44] The conference also considered the question of establishing an Islamic Solidarity Fund. As noted above, one reason for the initially lukewarm response of Arab countries to the idea of a joint fund was that that idea had originated with Iran. In the case of the Islamic Development Fund, however, Iran showed a lack of enthusiasm and did not contribute to the fund when it was established, since it was essentially a Saudi project headquartered in Jeddah.

Thus, while Arab countries were frantically organising new institutions, Iran and Venezuela were channelling most of their aid through other means – bilaterally in the case of Iran, and through different inter-American organisations in the case of Venezuela.

OPEC countries also contributed to the new international mechanisms created to deal with the economic problems of the post-October 1973 era. One of the most important of these mechanisms was the

IMF Oil Facility, which was decided upon at the January 1974 meeting of the IMF's Committee of Twenty. In the same vein, OPEC members contributed to the UN Emergency Fund created at the Sixth Special Session of the UN General Assembly, as well as to the World Bank and to other multilateral organisations, both new and old.

Thus, when the major shift in oil power began in the early 1970s, OPEC countries were in agreement on the need and desirability to assist the developing countries, to cooperate with them in international conferences, and to facilitate the adjustment process of the world economy to the new conditions. But the OPEC countries did not adhere to a set of common specific guidelines on how to proceed in this direction.

One of the consequences of divergences in view among OPEC members was that these divergences helped the industrialised countries in their efforts to separate OPEC members from one another and from other developing countries. One tactic used to isolate OPEC members from other developing countries was the effort to establish a dialogue solely between OPEC and the industrialised countries. There were also hints at giving some OPEC members more influence in international economic organisations, such as the IMF and the IBRD. And there were unofficial suggestions about establishing some kind of link between certain OPEC members and the OECD.[45]

However, the weakening of OPEC-Third World solidarity was prevented by the fact that OPEC members – despite their particular interests and objectives – were themselves also developing countries. Moreover, OPEC countries – particularly the Arabs – needed the support of other developing countries for their own political and economic goals. An OPEC-developing country split was also prevented by the fact that some Western countries, particularly the United States, used high-handed tactics, such as the threat to use force in the Persian Gulf.

The Second Phase of Economic Negotiations and the Role of OPEC

After the failure of the UN General Assembly's Sixth Special Session (1974), there was a general sense that negotiations between the industrialised and developing countries should at first be conducted within smaller groupings, and suggestions were aired to this end. In order to study the new developments and adopt a common position, at the suggestion of Algeria an extraordinary conference of OPEC was convened on 26 January 1975. The conference welcomed in principle the idea of establishing a dialogue between smaller groups of developing and industrialised countries. The conference then decided that a summit meeting of OPEC heads of state should be convened to discuss international economic questions and OPEC positions on them. The summit was held in Algiers in March 1975 and produced a Solemn Declaration, which is the most important OPEC document so far on the subject.[46]

The first part of the Solemn Declaration reiterated the right of OPEC members 'to develop their natural resources, to exploit them and to fix their prices'. It also rejected 'any idea or attempt to infringe on these basic rights'.[47]

The second part of the Declaration dealt with the causes of international economic crises. It observed that: 'The current international economic crisis is due basically to great differences in the economic and social progress of the various people; these differences, of which the backwardness of the developing countries is one feature, are basically the result of foreign exploitation, which perpetuates these differences.' The Declaration then rejected 'all allegations which attribute the responsibility for the present instability of the world's economy to the price of oil'.[48]

In the third part of the Declaration, the heads of OPEC states 'condemn[ed] the threats that have been made, the propaganda campaign, and other measures taken, culminating in the accusation levelled at the OPEC member countries that they wish to undermine the economy of the developed countries'. They also 'denounce[d] any attempt by the consuming nations to form cartels with a view to a confrontation; condemn[ed] any plan or strategy aimed at economic or military acts of aggression by these or other cartels against any member countries of OPEC'. Then, once more, they 'emphasise[d] the solidarity which unites their ranks in defense of their peoples' legitimate rights, and declare[d] their readiness, within the framework of that solidarity, to take immediate and effective measures to oppose these threats by adopting a united policy whenever it is called for, particularly in the event of aggression'.[49]

The fourth part of the Declaration dealt with OPEC aid. The part dealing with aid to developing countries read as follows:

> Once again the kings and presidents stress the mutual solidarity which unites their countries with other developing countries in their struggle to overcome their backwardness. . .
>
> They realise that the developing countries suffer worst from the world economic crisis. Consequently, they stress anew their determination to implement measures to strengthen their coopera-

tion with these countries. They are also prepared to participate within the limits of their resources in implementing the special international program drawn up by the UN and to give additional special allocations, loans, and grants to the developing countries. In this connection they have agreed their special program for financial cooperation to aid the worst hit developing countries in the best possible manner, especially to help them overcome their balance of payments difficulties.

They have also agreed to coordinate these financial measures with long term loans for the development of the economies of these countries.

To help improve the use of the agricultural potential of the developing countries, the kings and presidents have decided to encourage the production of fertilisers and to provide the latter at favourable terms to the countries which have been badly affected by the economic crisis. They stress their readiness to cooperate with other raw material exporting developing countries in their efforts to obtain a fair price for their exports. . .[50]

This Solemn Declaration had an important impact, in that it pre-empted the industrialised countries' efforts to establish an exclusive dialogue with OPEC and to keep it confined to energy.

The Paris Conference on International Economic Cooperation (CIEC)

As noted earlier, since the beginning of 1973 France had demonstrated more receptivity to the demands and views of oil producing and other developing countries. It also attempted to bridge the gap between developing and Western countries – particularly the United States. A first meeting of industrialised, developing, and oil-producing countries was arranged and took place in Paris from 5-17 April 1975. This meeting was called to decide on the membership and the agenda of the main conference. Yet sharp differences of approach concerning the mandate of the conference appeared from the very beginning. For example, the US representative made clear in his opening statement that the United States was adamant that the work programme to be developed for the conference should concentrate on the specifics of energy and directly related matters, and not become diluted with parallel discussions of other less-germane issues, however important they might be. The United States also favoured having a limited number of participants in the full conference.

By contrast, OPEC members felt that, since the energy crisis was a symptom and not the cause of global economic crisis, discussions should concentrate on the whole range of global economic issues and not on energy alone.[51]

The European countries – members of the EC – were more cautious and non-committal in their statements, and in general were more prepared to compromise. Meanwhile, delegates from India, Zaire, and Brazil – representing the Third World – focused mainly on the problems of developing countries in general.

The first Paris preparatory meeting thus ended in total failure, with each group refusing to yield on its position; and all efforts at mediation by Iran and Algeria failed.

The reason for the lack of a spirit of compromise on the industrial-state consumers' side – particularly on the part of the hardliners – was a belief that

> . . . the balance of power and market forces are turning against the oil producers, and therefore the industrialised consumers would be better advised to wait and see how the situation develops rather than get locked into radical new long-term agreements of a global character on prices of oil and other strategic raw materials which could turn out to be unfavourable to them.[52]

For their part, the developing countries came to the conclusion that

> . . . OPEC's energy is and will remain the trump card which can be and must be used as a lever to bring about the ultimate goal of a new economic order characterised by a real and substantial transfer of wealth from the industrialised world to the developing nations.[53]

As time went by, however, it became clear that OPEC was not able to use this trump card in any effective manner. Several reasons accounted for this failure, among which was the unwillingness of certain major OPEC members – Saudi Arabia, in particular – to agree to measures that would have made OPEC's threats more credible and thus capable of pressuring the industrialised countries into compromise.

There were also economic trends unfavourable to OPEC. For example, the mild winter of 1973 and the economic recession in the industrialised countries had reduced the demand for oil. Also, large expenditures by oil producers, as well as their financial assistance both to developing and industrialised countries, had diminished the importance of the problem of recycling petro-dollars. It had become clear that the estimates of oil-producer surpluses were grossly exaggerated. In sum, by 1975 the industrialised world had managed to cope with the oil crisis much better than it had at first expected. The policies of some OPEC members, however, had greatly contributed to this success. For instance, even before the effects of the economic slackening in the West were felt in the oil market, Saudi Arabia was asking for the reduction of oil prices. Some of the political and economic reasons for Saudi behaviour have already been mentioned. Some other factors accounting for the Saudi attitude were the following:

(i) since the oil crisis coincided with the rise in the popularity of communist and socialist parties in Italy and France, the Saudis became truly concerned about the effects of a prolonged economic recession on the social and political fabric of these countries. Given the deep-rooted aversion of the Saudis to communism, this proved to be a potent factor in determining their policies;

(ii) the Saudis had embarked on an armament programme with US cooperation, which had started the so-called US-Saudi special relationship. Although this was never explicitly mentioned, the special relationship was to a large extent based on the bartering of oil for security; and

(iii) there was genuine concern among Saudis that further increases in the price of oil would reduce demand for it and also encourage the speedy development of alternative sources of energy, thus keeping Saudi oil in the ground.

Given the conditions of oversupply of oil, OPEC's logical choice was to curtail the production and increase the price of oil, or at least to hold out the spectre of increasing prices as a means of obtaining concessions from the Western countries. But from the very beginning, Saudi Arabia made it clear that it would not go along with such a policy.

During the whole period of crisis, the Saudis never talked about cutting production or increasing prices; rather, they threatened not to press for price reductions or to abandon their moderating role within OPEC. Thus, when the Paris preparatory conference failed, Saudi officials made some statements to this effect. For instance, while visiting the US in May 1975, Sheikh Yamani warned US officials that, in case of a confrontation, Saudi Arabia might have to abandon its moderate stand.[54]

The United States responded to these Saudi initiatives in the following way. In a speech on 13 May 1975, the US Secretary of State said: 'The US is prepared to attend a new preparatory meeting.' He added that: 'US thinking on the issue of raw materials, and the manner in which it can be addressed internationally, has moved forward.'[55] However, it is difficult to determine whether or not the US took seriously the Saudis' warning (and that of other oil producers), and as a result moved away from its original position *vis-à-vis* this issue. Given the later intransigence of the United States and most of the other Western countries during the meetings of the Conference on International Economic Cooperation (CIEC), it could be assumed that the apparent shift in US policy was a tactical ploy to strengthen Saudi Arabia's position within OPEC and among developing countries, thus enabling it to continue playing its moderating role, as well as keeping more radical members of OPEC from pressuring the West. The desire to placate the French also played a certain role.

Yet whatever the real reasons behind the change in the US attitude, this shift brightened the prospects for reconvening the conference. Furthermore, in June 1975 the IEA's Board of Directors agreed on a new set of guidelines for relaunching the dialogue with the oil producers and other Third World countries. These guidelines were an improvement over the revised US position and moved more closely in line with the demands of the Third World countries. The member countries of the IEA agreed that the dialogue should deal with three main questions – namely, energy, raw materials, and problems of development. They also agreed that three separate commissions should be set up for this purpose, with each having equal weight and importance.

In view of these changes, the participants in the first preparatory meetings (7-15 April 1975) met again in Paris from 13-16 October and agreed to hold a Plenary Conference at ministerial level in Paris beginning on 19 December 1975.

At its first meeting, the conference decided to organise four commissions dealing with the following issues: energy, raw materials, development and finance. During this meeting, the OPEC/developing country group and the industrialised countries submitted working papers on the issues to be discussed by each commission. As could be seen from the texts of the working papers, one submitted by seven OPEC/developing countries (Saudi Arabia, Brazil, India, Iran, Zaire, Venezuela) and the other by the United States, there were deep divergences of views between the two groups.[56]

The Paris Conference on International Economic Cooperation (CIEC) lasted two years, but it did not achieve any more results than had the two special sessions of the UN General Assembly. This was so because the developing countries were interested in profound structural changes in the international economic system, whereas the industrial nations were only prepared to discuss minor concessions on trade and aid. Indeed, the industrialised countries did agree to contribute $1 billion to a Special Action Programme in order to help meet on concessionary terms the urgent needs of the low-income countries. Of this amount, $385 million was entrusted by the European Community to the International Development Association (IDA).

The developed countries also agreed in principle to increase their Official Development Assistance (ODA) in real terms, directing part of it to the expansion of food production in developing countries. In the trade area, agreements were of a very vague nature.

At the end of the 1977 session of CIEC, the dialogue on North-South relations in its more comprehensive aspect was again transferred to the United Nations. The specific issues were scattered among several bodies. For instance, the issue of commodities was left to UNCTAD; financing to the IMF-IBRD Development Committee; external debt to both UNCTAD and the Development Committee; development and balance of payments to IMF and IBRD; and the question of access by the developing nations to export markets to the GATT.[57]

Thus, even with the assistance of the oil producers, the developing countries did not succeed in obtaining real concessions from the industrialised countries. However, for several reasons this was to be expected. First, under the euphoric conditions created by OPEC actions in 1973-4, both OPEC and Third World countries had overestimated their leverage on the industrialised countries and the degree to which the balance of economic power had shifted in their favour.[58] Likewise, OPEC members did not fully appreciate their vulnerability to possible Western retaliatory actions – particularly military actions. Second, the developing countries did not fully realise some important divergences of political and economic interests between themselves and some of the major OPEC members, in particular Saudi Arabia and – to a lesser extent – other Persian Gulf oil producers. This factor had a significant impact on the fate of industrialised-developing country relations and dialogue.

Although OPEC's power had been grossly exaggerated, nevertheless its oil bargaining power could have been used more effectively in negotiations with the industrialised countries. Yet the OPEC members – some more than others – succumbed to the delaying tactics of the industrialised world. The timing of the Paris Conference itself is interesting: in 1976 the industrialised world was beginning to emerge from the economic recession; the Middle East peace process was continuing, thus minimising any immediate danger of an oil embargo or other retaliatory action by the Arabs; and the world was experiencing an oversupply of oil while OPEC was unable to agree on any production cutback. It was no surprise, therefore, that the industrialised countries were unwilling to make any concessions.

V Recent Developments in OPEC-Third World Relations

Since the end of the 1977 meeting of CIEC, debate on the reform of the international economic order has continued within the UN system. However, not only can no major progress be reported on any of the 25 important items incorporated in the Programme of Action for the establishment of a New International Economic Order (NIEO), disagreement between the developing and industrialised countries has deepened regarding the proper forum for the conduct of global negotiations.

The 1980 UN special session was the last major effort to find an acceptable formula for global negotiations. However, it did not succeed, largely as a result of the rigid position of the United States and most of the other industrialised countries. And consequently, the global economic negotiations were stalled.[59] The Cancun Summit of October 1981 tried to rekindle the dialogue again without much success. In fact, the summit almost did not take place because of US opposition, but when it was finally agreed that the summit would be essentially an opportunity to exchange views rather than to negotiate, the United States agreed to take part. However, nothing concrete came out of Cancun either, and with the shift in US policy towards more conservatism, the prospects for the resumption of meaningful negotiations on global economic issues do not seem very bright.[60]

The only marginal success has been an agreement to establish a Common Fund for Commodities to help stabilise the market prices of some basic raw materials. However, the fund agreed upon is a far cry from the original proposals. Originally, it was supposed to have resources of up to $6 billion, but according to the agreement finally reached in June, 1980, its resources are only $750 million. OPEC countries agreed to contribute $200 million to the Fund and also to pay the $1 million share of each of the 25 least developed of the developing countries.

Relations between OPEC and the Third World have now reached an important point. When OPEC was founded, it was welcomed by the Third World as a proof of the Third World countries' cooperative potential. After 1973, Third World countries supported OPEC's action out of a sense of Third World solidarity, and also because they expected financial assistance and other benefits from economic cooperation with OPEC, as well as the use of OPEC power in the bargaining process with developed countries. But with the failure of international negotiations to yield any tangible results, and with the general rise in oil prices (only abated by the global recession of 1981-2), a large number of developing countries are beginning to question the wisdom of cooperation with OPEC. Already during UNCTAD V in Manila in 1979, some developing countries demanded the inclusion of the price of oil in the negotiations – something that the OPEC countries have always refused to accept. The dissatisfaction of developing countries with OPEC increased after the last round of oil price increases in 1979-80, thus causing serious strains in OPEC-developing country relations. Some developing countries, such as Bangladesh, have voiced increasing criticism of OPEC price and aid policies.[61] The industrialised countries in turn once again seized the opportunity, and actively tried to drive a divisive wedge between OPEC and the rest of the Third World countries. But this time the industrialised countries might be more successful. The possibility of such a development was not lost on the OPEC countries and prompted them to take action to prevent it. The Secretary-General of OPEC was reported to have said:

> We in OPEC are, of course, used to being treated as a convenient scapegoat. But in recent times the campaign against the organisation has assumed worrying proportions. . .and is highly successful. The smear campaign has taken a new and worrying twist because of the subtle efforts being made by the industrialised countries to drive a divisive wedge between OPEC and its Third World brothers.[62]

However, anti-OPEC propaganda is not the only reason for increased tensions between OPEC and the Third World. The fact is that the external debt of developing countries is reaching alarming proportions.[63] Furthermore, financial experts predict that developing countries will have more limited access to international capital markets as a result of their excessive indebtedness. Therefore, there will be even more pressure on OPEC countries and the international lending institutions to increase their assistance to developing countries. Since the oil price increases of 1973, OPEC countries have given considerable amounts of aid to developing countries, but this assistance has not offset the negative effect of the oil price increases, and it is doubtful that it could do so in the future, unless there is a massive increase in the volume of OPEC aid. The developing countries are becoming increasingly sceptical that OPEC aid can be enough to offset their losses, and they are questioning their community of interest with OPEC. Even Rene Ortiz, the then OPEC Secretary-General quoted in the interview above, admitted that what he called 'the indivisibility of relations between OPEC countries and other developing countries' has been strained by rumblings of discontent from within the ranks of the Third World and what he saw as divisive tactics by the industrialised nations.[64]

OPEC has been sensitive to these developments, and, since 1978 when its Long Term Strategy Committee was established, it has been trying to develop a new strategy to deal with the problems of the Third World. Details of OPEC's strategy were expected to be unveiled at the Organisation's twentieth anniversary meeting, to be held in Baghdad in November 1980, but it was cancelled because of the Iran-Iraq war. Nevertheless, some aspects of the new strategy that OPEC seems to have been considering have already become clear. In general, OPEC seems to be adopting a more coherent approach towards the problems of the Third World. Turning the OPEC Special Fund into a fully-fledged development agency, plus increasing its resources (so far exceeding $4 billion), is a good example.

OPEC members have also presented a number of other proposals. For instance, Venezuela and Algeria have called for a further substantial increase in the OPEC Fund's resources (up to $20 billion).

Iraq has also presented a proposal that was adopted in principle by OPEC's Long Term Strategy Committee. This proposal – which incidentally is similar to Iran's original proposal in 1974 – calls for the establishing of a new global Fund for Energy and Development. This fund is supposed to be a joint effort between OPEC and other countries, and its resources would be provided by contributions both by OPEC and by industrialised nations. The amount contributed by the industrialised countries would depend on the annual rate of world inflation as reflected in the price of goods and services exported by the donors. The rate of OPEC's contribution would reflect 'the adjustment of oil prices on account of inflation on oil exports to other countries.[65] The developing countries would not be required to contribute to this fund financially, but would be full members and have equal voting rights.

Another proposal was made by Iran – namely, to reimburse developing countries on a grant basis for the financial burden resulting from oil price increases. To do this a new OPEC Fund would be established to which the oil producers would contribute 10 per cent of their total additional revenues.[66]

It is difficult to predict whether any of these schemes will ever come into being. The first imponderable is, of course, the future of oil markets and thus the level of OPEC revenues. This is so because, even though OPEC maintains that its aid 'is not contrived in its totality as a process for compensation', nevertheless OPEC's oil revenues are the 'enabling factor' of its aid.[67]

Moreover, if OPEC's history is any guide, no system of aid that introduces a higher measure of automaticity into OPEC's aid and its management will be acceptable to its richest and most well-endowed member, Saudi Arabia. This is logical since, under any such scheme, Saudi Arabia will end up paying more than any other OPEC member and having less than equivalent control over the use of funds.

VI Conclusions

The purpose of this chapter has been to illustrate how OPEC's nature as an institution, the characteristics of its members, and its methods of work have also affected its relations with the Third World countries, including its approach to the question of aid to these countries. In the course of this chapter, it was clearly demonstrated that, far from being a tightly-knit and homogeneous institution with power to set the policies of its members, OPEC is an amalgam of countries deeply divided along ethnic and political lines, with serious differences in their resource mix – including petroleum reserves – and their economic needs. These differences are also reflected in OPEC's working methods.

A principal consequence of this situation has been that, more often than not, OPEC has been reactor rather than initiator, responding to external circumstances rather than trying to shape them. In general, whenever these circumstances have required it, during, for example, the period of the oil companies' total dominance, OPEC members have managed to overcome their differences. Under opposite conditions, by contrast, differences among OPEC states have generally proved too strong.

Indeed, since 1973 external circumstances, despite periodic fluctuations, have favoured OPEC, but differences among its members have thereby been exacerbated. Moreover, as demonstrated above, a similar pattern has existed in OPEC-Third World relations. Thus, for example, until 1971 there indeed was a community of interest between OPEC and other developing countries. But oil price increases following the Teheran agreement began to erode that community, and after 1973 the gap between OPEC and developing countries progressively widened, although for a few years OPEC refused openly to acknowledge it. The gap has been particularly marked in the case of those OPEC countries that have large oil reserves, large monetary surpluses, and low absorptive capacity. But there is also a gap between other OPEC members and developing countries in regard to such issues as the price of oil and the development of alternative energy sources.

Nor, because of all these factors, could the OPEC countries agree among themselves on how to help the developing countries, or on concrete and unified action towards the industrialised countries in order to advance Third World interests and promote reform of the international economic system. Regarding the specific issue of aid, OPEC's internal disarray was reflected in its incapacity to agree to set up a single large collective aid institution. On the contrary, following their own special needs and interests, OPEC members chose a variety of ways to channel their aid, although they made a largely-symbolic bow to OPEC solidarity by creating the OPEC Fund.

Important as they are, however, intra-OPEC differences have not been the only or even the most important reasons for the behaviour of its members. Determining reasons, in fact, have related to the nature of OPEC countries, their societies, and their place in the international system. In essence, they began as underdeveloped countries with one principal source of income; their technological bases have been weak and they have lacked trained manpower; their political and social institutions are not capable of meeting the requirements of rapid change, and they have faced serious internal contradictions. Furthermore, the key members of OPEC are located in the strategically important region of the Middle East, and thus they are highly permeable to the great powers and have serious external dependencies.

The combination of these factors has made these countries highly vulnerable to retaliatory actions by a variety of regional and international actors. As a result – as the next chapter will make clear in detail – mitigating the negative implications of these factors, rather than trying to achieve some ideal of Third World solidarity, has become the prime objective of these countries, and has asserted strong claims on the use of their oil and financial assets.

Notes

1. For example, the first Secretary General of OPEC, Dr Fuad Rouhani, used this argument while explaining the reasons behind the creation of OPEC. After quoting the President of Columbia, who had said Columbia had lost more as a result of decline in the price of its coffee than it had received in aid from the alliance for progress, he said: 'This situation, which applies to petroleum too, is aggravated by the fact that the price of manufactured goods which our countries have to buy from the industrial countries continue to increase year after year.' *Text Of Speech Delivered By Mr Fuad Rouhani, Secretary General at the II Consultative Meeting in Geneva*, Geneva: OPEC Public Relations Department, 1963; p. 3.

2. Algeria is one OPEC member which has used this argument. See A.A. Kubbah, *OPEC, Past and Present*, Vienna: Petro-Economic Research Center, 1974, pp. 129-30.

3. Fuad Rouhani, *A History of OPEC*, New York: Praeger, 1972, p. 76.

4. Zuhayr Mikdashi, *The Community of Oil Exporting Countries: A Study in Governmental Cooperation*, London: G. Allen and Unwin, 1972, pp. 28-9.

5. Emile Bustani, *Marche Arabesque*, London: Robert Hale Ltd, 1961, p. 159.

6. Ibid., p. 141.

7. Syria maintained that a unified Arab oil policy should be based on the following principles: '(1) Arab oil revenues should be distributed among the Arab countries according to individual need for industrialisation and raising their standards of living; (2) the oil transportation industry should be regarded as an integral part of the oil production industry.' David Hirst, *Oil and Public Opinion in the Middle East*, London: Faber & Faber Ltd, 1966, p. 106.

8. Ibid., pp. 109-10.

9. Venezuela's active role at such an early stage is explained by the fact that commercial production of oil in Venezuela had started as early as 1917, thus giving the Venezuelans a better understanding of oil and problems related to it. Moreover, Venezuela, which by 1945 had managed to establish the 50-50 principle in its relations with the oil companies, suffered from the competition of lower-priced Middle East oil. In fact, the oil companies increased oil production in the Persian Gulf in order to warn Venezuela against making heavier financial demands on them. Thus the creation of a cooperative front of oil producers served Venezuela's interests well. See Fuad Rouhani, *A History of OPEC*. On the Venezuelan views and activities in oil matters prior to the establishment of OPEC, also see *Documents, Speeches and Venezuelan and World Views Relating to the Antecedents and Creation of OPEC*, the Venezuelan Ministry of Mines and Hydrocarbons: Division of Petroleum Economics, General Secretariat of the Presidency, 1961.

10. Zuhayr Mikdashi, *The Community of Oil Exporting Countries*, p. 31.

11. Fuad Rouhani, *A History of OPEC*.

12. The unilateral nature of oil company decisions seemed to have particularly angered the oil producers, as the following statement by the Shah of Iran illustrates: 'Our fundamental point is that while these actions are taken without our

knowledge, market conditions and the principle of commercial competition might justify lowering of prices, in which case it would not be difficult to convince us. But if this is not the case, then we will not accept it. At any rate, if this is done without our knowledge, even if it is basically correct, it cannot be acceptable to us.' *The Sayings of H.I.M. The Shah About Oil, July 1953-July 1975* (Tir 1331-Tir 1353), Teheran: Ministry of Information and Tourism, August 1975, pp. 32-3, (author's translation from the Persian text).

13. David Hirst, *Oil and Public Opinion*, pp. 111-12.

14 During the Middle East War of June 1967, and later following Israel's occupation of Arab territories, some Arab states sought to balance their military weakness by resorting to the oil weapon. Thus the Arab ministers of finance, economy, and oil met in Baghdad on 3 and 4 June and decided to impose a selective oil embargo on petroleum going to certain specific destinations: the United States, the United Kingdom, and to some extent West Germany. The embargo, however, proved to be ineffective. As the Saudi minister of oil later commented, it 'hurt the Arabs themselves more than anyone else' and the only ones to gain any benefit from it were the non-Arab oil producers. *Middle East Economic Survey*, Vol. XI, No. 32, 7 June 1968, p. 1.

In order to reconsider the situation, another conference of the Arab ministers of finance, economy, and oil was held in Baghdad from 15 to 20 August 1967. In this conference, two diametrically opposed solutions were proposed. Iraq, supported by Algeria, advocated a three-month total stoppage of Arab oil exports. Saudi Arabia, Kuwait and Libya, which had suffered heavy financial losses as a result of the selective embargo, suggested a positive policy of maximizing oil revenues. They urged the use of oil proceeds to support the war-stricken Arab states in their efforts to regain and protect their territorial integrity.

At the end, the latter solution was adopted at the Arab Summit Conference meeting in Khartoum on 29 August 1967. The conference concluded that 'oil flow could itself be used as a positive weapon in that Arab oil represents an Arab asset which could be used to strengthen the economies of those Arab states which were directly affected by the aggression, thereby enabling them to stand firm in the battle.' (Res. 4 – *MEES,* Vol. X, No. 45, 8 September 1967, p. 3.)

Having thus prevented future losses of income, Saudi Arabia, Kuwait, and Libya offered financial assistance on an annual basis to Egypt, Syria, and Jordan.

The unsuccessful oil embargo, therefore, also led to the direct involvement of Arab oil producers in the struggle against Israel, through their financial support of the three confrontation states. This was also the start of massive intra-Arab aid that has continued since then.

15. Zuhayr Mikdashi, *The Community of Oil Exporting Countries,* p. 106.

16. Adib al-Jader, *MEES Supplement*, vol. XI, no. 12, 19 January 1968, p. 1.

17. Ibid., p. 2.

18. *MEES*, vol. XI, no. 32, 7 June 1968, p. 6.

19. 'Summary of OAPEC Charter' *MEES*, vol. XI, no. 12, 19 January 1968, p. 5. For a detailed study of OAPEC's history and evolution, see Mary Ann Tetreault, *The Organization of the Arab Petroleum Exporting Countries: History, Policies, and Prospects*, London: Greenwood Press, 1981. Part of the change in the nature and objectives of OAPEC resulted in its involvement in joint intra-Arab oil ventures. The following are examples of intra-Arab ventures organised under OAPEC: Arab Maritime Petroleum Transport Company (AMPRTC), founded in 1972; Arab Shipbuilding and Repair Yard Company (ASRY), founded

in 1974; Arab Petroleum Investment Corporation (APICORP), founded in 1975; and Arab Petroleum Services Corporation (APSC), founded in 1977.

20. OPEC began in 1960 with five members: Iran, Iraq, Kuwait, Saudi Arabia, and Venezuela. It now has twelve full members, after the addition (in chronological order) of Qatar, Libya, Indonesia, Abu Dhabi (now the United Arab Emirates), Algeria, Nigeria, and Equador. OPEC has one associate member, Gabon. Two applications for membership – from Trinidad and Tobago and Congo (Brazzaville) were rejected because of the low volume of their oil exports. OPEC's statute distinguishes among three categories of members: Founding Members, Full Members, and Associate Members.

According to Resolution I.2, any country with a substantial net export of crude oil can become a member, if it is unanimously accepted by all five Founding Members of the organisation. Furthermore, according to the paragraph C of Article 7 of OPEC's statute, in addition to being a substantial net exporter of petroleum, an applicant must have 'fundamentally similar interests' with OPEC's other members. See: *Text of OPEC Statute*, Vienna: Information Department of OPEC Secretariat, 1971, p. 7.

21. Article 11, paragraph B, ibid., p. 9.

22. For instance, when Iraq was having problems with its concessionnaires, OPEC in several resolutions gave verbal support to Iraq, but none of the members did anything that could have really helped it.

23. This was the case in 1965, when Libya decided to apply the terms of the 1964 OPEC settlement with major companies – regarding royalty expensing based on posted prices – to all companies operating in Libya, including a large number of independents. At that time, the OPEC Conference adopted a strongly-worded resolution, recommending that:

> The governments of the member countries of OPEC, until such time when those title holder companies operating in Libya undertake to comply with the obligations of Articles 11 and 12 of the Royal Decree of November 22, 1965, should not grant any new oil rights of any nature whatsoever or enter into any new contracts concerning the exploration and/or exploitation of new areas to parent countries of said title holder companies, to the affiliated or subsidiary companies of any of them or to any other company in which one of the title holder companies has an interest of 10 per cent or more. . .

OPEC Resolution X.63, *Resolutions of the Tenth Conference in Vienna from 15th to 17th December 1965.* Vienna: OPEC Public Relations Department, p. 105.

24. *OPEC Statute*, Vienna.

25. *OPEC Bulletin*, vol. XI, no. 14, 5 May 1980, p. 45.

26. Ibid.

27. OPEC Resolution XVI.90, reproduced in *OPEC Official Resolutions and Press Releases, 1960-1980*, New York: Pergamon Press, pp. 80-3.

28. Text of Resolution XXI.120. Reproduced in Ibid., pp. 99-100.

29. Notice, for example, the following statement by the Shah of Iran during a speech on the occasion of the opening of the Iranian Parliament in October 1970: 'We are determined to use our oil for the advancement of our country. This is in accordance with the resolution passed at the Seventh Session of the United Nations' General Assembly in 1952 which clearly recognises the sovereign right of all states to use their natural resources for their economic development and progress. . .' *Sayings of H.I.M. The Shah About Oil*, pp. 65-6.

30. *MEES*, vol. XIV, no. 17, 19 February 1971, p. 6 (emphasis added).

31. Thus, for example, in an interview immediately after the oil price increase

of 1973, he said that the oil exporting countries could create a development bank which could finance energy development plans in the Third World countries. Referring to the specific case of Iran and India, he said that Iran could expand the joint Irano-Indian refinery in Madras, as well as establish new refineries and other petro-chemical plants. *The Sayings of H.I.M. The Shah About Oil*, p. 106.

32. The text of President Nixon's letter was published in *MEES Supplement*, vol. XVII, no. 12, 11 January 1974, p. 11.

33. *Middle East Economic Digest*, vol. 18, no. 5, 1 February 1974, p. 126.

34. *MEED*, vol. 18, no. 6, 8 February 1974, p. 148.

35. Ibid., p. 15.

36. Ibid., p. 148.

37. *MEED*, vol. 18, no. 5, 1 February 1974, p. 126.

38. See, for example, Nazli Choucri, *International Politics of Energy Interdependence: The Case of Petroleum*, Lexington, Massachusetts: D.C. Heath & Co., 1976, pp. 91-100.

39. According to an Iranian ex-official involved in the elaboration of this Iranian proposal, the Saudis would have opposed any plan that was proposed by Iran. Nevertheless, had Iran first consulted the Saudis and had been prepared to present the scheme as a joint Saudi-Iranian plan, Riyadh might have accepted it. But given the Shah's concern with boosting his own prestige, it was not prepared to follow this course.

40. See 'No Kuwait Money for Iranian Fund', *MEED*, vol. 18, no. 11, 15 March 1974, p. 294.

41. Quoted from a Saudi source in *MEES*, vol. XVII, no. 25, 12 April 1974, pp. 1-2.

42. The OPEC Special Fund (OSF) was first established as an international account collectively owned by the contributing parties. However, the OSF was an independent institution with its own separate headquarters and administrative apparatus and was not part of the regular OPEC organisation and its secretariat. However, in 1980, the OSF was converted into a full-fledged aid organisation, and from then on would be called the OPEC Fund for International Development. The decision to convert the OSF was reached at the meeting of OPEC finance ministers in Vienna on 27 May 1980. At the same time, the meeting approved an additional increase of $1.6 billion in the Fund's resources. 'Communique of OPEC Finance Ministers Meeting', reproduced in *MEES*, vol. XXIII, no. 33, 2 June 1980, p. 2. For more details on various proposals for a collective OPEC aid institution, see Ibrahim F.I. Shihata, *The OPEC Fund For International Development*, London: Croom Helm Ltd, 1983.

43. *MEED*, vol. 18, no. 9, 1 March 1974, p. 23 (emphasis added).

44. The bank was established in 1975.

45. For a detailed study of this, see 'OPEC, the Trilateral World, and the Developing Countries: New Arrangements for Cooperation, 1976-1980', a report of the Trilateral Task Force on Relations with Developing Countries to the Executive Committee of the Trilateral Commission, by Richard N. Gardner, Saburo Okita, B.I. Udnik, 1975. See also: Kai Bird, 'Co-Opting the Third World Elites: Trilateralism and Saudi Arabia', in Holly Sklar (ed.), *Trilateralism: The Trilateral Commission and Elite Planning for World Management*, Boston: Southend Press, 1980, pp. 341-52.

46. Text of the Solemn Declaration, reproduced in *MEED*, vol. 19, no. 11, 14 March 1975, pp. 8-10. (See Appendix for the full text.)

47. Ibid.

48. Ibid.

49. Ibid.

50. Ibid.

51. After the session, the Algerian delegate said that the meeting's failure resulted from the United States' 'unbending adherence to their rigid position' – isolating oil from other issues – 'despite five compromise suggestions put forward by the developing countries'. *MEED*, vol. 19, no. 16, 18 April 1975, p. 5.

52. *MEES Supplement*, vol. XVIII, no. 26, 18 April 1975, p. 2.

53. Ibid.

54. *MEED*, vol. 20, no. 19, 23 May 1975, p. 7.

55. Ibid.

56. For the text of the working documents, see *MEES Supplement*, vol. XIX, no. 9, 19 December 1975, pp. i-iii.

57. Ibrahim F.I. Shihata, *The Other Face of OPEC: Financial Assistance to the Third World*, New York: Longman, 1982, pp. 83-5.

58. On OPEC's dependence – particularly financial – on the industrialised countries, see: Anindya K. Bhattacharya, *The Myth of Petro Power*, Lexington, Massachusetts: Lexington Books, 1977, pp. 71-6.

59. See *Journal of Commerce*, 3 September 1980, pp. 1, 23.

60. See 'Pragmatism at Cancun', *Far Eastern Economic Review*, 30 October-5 November 1981, pp. 59-60.

61. Ibid., p. 60.

62. *Far Eastern Economic Review*, 1 August 1980, pp. 85-6.

63. According to the latest study published by the OECD at the end of 1982, the medium and long-term external debt of the developing countries had reached as high as $626 billion. Moreover, debt service problems of these countries have become particularly serious in the last few years, as a result of high interest rates in the industrialised countries. For instance, in 1982 debt service payments of the developing countries amounted to $131 billion, of which $60 billion was in interest payments. See the *Christian Science Monitor*, 17 December 1982, p. 11.

64. *Far Eastern Economic Review*, 1 August 1980, p. 86.

65. Ibrahim F.I. Shihata, *The Other Face of OPEC*, pp. 13-16.

66. Ibid.

67. Ibid.

2 THE POLITICS OF OPEC AID

The nature of OPEC as an organisation has kept its members from channelling their assistance to developing countries through a single, large, collective institution. The result has been the disbursement of the bulk of OPEC's aid through bilateral channels, other regional channels, and to a lesser extent international channels. The foregoing thus implies that the politics of OPEC aid should be analysed at several levels.

First, it is important to discuss the politics of that portion of aid that has been channelled through the OPEC Fund for International Development: in order words, collective OPEC aid. However, this represents a very small part of total OPEC aid.

Second, it is important to discuss the politics of aid given by *individual* OPEC countries, that is, national aid. There are two parts to this issue, as well.

Arab Members of OPEC. This subject requires the more extended discussion, since six of OPEC's 13 members are Arab states, and they also have the largest share of OPEC's oil reserves and financial surpluses. In fact, since the end of Iranian aid and with the recent financial problems of OPEC's non-Arab members, OPEC aid is now essentially that of the Arab states and is likely to be so in the future, as well. This discussion will examine Arab aid in its totality and will analyse its uses for the achievement of both common Arab objectives and the objectives of individual Arab countries.

Non-Arab Members of OPEC. This aspect of the subject can best be dealt with through discussion of aid given by Nigeria and Venezuela. Despite the comparatively low level of aid provided by these two countries – particularly Nigeria – it would be valuable to look at their experience because they operate in different regional contexts and have political traditions different from those of OPEC's other member states. Since three other members of OPEC – Indonesia, Ecuador, and Gabon – do not have aid programmes, they will not be discussed. Aid programmes of the two remaining OPEC states – Iran and Saudi Arabia – will be discussed in Chapter 3 as special case studies.

Since a study of the politics of OPEC aid needs to be set in context, this chapter will include a brief conceptual introduction to the politics of foreign aid in general, including traditional motives for granting that aid.

I Conceptual Framework

Granting aid to another country is basically a political decision and as such, therefore, a nation's aid programme is first and foremost a tool of its foreign policy.[1] The historical record of foreign aid provided by traditional donors has amply proved this point. Among the objectives they have tried to achieve through aid, thus serving as its primary motivations, most important have been those in the realms of security, politics, ideology, and economics.

However, the relative impact of each of these objectives in shaping the aid policies of individual donors – as well as to a large extent the nature and content of their aid – has not been uniform at all times. Rather, the relative impact of specific objectives on the donors' policies, both in general and in specific cases, has depended on a variety of factors, including the donors' security, political, and economic needs and interests; the nature of threats posed to those interests; the regional and international contexts within which donor countries have had to act; their ideologies or the general social, economic, political, and cultural philosophies to which they have adhered; their leadership characteristics, and the nature of their decision-making structures and processes.

More often than not the aid policies of the traditional donors have also been determined by a *combination* of these factors, reflecting the fact that a nation's security, political, and economic interests are generally interconnected. Developments that have affected a particular set of these interests could have and generally have had implications for the others.

For example, the maintenance of reliable sources of supply of raw materials has often been a principal economic objective of the traditional aid donors. Yet this factor has also had significant security implications, since the lack of such reliable sources of supply could undermine the economic strength of a donor-state and thus its capacity effectively to provide for its security through adequate military power or other means. Similarly, the traditional donors' propensities to propogate their political ideologies or their particular types of social and economic philosophy have been based partly on the assumption that nations with similar ideologies or philosophies are more likely to be friendly towards one another than nations not sharing such attitudes. Thus ideological compatibility could be seen to have security implications.

This linkage between ideology and security was particularly close during the 1950s, when the international political system was deeply polarised along rigid ideological lines into the so-called Socialist Camp and Free World. Although a number of developments, such as the deep schism within the Socialist Camp, later demonstrated that ideological compatibility may not subdue other elements of interstate rivalry and conflict, in general those nations sharing similar ideologies – in the absense of other divisive factors – have tended to be less hostile towards one another.

Yet to emphasise that, over the last three decades, aid has essentially been used to achieve a wide range of national objectives, is not to imply that the traditional aid donors have never been concerned with the recipients' social and economic development. On the contrary, for several reasons this objective has played an important role. But again, the primary motivating factor for aid has been the security and political implications for the donors of the recipients' underdevelopment. For example, during the 1960s major Western aid donors viewed underdevelopment and poverty in the Third World as being against their own security and political interests, since underdevelopment and poverty tended to destabilise Third World societies, promote radicalism, and create opportunities for the West's competitors to gain influence in these countries and thus to weaken the Western position within overall East-West competition.

In time, a number of significant changes in the international political system, resulting from developments such as the process of decolonisation, the creation of the United Nations, and – most important – drastic changes in the nature of weaponry and warfare, altered the nature of global competition for power. Thus the battle for territories and colonies was replaced by the battle for the hearts and minds of peoples in Third World countries. Within this new context, the capacity of the economically-advanced nations to contribute to the development of Third World nations acquired new importance. In addition, the advanced countries committed themselves, within the UN framework, to improve the economic conditions of the less advanced countries. In fact, this was viewed as essential for the maintenance of international peace.

More importantly, Third World nations gradually gained more capacity – although still limited – to retaliate against advanced-country neglect of their developmental needs. One easy way of doing this was to turn to the rival camp.

As a result of these multifaceted developments, a greater linkage was established between particular interests of the traditional aid donors and the developmental needs of the recipients. Despite this linkage, however, those donor interests remained the primary motive behind the granting of foreign aid, and the requirements of securing those interests the primary determinant of the aid's content and nature.

Within this general context, aid has traditionally been provided for the following motives:

Security. In this category, aid essentially has been used either to ward off a particular, clearly-identifiable danger, or to improve the donors' broader security environments.

Political and Ideological. These motives have traditionally been an extension of the donors' security interests, closely related to the creation or maintenance of regional and international environments congenial to those interests. However, this has essentially been true of long-term political goals. By contrast, short-term political goals which have influenced aid policies have been related to creating, facilitating, or maintaining favourable conditions for achieving more long-term objectives or diplomatic goals, such as gaining either support for the donor-nations' positions in international organisations or concessions in bilateral and multilateral negotiations. Other political goals have traditionally been related to gaining good will – usually in countries in which the donor has had no specific security, political, or economic interest; to enhancing the donor's prestige; and to promoting the donor's particular culture.

Economic. Major economic motives for aid have been the following: to secure access to raw materials; to maintain and/or expand export markets; and to protect private capital and to create a favourable investment climate.

This short conceptual introduction to traditional motives for aid does not exhaust the subject. But it has been important to set the stage for the discussion that follows – namely, to identify and analyse real motives rather than declaratory stances behind OPEC aid.

II Collective OPEC Aid

Of all the aid granted by OPEC members, assistance provided by the OPEC Special Fund – now the OPEC Fund for International Development – has been least affected by any particular security, political, economic, or other interest, since this aid was not designed to help OPEC members achieve such goals. That fact, in turn, largely explains the low percentage of OPEC members' aid channelled through their collective aid institution. Yet this does not mean that OPEC Fund aid has had no other purpose than the social and economic development of the recipients. Quite the contrary, it has been supposed to serve two important purposes: to help offset the negative impact of oil price increases on OPEC-Third World relations and thus to gain good will for OPEC; and to preserve and enhance OPEC's prestige among Third World countries.

Still, OPEC Fund assistance in general has not been tainted by individual interests of member countries.

By its own testimony, the OPEC Fund's only declared objective is: 'The strengthening of financial cooperation among developing countries through providing untied financial assistance to these countries without any conditions of a political nature.'[2] In the process, the Fund's operations have been governed by the principle of universality: 'No developing country affected by economic and financial problems will be excluded because of its geographical location or political orientation.'[3] Indeed, since the Fund began operating, it has to a great extent remained faithful to these principles.

In addition, its operations have also been influenced to some extent by principles developed in the context of the so-called New International Economic Order (NIEO). In fact, the Fund was created to demonstrate the solidarity of OPEC countries with aspirations of other developing countries, as articulated within the NIEO framework. The Fund's first annual report states that 'The OPEC Special Fund was established as one of the many instruments of change and policy tools required for shaping the New International Economic Order.'[4]

Some other OPEC actions – largely carried out through the OPEC Fund – have also been justified as helping to achieve the objectives of the NIEO. These have included large contributions to the International Fund for Agricultural Development and contributions to help establish a Common Fund within the context of UNCTAD's Integrated Programme for Commodities (IPC).

Yet despite their commitment to the objectives of the NIEO, OPEC countries have refused to shoulder a disproportionate burden. In regard to the Common Fund, for example, OPEC members have resented pressures from industrialised countries to provide a larger share of financial resources. Thus, at the negotiating conference on the Common Fund (15 March 1977), the OPEC Fund's Director General reiterated OPEC's support within the general framework projected by UNCTAD, but then said:

> OPEC countries, which account for less than 3.5 per cent of the trade shares in the 18 Nairobi commodities, should not be treated in the context of the Common Fund as a distinct and separate category. They may participate in the Fund's equity capital in the same manner as other developing countries, according to agreed criteria applicable to all developing countries.[5]

However, given the symbolic importance attached by the developing countries to the Common Fund, the OPEC Fund wished to show its commitment to developing-country objectives. It expressed readiness to provide support to the 29 least-developed countries (as defined by the United Nations) to enable them, if they wished, to meet part of their contribution to the projected Common Fund. Later, when agreement was finally reached in 1980 to set up the fund, albeit on a reduced scale, OPEC members contributed almost one-third of its resources, as well as the share of 29 least-developed countries ($1 million each).

The OPEC Fund's commitment to the objectives of the NIEO has also led it to assist projects that encourage cooperation among developing countries, since the expansion of intra-developing country cooperation was highly recommended by the Programme of Action for the establishment of the NIEO.[6] A good example has been cooperation between the OPEC Fund and the United Nations Development Programme (UNDP) in providing technical assistance to regional projects.

Also, the essentially non-political nature of the OPEC Fund has led to its application of internationally-set criteria in the selection of recipients for its aid.[7] The Fund has also not tried to impose its own preferred development strategy, in order to avoid being accused of interference in the recipients' economic affairs. Contributing to this approach, however, have been the Fund's inherent limitations, including the limited nature of its resources and its lack of trained staff in adequate numbers. These factors, plus the Fund's desire to extend aid to as many countries as possible, have meant that its aid has seldom been large enough to have a decisive impact on recipient countries' economic development planning.

Similarly, the Fund's aid has not had a great political impact, particularly in creating recipient-country dependence. However, certain aspects of the Fund's operational style have tended to perpetuate developing-country dependence on the existing international development institutions. Among these practices has been the Fund's emphasis on co-financing projects already approved by the World Bank, and for which the Bank is the executing agency. Also, through the same process of co-financing projects with OPEC members' own national aid agencies – essentially Arab agencies – the Fund has indirectly helped to advance these agencies' purposes and to consolidate their positions among the developing countries. Moreover, this particular practice has been in conflict with the Fund's declared objectives relating to the realisation of NIEO objectives, since neither the World Bank nor the OPEC national aid agencies have been particularly committed to the NIEO.

III National OPEC Aid

Common Factors in Arab Aid

The aid policies of the Arab members of OPEC have been motivated first and foremost by their security, politico-ideological and economic objectives, both at the level of individual Arab countries and at a Pan-Arab level. As such, therefore, Arab aid has been deeply affected by intra-Arab politics, including deep-rooted political and ideological divergences and conflicts of interest among the Arab countries.

One of the paradoxes of Arab politics is that, despite their divergences, the Arab countries at least in theory are committed to the ideal of Arab unity and to some common Arab political and economic objectives. Given this commitment, they agree that their new wealth should be used to achieve these objectives. Yet given their divergences, they disagree on the exact nature, order of priority, and best means to achieve these goals. Thus through its financial leverage, every major Arab donor has tried to influence the evolution both of intra-Arab relations and relations between Arab and Third World countries in directions more akin to its own interests and ideological preferences. This is not to say that Arab countries have been totally insensitive to the aspirations of the developing countries. It is simply to stress that their individual and common objectives and interests have had priority over other considerations.

Security and Political. For the past 30 years, the paramount security and political concern of the Arabs has been the creation of the Jewish state of Israel and its expansion at the expense of Arab lands. Yet for a long time, the burden of meeting this threat was borne principally by Egypt and to a lesser extent by Syria and Jordan. Nor was this surprising, since, until 1967, Egypt no doubt was the strongest and most influential member of the Arab world, by virtue of its size and more advanced economy and military power. Since Egypt bore the brunt of fighting Israel, it also acquired the capacity to determine Arab policies towards Israel, and became in Arab eyes the real defender of Arab rights.

But Egypt's defeat in the war of June 1967 changed the situation. The loss of large portions of Arab territory to Israel, plus Egypt's military losses and economic problems – resulting partly from President Nasser's socialist policies and the strains of a drawn-out war in Yemen – seriously eroded its position in the Arab world. At the same time, while Egypt's position was being eroded, a number of other Arab countries – conservatives like Saudi Arabia, Libya, and Kuwait – were acquiring new wealth as a result of changes in relations between oil-producing countries and oil companies. And they were prepared to use this new wealth to gain influence.

Nasser's revolutionary policies and his tactics of appealing directly to Arab populations had long caused concern among these conservative oil-producing countries and had provoked their antagonism towards Egypt. For instance, Saudi Arabia was a direct target of Nasser's revolutionary politics. For most of the time, Egypt limited itself to propaganda warfare; but its armed intervention in the Yemeni civil war changed the situation. For the first time, another Arab country – Saudi Arabia – saw its security directly threatened by the proximity of the Egyptian army.

Saudi Arabia reacted to this threat, first, by actively supporting the conservative factions in Yemen; and second – after King Faisal assumed power – by engaging in extensive diplomatic efforts aimed at establishing closer contacts and cooperation among countries opposed to Nasser and his interventionist policies.[8] For example, in order to broaden support for his policies, King Faisal appealed to the concept of Islamic solidarity, using it as a convenient ideological alternative to Nasser's Arab socialism.

In pursuit of this policy, King Faisal proposed the convening of a conference of heads of state of Islamic countries. But in order to prevent this conference from appearing to be an anti-revolutionary (and particularly an anti-Nasser) device, he proposed to include such revolutionary regimes as Syria, Egypt, and Algeria. But in practice, Faisal focused his efforts on those conservative Islamic countries whose relations with Cairo were cool at best.

Saudi Arabia's efforts, however, did not succeed in eroding Egypt's influence in the Arab world.[9] But then the 1967 war drastically changed the intra-Arab balance of power. With Egypt's military and economic power dissipated and its moral influence radically reduced, no single Arab country could any longer claim overwhelming influence on the shape of Arab politics. Rather, from then on Arab politics were subjected to influences emanating from the newly-emerged centres of power.

The most important of these new centres were the Arab oil producers. Taking advantage of Arab disenchantment with Nasserite tactics and policies, these countries set out to influence more effectively the future development of Arab politics by using their new wealth. The Saudis were at the head of these countries and organised and coordinated their actions. Thus the Arab oil producers offered their assistance to Egypt; but in return they exacted a price: 'The price was a political one – concessions on the part of Egypt and its willingness to reassess its dominant political posture in the region in exchange for economic support.'[10]

Egypt agreed to pay the price to a very large extent, by patching up its differences with Jordan and Saudi Arabia, by recalling its army from Yemen, and by stopping direct propaganda attacks on Arab monarchies.[11] However, although the Arab oil producers used their financial power to exact concessions from Egypt, their assistance was not merely a cynical exercise in the use of financial power for political ends. Quite the contrary, in order to make their assistance acceptable and their participation in the development of Arab strategy legitimate, the oil producers had to use collective Arab channels. Thus the decision to pay subsidies to Egypt, Syria, and Jordan was taken at the Khartoum Conference of Arab heads of state and, as such, was a joint Arab decision to meet a common Arab challenge. Moreover, the 'subsidies' were only one of several means suggested by the Arab countries to deal with the Israeli threat, and the oil producers had to bargain hard in order to gain Arab acceptance.[12]

What the foregoing implies, therefore, is that despite changes in the intra-Arab balance of power in favour of the oil producers – which in turn had increased their influence in the Arab world – the peculiarities of Arab politics imposed limitations (and still do) on their ability to pursue their individual interests in disregard of wider

Arab interests. Thus, like all other Arabs, the oil producers had to find some kind of Pan-Arab formula to achieve their own interests.[13]

One consequence of the relative shift in the intra-Arab balance of power was that the Arab strategy for dealing with Israel shifted from that essentially of military confrontation to that of finding a political solution. However, before the Arabs could adopt this strategy, they had to go through one more war. That took place in October 1973 and was much broader, in so far as Arab participation – albeit indirect – was concerned. The Arab oil producers played a major role by imposing an oil embargo on those states supporting Israel. The psychological effect of the embargo, plus its impact on global oil markets, was very deep indeed. The wealth and power of the oil producers were greatly enhanced as a result of these events. Moreover, the Arabs (mainly Egypt) scored some military victories over Israel that were very effective in restoring their pride. Buoyed by their new sense of pride and their new wealth, the Arabs felt confident enough to pursue the path of a political solution to their conflict with Israel.

Thus they set out to convince international public opinion of the rightness of their cause and to win the support of as many countries as possible. Of course, the Arabs had tried this before, but after 1973 their financial means and their control over the world's key source of exportable oil gave them potent means of persuasion that they have used to good effect.

The Arabs successfully used their financial assets in various forms – such as aid to developing countries and investment in industrialised countries – to gain support for their cause. Extensive trade, economic, and financial relations between the Arab oil producers and European countries, plus the development of such initiatives as the Euro-Arab dialogue and the Trilateral Cooperation, greatly contributed to changes in European attitudes towards the Arab-Israeli conflict. However, once limitations of European capacity or willingness to make changes required by the Arabs became apparent, these initiatives also gradually died out.

Concerning relations with the Third World, Arab-African relations reflected particularly well the interplay of a wide range of different factors. As a measure of the efficacy of aid in achieving common Arab goals, it is useful to make a brief study of the impact of Arab financial power in changing the attitude of African countries towards the Arab-Israeli conflict.[14]

Afro-Arab Relations. Relations between African and Arab nations have had a number of particular features. For instance, the fact that eight of the 22 members of the Arab League are also members of the OAU, plus a shared history of colonial domination and anti-colonial struggle, creates special bonds between them. Moreover, most Arab countries historically have supported African nationalist movements and later the liberation movements in southern Africa. At times, important Arab and African leaders – such as Nasser and Nkrumah – have held similar ideological views and have tried to organise Arab-African co-operation.[15]

Indeed, any judgement on Arab economic aid to Africa and the political rewards for the Arabs would be incomplete and prone to error if it did not take due account of these historical factors. As one expert has pointed out:

> It is important to remember the early efforts at forging solidarity between the Arab world and Africa because there is a mistaken, but common, view that the present cooperation between Arabs and Africans is based purely on expedience and self-interest.[16]

Nor can African support of the Arab cause or the breaking of relations with Israel be directly attributed to African expectations to receive cheap oil or financial aid. In fact, 'by the time the Organisation of Petroleum Exporting Countries dramatically raised the price of oil, much of Africa had already sided with the Arabs on the Palestine question'.[17] Even African countries critical of OPEC's oil price increases took pains to distinguish between the increases and the Palestinian question.

In many instances, in fact, African support predated the sharp increase in Arab revenues and the flow of Arab aid to Africa. Rather, this support for the Arab cause seemed, to a considerable extent, to have been the result of strains in African-Israeli relations, because of the latter's being part of the Western world, and particularly because of its close relations with the racist regimes of South Africa and Rhodesia. As one expert has put it, this is not to say that Israel was never genuinely interested in identifying with liberation forces in Africa, 'but the Israelis became hampered by their bed-fellow'.[18]

To quote the same expert:

> On the one hand Israel was virtually the fifty-first state of the U.S.A., with a massive American commitment to its preservation, and massive American contributions to its maintenance and up-

> keep. In that respect Israel was a piece of the Western world deposited in the heart of the third world. On the other hand there were the Israeli connections with white dominated southern Africa. South Africa was the second largest non-governmental external financial contributor to Israel's funds.[19]

Inevitably, therefore, Israel found itself siding with the Africans' enemies.[20]

At the same time, there has been a qualitative difference between African support given to the Arab cause and the severing of relations with Israel. But even here, not all African countries broke relations with Israel solely to get Arab aid. Rather, Israel's policies caused the initial shift in the African attitude. For example, a major Israeli mistake was to help Idi Amin oust Milton Obote. One reason for Israel's decision was Obote's pro-Arab inclinations during his last year in office. This event heightened the Africans' concern over a similar role that Israeli training and technical assistance personnel might play in their own countries.[21]

Beyond African support on Palestine and severing ties with Israel, the African response to the Arabs has to a very large extent been influenced by the prospect of large amounts of Arab aid and investment. For instance, high expectations were raised in Africa about prospects for development by combining Arab money and African natural resources. The Arabs' euphoric mood and statements about their ability to help Africa raised African expectations even further.[22]

Thus, when both Arab aid and investment proved to be much less than expected, the Africans began to react sharply, although the degree of their negative reaction differed from country to country and was very much influenced by the ideological inclination of each country.[23]

In order to prevent feelings like these from damaging Arab-African relations, the Arab countries took certain measures. One was the creation of the Arab Bank for African Development, which was decided upon at the Arab Summit of 1973 in Algiers and became operational in 1975.[24] At first, the Africans did not receive the Bank with great enthusiasm. The initial capital proposed was judged inadequate; the capital was later increased. Also, Africans feared that this new institution might compete with the African Development Bank or at best duplicate its operations.

The path of Afro-Arab cooperation has proved to be full of pitfalls. Principal problems have been caused by political, economic, ideological and even psychological conflicts, both within each group and between them.

The underlying psychological problem has been the African fear that the Arabs might use aid to impose their cultural and religious values and to expand their influence beyond reasonable levels. In fact, the African countries have been wary of a new Arab-Islamic colonialism replacing or supplementing European colonialism in Africa.[25]

However, what has most worried the Africans has been the intervention of some Arab countries in intra-African disputes, as well as the spillover of intra-Arab conflicts into Africa (for example, the Libyan interventions in Chad and Uganda, or the Arab support for the Muslim Eritrean rebels in Ethiopia). These have endangered fundamental principles (for example, non-interference in internal affairs and the sanctity of colonial boundaries) upon which the very fragile foundations of African unity have been based. Furthermore, intra-Arab conflicts and rivalries have brought yet other sources of division to a continent already torn by deep tribal, political, and ideological differences, for example, the conflict between Algeria and Morocco over Western Sahara.[26]

As a final factor, Arab countries have not yet developed a common, cohesive strategy for their own regional, political, and economic cooperation, and thus are unable to approach the African countries with concrete plans for Afro-Arab cooperation. As a result, every Arab country with financial means has embarked on its own aid and influence adventure in Africa, mostly to the disappointment of the African countries, thus intensifying fears of Arab influence.

In sum, therefore, in theory there have been infinite possibilities for close Arab-African cooperation; and the increase in Arab oil revenues raised hopes as to their speedy realisation. But such an eventuality certainly does not lie in the near future. Nevertheless, it is important to note that there has been more behind this failure than the above factors, including barriers to regional cooperation among the developing countries in general.

Economic. Following political goals – essentially related to the question of Palestine – the most important common Arab goal has been the social and economic development of the Arab world. This goal has been important because of its significance for general Arab revival. But, again, it has also been important because of its implications for the future of Arab-Israeli relations and thus for common Arab security. In fact, since their defeat at Israeli hands in 1948, the Arab countries have attributed their incapacity to meet Israel's challenge not only to the lack of concerted Arab action, but also to the underdeveloped state of Arab economies and technological bases. Thus for three decades the Arabs have tried to take joint measures to speed up Arab economic development and cooperation, hoping that the culmination of these efforts would lead to Arab economic unity at some future point.

The first step to coordinating Arab actions was the signing of the Joint Defence and Economic Cooperation Treaty in June 1950, although – even before then – a principal objective of the Arab League charter had been the promotion of Arab economic cooperation. But the Joint Defence and Economic Cooperation Treaty was more specific. The treaty created an Arab Economic Council which, in cooperation with the Economic Committee of the League, was to suggest ways and means to promote Arab economic development, closer cooperation, and more effective coordination among Arab countries.[27]

But this Council remained largely ineffective, since it did not become autonomous until 1959. Nevertheless, in 1957 the Economic Council produced a Convention for Economic Unity which, again, remained ineffective until 1962. These efforts were followed by the creation of a Council for Arab Economic Unity (CAEU) to implement the 1957 Convention, but another two years passed before CAEU had enough members to become operational. In the same year (1964), an Arab Common Market was created by the Arab Economic Council to mark the first step towards economic unity. These last two steps were perhaps the most spectacular actions taken on the path to Arab economic unity.[28]

Nevertheless, for a long time Arab efforts at economic cooperation were not particularly successful, principally because of lags in the implementation of agreements caused by intra-Arab political conflicts. As one expert put it, implementation 'remained all through at the mercy of the political climate, and therefore has witnessed severe discontinuities as a result of the erratic course of political relations'.[29]

Despite their significance, political divergences have not been the only cause of a lack of progress in Arab economic cooperation. Other major barriers have been essentially economic, including differences among Arab economies in the level of their development; their competitive rather than complementary natures; and their different colonial legacies.[30]

However, most experts have argued that economic problems have not been insurmountable, and that the political and psychological barriers have been the most intractable.[31] For example, in response to the popular Arab belief in the virtues of unity, the Arabs have adopted ambitious resolutions calling for complete unity, yet at the same time have refused to implement modest measures of cooperation, fearing that this might reduce their freedom of action or independence.

However, since the oil revolution, certain changes – both in the economic conditions of a number of countries and in their political perspectives – have boosted intra-Arab economic cooperation. Although the results thus far are not conclusive, these changes could make a more limited, pragmatic cooperation almost a necessity for a large number of Arab countries.

The most significant of these changes has been the dual phenomenon of a development boom in Arab oil producing countries and their greater degree of involvement in the mainstream of Arab political life. The oil producers' development boom has created real bonds of economic interdependence among the Arab countries that have even survived political conflicts. This newly-emerged Arab interdependence has derived mainly from certain characteristics of the Arab oil producers, particularly those with large foreign exchange surpluses. For example, they have had small populations; underdeveloped technological bases – even compared to some other Arab countries, resulting in acute shortages of skilled manpower; very small or no agricultural bases; small domestic markets; and limited access to productive investment outlets, as compared with non-productive investments (that is, real estate and currency markets).

The combination of these factors has, in turn, led to an influx of labour from heavily populated and technologically more advanced Arab countries to the oil producers and a reverse flow of worker remittances. For example, today the economies and social services of countries such as Saudi Arabia, Kuwait, the UAE, and Libya cannot operate without foreign labour. Thus, even in times of political conflict, nothing has been done to interfere with this aspect of intra-Arab relations. For instance, in the past few years, Egypt and Libya have several times reached the brink of war or gone slightly beyond, but nothing has been done by either side to interfere with the work of Egyptians in Libya. Also, when Arab governments decided to penalise Egypt for signing a separate peace treaty with Israel, they exempted Egyptian immigrant workers from retaliatory measures, stating that they did not want to harm the Egyptian people. No doubt this factor did play a role, but the real reason was that these countries could not do without the Egyptian workers. Nor could Egypt retaliate by calling its citizens home, since it also needed their remittances.

From a long-term perspective, too, the oil producers will need Arab and other developing countries as export markets and investment outlets. Moreover, at times tensions between Arab oil producers and industrialised countries have alerted the former to the potential risk that the latter might in the future exploit Arab dependence – on imported food.[32] Here, the answer could lie in a combination of the oil-producers' financial resources and the agricultural potential of other Arab countries.

For all these reasons, therefore, since oil-producer income went up – and particularly since 1974 – a number of plans for Arab economic cooperation have been resurrected and the number of Arab joint ventures has increased. With regard to encouraging Arab economic cooperation, the most significant step has been the creation of the Arab Fund for Social and Economic Development – based on the original idea of an Arab financial institution. Another example has been the establishment of the Arab Authority for Agricultural Investment and Development and the Arab Monetary Fund.

The small oil producing countries of the Persian Gulf, particularly Kuwait, have been especially active in promoting regional schemes and in developing the necessary legal and institutional frameworks for the free movement of capital among the Arab countries. Political and economic interests have contributed to this attitude. From a political point of view, these countries have thought that their security and other interests would be best served within the context of a more interdependent Arab world that would give them some measure of protection against the ambitions of larger but resource-poor Arab states.

Economically, too, they would benefit from closer Arab cooperation, since their own individual resources and market size do not allow the development of diversified economic bases.

However, despite considerable progress, Arab economic cooperation has in general fallen short of expectations, again largely because of political tensions and deficiencies in infrastructure in Arab countries. As a result, the level of financial transfers from oil producers to other Arab countries has fallen far below the initial hopes of the potential recipients. Given these problems, the Arab oil producers of the Persian Gulf have embarked on their own more limited regional cooperation.[33] Intra-Gulf cooperation received a major boost with the creation of the Gulf Cooperation Council in 1981.

Religion. Another common Arab goal is the promotion of Islamic solidarity and the consolidation – and whenever possible the spread – of Islam and Islamic culture. Two basic reasons account for this:

1. Arabism and Islam are closely related. Islam originated in Arabia and the Muslim Holy Book is written in Arabic. In the minds of most Arabs, Islamic culture is synonymous with Arab culture. Thus, the revival and expansion of Islamic culture has often been viewed as helping the flourishing and expansion of Arab culture.
2. Islam has been important for the promotion of the Arab cause in the Arab-Israeli conflict. Indeed, the level of support among Muslim countries increased after the June 1967 War and Jerusalem's falling under Israeli occupation. Since Jerusalem is the most sacred Muslim holy place after Mecca and Medina, Arabs have believed that sharpening Islamic identity among Muslim countries would increase concern for the future of Jerusalem, and thus give the Arab-Israeli conflict an Islamic dimension.

Historically, however, the Arab countries have used Islam as a means of advancing their own interests, although in the process they have created such momentum that they themselves could no longer overlook Islam's demands. As noted earlier, for example, King Faisal's desire to find an alternative to Nasser's Arab Socialism and to create an anti-Nasser coalition led him to organise the Islamic Conference. More recently, Libya has used the Islamic factor to expand its influence in those non-Arab African countries that either have a Muslim majority or have large Muslim minorities.

Foreign aid has played some role in the effort to promote Islam. But the Arab countries have relied essentially on bilateral channels, and the only joint Arab action has been the creation of an Islamic Development Bank.

In sum, therefore, there have been three main factors leading to cooperation among Arab states that have had an impact upon their aid policies: direct concerns about the Arab-Israeli conflict, economic development, and the role of Islam.

Specific Factors of Arab Aid

The aid policies of individual Arab donors have also been deeply affected by those factors that have affected their aid at the Pan-Arab level. However, at the level of individual Arab countries, the relative impact of each of these factors has not been equal for all. This situation in turn has resulted from considerable differences existing among

Arab donors in regard to their sizes, populations, resource mixes – beyond oil – leadership characteristics; and most important, their geo-strategic conditions and the nature of threats to their security.

Security. Security considerations have been the most influential factor in determining the aid policies of a number of Arab donors, whereas their impact in the case of two Arab countries – namely, Libya and Iraq – have not been very significant. Security considerations have been paramount in the cases of small Persian Gulf donors – namely, Kuwait, the UAE, and Qatar. This fact has derived from the essential characteristics of these countries, which create special security problems for them. The most important of these characteristics have been the following:

(a) they are small, with fabulous wealth that has enticed the envy and greed of their neighbours and other fellow-Arabs;
(b) their non-oil resources are meagre;
(c) they have small indigenous populations, a fact that has put severe limitations on their ability to develop viable military forces;
(d) they have large non-indigenous populations which, together with their religious divisions, could be a source of subversion and domestic unrest;
(e) given the conservative nature of their governments, in the past they have had – and still do – legitimacy problems with large segments of Arab opinion;
(f) the institutional capacities of their governments are not fully developed yet; and
(g) geo-strategic conditions have not been favourable: they are located in a zone of great power rivalry and thus have been highly permeable to outside forces. Moreover, they have faced far stronger neighbours vying for regional leadership, a situation that has created an unstable regional environment for them. Also, some of these countries have been openly coveted by some of their stronger neighbours.

The combination of these factors has created special security problems for these countries, the most important of which have been direct military take-over attempts by their larger and stronger neighbours; a deteriorating regional environment; and internal subversion by radical Arab or other forces, in some cases using immigrant populations.[34]

For example, concerning the threat of a direct military take-over, since the very early days of its independence in 1961, Kuwait faced such a threat from Iraq, which laid claim to its territory. This claim did not go beyond words and was warded off by the sending of 6,000 British troops to Kuwait. Nevertheless, it was a big disappointment for Kuwait.

Other Persian Gulf countries have not had the same traumatic experience as Kuwait. But they have also been potentially vulnerable to such threats. Thus part of the aid of these countries has been aimed at warding off this kind of threat.[35]

The other major threat to these countries has been a deteriorating regional security environment. In fact, this has meant that the predominance of hostile forces in regions of interest – both immediate and more distant – would be hazardous to their security and would thus have needed to be prevented. Since these countries have lacked the military potential to deter these forces, they have essentially relied on aid to neutralise and pacify existing hostile forces; to moderate – as far as possible – the positions of hostile forces; and to strengthen existing moderate and friendly forces. The Gulf countries have applied this strategy in their immediate region – the Persian Gulf – in the Arab world, and in their peripheries.

Extensive aid given by the Gulf countries to the Arab confrontation states – as well as to such radical states in the Gulf region as South Yemen, and to such peripheral states as Pakistan, Somalia, and Sudan – has all been justified in terms of the above factors.

Moreover, at the global level the Gulf countries have essentially viewed their security interests as being linked to those of the Western world, although they have proclaimed non-alignment and – particularly Kuwait – have followed a more even-handed policy towards the East-West conflict. Thus through their aid they have tried to strengthen Western positions in the above-mentioned regions.

The danger of internal subversion has been the other serious threat to the security of the Gulf countries. As noted earlier, this threat has essentially derived from the following sources: leadership characteristics of these countries – which are conservative and thus disliked by the radical Arabs; resentment by poorer Arab countries of their riches; and the presence of large non-indigenous populations with grievances of their own which have been manipulated by hostile forces.[36]

The negative impact of these conditions has been further intensified by the existence of religious and other divisions within these countries, as well as by social and political stresses caused by development and rapid change.

Again, these countries have used aid to reduce such threats. By giving aid, they have tried to show first the Arab world and then the international community that they are responsible members of that community, ready to help others. In this way, they have hoped to convince potentially or actually hostile forces – and countries – that friendship or at least benign neutrality towards them would be more beneficial and financially-rewarding than hostility.[37] Large contributions by the Gulf countries to such forces as the Palestine Liberation Organisation have been examples of this type of aid.

In sum, therefore, the most important function of the aid extended by these countries has been to serve as security insurance for them.

Unlike the Gulf countries, security has not been the primary motivation for Libyan and Iraqi aid. Again, this fact has derived from these countries' particular conditions and the nature of threats to their security. Thus unlike the Persian Gulf countries, Libya and Iraq have not faced the danger of a direct military take-over by their neighbours. In Iraq's case, its size and its military strength have been serious barriers. Libya has been relatively more vulnerable despite a large inflow of arms, since – given its manpower problems – the efficiency of its armed forces has been doubtful. Moreover, some of Libya's neighbours, notably Egypt, have been militarily stronger and potentially could threaten its security. Indeed, strained relations between Libya and Egypt since their failed attempt at unification in 1971 have – as noted earlier – on two occasions brought them to the brink of war, and once slightly beyond. Even so, in view of Libya's size and the absence of an acceptable pretext – such as a long-standing territorial claim such as exists in the case of most Persian Gulf countries – a direct military take-over attempt by Egypt is unlikely.[38]

Also, Libya and Iraq have not faced the same problems of internal subversion as have the Persian Gulf countries. Although vastly different from one another, their societies are more homogeneous and stable.[39]

Also, being among radical Arab countries, they have not faced the challenges of radicalism as have the Persian Gulf countries. However, in the case of Iraq – with its rapid shifting of alliances and political directions – this situation has been changing.

Political and Ideological. In the cases of the Persian Gulf donors, political and ideological considerations have been the second most influential factor determining their aid policies. However, for these countries political interests have indeed been an extension of their security needs. Thus these factors have tended to intensify the impact of security considerations. Beyond this, factors such as increasing their standing in the Arab world and internationally have also been important.

By contrast, for Libya and Iraq, political and ideological factors have been the primary influences. Moreover, in the case of both countries, leadership ambitions in the Arab and Third Worlds have also played a larger role. Thus, for example Iraq's militant Ba'athist Arab nationalism and anti-Zionism led it to refrain from financially assisting the confrontation states, as was decided by the Khartoum Conference of 1967.[40] Iraq's ideological preferences initially also affected its choice of aid recipients, among Third World countries as well as multilateral agencies. Thus Iraq initially favoured socialist-oriented Third World countries or at least those that were not closely identified with the West.

Also, during the years 1974-7 Iraq did not contribute to the IMF or the IBRD, including the IMF Oil Facility. Reasons cited for the last-named decision were that this facility had helped the industrialised countries and Israel more than the developing countries, and that Iraq had warned the Arab countries not to participate in it. The Baghdad daily, *Al-Thawra*, organ of the Ba'ath party, wrote that:

> The United States has for some time been applying pressure on a number of Arab countries to place $12 billion dollars at the IMF's disposal in order to permit the fund to increase its loans to the developing countries. The industrial countries are in the habit of launching one financial facility after another under the flimsy pretext of aiding the developing countries whereas in fact their main objective is to gain control over more of the Arab oil producers' funds.[41]

However, with changing Iraqi policies after 1978, Iraq's attitude towards aid has also changed. Already by 1974, despite its radical posture and its close links with the Soviet Union, Iraq had begun to expand its relations with a number of Western and some developing countries.[42]

This westward shift in Iraq's policies was later accentuated by a number of regional and intra-Arab developments such as the Iranian revolution and Egypt's isolation after its peace treaty with Israel.

Thus, sensing the leadership opportunities provided for it by these events, Iraq embarked on active diplomacy aimed at gaining regional supremacy and greater influence in the Arab and Third Worlds, largely through patching up old differences and in general adopting a more moderate and less ideologically-rigid approach.

Regarding the aid issue, this new activist policy led Iraq to become more vocal in OPEC and to present new initiatives. On a bilateral level as well, Iraq took a number of initiatives and expanded the geographical scope of its aid.[43]

In addition, regional rivalries also played a role in the direction of Iraq's aid. For example, since 1976 Iraq has given considerable aid to Jordan – in excess of the latter's share of the funds allocated to the confrontation states. Rivalry with Syria – as well as access to Jordan's Mediterranean ports – have been primary motivations. Rivalry with Iran also might have been one reason for Iraq's considerable aid to India.

In Libya's case, as well, political and ideological factors have played a determining role in shaping its aid policies. The dominant ideology has been Qaddaffi's views on the economic and political organisation of the Arab and Third Worlds, enunciated in his so-called third theory.[44] Principal tenets of Qaddaffi's third theory have been Pan-Arabism, anti-Zionism and Islam. Qaddaffi's ideology has also been anti-Western because of the West's support for Zionism.

In its relations with the Arab countries, including those aspects related to aid, Libya has essentially applied Pan-Arabist criteria. Thus Libyan aid to Jordan was suspended after Qaddaffi came to power in 1969. By contrast, Libyan aid to Egypt continued until the westward shift in its policy became irreversible. However, even the so-called progressive Arab regimes – Syria and Iraq – have not been immune to Qaddaffi's criticism on the basis of their laxity towards the achievement of Arab unity. This feeling, in turn, has affected the level and the degree of continuity of Libya's aid to these countries.[45] Moreover, Qaddaffi has used the lure of aid to encourage Arab countries to move towards unity.[46]

In addition to anti-Zionism and Pan-Arabism, Islam has been a strong component of Qaddaffi's ideology. He has believed that Islam is the best answer to the Third World's problems, and for the Islamic countries a return to Islamic principles is the best solution to their difficulties.[47]

In Qaddaffi's view, Libya's Islamic revolution was the beginning of Muslim awakening, and therefore the Libyans have a special responsibility to spread Islamic revolution to other countries.[48] Qaddaffi's theory of Islamic revolution has not only provided him with a pretext to intervene in Afro-Asian countries, but it has also served his anti-Israeli objectives, since in his view being a Muslim revolutionary and being anti-Israeli are the same.

Regarding the question of Libyan aid, Qaddaffi's philosophy has had a certain influence. In Africa, for instance, Libya's aid to Idi Amin, despite his close relations with Israel, stemmed from his being Muslim. Qaddaffi apparently believed that Amin's relations with Israel were out of necessity and – if given an alternative – being a Muslim he would not continue these relations. Libya's support to the Eritrean Liberation Front derived largely from feelings of Islamic solidarity, compounded by the desire to undermine the pro-Western regime of Ethiopia under Haile Selassie. Also, acting under the impulse of Qaddaffi's anti-Zionist feelings, according to some accounts Libya offered Burundi $75 million in aid in exchange for the latter's severance of diplomatic relations with Israel.[49]

However, whenever Libya's ideological preferences have conflicted with its other vital interests, the latter have prevailed – as the ebbs and flows of its policy in Chad over the last several years have clearly illustrated.[50] In Libya's relations with Asian countries, as well, ideological considerations (especially Islam) have been important.

Libya's desire to diminish Western influence among certain countries and to expand Arab and Islamic cultures among them has been another factor affecting its aid policies. The best example of such influence has been Libya's aid to Malta to enable it to close the British/NATO base on the island.[51]

Economic. Traditional economic factors – such as access to sources of raw materials and development of export markets – have played little or no role in determining the aid policies of Arab donors at the national level. However, the desire to create favourable investment climates for their surplus capital and to gain access to the human and technological bases of some countries have been important factors. The former has been particularly important in the case of the Gulf countries, with Kuwait again taking the initiative. However, this factor was more significant at the beginning of the oil revolution when there was more OPEC interest in Third World countries as possible investment outlets. The following statement by a Kuwaiti expert illustrates this point:

To the extent that Western economies are unprepared for raising

> direct investments by oil producing nations, growing proportions of Arab oil surplus will inevitably begin to find their way to such outlets in the lesser developed African and Asian countries where rates of return could be higher... To this effect, surplus countries would find it imperative to complement their direct investments with soft lending for capital overhead projects that are essential to make their commercial direct investments profitable in the lesser developed countries.[52]

However, this consideration seems to have lost some of its significance for Arab financial-surplus countries, which have invested the bulk of their surplus funds in the industrialised countries. For example, of approximately $75 billion of Kuwaiti-invested funds, only 5 per cent has been invested in the developing countries, including those of the Arab world. If the Arab countries are excluded, the developing countries' share of Kuwait's investments would drop to a bare minimum.[53]

In the case of Libya, by contrast, the desire to have access to manpower and technological bases has played an important role, although investment-related considerations have not been insignificant.[54]

However, in the case of Iraq, the traditional motive of securing safe export markets seems to have played a role. Iraq has shown a desire to establish long-term oil-sale relationships, thus ensuring safe markets for its oil. This motive could account for the large share of credits for oil purchases in total Iraqi aid.

The least influential economic factors have been those related to Third World aspirations for systemic reforms and a more systematic and mutually-beneficial partnership with OPEC countries. There have been no indications that conscious efforts were made to develop such aid policies which could contribute to the achievement of these goals. However, this has been true of both pro-Western conservative and radical Arab countries, despite the latter's rhetoric. However, the conservative countries, like those of the Gulf, have had more open and close cooperation with Western dominated international development and financial institutions.

Principal Characteristics of Arab Aid

The preceding illustrated that the principal purpose of Arab aid at the national level has also been to meet security, political, and other needs of the Arab countries, and to achieve their primary objectives in this regard. Thus Arab aid at the national level – as well as at the Pan-Arab level – has been highly political. This situation, in turn, has had a number of implications for the nature of Arab aid, the most important of which have been the following:

1. High geographical concentration on Arab and Islamic countries, particularly the three Arab confrontation states.
2. The application of most favorable terms to Arab countries, particularly the three Arab confrontation states, which have received the bulk of Arab aid in grant form.
3. The disbursement of the bulk of aid through ministries of finance – or similar institutions – rather than through national development institutions.
4. The disbursement of the bulk of multilateral aid through Arab agencies.

In addition, lacking any particular concern with the developmental impact of their aid on the recipients, the Arab countries have tended to follow established – and safe – patterns of development assistance, favouring project aid, except in the case of the Arab confrontation states which have received the bulk of their aid in the form of general budgetary support. In choosing projects, they have tended to favour sectors such as infrastructure which are more visible and also are considered safe for the lender.

The following tables provide more details regarding the volume and principal characteristics of Arab aid at the national level.

1. Kuwait

Table 2.1 Volume of Kuwait ODA ($US millions)

Year	Committed	Disbursed	GNP(%)
1973	378.8	345.3	5.76
1974	838.9	621.5	5.70
1975	1,190.0	975.1	6.52
1976	755.5	526.9	3.23
1977	–	–	–
1978	–	1,300	6.4
1979	–	1,055	5.1
1980	–	1,188	4
1981	–	685	1.98

Note: The 1983 *Annual DAC Review* was published in December 1983.
Source: *Annual DAC Reviews*, 1974-82.

Table 2.2: Concessionality of Kuwait ODA

Year	% of Grants in Total Commitments	% Grant Element in ODA Loans	% Grant Element in Total ODA
1974	80.1	41.2	88.7
1975	74.2	50.5	87.3
1976	57.9	46.7	77.6
1979	–	–	74.3
1980	–	–	87.8
1981	–	–	74.4

Source: OECD, *Annual DAC Reviews*, 1974-82.

Until 1978 Egypt was the principal recipient of Kuwait's aid. After the cessation of aid to Egypt following the Camp David agreement Syria became principal recipient of Kuwaiti aid followed by Bahrain, Jordan, and Lebanon. Other important recipients of Kuwaiti aid have included the two Yemens and Somalia. In addition as early as 1953 Kuwait extended aid to smaller Gulf sheikhdoms now members of the UAE and the Yemens and Oman. Since 1966 this type of aid has been dispensed through the General Board for the South and Arabian Gulf. Most of this type of aid has been for health, education and other social services. Between 1966-9 the Board had given $14.6 million in aid. Aid through this channel increased considerably between 1975-81 as Table 2.3 illustrates.

It is important to note that the bulk of Kuwaiti aid in grant form has gone to the Arab confrontation states, the Palestinians and a few other states. Regarding the distribution of Kuwait's multilateral ODA, the bulk of it has been extended through Arab organisations, followed by the OPEC fund, the World Bank Group, and the IMF. The UN agencies have received the lowest share.

Table 2.3: Kuwait's ODA Contributions to Multilateral Organisations (disbursements in $US millions)

	1973	1974	1975	1976	1977	1978	1979	1980	1981
UNDP	0.4	0.4	0.4	0.5	0.5	0.5	0.5	0.6	0.6
UNRWA	0.2	0.4	0.4	1.4	–	0.6	2.1	0.6	0.6
WFP[a]	–	0.1	2.7	1.6	0.2	0.2	–	0.4	0.5
IFAD	–	–	–	–	–	36.0	–	–	–
IBRD[b]	–	–	–	20.0	–	–	–	32.9	0.8
IDA	4.4	9.0	9.0	9.0	66.7	70.8	70.4	–	66.0
IFC	–	–	–	–	–	2.9	3.2	4.2	–
AFDF	–	–	–	1.0	1.0	1.1	1.1	–	2.0
OTHER UN	–	0.1	0.1	3.0	0.1	1.0	0.3	0.5	2.7
TOTAL	5.0	10.0	12.6	36.5	74.5	123.9	88.5	40.7	74.7

Note: a. Including FAO Trust Funds for agricultural projects in Middle Eastern countries; b. Including contributions to IFC and Third Window lending facility; c. Trust fund.

Source: OECD, *Aid From OPEC Countries*, 1983.

Table 2.4: Volume of Disbursement by the General Board

Year	Amount in $US millions
1975	25.4
1976	34.4
1977	41.4
1978	42.4
1979	42.2
1980	44.9
1981	50.8

Source: OECD, *Aid From OPEC Countries*, 1983.

Table 2.5: Kuwait's ODA Contributions to OPEC/Arab Organisations (disbursements in $US millions)

	1973	1974	1975	1976	1977	1978	1979	1980	1981
AFESD	28.5	8.2	16.6	49.3	19.6	20.4	20.4	69.0	45.4
BADEA	–	–	10.0	5.6	45.0	6.7	6.7	6.7	–
IsDB	–	–	24.3	23.1	23.4	25.0	25.8	–	–
OPEC Fund	–	–	–	17.9	1.2	6.1	16.5	27.5	33.4

Source: OECD, *Aid From OPEC Countries*, 1983.

2. *The UAE*

Table 2.6: Volume of UAE ODA ($US millions)

Year	Committed	Disbursed	% of GNP
1973	318.1	288.6	12.03
1974	676.6	510.6	6.66
1975	1,123.6	1,046.1	11.79
1976	1,181.4	1,021.9	10.23
1977	–	–	–
1978	–	–	–
1979	–	1,114	5.87
1980	–	1,062	3.96
1981	–	799	2.88

Source: *Annual DAC Reviews*, 1974-81.

Table 2.7: Concessionality of UAE ODA

Year	% of Grants in Total Commitments	% Grant Element in ODA Loans	% Grant Element in Total ODA
1974	84.2	49.3	92.2
1975	56.1	62.7	69.3
1976	74.7	35.5	77.4
1980	87	–	84.6
1981	–	–	95.4

Source: *Annual DAC Reviews*, 1977-82.

Table 2.8: UAE's ODA Contributions to Multilateral Organisations (disbursements in $US millions)

	IFAD	UN Agencies	IBRD IDA IMF	Reg. Dev. Banks	Arab Agencies	OPEC Fund	Total	% GNP
1973	–	0.2	–	–	4.7	–	4.9	0.22
1974	–	10.3	–	–	32.2	–	42.5	0.59
1975	–	7.2	5.0	–	62.5	–	74.7	0.83
1976	–	3.3	–	–	40.1	8.5	51.9	0.45
1977	–	0.9	0.1	–	241.8	0.5	243.3	1.67
1978	5.5	1.4	11.0	–	110.1	2.7	130.7	0.92
1979	5.5	1.3	6.1	5.5	60.8	7.5	86.7	0.46
1980	5.5	3.2	1.0	5.3	31.7	12.5	59.2	0.22
1981	–	1.5	–	–	33.2	15.2	49.9	0.18

Source: OECD, *Aid From OPEC Countries*, 1983.

UAE aid has also been highly concentrated geographically in the Arab countries. In addition to grants to the confrontation states, according to OECD figures 81 per cent and 95 per cent of the Abu Dhabi Fund's loan commitments for 1978 and 1979, respectively, were to Arab countries. In 1980, too, almost nine-tenths of bilateral grants benefited the Arab countries. Grants for non-Arab countries were small, with the exception of Pakistan. In the case of Abu Dhabi, too, multilateral ODA has constituted a small share of total ODA, particularly if contributions to Arab/OPEC institutions are excluded. Among multilateral organisations with broad membership, UAE aid has been more evenly distributed among the UN agencies and the World Bank Group. Among the regional banks, the UAE has contributed to the African Development Bank.

3. Qatar

Since 1977, most of Qatar's aid has consisted of grants to confrontation states. Qatar's aid also has been highly concentrated on the Arab countries. The share of multilateral ODA has not been very high in Qatar's total ODA, and most of it has been to Arab institutions.

Table 2.9: Volume of Qatar ODA ($US millions)

Year	Committed	Disbursed	% GNP
1973	93.1	93.7	15.62
1974	227.7	185.2	9.26
1975	369.1	338.9	15.62
1976	138.3	175.1	7.40
1977	–	194.0	–
1978	–	100.0	–
1979	–	250.0	5.6
1980	–	319.0	4.80
1981	–	175.0	2.64

Source: *Annual DAC Reviews*, 1974-82.

Table 2.10: Concessionality of Qatar ODA

Year	% of Grants in Total Commitments	% Grant Element in ODA Loans	% Grant Element in Total ODA
1974	71.9	51.7	81.5
1975	69.9	43.1	77.8
1976	87.7	47.7	93.2
1979	–	–	97.2
1980	–	–	86.1
1981	–	–	100.0

Source: *Annual DAC Reviews*, 1977-82.

Table 2.11: Qatar's ODA Contributions to Multilateral Organisations (disbursements in $US millions)

	IFAD	UN Agencies	IBRD IMF	Reg. Dev. Banks	Arab Agencies	OPEC Fund	Total	% GNP
1973	–	0.2	–	–	0.9	–	1.1	0.18
1974	–	0.5	–	–	15.3	–	15.8	0.79
1975	–	0.4	–	–	35.1	–	35.5	1.64
1976	–	1.8	2.0	–	42.4	4.9	51.1	2.08
1977	–	1.4	–	–	10.8	0.3	12.5	0.50
1978	3.0	0.8	2.8	–	48.9	1.4	56.9	1.96
1979	3.0	0.8	1.0	–	12.8	4.0	21.6	0.46
1980	3.0	0.5	1.3	–	21.7	6.8	33.3	0.50
1981	–	2.3	–	–	7.6	8.3	18.5	0.28

Source: OECD, *Aid From OPEC Countries*, 1983.

4. Iraq

Table 2.12: Volume of Iraqi ODA ($US millions)

Year	Committed	Disbursed	% GNP
1973	115.7	11.1	0.21
1974	497.7	422.9	3.99
1975	370.8	215.4	1.63
1976	181.3	96.7	0.60
1977			
1978	559	146	0.66
1979	–	47	2.53
1980	–	829	2.12
1981	–	143	0.37

Source: *Annual DAC Reviews*, 1974-82.

Table 2.13: Concessionality of Iraqi ODA

Year	% of Grants in Total Commitments	% Grant Element in ODA Loans	% Grant Element in Total ODA
1974	59.0	42.9	78.2
1975	74.1	56.6	88.8
1976	46.4	47.3	71.7
1979	–	–	81.8
1980	–	–	87.7
1981	–	–	87.3

Source: *Annual DAC Reviews*, 1974-82.

Table 2.14: Iraq's ODA Contributions to Multilateral Organisations (disbursements in $US millions)

	IFAD	UN Agencies	IBRD IMF	Reg. Dev. Banks	Arab Agencies	OPEC Fund	Total	% GNP
1973	–	0.3	0.7	–	7.1	–	8.1	0.16
1974	–	0.9	–	–	48.1	–	49.0	0.46
1975	–	0.9	–	–	19.1	–	20.0	0.15
1976	–	1.1	–	–	42.8	–	43.9	0.27
1977	–	0.7	–	–	33.1	0.5	34.3	0.18
1978	20.0	4.0	4.9	–	22.8	–	51.7	0.23
1979	–	1.7	5.3	–	34.5	2.5	44.0	0.13
1980	–	6.7	7.1	–	36.3	4.5	54.6	0.14
1981	–	0.5	–	–	19.8	5.5	25.8	0.08

Source: OECD, *Aid From OPEC Countries*, 1983.

However, UNCTAD's *Financial Solidarity for Development* has cited the percentage of overall grant element of Iraq's ODA as 77 per cent and 88 per cent for 1974 and 1975, respectively.[55]

The level of geographical concentration of Iraq's aid has also been very high. For instance, according to UNCTAD, in 1974 94 per cent of all Iraqi bilateral aid went to four countries – India, Lebanon, Sudan and Syria. OECD sources, however, have cited Egypt as the principal recipient. Since 1978, Jordan, Syria and the West Bank have accounted for the bulk of Iraqi commitments. But in terms of disbursements, the situation has been less clear. For instance, it is unlikely, after the outbreak of the Iran-Iraq war and Syria's support for Iran, that any funds have been disbursed to Syria. Among non-Arab countries, India has been the principal recipient of Iraqi aid.

Iraqi aid beyond that to confrontation states has been largely tied to the purchase of oil. But the share of aid tied by project has not been very high. As far as multilateral ODA is concerned, most of Iraq's contributions have been to Arab agencies.

5. Libya

Table 2.15: Volume of Libyan ODA ($US millions)

Year	Committed	Disbursed	% of GNP
1973	238.4	214.4	3.32
1974	266.9	147.0	1.32
1975	291.6	261.1	2.13
1976	217.2	103.6	0.67
1977			
1978	569	140	–
1979	–	105	0.45
1980	–	281	0.92
1981	–	105	0.37

Source: *Annual DAC Reviews*, 1974-82.

Table 2.16: Concessionality of Libyan ODA

Year	% of Grants in Total Commitments	% Grant Element in ODA Loans	% Grant Element in Total ODA
1974	55.4	42.1	74.2
1975[a]	96.0	53.5	98.2
1976	63.2	27.2	73.2
1979	–	–	100.
1980	–	–	97.9
1981	–	–	86.7

Note: a. UNCTAD, however, cites the grant element of Libyan ODA as 99.3 per cent for 1975.
Source: *Annual DAC Reviews*, 1974-82.

A principal characteristic of Libyan aid has been the large gap between commitments and disbursements, particularly in aid given to the confrontation states. Thus, for example, of $487 million committed to Jordan and Syria at the 1978 Baghdad Summit Conference, nothing was disbursed by 1980.

Regarding geographical distribution of Libyan aid, in terms of actual disbursements Egypt and Pakistan seem to have been the largest recipients in the period between 1973 and 1976. Other principal recipients appear to have been the PDRY, Syria, Vietnam, Guinea, Uganda, Gabon and Malta.

The bulk of Libyan aid has been untied both by source and by end-use. Multilateral contributions largely to Arab – and some African – institutions have accounted for the largest part of Libyan aid: two-thirds of total disbursements in 1979.

Table 2.17: Libya's ODA Contributions to Multilateral Organisations (disbursements in $US millions)

	IFAD	UN Agencies	IBRD IMF	Reg. Dev. Banks	Arab Agencies	OPEC Fund	Total	% GNP
1973	–	1.3	–	15.5	11.3	–	28.1	0.44
1974	–	1.0	–	–	13.4	–	14.4	0.12
1975	–	1.3	–	2.4	89.3	–	93.0	0.82
1976	–	1.6	–	4.8	48.6	11.0	66.0	0.45
1977	–	2.2	–	4.9	69.3	–	76.4	0.43
1978	6.6	2.5	1.0	–	77.6	3.6	91.3	0.53
1979	6.7	2.3	–	–	68.7	8.9	86.6	0.37
1980	6.7	3.8	2.8	–	34.3	15.1	64.0	0.21
1981	–	7.7	1.7	2.6	33.4	18.4	63.8	0.11

Source: OECD, *Aid From OPEC Countries*, 1983.

6. *Algeria*

Algeria is among the OPEC members whose economic needs far exceed their oil revenues. As such, therefore, Algeria has not been a major OPEC donor. Yet Algeria has contributed to Arab, OPEC, and international institutions. It has also had a small bilateral aid programme concentrating on a few Arab countries such as Syria, Lebanon, the PDRY, and a few African countries.

Table 2.18: Volume of Algerian ODA ($US millions)

Year	Committed	Disbursed	% of GNP
1973	23.0	25.3	0.31
1974	63.7	46.9	0.39
1975	59.6	40.7	0.30
1976	77.9	53.6	0.34
1977			
1978	–	40[a]	–
1979	–	272	0.87
1980	–	83	0.21
1981	–	65	0.16

Note: a. This figure is approximate.

Source: *Annual DAC Reviews*, 1974-82.

Table 2.19: Concessionality of Algerian ODA

Year	% of Grants in Total Commitments	% Grant Element in ODA Loans	% Overall Grant Element of ODA Commitments
1974	97.1	50.5	98.5
1975	77.3	38.7	86.5
1976	43.9	38.7	65.6
1979	–	–	77.4
1980	–	–	83.3
1981	–	–	95.5

Source: *Annual DAC Reviews*, 1974-82.

Table 2.20: Algeria's ODA Contributions to Multilateral Organisations (disbursements in $US millions)

	IFAD	UN Agencies	IBRD IMF	Reg. Dev. Banks	Arab Agencies	OPEC Fund	Total	% GNP
1973	–	0.4	–	–	3.4	–	3.8	0.04
1974	–	10.5	3.7	23.0	6.1	–	43.3	0.34
1975	–	0.1	–	–2.5	13.3	–	10.9	0.07
1976	–	0.6	–	3.0	–	5.6	9.2	0.05
1977	–	1.1	–	5.9	24.6	0.3	31.9	0.16
1978	3.3	1.0	–	6.3	22.1	3.1	35.8	0.14
1979	3.3	0.8	–	–	29.6	2.8	36.5	0.12
1980	3.3	1.0	–	–	30.7	7.6	42.6	0.11
1981	–	0.8	3.4	6.0	23.3	9.2	42.7	0.10

Source: OECD, *Aid From OPEC Countries*, 1983.

In addition, a common trait of Arab aid seems to have been the lack of a coherent development strategy and a well-planned aid policy which would take into account the principal needs of the developing countries.

Efficacy and Impact on Recipients

In general, the Arab countries have used aid with considerable success to achieve both their collective and individual objectives. For example, at a Pan-Arab level, Arab aid has played an important – although by no means determining – role in enhancing Third World support for the Arab cause against Israel. Likewise, aid has increased Arab prestige and influence among the Islamic countries.

However, the greater involvement of the Arab countries has not always been welcomed by recipients, largely for the following reasons:

1. Arab involvement in some cases has also meant the extension of intra-Arab divisions and disputes to other regions. This has been particularly true of Africa, where Arab involvement – for reasons discussed earlier – has been more extensive, and where the interaction between aspects of Arab and African politics has been close. Two good examples have been (a) the problems faced by the Organisation of African Unity (OAU) as a result of Arab divisions over the conflict in the Western Sahara, and (b) relations with Egypt after the latter signed a peace treaty with Israel.
2. A number of Arab countries have emphasised the promotion of Arab-Islamic culture among other Third World countries, particularly those which either are Muslim or have significant Muslim minorities. Again, Africa has been the primary focus of such activities, and many African countries have come to resent deeply this aspect of Arab involvement. Beyond the fact that Arab efforts to promote Arab-Islamic culture has had close similarities to past Western cultural colonialism, and thus are resented by those who have been subjected to it, these efforts have tended to exacerbate ethnic and religious divisions in these countries, thus undermining their socio-political cohesion and stability. Moreover, some Arab countries have used promotion of Islam as a vehicle for their own ambitions.[56]

The net effect of this situation, in turn, has been a dilution of Arab influence and prestige among Third World countries, and thus a reduced rate of efficacy of Arab aid.

At the national level, Arab aid has been most effective when it has essentially tried to neutralise an enemy or to moderate its policies towards the donor, and in some cases towards a whole range of regional and international issues. Thus, for example, the Arab countries of the Persian Gulf have been quite successful in reducing the threat of radical Arab countries and groups – such as the PLO – to their security through massive use of aid. Likewise, aid has in many cases been very influential in inducing change in the policies of recipients along lines more congenial to the donor. Egypt and Somalia are good examples of this effect of aid.

Beyond this, however, the capacity of the Arab donors to manipulate the foreign or domestic politics of recipients and to impose choices on them has been fairly limited. This has been particularly true of the principal recipients of Arab aid, especially that disbursed by the Persian Gulf countries. For example, although the Persian Gulf countries through their aid managed somewhat to neutralise Syria, they were not able to force it to abandon its alliance with the Soviet Union. Likewise, these countries were not able to dissuade Egypt from signing its peace treaty with Israel by threatening to cut aid.

This situation, in turn, has reflected the underlying weakness of principal Arab donors – especially the Persian Gulf countries – in other aspects of national power. It has also illustrated the inherent limitation of foreign aid as an instrument of foreign policy, particularly in the absence of other elements of national power. Moreover, the limited impact of aid in achieving donor objectives has not been confined to the foreign policy of the recipients. Rather, there is no evidence that the Arab donors have had any significant influence on the economic policies of recipients, particularly at a macro-economic level. In addition to the factors cited above, this situation has been due to the fact that principal Arab donors have lacked trained manpower and technical know-how essential for the assertion of economic preferences on recipients. The corollary of the limited efficacy of Arab aid has been the limited degree of dependence of recipients on this aid. Again, principal recipients of Arab aid have been in a better position. This has derived from the fact that aid to these countries has been designed either to dissuade them from taking hostile actions towards the donors, or to provide specific services to the donors. In the case of other countries which have not been principal recipients of Arab aid, the small share of Arab aid in their total receipts of external aid has accounted for its lack of serious implications for the recipients' political and economic dependence on the former. The fact that many recipients of Arab aid have been better endowed in regard to other components of power has contributed to this situation.

Non-Arab OPEC Donors: Nigeria and Venezuela

Nigerian and Venezuelan aid policies have been similar to those of the Arab countries and Iran in that they have reflected their salient national characteristics as well as their particular security, political, and economic needs. Moreover, Venezuela and Nigeria, too, have used aid essentially as an instrument of national policy. Nevertheless, they have differed in a number of respects from the previously-discussed countries, as well as from Saudi Arabia and Iran. For example, security considerations have played a much smaller role in determining their aid policies. By contrast, aspirations for regional leadership have been important factors. Also, traditional economic motives for aid have had a bigger impact in their cases.

Although very different from each other, Venezuela and Nigeria have shared a number of characteristics. For example, both countries have belonged to that group of OPEC members whose economic development needs over the long term have exceeded their revenues. They both have been regional powers, with aspirations for regional leadership. They both have been activist members of the Third World and the non-aligned movement, and as such have been champions of reducing great-power influence in their respective regions. As such, they have also been more deeply committed to the reform of the international economic system.[57] And both of them have been rather unusual among OPEC states – and indeed most of the Third World – with their more-or-less democratic systems of government.

In addition to these essential characteristics, there have existed a number of other similarities between Venezuela and Nigeria in respect to their economic development prospects, their security environment, and their security needs.

For example, neither Nigeria nor Venezuela has been faced with the same security threats as, for instance, the Persian Gulf members of OPEC. Moreover, being large countries with large populations, their capacity to develop viable military forces has been quite good. In the case of Venezuela, the danger of internal subversion by outside forces, through the exploitation of internal divisions, has not been very high. Nigeria, given its religious and ethnic divisions, has been more vulnerable.[58] Both countries, however, have been concerned about the deterioration of their security environment as a result of regional conflicts that have also reflected big-power rivalries in their regions.[59]

There have also been similarities between the two countries in regard to their political objectives and aspirations. Thus, for example, both have been influenced by requirements of regionalism and regional solidarity.[60] In the case of Nigeria, the issue of Apartheid and South Africa's impact on Black Africa have also been very important.

From an economic point of view, as well, Nigeria and Venezuela have had a lot in common as aspiring industrial states. As such, they have shared in the need to develop outlets for their manufacturing industries and also in some cases to secure access to raw material sources. In turn, the aid policies of these two countries to a considerable extent have reflected their needs, their political outlook, and the requirements of their particular security environments.

Thus, for example, Venezuela's contributions to the OPEC Fund, the IMF oil facility, and the World Bank have emanated from its vision of itself as a loyal member of OPEC and a responsible member of the international community. Its setting up of a $500 million Trust Fund, to be administered by the Inter-American Development Fund, has reflected Venezuela's commitment to the objectives of Latin American solidarity. By contrast, its setting up of a $25 million Trust Fund to be administered by the Caribbean Development Bank, and its contribution to the Andean Development Corporation, have reflected the importance it has attached to these regions in terms of their significance for its security, and also as export outlets. Venezuela has extended other bilateral assistance to a number of Caribbean, Central American, and other Latin American countries for a variety of security, political, and economic reasons.[61]

Regarding Venezuela's objectives – beyond those discussed earlier – the reduction of the negative impact of oil price increases on Latin American countries, and a desire to contribute to the improvement of their export-earning capacity seem to have dominated.[62] Venezuela also seems to have shown greater awareness of the need to avoid duplicating the efforts of existing institutions, but rather tries to complement them.[63] In so far as sectoral distribution of its aid has been concerned, Venezuela in theory has favoured agriculture and those projects which would contribute to intra-regional economic cooperation. In practice, however, the available data do not indicate any clear pattern of sectoral preference. As far as the terms of aid are concerned, Venezuelan loans have in general carried 8 per cent interest and have had 30-year maturity and five years' grace period. Unlike Arab members of OPEC, Venezuela has shown flexibility in regard to local cost financing.

Nigeria has followed a similar pattern in extending aid. Thus, for example, Nigeria has created a Trust Fund in the amount of $80 million to be administered by the African Development Bank.[64]

In addition, Nigeria has contributed to the OPEC Fund, the Commonwealth Fund for Technical Assistance, and the Technical Assistance Fund of the UN Commission for Africa. It has also given bilateral aid to a number of African countries and liberation movements for both development and purely political purposes.[65]

Nigeria has also used aid to encourage economic and political integration of the West African countries, through the financial commitments which it has undertaken within the Economic Community of West African States (ECOWAS). This policy in turn has reflected several basic principles of Nigerian foreign policy, such as commitment to the concept of African unity, reduction of French influence in West Africa, and the establishment of a leadership role for Nigeria in the region.[66] However, economic factors such as access to export markets have also been influential in Nigeria's aid policies.[67]

Regarding types of aid, Nigeria seems to have favoured technical assistance – through its contributions to different technical assistance funds – as well as to some extent rural development. Most of Nigeria's aid has been programme aid. Project aid has been largely tied to the supply of Nigerian goods and services.[68]

Table 2.21: Volume of Venezuelan ODA ($US millions)

Year	Committed	Disbursed	% of GNP
1973	18.1	17.7	0.11
1974	112.4	58.8	0.23
1975	11.6	30.0	0.11
1976	145.2	65.0	0.21
1977			
1978	–	109.0	0.28
1979	–	83.0	0.18
1980	–	130	0.23
1981	–	67	0.10

Note: The terms of the $500 million Venezuelan Trust Fund have not been concessional since the average interest rate charged on the loans under this programme has been 8 per cent.

Most of Venezuelan ODA has been disbursed multilaterally, and its bilateral aid has been essentially non-concessional. However, loans under the Mexican Venezuelan oil agreement should have qualified as ODA.

The share of world-wide multilateral organisations for the years 1979 and 1980 were 67.2 per cent and 60 per cent of total Venezuelan ODA.

Source: *Annual DAC Reviews*, 1974-82.

Table 2.22: Venezuela's ODA Contributions to Multilateral Organisations (disbursements in $US millions)

	1973	1974	1975	1976	1977	1978	1979	1980	1981
UNDP	0.9	2.7	1.5	—	3.6	2.0	2.2	2.1	2.2
UN Special Account	—	30.0	23.4	26.4	—	—	—	—	—
WFP	0.1	0.1	—	0.1	—	—	0.1	0.1	X
IFAD	—	—	—	—	—	22.0	44.0	—	—
Other UN	X	0.3	0.1	0.1	0.2	0.2	0.2	0.4	0.2
IBRD	—	—	—	10.0	—	—	—	—	—
IMF (Trust Fund and Subsid. Acct.)	—	—	—	1.7	1.8	16.6	18.0	21.6	—
IDB	16.7	—	—	16.5	19.6	29.6	10.0	52.5	—
Carib. DB	0.5	5.4	5.4	0.5	0.2	0.6	—	0.2	7.7
OAS	—	0.7	0.1	4.4	3.0	3.7	3.0	1.4	7.7
OPEC Fund	—	—	—	33.3	1.5	7.7	24.4	42.0	51.6
TOTAL	18.2	39.2	31.4	93.0	19.7	81.8	101.9	120.3	62.7
% GNP	0.11	0.15	0.11	0.29	0.05	0.21	0.21	0.20	0.09

Source: OECD, *Aid From OPEC Countries*, 1983.

Table 2.23: List of Projects Financed by the Venezuelan Trust Fund in 1976

Country	Programme or Project	Amount in $US millions
Costa Rica	Fishing Development	3.6
Ecuador	Industrial Loan	17.0
	Cement Factory	
	Selva Alegre	12.6
Guatemala	Hydroelectric of Chixoy	35.0
Peru	Industrial Loan	15.0
Jamaica	Credit to Exports	0.5
Argentina	Credit to Exports	5.0
Chile	Credit to Exports	1.0
Brasil	Credit to Exports	5.0
Mexico	Credit to Exports	5.0
TOTAL		99.7

Table 2.24: List of Projects Financed by the Caribbean Trust Fund

Country	Borrower	Amount US$
Guyana	Small Industries Corporation	1,960,780
Jamaica	Jamaica Development Bank	4,399,600
Bahamas	Water Sewerage Corporation	3,245,000
TOTAL		9,605,380

Table 2.25: List of Projects Financed in Jamaica in 1976

Loan No.	Programmes	Amount Bs.
CE-JAM-01-25	Improvement and repairing of roads	21,720,000.oo
CE-JAM-02-26	Third Highway Project	14,100,000.oo
CE-JAM-03-27	Rural Electrification	5,666,100.oo
CE-JAM-04-28	Airports Development	15,980,000.oo
CE-JAM-05-40	Sites and Services Project	7,063,738.oo
CE-JAM-06-41	Extension of the Water Supply System for Montego Bay and Falmouth	7,554,800.oo
	TOTAL	72,084,638.oo

Source: IDB.

Table 2.26: List of Projects Financed in Central America in 1976

Country	Project	Borrower	Amount Bs.[a]
Costa Rica	(1) Hydroelectric of Arenal	Central American Institute of Electricity	25,755,000.oo
	(2) Highway San José-Siquirres, San-José-Puerto Viejo	The Republic	12,877,500.oo
	(3) Fishing Development	The Republic	2,489,650.oo
	(4) Caldera Dock	The Republic	14,190,000.oo
	(5) Construction and repairing of roads	The Republic	12,019,000.oo
	(6) Agricultural Development	The Republic	9,014,250.oo
El Salvador	(7) Sixth Potency Project	Executive Hydroelectric Commission of Rio Lempa	43,953,686.48
	(8) Sugar Mill of Jiboa	Salvadorian Institute of Industrial Development	37,596,624.oo
Guatemala	(9) Hydroelectric of Chixoy	The Republic	140,804,547.95
Nicaragua	(10) Eighth Potency Project	National Enterprise of Light and Energy	68,971,949.10
Panama	(11) Hydroelectric of Bayano	Institute of Hydraulic Resources and Electrification	19,316,250.oo
	(12) New International Airport of Tocumen	Civil Aeronautics Administration	42,066,500.oo
	TOTAL		429,054,957.53

Note: a. A Bolivar is equivalent to $US 0.769.

Table 2.27: Volume of Nigerian ODA ($US millions)

Year	Commitment	Disbursement	% of GNP
1973	4.6	4.7	0.04
1974	15.7	15.3	0.07
1975	35.8	13.9	0.05
1976	136.4	82.8	0.28
1977	–	64.0	–
1978	–	38.0	–
1979	–	31.0	0.04
1980	–	42.0	0.05
1981	–	14.9	0.17

Note: Multilateral contributions constitute the bulk of Nigerian aid as well. Of this, world-wide multilateral institutions account for 58.6 per cent and 30 per cent of Nigerian ODA for the years 1979 and 1980, respectively.

Source: *Annual DAC Reviews*, 1974-82.

Table 2.28: Nigeria's ODA Contributions to Multilateral Organisations (disbursements in $US millions)

	IFAD	UN Agencies	IBRD IMF	Reg. Dev. Banks	Other	OPEC Fund	Total	% GNP
1973	–	0.4	–	–	–	–	–	X
1974	–	0.3	–	7.8	0.6	–	8.7	0.03
1975	–	0.5	–	7.8	1.6	–	9.9	0.03
1976	–	0.6	–	39.9	1.7	14.8	57.0	0.19
1977	–	0.2	–	46.7	1.3	0.7	48.9	0.10
1978	8.7	2.0	–	11.2	0.6	3.8	26.3	0.05
1979	8.7	0.8	–	3.2	5.0	11.0	28.7	0.04
1980	8.7	1.2	–	–	2.6	20.1	32.6	0.04
1981	–	4.2	24.6	87.7	–	24.0	140.5	0.16

Source: OECD, *Aid From OPEC Countries*, 1983.

Table 2.29: Regional Distribution of Nigerian Trust Fund Loans (UA millions[a])

Region	Number of Projects	Amount of Loan Approved	(%)
Central Africa	1	2.25	3.50
East Africa	4	15.68	24.36
North Africa	–	–	–
West Africa	11	46.44	72.14
Grand Total	16	64.37	100.00

Note: a. UA is a unit of account based on a basket of currencies and is equal to one SDR.

Source: The African Development Bank, *Annual Reports*, 1979, 1980.

Table 2.30: Sectoral Distribution of Nigerian Trust Fund Loans (UA millions)

	Agriculture	Transport	Telecommunications	Energy	Water and Sewage	Industry and Development	Education	Total
Cumulative amount of loans	8.55	18.37	10.10	7.60	5.22	7.43	8.10	65.37
Cumulative amounts as percentage of total	13.08	28.10	15.45	11.63	7.98	11.37	12.39	100.00

IV Conclusions

The most obvious and important conclusion to be drawn from the foregoing analysis is that all OPEC countries have used aid as a principal instrument of their security and foreign policies, in order to achieve specific goals and to meet specific needs. However, the role of aid as an instrument of policy has not been equally important in the cases of all OPEC countries. Rather its relative importance for individual OPEC members has depended on two factors: other instruments of policy available to individual countries and the size of monetary surplus. Nevertheless, for principal OPEC donors, aid has been the most important instrument of security and foreign policy.

The second conclusion relates to the motivations for OPEC aid. For the majority of OPEC members, including the largest donors, security has been the primary motivating force, and the percentage of aid given for this purpose has been the largest in total OPEC aid. As far as individual donors are concerned, the share of security-related aid has reflected their geostrategic conditions, the seriousness and nature of threats to their security, and their strengths and weakness in other components of national power. Thus the share of security-related aid has been highest in the case of the Persian Gulf countries, including Iran, whereas it has constituted a lower percentage in the case of countries such as Venezuela, Nigeria, Algeria and Libya.

Political and ideological considerations have been the other important motive for OPEC aid, in most cases, however, intensifying the impact of security considerations.

Economic considerations have generally played a secondary role. Their impact, however, has related somewhat to the level of economic development of the donors and to particular characteristics of their economies. Thus, those donors with a relatively more-developed economy and high future aspirations have used aid to secure export markets or reliable sources of supply.

The geographic scope of OPEC aid has essentially been limited. Thus 'regionalism' rather than 'globalism' has determined the distributional pattern of OPEC aid. This has been particularly true of national OPEC aid as compared to collective OPEC aid. This situation, in turn, has partly resulted from the predominance of security as a motivating factor for OPEC aid, since the security perimeter of OPEC countries has essentially been limited to their immediate regions. Consideration of ethnic and religious solidarity – such as Arabism and Islam for the Arab donors, and Latin and African solidarity for Venezuela and

Nigeria – have further strengthened the regionalist character of OPEC aid.

Third, the predominance of security and political factors as motivating forces for OPEC aid, and the aid's important role as an instrument of national policy, have resulted in the very large share of bilateral aid in total OPEC aid. However, there has also been a direct link between the volume of aid and its significance as an instrument of policy, and the percentage of bilateral aid. Those countries with large foreign aid programmes have chosen bilateralism whereas others (for example, Algeria and Nigeria) have favoured multilateral channels.

The fourth conclusion relates to the impact of OPEC aid on the recipients and its role in their development. In view of the political nature of OPEC aid, combined with the pressing security and political needs of the donors, considerations of the developmental impact of their aid have not played a major role in the case of most OPEC donors. Likewise, the potential role of aid in achieving Third World objectives has not entered the calculations of principal OPEC donors. However, since in most cases aid by OPEC members has been in exchange for security, their capacity to influence and manipulate recipients in most cases has also been limited.

Table 2.31: Motives for OPEC Aid and Relative Importance of Key Factors

	Security	Political/Ideological	Economic
Algeria	Low	High	Low
Iran	High	Medium	High
Iraq	Low	High	Medium
Kuwait	High	Medium	Low
Libya	Low	High	Medium
Nigeria	Low	High	High
Qatar	High	Medium	Low
Saudi Arabia	High	High	Low
UAE	High	Medium	Low
Venezuela	Low	High	High

Notes

1. See, for example, E.K. Hawkins, *The Principles of Development Aid*, Harmondsworth, England: Penguin Books, 1970, p. 25.
2. The OPEC Special Fund, *Basic Information*, Lancashire, England: Penworthan Press, December 1976, p. 2.
3. The OPEC Special Fund, *First Annual Report*, 1976, p. 12.

4. Ibid.

5. The OPEC Special Fund, *Second Annual Report*, 1977, p. 9.

6. Ibid.

7. Ibid., p. 8. The Fund's initial selection of projects for lending was done on the basis of the following rules: per capita income as an index of relative poverty; population as a proxy for size; the deficit in current account in 1974-5 as a measure of liquidity and financial problems; and net oil imports in 1973 as a sign of energy-import dependence.

8. See Malcolm Kerr, *The Arab Cold War*, London: Oxford University Press, 1971, pp. 109-10.

9. Faisal's Islamic initiative had very limited success for several reasons. First, 'it was easy for Faisal's critics to deride the religious rectitude of such fun-loving monarchs as King Hussein or the Shah, or of secularists like Bourghiba and the Turkish leaders . . .'; and second, 'none of the governments Faisal approached were eager to quarrel with Egypt with the exception of Iran and Tunisia, which were already doing so . . .' Ibid.

10. Nazli Choucri, *International Politics*, Lexington, Mass.: D.C. Heath, 1976, p. 93.

11. However, this did not mean that Egypt in the future would refrain from exploiting certain situations in Arab countries and from trying to turn them to its own advantage. See Ruth First, *Libya, the Elusive Revolution*, Harmondsworth, England: Penguin Books, 1974, p. 113.

12. For instance, after the failure of the selective oil embargo during the 1967 war, a conference of Arab Ministers of Finance, Economy, and Oil was held in Baghdad from 15 to 20 August 1967. At this conference, Iraq and Algeria proposed a three-month total stoppage of Arab oil exports. By contrast, Libya, Saudi Arabia, and Kuwait urged the use of oil proceeds to support the war-stricken Arab states in their efforts to regain and protect their territorial integrity. The final decision, however, was left to the Summit Conference of Arab heads of state in Khartoum which finally opted for the second alternative.

13. For an excellent study of this aspect of Arab politics, see Michael C. Hudson, *Arab Politics: The Search for Legitimacy*, New Haven: Yale University Press, 1977.

14. The impact of Arab aid on the political attitudes of other developing countries has been minimal. For example, most of the Asian countries, for reasons of religious, political, or ideological affinities, had supported the Arabs in their conflict with Israel long before the October War. However, as far as support for OPEC is concerned, expectations of aid, as well as the hope that OPEC's power might extract concessions from the industrialised countries in negotiations regarding the reform of the international economic order, have played a significant part.

15. Arab-African relations have not always been easy. For instance, it took Nasser some time to convince Nkrumah of the legitimacy of the Arab cause. 'As late as 1960, in a speech to the General Assembly of the United Nations, Nkrumah called upon the Arabs to recognise realities – implying that since Israel was a reality, the Arabs might as well recognise it in spite of any presumed injustice which might have been committed at the time it was created.' But later Nkrumah signed the communique of the conference of radical African countries held in Casablanca in 1962, declaring Israel a 'tool of neo-colonialism'. Ali Mazrui, *Africa's International Relations: | The Diplomacy of Dependency and Change,* Boulder, Colorado: Westview Press, 1977, p. 138.

16. E.C. Chibwe, *Afro-Arab Relations in the New World Order*, London: S. Friedman, 1977, p. 19.

17. For instance, 'members of parliament and journalists in Nariobi have regularly criticised the Arabs for making life difficult for those in the less developed countries, despite the fact that Africa has shown solidarity with the Arab

cause'. Therefore, 'the Finance Minister, Unwar Kibaki, reminded Parliament that Kenya severed diplomatic ties with Israel not for financial gains but as a matter of principle'. Ibid., p. 20.

18. Ali Mazrui, *Africa's International Relations*, p. 136.

19. Ibid.

20. In contrast with Israel, the Arabs have shown remarkable consistency in their support for important African causes such as the issue of Apartheid and the whole problem of racist regimes in southern Africa. They have also seized every opportunity to point out the contradictions between Israel's claims of support for the Africans and its actions.

21. Uganda broke relations with Israel on 30 March 1972, followed by Chad on 28 November and the People's Republic of the Congo on 31 December. In 1973, Niger, Mali, and Burundi broke relations, as did a number of other African countries such as Guinea, Tanzania, and Kenya. Each of these countries had special reasons in addition to the more general factors referred to here. Some did so out of religious or ideological affinity with Arabs, and some for reasons of internal politics. Countries like Zaïre, Senegal, Ivory Coast, and Ethiopia (under Haile Selassi) did so mainly because they did not want to be isolated from continental African diplomatic trends. Nevertheless, there have been cases of cash payments by Arab countries, particularly Libya, in exchange for the severing of relations with Israel. For instance, shortly after Chad broke diplomatic relations with Israel, President Tombalbaye visited Libya, and during this visit a $91.2 million Libyan loan to Chad was announced. Idi Amin of Uganda also received financial help from both Libya and Saudi Arabia. Victor T. Levin and Timothy W. Luke, *The Arab-African Connection: Political and Economic Realities*, Boulder, Colorado: Westview Press, 1979, p. 12. To an extent, the fear of punitive action by the Arabs did influence African decisions.

22. See the statement of the Egyptian Under-Secretary of Foreign Affairs on 27 November 1973, quoted in E.C. Chibwe, *Afro-Arab Relations*, pp. 42-3.

23. In 1975, President Mobuto of Zaïre became the first African leader openly to criticise Arab aid for African states that were hit by the 1973 price rises. In an interview with the Cairo daily, *Al-Ahram*, he hinted that African states might be tempted to restore links with Israel because of the Arab failure to replace Israeli advisors and technicians. *MEES*, vol. 19, no. 12, 21 March 1975, p. 11. Zaïre has since restored relations with Israel.

Other African countries whose support of the Arab cause was based more on principle than expedience – although harshly critical of Arab oil producers and their aid and investment policies – did not make any connection between these two issues. For instance, Julius Nyerere of Tanzania has always been a firm supporter of the Arab cause in the Arab-Israeli conflict, but has also been very critical of OPEC countries.

In general, as far as African support for OPEC is concerned, expectations of aid and investment have played a significant part. Even here, however, the realisation that non-cooperation with OPEC would not mean more aid from, or better treatment by, the industrialised countries has been more important.

24. The Bank is referred to as BADEA, its French abbreviation. The Arabs also established a special fund to finance part of the oil purchases of African countries, plus a Technical Development Fund. Furthermore, they tried to create links between the Arab League and the Organisation of African Unity, and to establish permanent mechanisms for economic and political cooperation between the Arabs and African countries. These efforts culminated in the convening of the Arab-African Summit in Cairo on 9 March 1977.

25. The history of the Arab slave trade in Africa – which has long been exploited by the European powers – somewhat justifies African fears of excessive

Arab influence. 'The Arab record in the slave trade featured prominently in history books and the British liked to justify their colonial presence in Eastern and Central Africa by arguing that the original motivation was to suppress the Arab slave trade.' Ali Mazrui, *Africa's International Relations*, p. 134. Moreover, the Arabs at times have shown themselves capable of excessive ethnic and cultural pride.

26. Another fear of the African states, particularly those with substantial Muslim minorities, has been that the efforts of some Arab countries – such as Libya – to spread Islam in Africa might create additional conflicts in the continent along religious lines, or exacerbate existing ones.

27. 'In 1953, before the formation of the Council of Arab Economic Unity (CAEU), the Economic Council of the Arab League had decided to draw up the Convention for Facilitating Trade and Regulating Transit (CFTRT) among member countries . . . Parallel with the CFTRT, the Agreement for the Settlement of Payments for Current Transactions and the Transfer of Capital (ASPTC) was formulated in 1965.' Yusif Sayigh, *The Economies of the Arab World*, London: Croom Helm, 1978, p. 705.

28. The Economic Council of the Arab League had taken several other measures that had not been fully implemented. Ibid. For instance, the payments agreement among the Arab countries has remained a dead letter, whereas the trade and transit agreement has been very slowly implemented. The League also made plans for an Arab Development Bank. Thus the Arab Financial Institution for Economic Development was officially created in 1959. The League had also made plans for a joint Arab Potash Company, an Arab Oil Tanker Company, an Arab Navigation Company, and an Arab airline. Until recently, most of these schemes were not implemented.

29. Ibid.

30. For example, cooperation between Arab countries of North Africa and the rest of the Arab world has been limited and difficult to achieve. For details, see Ibid., pp. 706-7. Similar problems have existed, and still do, among Arab countries of the Mashriq, although in their case competitive economies rather than colonial links have been the main cause. For details, see Ragaei El-Mallakh, *Economic Development and Regional Cooperation: Kuwait*, Chicago: University of Chicago Press, 1968, p. 169.

31. See Yusif Sayigh, *Arab World*, p. 708, and Ragaei El-Mallakh, *Economic Development*, p. 170.

32. During the oil crisis and since then, voices have been heard that the West – particularly the US – should use its agricultural power. Recently, again, there has been talk of using the US agricultural power as a countermeasure for OPEC action. Statements are made to the effect that 'If the OPEC demands and gets higher prices from Americans for its oil, why can't the U.S. use its vast amounts of grain as an economic weapon, too! The matter is even debated in the Congress, which is debating the question of establishing a National Grain Board, which would set the price of grain to be exported and approve sales to foreign countries. The proponents of this proposal such as Representative James Weaver think that a US grain board should cooperate with similar boards in Canada and Australia to raise the price of grain on the world market and get tough with OPEC grain customers.' 'The Grain Weapon: Towards a New Cartel?', *The Boston Sunday Globe*, 5 August 1979, p. 71.

33. A good example of this attitude was the setting up of the Gulf Organisation for Industrial Consulting in 1976, whose membership has included Saudi Arabia, Iraq, Kuwait, the UAE, Bahrain, Qatar, and Oman, and whose principal objective has been to achieve industrial cooperation and coordination among the member states.

According to its Secretary General, the main characteristic of this organisation has been its 'pragmatism'. For example, even after eight years GOIC's recommendations are not binding on member states, and Article 11 of its charter said that 'nothing in this agreement may restrict the freedom of the member states to retain their industrial development organisations or restrict the freedom of those states to receive technical assistance on the national level from Arabian, regional, and international organisations'.

The rationale behind this approach was that previous Arab efforts at cooperation had failed because they were too ambitious and often based on wrong hypotheses. The Gulf countries did not want to repeat that mistake. The GOIC Secretary General summed this up in the following way: 'The lack of success of Arab unity efforts is that they start with a hypothesis that is not really true. It's like tailoring a suit for the wrong customer; it may be very nice but it does not fit.' 'Gulf Industrialization: Tailoring a Suit that Fits', *The Middle East*, April 1981, no. 78, pp. 70-1.

34. Since the Iranian revolution, Iranian-inspired religious subversion has also become quite threatening.

35. As far as Kuwait was concerned, the following statement is instructive: 'In spite of General Kassem's arrogant response, the rest of the Arab states agreed to recognise the Shaikhdom as an independent state and Kuwait was admitted as a member of both the Arab League and the United Nations. The price of these Pan-Arab mercies, however, was a share in Kuwait's oil revenues.' David Holden, *Farewell to Arabia*, London: Faber & Faber, 1966, p. 169.

36. In fact, at times radical Arab countries have hinted that if they did not get a share of oil wealth, they might use force. For instance, according to one expert, the Egyptian delegate to the First Arab Oil Congress had said: 'We are not asking for a gift, but for a national right, and if the oil-producing countries refuse to share with us the gift which God has bestowed on them, then the time will come when we will get our share through force.' Michael Fields, *A Hundred Million Dollars a Day*, London: Sidgwick and Jackson, 1975, pp. 149-50.

37. Kuwait was the first Arab country to try to make this point. Thus according to one expert, when Kuwait established its development fund in 1962, its principal aim was: 'to show the world, and the Arab countries in particular, that Kuwait is a responsible member of the international community and ready to use its wealth to help those in need'. Robert Stephens, *The Arabs' New Frontier*, London: Temple Smith, 1973, p. 46. According to another expert, the Kuwait Fund's loans were 'unofficially but with perfect clarity' understood 'from Casablanca to Baghdad' to have been 'the first instalment of Kuwait's protection money'. David Holden, *Farewell to Arabia*.

38. Moreover, unlike the Gulf countries, Libya has chosen the military option to protect its security. In addition to the build-up of its conventional defence, Libya has apparently tried to acquire nuclear weapons. This desire, in turn, has affected the direction of Libyan aid. Thus some experts think that large Libyan aid to Pakistan was prompted by this factor. According to one source, 'In 1977 and 1978, Qaddaffi paid untraceable Libyan cash to finance the Pakistani nuclear project near Islamabad which is expected to produce a testable weapon soon.' J.K. Cooley and L. Kaufman, 'Deterring a Qaddaffi Bomb', *The Washington Post*, 23 December 1980, p. A15.

Later, relations between Pakistan and Libya became less cordial and it seemed that by 1979 nuclear cooperation between the two countries was terminated. The Saudi factor might have played a role in it, in view of now extremely close Saudi-Pakistani relations. It was conceivable that the Saudis offered to match and even surpass Libyan aid to Pakistan, if the latter ended its nuclear connections with Libya.

Before trying to develop a nuclear capacity through cooperation with more advanced Third World countries, Qaddaffi may have tried to buy an atom bomb. See 'Kaddafi Hopes to Buy an Atom Bomb', *Africa Diary*, vol. XV., no. 5, January 29-Feburary 4, 1975, p. 7295.

39. Iraq, however, has had serious problems emanating from its internal ethnic and religious divisions. These problems, particularly those caused by religious differences, have been exacerbated by the Islamic revolution of neighbouring Iran, and by the latter's efforts to generate a similar Shi'a-inspired revolution in Iraq. Recently, the activities of Libyan exiles and opposition at home have been creating a number of internal security problems for Libya.

40. However, in addition to ideological preferences, roles were also played by Iraq's political instability and later by the preoccupation of the Ba'athist regime – which came to power in July 1968 – with problems of internal consolidation, plus the relatively low level of Iraq's oil income. Thus Iraq's more active participation in both intra-Arab and international aid efforts reflected its emergence from isolation. See Madjid Khaduri, *Socialist Iraq*, Washington, DC: The Middle East Institute, 1978, pp. 172-3.

41. *MEES*, vol. XX, no. 31, May 23, 1977, p. 11.

42. France, Italy, later West Germany, and Brazil and India were among Iraq's major economic partners. Edith Penrose and Ernest Benn, *Iraq: International Relations and National Development*, Boulder, Colorado: Westview Press, 1978, pp. 436-9.

43. For instance, on 10 December 1979 Iraq's Oil Minister, Mr Tayeh Abdul-Karim, declared that, under a temporary aid programme for those LDCs that have direct crude oil contracts with Iraq, Iraq had extended $200 million in the form of interest-free loans to twelve countries in regard to crude oil price increases in the period from 1 June to 31 December 1979. *MEES*, vol. XXIII, no. 9 17 December 1979, p. 7. Later this amount was disbursed among the following countries: Tanzania, Kenya, Madagascar ($70 million), India ($104 million), Pakistan ($19.5 million), Vietnam ($6.5 million). *MEES*, vol. XXIV, no. 33, 13 August 1980, p. 8 and *MEES*, vol. XXIII, no. 40, 21 July 1980, p. 11.

44. Initially Qaddaffi was reluctant to articulate his views, and he was cautious in applying them to his relations with Arab countries. This attitude resulted partly from his intense admiration for Nasser. When Qaddaffi came to power, Nasser's image was tarnished by Egypt's defeat in the 1967 war but he was still the leader of the Arab world. Thus Qaddaffi showed intense admiration for him and accepted the second position for himself. But after Nasser's death, he came to consider himself as Nasser's successor and the real custodian of the Nasserite legacy and the ideals of Pan-Arabism.

45. For instance, according to press reports some years ago, Qaddaffi promised Syria to finance its arms purchases from Russia, but when Hafiz Assad went to Russia to negotiate the terms, he found that Libya had backed out. *The Washington Post*, 30 July 1979, p. A8.

46. According to one report, Major Abdessalam Jallud, second in command to Qaddaffi, during a visit to the Yemen Arab Republic in the spring of 1980 presented a programme of military and economic assistance on the condition that North Yemen immediately join with the PDRY. The package offered by Libya was quite extensive and included: Libyan commitment (1) to supply the YAR with the latest Soviet military equipment, and the payment of the cost of Soviet advisers necessary for training the Yemenis with the new weapons; (2) to supply the YAR with oil for a five-year period at a nominal price far below the world price and to construct oil refineries; and (3) to make up any deficits in the Yemeni budget and to pay employee salaries for five years. *Strategy Week*, vol. VI, no. 25, 23 June 1980, p. 5. Of course, the desire to draw the YAR out of the Saudi sphere of influence must have played a role.

47. Qaddaffi has believed that the reason for the backwardness of the Islamic countries is that they have forsaken Islam, and in this way have brought upon themselves the wrath of God that has manifested itself in the form of 'backwardness, imperialism, reactionary style of life, and a dictatorship installed over them from within'. From Qaddaffi's speech on 19 November 1978, quoted in Raymond N. Habiby, 'Mu'amar Qadhaffi's New Islamic Scientific-Socialist Society', *Middle East Review*, vol. XI, no. 4, Summer 1979, p. 32.

48. Qaddaffi, in the speech referred to above, said: 'You Libyans are to play a big role in leading the new revolution, the revolution of the emancipation of Islam, the emancipation of the masses ... You are to play a leading role in preaching the Islamic revolt. . .' Ibid., pp. 32-3.

49. Brian Crozier, *Libya's Foreign Adventures*, Conflict Studies, no. 41, London, The Institute for the Study of Conflict, December 1973, p. 13.

50. During Chad's lengthy civil war, Qaddaffi has supported diverse factions in the country at one time or another, including non-Muslims against Muslims.

51. The British/NATO base in Malta was finally closed in March 1979. The Maltese Prime Minister, Dom Mintoff, is reported to have said that 'Without their help [the Arabs] it would have been impossible to close the British base.' *MEED Special Report on Malta*, May 1980, p. 5.

52. Hikmat Nashashibi, 'Other Ways to Recycle Oil Surpluses', *Euromoney*, August 1974, p. 52.

53. Two-thirds of Kuwait's funds are invested in the United States, 27.6 per cent in Europe, and 11 per cent in other countries, including Japan. *MEED*, vol. 25, no. 8, 20 February 1981, p. 7. However, this has not been totally the Gulf countries' fault. Lack of adequate economic and social infrastructure in the developing countries, plus the danger of political instability, have proved a very serious handicap. In fact, one Gulf country – Kuwait – could be given some credit for having tried to create conditions, at least in the Arab world, which could make investments safer and thus more possible. For instance, Kuwait initiated the Inter-Arab Investment Guarantee Corporation (IAIGC) with the Kuwait Fund for Arab Economic Development (KFAED), taking the lead as early as 1966 when it proposed this step to the First Arab Industrial Development Conference. Later, KFAED convened a meeting of Arab financial experts to study the different aspects of the question. By 1970, KFAED had prepared a draft convention, and by the beginning of 1973 the convention had received the approval of 13 Arab countries. Michael Fields, *A Hundred Million Dollars*, pp. 158-9.

54. As a result of this consideration Libya's aid has largely gone to those Muslim countries – Pakistan and Turkey – that could be useful to it either from a military point of view or as sources of skilled labour and investment outlets. For instance, part of the agreements signed with Turkey also were related to the establishment of an armaments industry producing small arms and ammunition, as well as providing large numbers of Turkish workers for Libya's development plans. *Africa Diary*, vol. XV, no. 7, 14-25 February 1975, p. 7320.

55. *Financial Solidarity for Development: Efforts and Institutions of the Members of OPEC*, 1973-1976 Review, TD/B/C.7/31, p. 38.

56. Libya, for example, has tried to increase its influence in Africa by manipulating Muslim populations of the African countries. In some cases, Libya has tried to subvert these populations. For example, according to a former ally of Qaddaffi, Chaibo Bishara of Chad, Libya has been training 5,000 legionnaires in order to establish Islamic governments in Chad, Niger, Mali, and Senegal. *Strategy Week: Mid-East-Africa-Asia*, vol. VI, no. 27, 13 July 1980, p. 4.

57. In the case of Venzuela, this commitment has derived from its history of struggle for economic emancipation, symbolised by the decisive role that it

has played in the creation of OPEC. Consequently, Venezuela has believed that OPEC's effectiveness has depended on its solidarity with the Third World and its contribution to the establishment of a NIEO. See Robert D. Bond, 'Venezuela's Role in International Affairs' in Bond (ed.), *Contemporary Venezuela and Its Role in International Affairs*, New York: New York University Press, 1979, pp. 244-5.

58. According to some reports, Libya was involved in the violence which erupted in Nigeria's Kano region by Islamic fundamentalists, and as a result Nigeria has been becoming increasingly concerned about Libyan ambitions in Africa. *The Christian Science Monitor*, 26 December 1980, p. 3.

59. Venezuela has been concerned about the impact of Cuban activities in Central America which have tended to polarise the region and to reduce the chances for the development of moderate and democratic governments there. Nigeria, in view of Libya's activities in Chad and other African countries, has become increasingly concerned with the implications of Libya's ambitions.

60. For example, Venezuela's political outlook in Latin America has been influenced by the Bolivarian vision of a United Latin America. Such Venezuelan actions as the creation of a Systema Economica Latin Americano (SELA) illustrated this point. In the case of Nigeria, the concept of African unity has been quite influential. For an analysis of the impact of this and other similar concepts on the Nigerian policy see: Oyeleye Oyediran (ed.), *Nigerian Government and Politics Under Military Rule 1966-77*, New York: St Martin's Press, 1979.

61. For example, according to some reports, Venezuela has given $120 million in aid to the Sandinista regime in Nicaragua in order to moderate its policies. *The Wall Street Journal*, 6 January 1981, p. 34, and aid to Jamaica in the amount of $22.5 million ($2.5 million to the Bank of Jamaica and $20 million to the government of Jamaica) has partly been to gain access to its bauxite resources for Venezuela's aluminium industry.

Aid has also been given to Peru, Honduras, El Salvador, and the Dominican Republic for the financing of oil purchases from Venezuela and for a variety of development projects. Another oil-related project has been the Venezuelan-Mexican agreement to lend back to the purchaser 30 per cent of the cost of oil at 4 per cent over two years or 2 per cent over 20 years to be used to develop their energy resources.

62. Venezuela's plan to set up a special fund for the regulation of the price of coffee of the Central American countries, through agreements between the Venezuelan Investment Fund and these countries' central banks, illustrated this point. This decision was reached at a meeting of Central American governments in Guyana in December 1979. *Venezuela Up To Date*, January 1975, p. 4.

63. For example, in announcing Venezuela's decision to set up a trust fund at the 15th Annual Meeting of the IDB in April 1975, Venezuela's governor said that the funds would be a 'Fund for developing the region's productive and exporting capacity, and not one for strengthening the physical infrastructure for which purpose international services of financing are already available.' *Inter-American Development Bank Annual Report*, 1975, p. 31.

64. Among the recipients of the Trust Fund's loans have been Madagascar, Gambia, Liberia, and Burundi.

65. Recipients of Nigerian aid have included Mali, Senegal, Upper Volta, Chad, Niger, Ethiopia, Sierra Leone, Somalia, Zambia, Sudan, São Tomé and Príncipe, Angola, the African National Congress, and Mozambique. See Bolaji A. Akinyemi, 'Mohammed/Obasanjo Foreign Policy' in *Nigerian Government and Politics Under Military Rule*, p. 165.

66. The following passages from the speech by General Obasanjo (ex-President of Nigeria) at the Institute of African Studies of the University of

Ibadan on 30 April 1980 illustrated this point: 'There are countries in Europe, particularly the erstwhile colonial powers who derive substantial political and economic advantage from political fragmentation of West Africa and Africa. Such European countries are afraid of losing the benefits of political and economic imperialism and are always ready to instigate those African leaders who are more oriented towards Europe and European interests to decry progressive political ideas that can lead to a more integrated West African region.' In referring specifically to ECOWAS, he added, 'The West African region in particular is replete with colonially and externally inspired efforts at regional economic integration. Among these must be included the French-formed West African Customs Union in 1959 and the French-inspired West African Monetary Union in 1962. But the first genuinely internally inspired efforts at harmonization of trade and economies of the region was the establishment in 1975 of the Economic Community of West African States.' Referring to Nigeria's leadership potential he said, 'Nigeria, by combined accident of history and geography, has all the potential and making of leadership in West Africa and Africa. But we have to make haste slowly and show our good intentions to political and community leaders in West Africa and Africa not as an ambitious, domineering bully wanting to subjugate the rest of the region, but as an older brother who is endowed more than his other brothers and who genuinely wants to pull the family resources together on the basis of cooperation so as to improve the lot of each member of the family.' Text of Address, pp. 14-15.

67. For these reasons the Nigerian business community was ahead of the Nigerian government in pushing for institutionalisation of intra-West African economic relations when the Nigerian Chamber of Commerce became one of the leading lights in the formation of a West African Chamber of Commerce before ECOWAS was formed. Bolaji Akinyemi, *Nigerian Government*, p. 164.

68. *Financial Solidarity for Development*, T/D/B/C. 7/31, pp. 53-4.

3 CASE STUDIES: IRAN AND SAUDI ARABIA

Iran and Saudi Arabia are natural choices for case analysis because they represent two types of key OPEC member. In addition to its oil income, the former has significant non-oil resources; but at the same time it has major internal demands for resources, and thus has relatively little financial surplus to be devoted to foreign aid. By contrast, the latter has few resources besides oil, but also has a relatively low absorptive capacity and thus large financial surpluses. Moreover, these two countries, while sharing a number of characteristics, also differ from one another in regard to such important aspects as their geo-strategic conditions, components of national power, nature of alliances, historical experience, and principal instruments of policy.

PART ONE: IRANIAN AID POLICIES IN CONTEXT

Iran is almost unique among OPEC countries in terms of its geo-strategic situation, historical experience, and leadership characteristics. Iran also has special significance for two other reasons: first, it has a longer-run historical sense of the context within which aid policies must be meshed than is true, certainly, in the other Middle East members of OPEC, which are relative latecomers on the international scene.

Second, aid has been a secondary instrument of Iran's foreign policy for the following reasons: the relatively low level of Iran's financial assets, particularly compared to its development and other needs, and the availability of other instruments, including considerable military power. In turn, the combination of these two factors explains: (1) Iran's relatively late entry into the business of providing aid; (2) the erratic nature of its aid levels; and (3) the termination of its aid programme after 1979. Of course, Iran's revolution in that year was the proximate cause for the ending of its aid programme, but it also reflected Iran's financial shortcomings and its ability to pursue its national interests through other means.

What follows, therefore, is an effort to establish context and motivation for Iranian foreign aid, and to describe and analyse the Iranian aid programme in overall terms of foreign policy.

I Determinants of Iranian Aid Policy

As with other OPEC countries, security considerations were paramount in determining Iran's aid policies. In fact, Iran's leaders were quite candid in admitting that the ultimate purpose of its aid programme was to complement its overall security policy.[1] Iran's views of threats to its security, and thus its security needs, have essentially been determined by its geo-strategic condition and historical experience. The most consequential aspects of Iran's geo-political conditions have been its territorial contiguity to a great power (Russia/Soviet Union) and its location in a zone of great power rivalry. This situation in turn had caused Iran (and still does) to be subjected to pressures and military incursions by its great power neighbour, as well as by the extra-regional competing great power – historically, Britain and now the United States. Also, Iran had suffered as a result of occasional collusion between the competing powers and had several times even faced the danger of partition because of such collusion.[2]

By the time of the 1973 oil revolution, the negative aspects of Iran's geostrategic condition had been somewhat lessened, largely because of changes in the international system, plus internal changes both in Iran and in its great power neighbour, the Soviet Union. Yet Iran's basic security dilemma remained the same, since not all systemic changes served Iran's security interests.[3]

Thus, by this time the danger of a direct Soviet attack on Iran had subsided. Nevertheless, it potentially remained the most serious threat to Iran's security although the nature of this threat and its focus had changed. This was so despite improvement in Soviet-Iranian relations, since – given the persistence of certain systemic factors plus differences in Soviet and Iranian political and economic outlook and orientation – Moscow was not yet totally benevolent towards Iran.[4] In fact, a number of specific developments during the early 1970s had convinced Iran of the continuing seriousness of the Soviet threat and even its intensification, since, following those developments, the Soviet threat became more diffuse and no longer confined to Iran's northern borders and thus more difficult to deal with.[5] As a result, Iran feared that the Soviet Union was bent on pressuring it through a policy of encirclement by unfriendly countries.

The first of these developments was the Indo-Pakistani war of 1971 that resulted in Pakistan's dismemberment and during which the Soviet Union had supported India. Soviet-Indian ties were later strengthened further and were formalised by the signing of the Indo-Soviet friendship treaty in 1972. Pakistan's dismemberment was followed by a wave of internal unrest and the growth of separatist movements in its Northwestern province and Baluchistan. Baluchi unrest was very disturbing to Iran, given its own Baluchi population. The Iranians were particularly worried by evidence of direct and indirect – (through Iraq) Soviet involvement in these Pakistani events.[6] The Iranians feared that the rebel movement in Baluchistan, with Soviet and Iraqi help, could lead to the separation of this province from Pakistan and thus remove a buffer area on Iran's eastern border.

The second major event was the signing of the Soviet-Iraqi treaty of friendship in 1972, followed by Soviet arms deliveries to Iraq.[7] This was followed by Iraq's attack on Kuwait in March 1972 and increased border clashes with Iran. All these developments were viewed as signs of a Soviet policy of destabilising Iran and the Persian Gulf.

The third major event was the coup in Afghanistan in 1973 that removed King Mohammad Zahir Shah and established a Republican government. Although there is no clear evidence that the Soviet Union instigated the coup, it was generally believed that Moscow had prior knowledge, a factor that was not lost on Iran.[8] Added to these developments were increased Soviet influence in the Peoples Democratic Republic of Yemen (South Yemen) and Moscow's support – albeit indirect – to the Dhofari rebellion; Soviet activities in Somalia; and frequent Soviet naval visits to Persian Gulf/Red Sea ports, all of which developments exacerbated Iran's fears of Soviet intentions. Also troubling was the fact that these developments took place at a time of a relative retrenching of the Western presence from these regions, and of growing doubts in Iran about the security value of its Western alliance ties.[9]

Thus, by 1973, despite the reduced danger of direct Soviet attack, Iran strongly felt the pressure of Soviet power and military might.[10] In fact, this more pervasive and thus more threatening Soviet power more than ever before affected Iran's immediate security environment. Consequently, Iran's primary security objective was the reduction of the negative impact of Soviet power on Iran's regional environment.

In 1973, there was no threat of direct military attack against Iran from its neighbours – given its friendly relations with Pakistan and Turkey and its reasonably good relations with Afghanistan. Iran's essential problem in regard to these countries was the possibility of changes in regimes through subversion or internal turmoil – in Pakistan, for example. The only potential source of direct military attack was Iraq, because of the long history of animosity between Iran and Iraq and the latter's miliary capabilities. But in 1973, such a threat was less credible in view of Iraq's domestic problems – notably the rebellion by its Kurdish population. Nevertheless, Iraq was still a primary source of threat to Iranian security, since during the 1970s it had become a major source of subversion in the Persian Gulf – and indeed throughout the Middle East.[11]

Moreover, Iran was worried about Iraq's designs on other Gulf countries, especially Kuwait – designs that, if successful, would have led to the installation of more radical regimes that would have been more hostile to Iran, thus causing its security environment to deteriorate.

Consequently, beyond the threat from the Soviet Union and to some extent from Iraq, Iran was primarily preoccupied by regional subversion, focused on the Persian Gulf.[12]

Security Threats in the Persian Gulf

The importance of the Persian Gulf for Iran's security is evident:

(i) without its Persian Gulf ports, Iran would be a land-locked country;
(ii) Iran's most important natural resource – oil – is located in its south-western province of Khuzistan, bordering on the Persian Gulf;
(iii) Iran's political and economic viability depends on the free flow of oil from its Persian Gulf terminals; and
(iv) historically, the Persian Gulf has been the approach – (other than from Russia) – through which foreign powers have encroached on Iran's independence and rights. As such, Persian Gulf security is also psychologically very important for Iran.[13]

Despite its vital importance, the Persian Gulf did not become the focus of Iran's security and other interests until 1965, largely because of its preoccupation with the Soviet threat in the north, and British supremacy in the Gulf. However, following developments in the Arab world and in the Gulf region, Iran's attention by the late 1950s had begun to shift towards the Gulf.[14]

However, in 1968 when Britain announced its decision to withdraw militarily from the Gulf by 1971, the latter became Iran's primary security concern and the focus of its defence and foreign policies. British withdrawal presented Iran with two sets of problems. The first related to the Gulf's emerging political pattern and its potential impact on Iran's interests. Iran had a few unresolved issues with Britain (over Bahrain and a few other smaller islands) that it wanted to see settled before Britain left. It was also concerned about the strength and weakness of the emerging power structure in the Gulf. For Iran, already flanked by Iraq with its considerable military power, the prospect of having to face another Arab power across the Persian Gulf was not very appealing.[15] Yet the weakness of the new set-up was also disturbing to Iran, since this weakness could have made it an easy target of radical Arab subversion and thus a potential source of threat to Iran and to the stability of the Gulf, in general.

The other set of problems concerned the identity of the nations that would fill the power vacuum left in the Gulf by British withdrawal. Iran worried that this could be the Soviet Union, either directly or – more likely – through proxies.[16] Consequently, forestalling such an eventuality and thus combating regional subversion became Iran's other primary security objective. The following statement by an American expert succinctly illustrates this point: 'The Shah wants to preserve his own rule and he also wants to insulate his country against the kinds of revolutionary forces which have made a shambles of stability . . . in some Middle East countries. . .'[17]

In sum, therefore, Iran's security needs and objectives resulted from its geostrategic conditions, the nature of its regional environment, and the requirements of its political regime. But the extent of these objectives – or in other words the confines of Iran's security perimeter – was a function of the level of its military and economic capabilities, as well as the evolving characteristics of international and regional systems. By 1973, both Iran's own capabilities and changes in the regional and international systems had led it to define its security perimeter in broad terms, extending beyond the Gulf into the Indian Ocean. As a result, Iran became concerned about developments beyond the Persian Gulf and sought to reduce their negative aspects – a concern that foreshadowed its entry into foreign assistance.[18] Of course, the idiosyncrasies of Iran's leadership also had an important impact on the definition of its security perimeter.

Political/Ideological Motive

For many years, Iran's political objectives have been essentially determined by its security needs. Thus, the reduction of Soviet and Iraqi threats and the fight against regional subversion were also important Iranian *political* objectives. Furthermore, Iran was concerned about some aspects of systemic change. It feared that they might increase the risks of great power collusion at Iran's expense, and it wanted to forestall this development if it could. Also, Iran wanted to increase its capacity for autonomous action, to have a greater impact on the evolution of regional events, and to enhance its international prestige and standing.

By 1973, Iran's pursuit of these objectives had led it to develop a foreign policy whose basic objectives were the following:

(a) to minimise the great powers' presence in the region of the Middle East/Persian Gulf and the Indian Sub-continent, and their penetration of inter-regional affairs;
(b) to resolve intra-regional disputes in order to eliminate as far as possible the resort by regional countries to the superpowers for maintenance of their security or restoration of their rights;
(c) to promote moderate forces and to create incentives for moderate behaviour; and
(d) to present regional alternatives to problems of regional security and economic development.

The following statement sums up both Iran's principal political concerns and its policy choices to deal with them: 'Iran, anxious to avoid great power presence in the region, to maximize its autonomy, and prevent the prospect of being sacrificed on the altar of crisis management, had sought a regional formula to assure her security.'[19]

Iran's methods for achieving its policy goals were essentially pragmatic, flexible, and non-doctrinaire.[20] The lack of any particular ideological focus in Iran's foreign policy – in addition to a sense of political pragmatism – derived from its ethnic and cultural characteristics.[21] However, this stance did not always work in Iran's favour. In fact, despite its growing military and economic power, by 1973 Iran felt isolated – a feeling that contributed to some of its policy choices, including that of foreign assistance.[22]

In an interview with the Indian journalist R.A. Karanjia, the Shah illustrated Iran's search for a new ideological and philosophical focus for its foreign policy. The Shah said that his ultimate purpose in expanding Iran's relations with India, Pakistan, and Afghanistan was to bring about 'a renascent Aryan brotherhood of Iran, India, Pakistan, and Afghanistan . . .' in order 'to hold high the torch of a glorious, humanitarian and moralistic civilization'.[23]

This factor also contributed to Iran's generally globalist approach to issues related to international economic relations and problems of aid and development.[24] In addition, Iran's search for prestige also was another of its political objectives and derived essentially from perceptions of Iran's past and visions of its future – particularly on the part of the Iranian leadership.[25]

Economic Motives

Clearly, economic factors also affected Iran's policies, and did so in essentially two ways: (1) by adding an extra dimension to its security concerns – for instance, preoccupation with the Persian Gulf; and (2) by strengthening policy trends already generated by other factors. Also, economic needs generated by Iran's social and economic development plans had a critical impact on its foreign policy, as the following discussion will demonstrate.[26]

By 1973, Iran had made considerable progress in its social and economic development and had set ambitious goals for its fifth development plan (1973-8) – ambitions that were revised upwards after the unexpected rise in its oil income. The increase in Iran's oil revenues had also led it to adopt a new development strategy for the next 20 years. This strategy was based essentially on the twin principles of (1) high levels of oil production and export, and (2) rapid industrialisation to enable Iran to replace its oil revenues by earnings from industrial exports once its oil reserves were depleted. Parallel with its ambitious economic development plans, Iran had embarked on a vast social programme aimed at turning it into a true welfare state.

Although Iran's natural and human resources and the size of its domestic market warranted some optimism regarding its prospects for developing a diversified economic base, its ambitious fifth and sixth development plans entailed a vast number of urgent needs as well as some serious long-term problems. In turn, the requirements of meeting these needs and finding solutions for the more long-term problems affected (1) Iran's perceptions of its economic interests, within both the regional and international contexts; (2) consequently its approach to a wide range of global economic issues; and (3) the broad outlines of its foreign economic policies and even to some extent its foreign policy – leading to a programme of foreign assistance.

Access to Sources of Supply. Because of both Iran's ambitious development plans and the dramatic increase in the level of popular consumption following the oil boom, Iran's import needs had jumped to new heights. These needs could be roughly divided into three categories:

food and a wide range of raw materials; skilled manpower and technology; and industrial equipment. Nor were these needs of a temporary nature. As a result, securing reliable sources of supply at preferably more-or-less stable prices became an important objective for Iran and was one of the primary reasons – in some cases the only reason – for the expansion of Iran's relations with a number of countries.[27]

Access to Export Markets. As noted above, Iran's economic development strategy was based on rapid industrialisation to enable it to replace oil revenues by earnings from industrial exports.[28] Yet Iran faced enormous problems before it could become internationally competitive. Thus the need to establish export markets acted as an impetus for the expansion of Iran's relations with a number of Third World countries. It also affected Iran's outlook on global economic issues and its relations with the industrialised countries. However, there was a great deal of contradiction here among Iran's diverse interests. For example, not only did Iran – as an essentially pro-Western country – have a security and political interest in the health of Western economies, but also its own economy had become more rather than less dependent on the rate of economic growth of a few select industrialised countries. As a result, Iran could not be 'indifferent to a slowdown in the economies of the industrialised countries', let alone to their disruption.[29] Yet Iran's interests as an aspiring industrial nation differed from those of the industrialised countries in many regards.[30]

II Foreign Policy Instruments

The preceding discussion of Iran's various interests leads to an analysis of the methods chosen to secure those interests, within which foreign aid came to play an instrumental role.

By 1973, Iran's essential instruments of foreign policy were military power, diplomacy, oil, and economic cooperation – including trade, investment, and aid.

Military Power

Among these instruments, military power occupied first place in Iran's defence and foreign policies. Yet this emphasis was not always understood, even by Iran's allies.[31] Indeed, during the 1970s Iran's defence build-up became a matter of regional and international controversy, and many commentators attributed this tendency to the idiosyncrasies of Iran's leadership.[32]

However, while this aspect of the Shah's character was important, Iran's emphasis on military forces had more to do with its geostrategic conditions, the nature of threats posed to its security, its historical experience, and its resource base.[33] Thus, for Iran – which even after the oil price increase of 1973 had limited financial resources – compared to Arab members of OPEC, except Algeria – but was relatively rich in human resources, development of a viable defence force was an obvious choice. Moreover, the character of Iran's adversaries made the effectiveness of other instruments on their own (such as economic tools) – very doubtful.[34]

However, beyond a certain point – roughly 1976 – Iran's military ambitions came into conflict with its other objectives, in regard both to its economic development plans and its regional diplomacy. To the extent Iran persisted in its plans for military build-up, this was essentially due to the nature of its decision-making apparatus and the idiosyncrasies of its leadership.[35]

Diplomacy

Since the mid-1960s, Iran's active diplomacy contributed to its security and other objectives. As noted earlier, Iran perceived principal threats to its security deriving from the following sources:

(a) pressure by the great powers, either in competition or in collusion with one other;
(b) over-involvement of the great powers in regional affairs that, in Iran's view, could make it more vulnerable to their pressure, either directly or indirectly through third countries; and
(c) regional instability caused by intra-regional disputes and subversion. This last concern was linked to the second since, in Iran's view, regional disputes could be manipulated to the great powers' advantage.

Thus since the mid-1960s, and increasingly so during the 1970s, Iran's diplomacy was focused on (1) conflict resolution at the regional level – both as between Iran and its neighbours and among Iran's neighbours – and (2) minimisation of great-power involvement in regional affairs through, among other efforts, the offering of alternative regional models for dealing with security and economic problems.[36] After the oil price increases, Iran's diplomacy, particularly at the international level, focused on explaining Iran's (and OPEC's) position on global economic issues, mitigating the negative impact of industrial-country policies against OPEC; and promoting Third World views on global economic issues.[37] Needless to say, Iran used all its assets, both military and economic, in support of its diplomacy.[38]

Economic Instruments

In a general sense, Iran's most effective economic instrument has been oil, since it has been the source of its increased financial means and the principal engine of its economic development. Also, until its revolution Iran was the world's second largest oil exporter, and thus its capacity to influence the price of oil gained it access to international parleys dealing with global economic issues (for example, the Conference on International Economic Cooperation (CIEC)), and enabled it to promote its own and the developing countries' views.

Moreover, Iran's ability to provide oil on a long-term and assured basis – in some cases at concessional terms – enabled it to offset some of the negative impact of oil price increases on its relations with the industrial countries. It also increased its influence over the direction of the foreign policies of some Third World countries, along the line of its own preferences.[39] This ability also led to Iran's obtaining a foothold in the markets of some developing countries.[40]

Traditionally, Iran has also used trade to achieve its security and other foreign policy and economic goals. With its increased oil revenues in the early 1970s, Iran used trade and investment with more efficacy in its relations with the industrialised, socialist, and developing countries.[41] In relations with the industrialised countries, Iran used these instruments (1) to ease their balance of payment burdens and thus offset some of the contradictions in their relations with Iran; (2) to secure needed technology and other material for Iran's development plans; and (3) to get a foothold in their industrial sectors. In relations with the socialist and the developing countries, these instruments served to boost Iran's exports and to secure sources of supply of needed raw materials and manufactured goods.[42]

III Aid

It is evident from the foregoing discussion of Iran's interests and its tools of foreign policy – in comparison with those of other OPEC states – that 'aid' as traditionally defined has occupied a far less significant place as an instrument of foreign and security policy for Iran than for other major OPEC donors. In fact, Iran's leaders have consistently emphasised the theme of trade and economic cooperation rather than aid.[43]

This attitude has been natural and the logical consequence both of Iran's limited financial resources – compared to those of Arab members of OPEC – and of its large population and huge developmental needs. In fact, while promising Iranian participation in aid plans for the Third World, the Shah constantly emphasised that Iran could spend its 'last penny' on its own economic development.[44]

For the same reason, Iran – together with Algeria and Venezuela but unlike the Persian Gulf Arab countries – supported and even suggested *international* schemes for aid, since limits on financial surpluses argued against aid large enough to justify *bilateral* programmes. Thus these donors could not on their own reach most of the developing world with foreign assistance. Yet they could hope to attain influence in the Third World through multilateral aid programmes in the creation and operation of which they would have a major role. And it was only when prospects faded for establishing such a fund – because of Arab opposition – that Iran embarked on its aid programme.[45] However, as noted earlier, Iran still did not emphasise the theme of 'aid', but rather talked about economic cooperation. Iran's thinking is clearly illustrated by the facts that it did not establish a development fund like most other OPEC countries, and that its aid programme was headed by the 'Organisation for Investment, Economic and Technical Assistance of Iran' as part of the Ministry of Finance.

In addition, the limited nature of Iran's resources meant that it had to tailor its aid policy even more carefully than did some OPEC states with larger surplus resources, in order to advance its own political and economic interests. The following analysis of the principal characteristics of Iran's aid amply illustrates these points.

Principal Characteristics

Principal characteristics of Iranian aid during its short lifetime to some extent bore a resemblance to that of other OPEC members, except for volume trends, and reflected Iran's particular needs. These characteristics were as given below.

Falling Volume. The volume of Iranian aid has followed a downward trend, illustrating the impact of both falling oil revenues and political change, as indicated in Table 3.1.

Table 3.1: Volume of Iran's ODA ($US millions)

Year	Disbursement	% of GNP
1974	739.4	1.59
1975	936.1	1.79
1976	807.3	1.22
1977	315.5	0.38
1978	333.4	0.40
1979	25	0.03
1980	3	na

Source: *Annual DAC Reviews*, 1974-81.

High Geographic Concentration. Iran's bilateral aid has been highly concentrated in a few countries. For example, in 1974 and 1976 Pakistan accounted for 74 per cent and 82 per cent of Iran's bilateral aid respectively.[46] In 1975, India was the largest recipient of Iranian aid, followed by Egypt.

In fact, according to one Iranian source, the value of this geographic concentration, in relation to Iran's overall strategic objectives, was clearly understood within its leadership. For example, the Shah used to say that either Iran must increase its military budget by $2 billion in order to keep a new division on its frontier with Pakistan (in Iranian Baluchistan) or must help Pakistan improve economic conditions in its Baluchistan, thus contributing to stability in the region.[47]

Table 3.2: Principal Recipients of Iranian Aid, 1974-6 ($US millions)

Country	1974	1975	1976
India	940[a]	–	–
Bangladesh	125	–	–
Pakistan	580	–	–
Egypt	200	120	–
Afghanistan	10.0	0.1	–
Morocco	30.0	–	–
Tunisia	4.5	–	–
Syria	150.0	–	–
Turkey	11.9	–	–
Peru	100.0	–	–
Senegal	10.9	–	–
Gabon	–	3.0	–
Lesotho	1.0	–	–
Jordan	15.0	4.5	–
Maldives	–	1.0	–

Note: a. This includes $600 million to develop the Kudrumeh iron ore deposits.
Source: OECD, *Annual DAC Review*, 1979.

In addition to India and Pakistan, which held special strategic, political, and economic significance for Iran, other principal recipients fell roughly into the following categories:

1. Those Middle Eastern countries that had a history of hostile relations with Iran and with whom Iran wanted to improve its relations, as well as to encourage moderate tendencies. Egypt and Syria fall in this category.
2. Friendly African countries in the stability of whose regimes Iran was interested – notably Morocco and Tunisia.
3. Other neighbouring countries with which Iran wanted either to strengthen further its relations or to induce some changes in their policies. Afghanistan and Turkey are in this category.

Paramountcy of Non-development Motives. As illustrated by the pattern of geographic distribution of Iranian aid, security and political motives were very influential. Economic considerations also tended to strengthen the impact of political factors. As noted earlier, export promotion and the securing of sources of supply were the primary economic interests Iran promoted through aid.[48]

High Percentage of Bilateral Aid. Even though Iran initially favoured multilateral channels for aid – as its proposal for an international fund illustrates – when its suggestion did not lead to results it channelled the bulk of its aid bilaterally. For example, Iran did not contribute to IDA, to regional development banks, or to the Islamic Development Bank. Its multilateral contributions were limited to UN agencies and the UN Special Account.

The explanation for Iran's coolness towards the World Bank Group lies largely in the peculiarities of Iran's leadership. At the time, the Shah was unhappy over criticisms voiced by Bank officials on the wisdom of Iran's economic policies. He also realised that Iran did not have much influence within the Bank over decisions about the use of Iranian contributions. Thus Iran's attitude also reflected the traditional dislike of donor countries for relinquishing control over the use of their aid money.[49] The latter factor was also the principal reason for Iran's reluctance to contribute to the regional development banks. With regard to the Islamic Development Bank, Iran was reluctant to contribute to it because it was a pet project of Saudi Arabia, headquartered in Jeddah and dominated by the Saudis.[50]

Yet Iran did contribute to the IMF oil facility, in large part to

Table 3.3: Iran's ODA Contributions to Multilateral Organisations (disbursements in $US millions)

	IFAD	UN Agencies	IBRD IMF	Reg. Dev. Banks	Arab Agencies	OPEC Fund	Total	% GNP
1973	–	1.5	–	–	–	–	1.5	0.01
1974	–	22.5	–	–	–	–	22.5	0.05
1975	–	5.5	–	–	–	–	5.5	0.01
1976	–	5.6	1.7	–	–	54.6	61.9	0.10
1977	–	5.4	1.8	–	–	2.7	10.0	0.01
1978	41.6	0.4	1.9	–	–	13.7	57.6	0.08
1979	–	4.6	1.9	–	–	14.3	20.8	0.03
1980	–	4.0	–	–	–	28.7	32.7	0.04
1981	–	0.4	–	–	–	–	0.4	–

Source: OECD, *Aid From OPEC Countries*, 1983.

counter criticisms of oil-price increases. However, since the terms of this aid were not concessional, its inclusion in Iranian aid figures was a matter of controversy.[51] Also, when the OPEC Special Fund and the International Fund for Agricultural Development (IFAD) were set up, Iran made significant contributions to both. Iran's willingness to contribute to the OPEC Fund stemmed from the imperatives of intra-OPEC solidarity. Also, within the OPEC Fund Iran could gain more influence over decisions on the use of aid funds. With regard to IFAD, Iran took an active part in the negotiations leading to its establishment, and thus could influence its course. Also, IFAD's structure and voting system – equal rights for all participants regardless of the level of their contribution – resembled the proposals Iran had made earlier for an international development fund to include industrialised, OPEC, and developing countries.

These contributions, in turn, somewhat changed the ratio of multilateral to bilateral aid in total Iranian ODA. Thus, according to official Iranian figures, in 1976 multilateral *commitments* accounted for 56.2 per cent of Iran's Official Development Assistance (ODA), and OECD figures put the multilateral *disbursement* for that year at 10 per cent of Iran's ODA.[52]

Low Concessionality. The terms of Iranian aid were among the hardest of the OPEC donors, although the overall terms of Iranian ODA improved somewhat by 1976 because of large Iranian contributions to the OPEC Special Fund. Iran extended very few grants as opposed to loans and – although the interest Iran charged on its loans was not

Table 3.4: Concessionality of Iranian ODA, 1974-6

% of Grants in Total Commitments			% Grant Element in ODA Loans			% Grant Element in Total ODA		
1974	1975	1976	1974	1975	1976	1974	1975	1976
5.9	1.3	57.0	34.7	43.6	55.8	38.5	44.3	72.9

Source: *Annual DAC Review*, 1977.

much higher than the OPEC average – in view of their short maturity their grant element was low.[53]

Softer terms seem to have applied to general balance of payment support loans extended to countries Iran deemed particularly important, as well as to loans it extended for the purchase of Iranian goods.[54] The least-developed countries also tended to get softer terms, but the number and amount of bilateral loans extended to them were not considerable.

High Percentage of Tied Aid. In view of the large amount of oil credits extended by Iran, plus credits for the purchase of Iranian goods, the percentage of tied aid was higher in Iran's case than in that of the rest of the OPEC countries, although an exact percentage is hard to establish from available data. This practice reflected the relatively more-advanced state of Iran's economy, since Iran had more to sell and more incentive to develop its own economy.

Impact on the Recipients

As with any aid programme, the impact of Iran's aid should be evaluated from both short- and long-term perspectives. Such evaluation should also take into account both the economic and political consequences of aid. Unfortunately, this last task is complicated by a lack of available data, the subjective characters of political judgements, and the relatively brief duration of the Iranian aid programme against which to judge aid performance over an extended period of time.

It is safe to say that the short-term economic impact of Iranian aid was positive, or at least that it eased recipients' balance of payments burdens. Furthermore, with regard to Iranian influence on the development planning, available evidence indicates that Iran did not have any influence on the level of macro-economics. This was due partly to the fact that Iranian aid was given essentially for political purposes, and as long as it accomplished these purposes, the Iranians were not overly-concerned with the developmental impact of their aid.

Moreover, some countries – such as Pakistan – felt that aid they received from Iran was somehow their due. Indeed, as one Iranian source put it, 'they came to get their share of the oil money', and thus were not prepared to accept any conditions or meddling by Iran.

However, on a micro-economic level, Iran did have some impact on development planning in recipient countries. For example, by expressing its interest in certain industries, it could influence potential aid recipients to favour those industries. Yet in this regard, too, Iran's capacity for influence was limited by the nature of the economies of recipient countries.

Iran also tended to apply more rigorous conditions to the aid given to countries that were less important to it from a political and strategic point of view. For example, these countries received more project aid than general balance of payments support. Also, Iran imposed added conditions to ensure that both projects were completed and loans repaid on time. India, for example – unlike Pakistan – received mainly project aid from Iran.

Iran's most important project in India was the Kudrumeh iron ore project to which Iran committed $600 million. The agreement signed between the two countries included certain points that even led to criticism in the Indian parliament. For example, the disbursement of aid was synchronised with the completion of every stage of the project. Moreover, the Iranian executing agency (the National Iranian Steel Corporation) had to confirm progress before funds were disbursed. In addition, there were high penalties for the Indian government if the project were not completed on schedule. To prevent this from happening, the Indian government set up a three-man high-level committee to cut down on red tape and bureaucratic delays in regard – for example – to the importing of equipment.[55]

In regard to other specific projects, as well, Iran tried to ensure to the extent possible that they met the requirements of feasibility and profitability. And there were regular missions from Iran to recipient countries. But a coherent set of standards and procedures was not yet developed by the time Iranian aid came to a halt.

By contrast, evaluating the long-term impact of Iranian aid is almost impossible, largely because of the programme's short lifetime. For example, some of the projects to which Iran had committed funds were never even started. But what *can* be said is that, had Iran continued its aid programme, it could have had a positive impact from the point of view of development *only* if its political motivations were played down and also if it placed higher priority on being sensitive to the needs and priorities of recipients than on an almost-exclusive preoccupation with meeting Iran's own economic needs.

As far as the political impact of Iran's aid is concerned – particularly the dependence of recipients on the donor – again the short lifetime of Iran's aid programme makes thorough evaluation difficult. Yet it is safe to say that Iranian aid did not create dependence on the part of recipients, because of several factors:

(a) most important, Iranian aid only lasted a short time;
(b) the value of Iranian aid, although significant in the case of a few countries (for example, India, Pakistan, and Egypt), was not that important in comparison with aid these countries received from other donors;[56]
(c) given the strategic, political, and – to some extent – economic importance of these countries for Iran – and thus Iran's eagerness to improve its relations with them – they were in a good bargaining position *vis-à-vis* Iran;
(d) some of the recipients, such as India and Egypt, in many respects (including military power) were either superior (India) or at least equal (Egypt) to Iran. Moreover, in view of their other attributes (for example, size, population, and regional importance) they were capable of creating problems for Iran and of preventing realisation of some of its ambitions. This in turn limited Iran's leverage on them through aid; and
(e) other competitive sources of aid were available to Iran's aid recipients. For example, the Arab countries also courted Pakistan and provided it with large sums of money. In return, Pakistan developed close relations with the Arab countries, including those – such as Libya – that were openly hostile to Iran. Even though Iran expressed its displeasure with these relations, it could not prevent them.[57] Also, perhaps partly in competition with Iran, Iraq was eager to provide India with oil at concessional prices.

In summary, therefore, Iran's capacity to extend financial aid helped it realise some of its basic national goals, such as bolstering friendly countries and expanding its ties with the Indian sub-continent. However, in view of Iran's relatively-limited financial resources, the nature of its interests, and the characteristics of the principal recipients of Iranian aid, this assistance did not result in a situation of political dependency on the part of the recipients. Even in regard to countries – such as Pakistan – in which Iran had significant (but by no means predominant) influence, this influence derived more from Iran's military strength, its geographic proximity, and its regional conditions than from aid relationships.

PART TWO: SAUDI ARABIAN AID POLICIES IN CONTEXT

Since the oil revolution of 1973 Saudi Arabia has emerged as the largest OPEC aid donor. During 1975 and 1976, Saudi Arabia even ranked as the second largest global donor after the United States. Moreover, given its large oil reserves and financial assets, among OPEC countries Saudi Arabia is most likely to maintain large-scale foreign aid over a long period of time.[58]

Yet Saudi Arabia's wealth is accompanied by severe deficiencies in other components of national power. For example, Saudi Arabia's other natural resources and agricultural potential are limited.[59] Its population is variously estimated as being between 4 to 7 million, with the figure of 5 million probably closest to reality. Saudi Arabia is also faced with severe shortages of skilled and semi-skilled (indigenous) manpower, creating serious problems both for its economic development programmes and its plans for military expansion. Thus, despite tremendous wealth, Saudi prospects for creating a diversified economic base are not promising. Also, despite large amounts spent on military hardware and training, Saudi Arabia's capacity to develop military forces sufficient to defend itself and to maintain regional stability is in doubt.

Despite these shortcomings, since the late 1960s – and particularly during the last ten years – Saudi Arabia has become an important factor in regional and global politics, essentially through the use of its financial assets.[60]

Yet even generous use of its wealth has not completely shielded Saudi Arabia from threats to its security, nor given it undisputed influence even at regional or intra-Arab levels. Given these paradoxes in the Saudi situation, therefore, it is extremely useful to look at Saudi foreign aid, factors affecting its nature and direction, its efficacy as an instrument of foreign policy, and its impact on recipient countries.

I Determinants of Saudi Aid Policy

As with Iran, Saudi Arabia's security needs have had the greatest impact on its aid policies. However, the linkage in Saudi thinking between security and aid has been even closer than was the case with Iran, for the following reasons:

(a) The nature of Saudi leadership, whose 'most fundamental value is security, both in its internal and external manifestation . . .'[61]
(b) The country's resource base, which makes problematical the development of other elements of power -- such as military forces – thus putting a high premium on the judicious use of financial power to achieve its security objectives.

In comparison with OPEC's other Persian Gulf members, Saudi Arabia's geo-strategic situation and the nature of its alliances have provided it with a more favourable security environment, particularly concerning certain types of threat. Unlike Iran, for example, Saudi Arabia is not contiguous to a great power and thus has not been directly subjected to expansionist or other great-power pressures that could emanate from such a position. Nor is Saudi Arabia sandwiched between larger and stronger neighbours as are the smaller Gulf countries.

Combined with other factors such as Saudi Arabia's size and difficult terrain, this situation has greatly reduced the danger of a direct all-out attack on Saudi Arabia, without of course completely excluding it.[62]

Of even more significance is the nature of Saudi Arabia's alliance with the United States – an alliance which is qualitatively different from, for example, the one that existed betwen the United States and Iran.[63] The high degree of identity of US-Saudi interests, coupled with Saudi Arabia's vital importance to the United States, has almost guaranteed a US response to any direct attack on Saudi Arabia, as indeed experience has indicated.[64] In turn, this situation has eliminated direct military attack as a credible security threat to Saudi Arabia. Thus the most serious threats to Saudi Arabia's security have emanated from those factors that have adversely affected regional environments of interest to it, and have increased the danger of internal instability and subversion.

From the Saudi perspective, these factors have been radicalism of all shades – but particularly that of the left – and Zionism. In fact, the Saudis have seen a direct link between these two factors, at least concerning events in the Arab world and even to some extent in the Islamic world.[65] From the Saudi perspective, one particularly disturbing consequence of this linkage is that it has led to the growth of anti-Western – in particular anti-American – feelings, and has drawn some Arab and Islamic countries towards the Soviet Union. In turn this development has not only led to a deterioration in Saudi Arabia's security environment, but also, because of its identification with the West, has made it a direct target of radical attacks. Consequently, since the mid-1960s, and increasingly so since the 1970s, combating radical forces and reversing Zionist (Israeli) incursions in the Arab world have become the most important Saudi security objectives.

The geographical scope of these threats (and thus the focus of Saudi counter efforts) have still primarily been the Persian Gulf, the Arabian Sea, the Red Sea, the Horn of Africa, and the Arab world. But in view of (1) systemic changes (such as greater linkage between developments in different regions); and (2) the increase in Saudi financial and other capabilities, the geographical scope of the Saudi security environment has expanded. Thus, as was also true with Iran, the Saudis have become increasingly concerned with developments in peripheral regions, as well as with those developments that could lead to a shift in the global balance of power against the West.

Persian Gulf/Arabian Sea

The importance of the Persian Gulf to Saudi Arabia is obvious: Despite efforts to find alternative routes for the export of Saudi crude oil, a considerable part of Saudi oil still has to pass through the Persian Gulf. Moreover, one of Saudi Arabia's two planned major industrial cities – Jubail – borders on the Persian Gulf. Meanwhile, the Arabian Sea's importance to Saudi Arabia derives from its being a link between the Persian Gulf and the Red Sea – another zone of vital interest to Saudi Arabia.[66]

Within these regions, three types of development could be highly threatening to Saudi Arabia, and have been seen as such in Riyadh:

1. A change of regime in smaller Gulf countries in favour of radical forces.
2. A greater Soviet presence in the region.
3. A drastic change in the regional balance of power because of an increase in the power and influence of the two larger regional states – Iran and Iraq.

The Saudis have believed that such developments, particularly the first two, are most likely to happen as a result of intra-regional and intra-Arab conflict and the growth of radicalism in the Arab world, which could be caused partly by Arab frustration with the non-resolution of the Palestinian problem. However, the Saudis have also been aware of the impact of factors such as economic underdevelopment on the growth of radicalism.[67] As a result, the peaceful resolution of intra-regional and intra-Arab conflicts, plus the resolution of the Palestinian problem, has been part of Saudi Arabia's security strategy.[68]

In cases where Saudi preventive action against radicalism is no longer possible – for instance in the case of the two Yemens – Saudi policy has aimed at reversing the situation, at moderating its impact, or at least at preventing a contagious effect on itself or on other regional states.[69]

With regard to maintaining a favourable regional balance of power, Saudi Arabia has tried to achieve this objective in two ways:

(i) by extending its influence among the smaller Gulf countries through a variety of means – with mixed succsss in the past but with increasing success in the last two years; and[70]
(ii) by acting as a holder of the balance in the traditional sense of balance of power politics, by generally supporting the less-powerful or the less-threatening of regional states.[71]

Red Sea/Horn of Africa

Part of the Saudis' interest in the Red Sea has been similar to their interest in the Persian Gulf/Arabian Sea region. For instance, some Saudi crude oil is exported through Red Sea terminals, and also the second major Saudi industrial centre is based on the Red Sea port of Yanbu.

In addition, the Red Sea is of great geo-strategic importance to the Saudis in the context of the Arab-Israeli conflict, as well as in its position as a link between Africa and the Arab Middle East. Moreover, some of the world's most important maritime choke points – such as the Strait of Bab-al-Mandab and the Suez Canal – are on the Red Sea. Given the dependence of Saudi Arabia and other Gulf oil producers on the free flow of oil and thus their concern with the continued safety of maritime routes, Saudi preoccupation with the Red Sea has been understandable. Furthermore, a number of vitally-important Arab states – such as Egypt and Sudan – also border on the Red Sea, and thus have been vulnerable to developments in the non-Arab Red Sea regional states.

In turn, the importance of the Horn of Africa has derived from its position on the western flank of the Red Sea. Principal security threats to Saudi Arabia in the zone of the Red Sea/Horn of Africa have been similar to those it has faced in the Persian Gulf, namely growth of radicalism, leading to an increase in Soviet presence. The Saudis have also been wary of increased influence in this area by both Israel and rival Arab regimes, such as Libya. Also, as in the case of the Persian Gulf, the Saudis have felt that intra-regional conflicts, and particularly great power rivalry, have tended to destabilise the area. Thus the thrust of the Saudis' security strategy in this region has also been to combat radicalism, to eliminate Soviet influence, and to establish in the region moderate Arab influence under their own leadership.[72]

Saudi statements and actions have supported this analysis, as the priorities set by then Crown Prince Fahd – referred to earlier – regarding Saudi determination to get the Russians out of Somalia and to help Sudan resist Communist pressure clearly illustrated. The same was true of the Saudi contribution to the speedy acceptance of Djibouti in the Arab League. In applying its policy – as will be demonstrated later – Saudi Arabia has used its financial assets extensively.[73]

The Arab World

Needless to say, a large part of the areas discussed above is located in the Arab world. In fact, Saudi interest in these areas, particularly in the Horn of Africa, has derived partly from their proximity to Arab nations, and thus from the possible impact of developments there on intra-Arab relations.[74]

Within the Arab world, too, principal threats to Saudi security have emanated from the growth of radicalism, anti-Western sentiments, and the increase in Soviet influence. As noted earlier, the Saudis have seen a direct link between these developments and the lack thus far of a solution to the Arab-Israeli conflict and the Palestinian problem. This problem has been particularly important to Saudi Arabia, as it has been to other Gulf countries, in view of their vulnerability to Palestinian pressure and even subversion, because of their large Palestinian populations. As a result, since the late 1960s, the Saudis have set as a major security goal the moderation in behaviour of the Palestinian movement and of those Arab countries directly facing Israel – or at least a blunting of their opposition to Saudi Arabia because of the Arab-Israeli conflict.

In the Saudi perspective, given the link between the Arab-Israeli conflict and the chances to achieve these objectives, the search for a reasonable and lasting solution for Middle East conflict has also been a primary Saudi security objective.

The Saudi security problem in the Arab world has been partly related to its extreme wealth as compared with the poverty in most Arab states. This fact has made Saudi Arabia vulnerable to Arab nationalist propaganda, which has tended to portray Saudi wealth as belonging to the whole of the Arab nation.[75] In the hands of some Arab countries that have large populations and limited resources – such as Egypt – this ideology can become a potent weapon against Saudi Arabia. And since Egypt – and perhaps even Syria – have the military capacity to reach Saudi Arabia, it has not been able to ignore such a threat.[76]

Even more disquieting to Saudi Arabia would be a combination of two or more unfriendly Arab countries in the context of some sort of Arab unity scheme.[77] These considerations, therefore, have been added reasons for the Saudis to try combating radicalism in the Arab world – in all of its manifestations, including leftist and Arab nationalist – and, failing that, to try neutralising it as far as possible.

Other Security Threats

Saudi Arabia has also been concerned with developments on the periphery of the three principal regions discussed above that could lead to a shift in regional balances of power in favour of radical groups.[78]

Moreover, at the global level the Saudis have been concerned about developments whose cumulative effect could be a weakening of the Western position, since they have viewed their own fortunes as linked to those of the West.[79] Among such developments are major global economic changes triggered, for instance, by excessive oil price increases or by other oil-related issues. The Saudis see a direct link between these changes and global stability, and thus also with their own security. As a result, a number of Saudi policies, both within OPEC and in regard to global economic issues, have been conditioned by this overriding security concern.[80]

Political Motives

As with other OPEC donors, primary Saudi political interests have essentially been an extension of security needs. Thus Saudi Arabia's essential political interests have been (1) combating radicalism and subversive forces within its immediate security environment, the Arab world, and their periphery; and (2) preventing the spread of Soviet influence both in regions of direct interest to it and globally.

In more practical terms – given what the Saudis have seen to be at the root of the spread of radicalism, subversion, and Soviet influence – the search for a peaceful solution to the Arab-Israeli conflict, the peaceful resolution of intra-Arab and other regional conflicts, and the combating of Arab poverty became important Saudi political objectives.[81]

Next in importance have been (1) the preservation of a rough balance of power within the Arab world that would exclude the overwhelming predominance of any single Arab power; and (2) the enhancing of Saudi influence and prestige in the Arab world, the Islamic world, and internationally. Clearly, these objectives have been closely interrelated. Saudi concern with maintenance of the balance of power has stemmed essentially from the country's limitations – such as its small population and military weakness – that have disqualified it from leadership of the Arab world. Thus thwarted, Saudi Arabia has 'a strong interest in preventing the hegemony of any single Arab state in the region'.[82] Needless to say, under conditions of a rough balance, Saudi Arabia could use its financial assets to increase its influence and leverage, and hence its capacity to shape events. As a result, over the last three decades the Saudis have shifted their regional alliances – overcoming old rivalries and ideological differences, and sometimes even using non-Arab Middle Eastern countries to secure this objective.[83] They have also opposed Arab nationalist schemes of unity – while paying lip-service to them – as in the Saudis' view being anathema to the preservation of the balance of power. The Saudis have also feared that these schemes could become excuses for larger and stronger Arab countries to get their hands on Saudi riches.

With regard to the Islamic world, the Saudis have felt that they have a special claim to influence because Arabia is Islam's birthplace and the Saudis are the guardians of the holy sites of Mecca and Medina. In the Islamic world as well, however, Saudi policy has focused on those countries – such as Pakistan and Afghanistan – that are located on the periphery of Saudi Arabia's immediate security environment, or could otherwise be useful to it.[84]

In the last few years, Saudi interest in the Islamic world has increased further because of the emergence of a militant and radical brand of Islam propagated first by Libya and since 1979 by Iran. As a result, countering this type of Islam has become a central Saudi objective.

Ideological Motives

Ideological factors have affected Saudi Arabia's security and foreign policies – and hence its aid policies – to a great extent. The main reasons have been the nature of Saudi society and leadership. Saudi society is based on Islam, and Islamic law is rigorously applied in the country.[85] In addition, Islam has been the principal legitimising force for the Saudi leadership, both internally and in the Arab and Islamic worlds. Thus the Saudis have naturally frowned on those ideologies, notably Communism, that profess an atheistic view of the world and of human history. But Saudi anti-Communism has also derived from the fact that the most powerful proponent of Communism, the Soviet Union, has been the rival of Saudi Arabia's principal ally, the United States.

Important as these factors have been, however, Saudi anti-Communism has stemmed principally from the fact that – given the present constellation of regional and global balances of power and patterns of alliances – the Soviet Union and its allies have been seen as threatening to Saudi security and to its other political and economic interests.[86]

As noted earlier, until recently Islam had been an asset for Saudi Arabia in advancing its interests. But with the advent of militant and radical Islam, Islam's effectiveness in promoting this end has been challenged. Thus, for example, in deciding whether or not in the future to provide foreign assistance to certain Islamic countries, the Saudis might look more carefully for specific signs of friendship or for behaviour in line with Saudi interests, rather than for the simple profession of Islam.

Economic Motives

Traditional economic factors, such as access to export markets or to secure sources of raw materials, have not had a major impact on Saudi aid policies, as, for instance, they did on Iran's. This has resulted from Saudi Arabia's resource base. For example, although Saudi authorities have consistently talked about industrialisation and diversification of their country's economic base, prospects for achieving these goals have not been promising, and for the foreseeable future the Saudi economy will have to be based on oil. In addition, the Saudi industrialisation programme has been essentially based on industries that rely on oil and gas, a situation that has reduced the need for secure access to sources of raw materials. By contrast, the need for export markets could become important in the long term. But in view of the state of Saudi industry when the country first embarked on aid on a massive scale in 1973, this factor was not very influential either.

An economic factor that might have provided an additional reason for Saudi Arabia's aid to some countries has been its desire to create a more favourable investment climate, although such a direct link is hard to establish. What can be said, however is that – even if that were initially true – it has become less and less important in Saudi policy. Saudi experience in Egypt illustrated the dangers involved in investing in countries that were subject to radical and unpredictable political changes. This experience in turn strengthened Saudi Arabia's inclination to invest its surplus funds in the industrialised countries and generally in short-term monetary assets.[87]

What the foregoing illustrates is that – given Saudi Arabia's resource base, its development potential, its security needs, and its special links with the West, particularly with the United States, a high degree of convergence also developed between its economic interests and those of the West.[88] As a result (as was noted in Chapter 1) Saudi Arabia has not pushed for acceptance of the developing countries' demands, although it has given them verbal support. Another result – in comparison with Iran and some other OPEC countries – has been Saudi Arabia's channelling a relatively larger share of its development aid through such international organisations as the World Bank and IDA, and its lending massively to the IMF.[89]

II Instruments of Policy: the Role of Aid

The most important instrument of Saudi security and foreign policy has indeed been its tremendous financial resources, which since the late 1960s, in particular after the 1973 oil price increases, have given Saudi diplomacy a new dynamism and have greatly broadened its scope. This situation is not surprising, since Saudi Arabia's resource base has limited the availability of other policy instruments. For example, despite large sums spent on military build-up since the early 1970s, military power is even now only a modest instrument of Saudi policy. Nor has this situation been solely the result of shortcomings such as lack of trained manpower. Rather, the nature of Saudi Arabia's political system and the insecurities of its present rulers have led to deep feelings of ambivalence within the leadership in regard to the size, composition, and potential role of the armed forces in Saudi society and political system. In fact, such feelings have led to the creation of a considerable gap between Saudi capacities, at least in terms of military hardware, and the quality of command and control of Saudi armed forces. Even Saudi Arabia's capacity to deal successfully with internal security matters was questioned during the crisis over the seizure of the Grand Mosque in Mecca. There were even rumours at the time that foreign – that is, French – security forces had to be brought in to resolve the crisis.[90]

In addition to these factors, neither Saudi Arabia's geopolitical conditions nor its historical experience had led it to emphasise military forces – in sharp contrast to Iran.[91] But by the mid-1960s, circumstances both in the region and in Saudi financial capacity had changed dramatically, thus leading Saudi Arabia to develop its military forces.

With regard to Saudi use of financial assets as an instrument of policy, in general, detailed analysis is beyond the scope of this study. Suffice it to say that Saudi Arabia's capacity to affect the international financial system has been at the root of its influence. However, its influence has by no means been unlimited, given Saudi Arabia's own high stake in the present financial system.[92] Neveretheless, even within rather serious limitations, Saudi Arabia can – and does – influence the policies of other countries through its investment policies and its ability to have a major impact on international financial markets. This type of influence has applied particularly to Saudi relations with the industrialised countries. Also, Saudi capacity to lend large sums of money to the industrialised countries has been a further instrument of Saudi influence.

But perhaps even more important than these two factors has been the ability of Saudi Arabia to reward or punish industrialised and other countries by granting or denying them access to its large markets – making this the root of its influence.[93]

III Saudi Aid: Principal Characteristics

Before discussing the principal characteristics, efficacy, and impact of Saudi aid, it is important to emphasise certain points. For example, the volume of Saudi aid has undoubtedly been much higher than officially reported by Saudi authorities to relevant international organisations. Nor are the conditions under which this type of aid has been granted, or the purposes for which it has been used, publicly known. Certain transactions seem to have been made directly between the Saudi monetary institutions and the central banks of recipient countries, and total secrecy has been maintained both by the Saudis and by the recipients.[94]

The amount of specific loans or grants has sometimes been reported by official agencies at figures below actual transfers, and discrepancies have often existed between official figures and, for example, those reported by the press. Yet it is impossible to determine the real figures. Under these circumstances, therefore, the following analysis will be based on the official figures of Saudi development assistance, and will only be indicative of overall Saudi aid. This analysis, however, will be somewhat complemented by a separate analysis of Saudi military assistance programmes based essentially on information gathered from press reports and personal interviews. In doing so, however, the author is conscious of the fact that a sharp distinction cannot be made between ODA and assistance given for purely military purposes, since part of ODA – particularly if it is in the form of balance of payments or budgetary support – could be used for military purposes. At the same time, military assistance can have a developmental effect by releasing funds for development projects that would otherwise have been used for military purposes.

Military Assistance

The following analysis is also only indicative of Saudi military assistance and does not represent a complete accounting of this type of aid. Moreover, given the lack of official information (and the limited nature of unofficial information) the figures quoted here do not represent the exact amount of this type of aid.

Saudi Arabia's military assistance, as well as its overall aid programme, essentially began with the 1967 Khartoum Arab Summit Conference. However, at that time it made no distinction between military assistance and other forms of aid, and the so-called confrontation states – Egypt, Syria, and Jordan – that received Saudi aid had discretion to use it in any way they wanted, including for the purchase of military equipment. Later, however, the Saudis agreed to finance specific purchases of military hardware for those countries.

The most extensive Saudi military aid relationship has been with Egypt. For example, prior to 1973 when Egypt did not have a military supply relationship with the United States, the Saudis agreed to finance Egypt's purchase of Soviet arms.[95] Later, the Saudis undertook to finance Egypt's military build-up for a period of five years.[96] As part of this commitment, the Saudis paid several hundred million dollars for Egypt's acquisition of French *Mirages* and Aerospatial *Gazelle* helicopters. For example, the Stockholm International Peace Research Institute's Yearbook for 1977 recorded that Saudi Arabia had purchased 39 Dassault *Mirage* IIIs. This sale was confirmed by President Sadat in his May Day speech in 1979.[97]

In addition to financing Egyptian military purchases, Saudi military assistance to Egypt took the form of contributions to the development of its military industry.[98]

North Yemen is another country towards which Saudi Arabia has made specific military assistance commitments. The largest such package of purchases for North Yemen was worth $400 million and included F-5E aircraft, MG tanks, and armoured personnel carriers.[99]

Again, closer to home Saudi Arabia is believed to have helped Oman to strengthen its defences. Also, according to some reports, Saudi Arabia has financed Morocco's military purchases from the United States, the exact amount of which is not known. Furthermore, it has been widely believed that Saudi Arabia has been subsidising Morocco's war in the Western Sahara.[100] Somalia and Sudan are two other countries that have received Saudi military assistance. Military assistance to Somalia was part of the Saudi scheme of eliminating Soviet influence in that country.[101]

In addition to these types of military aid, a new kind of military assistance relationship has developed between Saudi Arabia and Pakistan that has involved (as noted earlier) the use of Pakistani armed forces in Saudi Arabia in exchange for financial aid.[102]

In sum, in order to understand Saudi Arabia's use of its financial resources to promote its interests, it is important to take into account military assistance as part of an overall strategy. While not strictly 'economic' aid, military assistance has served some of the same purposes in terms of promoting Saudi national goals and – while not itself directly promoting development – has met some particular requirements of recipients. In some cases, as well, these transfers of military resources can free other recipient resources for development purposes, where military effort would in any event have top priority. This discussion is thus a useful complement to that which follows on more direct forms of Saudi economic assistance.

Volume of Saudi ODA

As noted earlier, since 1973 Saudi Arabia has become one of the largest economic aid donors, as the following Table 3.5 illustrates.[103]

Saudi Arabia's Official Development Assistance (ODA) has shared many of the characteristics of aid provided by other OPEC countries, including the following:

Table 3.5: Volume of Saudi ODA ($US millions)

Year	Commitments	Disbursements	% of GNP
1973	568.2	304.9	3.75
1974	1,287.6	1,029.1	4.56
1975	2,790.1	1,997.4	6.01
1976	2,802.6	2,315.8	5.77
1977	–	2,400	4.30
1978	–	1,500	2.32
1979	–	2,300	3.00
1980	–	3,000	2.60
1981	–	5,798	4.77

Source: *Annual DAC Reviews*, 1979-82.

High Geographical Concentration

During the period under discussion, Saudi Arabia's economic aid has been highly concentrated in Arab countries of major interest to it in terms of foreign and security policy. Pakistan and Indonesia, located in two other areas of Saudi interest, have been similarly favoured. Until 1978, therefore, Egypt was the largest recipient of Saudi aid, a relationship that ended when President Sadat signed the peace treaty with Israel. For similar reasons of Saudi foreign policy interest, other principal recipients of Saudi aid have included Syria, Pakistan, Jordan, Sudan, North Yemen, and Indonesia. Most of these countries have received aid in the form of general budgetary or balance of payments support – which, as noted above, is fungible in terms of *military* support – in addition to aid tied to specific projects and disbursed through the Saudi Fund for Development (SFD).

Beyond funds provided to specially favoured countries, the geographical scope of Saudi aid provided through the SFD has been much broader, though of lesser volume. This type of aid, after all, has demonstrated Saudi Arabia's commitment to the social and economic advancement of the developing countries, and has been the 'prestige' entry for Saudi Arabia in the aid field. Thus it has touched a broader clientele.

Paramountcy of Non-development Motives

As illustrated by earlier discussion and the lists of principal recipients of Saudi aid, security and political considerations have largely determined the direction of Saudi aid.

Table 3.6: Geographical Distribution of SFD Loans

Region	Cumulative 1974-82	1980-1
Asia	49%	38.5%
Africa	48%	52.1%
Others[a]	3%	9.4%

Note: a. Latin America and Oceania.
Source: *Saudi Fund for Development Annual Reports*, 1980-1/81-2.

High Level of Concessionality. Compared with Iranian aid, for example, the concessionality of Saudi aid has been much higher, reflecting Saudi Arabia's greater financial surpluses beyond its own development and other internal needs. This practice has been reflected in a larger percentage of grants within total Saudi ODA. The following tables give some indication of the concessionality of total Saudi ODA, as well as the level of concessionality of loans provided by the Saudi Fund for Development:

Table 3.7: Concessionality of Saudi ODA

Year	% of Grants in Total Commitments	% Grant Element in ODA Loans	% Grant Element in Total ODA
1974	79.7	51.7	9.2
1975	46.1	43.1	69.3
1976	56.8	47.7	77.4
1979	–	–	62.1
1980	–	–	86.7
1981	–	–	75.9

Source: *Annual DAC Reviews*, 1977, 1982.

The Annual Report of the Saudi Development Fund for the year July 1977-June 1978, however, cited the average grant element of its loans as follows: African countries, 44 per cent; Asian countries, 45 per cent; and others, 33 per cent – thus illustrating the difficulties of compiling accurate data.

Yet these figures did not present the whole picture concerning the concessionality of Saudi ODA, and thus the following observations are necessary. Not surprisingly, the most concessional of Saudi Arabia's aid efforts – mostly provided in grant form – have been directed towards a handful of countries that, like the geographical concentration of Saudi aid, have been important to it in security and political terms.

Thus the large percentage of grants in Saudi Arabia's total aid for 1977 was explained by its massive aid to Egypt and other 'confrontation' states. By contrast Saudi assistance to other countries, particularly non-Arab countries, has essentially taken the form of loans made through the SFD and has had a much lower grant element. Despite these differences in Saudi aid as between different kinds of recipient, however, the concessionality of Saudi ODA, in general, has compared well with that of other OPEC countries.

Low Percentage of Tied Aid

Almost all Saudi ODA has been untied by source. For reasons cited above (for example, the relative lack of a non-oil export economy) Saudi Arabia has not used its aid to promote exports, and thus has not tied it to the purchase of Saudi goods. Moreover, unlike some other OPEC countries, such as Iran and Iraq, Saudi Arabia has not provided credits for the purchase of oil, although aid given by the SFD has been tied to specific projects. Aid given by Saudi Arabia through other channels – again, particularly to those few countries strategically and politically significant to it – has been in the form of general budgetary or balance of payments support, and thus has been completely untied.

Ratio of Bilateral Aid to Multilateral ODA

Among OPEC countries, Saudi Arabia has been the largest source of aid provided through multilateral organisations, reflecting its clear awareness of dependence upon, and need for influence over, developments in the overall global economy and international economic institutions. Although there have been fluctuations in the way Saudi Arabia has divided its multilateral ODA as between Arab/OPEC and traditional organisations, roughly half of Saudi multilateral ODA – in terms of disbursements – has gone to traditional organisations.

Regarding the multilateral share of Saudi Arabia's total ODA, the following figures are illustrative: in 1974, Saudi Arabia's total committed and disbursed multilateral ODA amounted to $240 million; in 1975, almost 10 per cent of Saudi ODA was disbursed through multilateral channels. Saudi contributions to IDA in 1979 amounted to $350 million.

The share of multilateral commitments fell in 1980. The following organisations were the principal recipients of Saudi aid: Arab aid agencies, $98 million; the OPEC Fund, $76 million; IFAD, $35 million; and WFP, $28 million. As a percentage of total ODA, the share of world-wide multilateral organisations was respectively 20.2 per cent and 3.1 per cent of Saudi ODA in 1979 and 1980.[104]

Table 3.8: Saudi ODA Contributions to OPEC/Arab Organisations (disbursements in $US millions)

Organisation	1973	1974	1975	1976	1977	1978	1979	1980	1981
OPEC Fund	–	–	–	54.6	3.0	15.3	44.7	75.7	92.1
AFSED	–	23.1	10.4	30.9	24.1	25.1	25.0	49.3	47.8
BADEA	–	–	25.0	25.0	–	16.6	–	33.3	–
IsDB	–	–	48.6	46.2	51.7	50.1	51.7	–	–

Source: OECD, *Aid From OPEC Countries*, 1983.

Table 3.9: Saudi ODA Contributions to the UN and Other Multilateral Organisations (disbursements in $US millions)

Organisation	1973	1974	1975	1976	1977	1978	1979	1980	1981
UNDP	0.4	1.5	1.5	7.5	2.7	2.5	2.5	2.5	2.5
UNRWA	0.1	1.0	10.0	11.2	3.2	6.3	3.5	5.0	5.0
UN Special Account	–	30.0	–	–	–	–	–	–	–
WFP	–	18.5	16.6	26.2	25.0	25.0	27.5	27.5	26.0
IFAD	–	–	–	–	–	35.2	35.2	35.2	–
Other UN	–	0.5	21.5	2.2	1.0	3.1	3.7	2.0	33.0
IDA	–	–	–	–	–	–	–	83.7	68.3
IMF	–	–	–	11.4	11.5	6.0	32.7	8.8	–
AFDF	–	–	–	1.0	–	1.7	–	3.3	–
Other	–	–	–	1.0	–	1.7	–	3.3	–
TOTAL	0.5	51.5	84.9	59.5	43.4	135.9	112.7	184.0	141.1

Source: OECD, *Aid From OPEC Countries*, 1983.

Table 3.10: Profile of SFD Loans, 1974-82 Committed

Country	No. of Projects	Total value in S.r. millions[a]
Bahrain	1	150/00
Bangladesh	6	87/640
Taiwan	6	70/630
India	3	45/900
Indonesia	10	795/60
Jordan	16	534/50
South Korea	2	246/05
Malaysia	7	378/75
Maldives		53/85
Nepal	2	106/00
Oman	2	169/00
Pakistan	6	620/20
Philippines	to be allocated	69/00
Srilanka	3	337/50
Syria	12	879/20
Thailand	2	175/00
Turkey	7	840/00
Yemen AR	13	75/43
Yemen PDR	2	120/00
Algeria	1	176/50
Botswana	3	87/40
Burundi	3	66/60
Cameroon	4	214/70
Cape Verde	2	35/40
Chad	2	106/00
Comoros	5	96/06
Congo	2	200/29
Djibouti	2	93/50
Egypt	6	638/43
Gabon	3	175/60
Gambia	3	50/18
Ghana	2	142/46
Guinea	7	292/00
Guinea Bissau	4	35/30
Kenya	6	42/99
Lesotho	1	15/12
Liberia	2	70/60
Madagascar	1	42/20
Mali	11	308/721
Mauritania	6	784/95
Mauritius	1	16/80
Morocco	3	355/00
Niger	6	168/30
Rwanda	3	130/15
Senegal	12	643/31
Sierra Leone	1	50/00
Somalia	4	521/80
Sudan	10	591/24
Togo	2	35/20
Tunisia	13	1060/50

Table 3.10 (Cont.)

Country	No. of Projects	Total value in S.r. millions[a]
Uganda	4	105/00
Upper Volta	3	164/60
Zaire	5	211/80
Zimbabwe	6	167/50

Note: a. A Saudi Riyal is equivalent to $US 0.2872.
Source: *Saudi Fund for Development Annual Reports*, 1980-1/81-2.

Table 3.11: Grant Element of SFD ODA Loans

Year	% Grant Element
1975	44.9
1976	43.0
1977	48.0
1978	44.4
1979	49.3
1980	46.6
1981	47.8
TOTAL:	46.4

Source: OECD, *Aid From OPEC Countries*, 1983.

Table 3.12: Sectoral Distribution of SFD Loans

Sector	Cumulative 1974-82	1980-1
Transport & Communication	37%	29%
Energy	22%	31%
Social	15%	19%
Industry	11%	8%
Agriculture	14%	13%
Others	1%	–

Source: *Saudi Fund for Development Annual Reports*, 1980-1/81-2.

Among international channels for multilateral aid, Saudi Arabia has favoured the World Bank Group instead of the United Nations, partly because of its perception that this Group has been more efficient than the United Nations, but partly also because of its close Western ties and its view that its interests have been more or less identical with those of the West.

Other Features

With regard to other aspects of Saudi aid, the following observations are in order:

Conditions attached to Saudi aid have generally been very few. This has been particularly true of the large sums of highly-concessional aid provided – mostly in the form of grants for budgetary and balance of payments support – to those Arab and Islamic countries that have been vitally important to Saudi Arabia. Thus Saudi Arabia has not had any control over the use of these funds, once disbursed. In making such grants, Saudi Arabia has rarely tried to affect the economic development policies of recipient nations. This has been so not only because of the political motives for this aid, but also because Saudi Arabia has lacked sufficient trained manpower and skilled staff to make accurate judgements about recipients' development policies.[105]

Occasionally, however, there have been exceptions when Saudi Arabia has tried to influence recipients' policies, by using the expertise and clout of the World Bank – or as one Bank official put it, 'hiding behind the Bank or the Fund'. For example, in 1980 Saudi Arabia decided to suspend payment of $300 million in budgetary support to Sudan, pending the outcome of that country's negotiations with the IMF for a standby agreement. In this case, the IMF was demanding that Sudan take certain economic and financial measures to improve its economic situation before it would agree to lend further funds to Sudan. At that time, of course, Saudi Arabia was also becoming concerned about Sudan's internal stability, which has been related to its economic performance.

In general, where Saudi Arabia has had an impact on the economic policies of its aid recipients, it has achieved this through its association with, and support for, positions taken by the World Bank or the IMF. At the same time, Saudi Arabia's lack of skilled manpower in the development field has also limited its ability to influence the policies of the international institutions to which it has contributed, in ways that could have made them more responsive to the needs of the developing countries. However, on occasion Saudi Arabia has made clear – as with the IMF Oil Facility – that it expected most of its contributions to these institutions to be made available to developing countries.

Likewise, lack of skilled manpower has influenced Saudi Arabia's decision to limit aid contributions through UN organisations, since it could not monitor their performance effectively. This factor has also helped to explain Saudi reluctance to support grandiose schemes for collective OPEC aid. Not having enough skilled people to place in such institutions, the Saudis have felt that decisions regarding the use of funds they contributed would at best be made by the officials of rival OPEC countries, such as Venezuela, Iran, or even Kuwait.

By contrast, when Saudi aid has been channelled through the SFD, at least indirectly and to a limited extent it has affected choices made by recipient countries. For example, the SFD has seemed to favour infrastructure projects, as well as projects that have had high visibility – thus tending to improve Saudi prestige and standing in recipient countries.[106]

The Saudis have attached few specific conditions to SFD loans. However, the SFD has made disbursement of its loans contingent on the timely completion of both projects and their specific stages. This fact has helped to explain why there has been a considerable gap between Saudi commitments and disbursements.

In addition, Saudi Arabia has influenced the economic planning and development prospects in a few countries where it has been highly involved and the recipient country has been highly dependent on Saudi aid. The best example has been North Yemen.

To make a final judgement about the impact of Saudi financial power on the social and economic development of North Yemen is beyond the scope of this study. But some experts have thought that Saudi manipulation of internal Yemeni politics, plus the practice of cutting back or suspending aid depending on political circumstances, 'has been disastrous' for Yemen's social and economic development. Some have even thought that Saudi Arabia has intended this result in order 'to ensure a steady supply of labor, if nothing else'.[107] But besides a few such cases, Saudi Arabia has not seemed to have influenced the economic development of recipient countries in any great measure, either positively or negatively.

Efficacy and Impact on Recipients

Saudi Arabia's record in using aid to achieve a range of objectives has included considerable success – success largely limited, however, to gaining the most basic of Saudi objectives, and also often requiring it to depend on other factors besides aid. As an example of one success through the use of aid, Saudi Arabia has generally managed to neutralise negative feelings towards it by some radical Arab states and forces – such as Syria and the PLO – and has largely prevented them from taking subversive or other hostile action against it.

Saudi aid has also helped to shift policies of some other Arab countries in moderate directions. This was true with regard to Egypt's change of policy after the 1967 war and particularly after Nasser's death, including better Saudi-Egyptian relations and the substitution of US for Soviet influence in Cairo. Yet even here, other factors had already created the changed circumstances within which Saudi aid could become an influential tool of policy. Thus Egypt's defeat in 1967 and its consequent weakening, not Saudi aid, were primarily responsible for changes in its foreign policy, although the latter factor also played a role. A decade later, in fact, events in Egypt graphically illustrated the limits of Saudi financial leverage on Egyptian policies. When President Sadat decided in 1977 to make peace with Israel, neither the threat of a cutback in Saudi and other Arab aid, nor the lure of its potential increase, had any effect on his decision. Of course, the fact that the United States, other Western countries, and the international lending institutions were prepared to increase their aid to Egypt contributed to the lack of Saudi leverage on Egypt.

More recently, threats of a cutback in Arab – including Saudi aid to Syria did not deter it from supporting Iran in the Iran-Iraq war, against the Arab consensus. Nor did it prevent Syria from rejecting the Fahd Peace Plan for the Arab-Israeli conflict, or from refusing to take part in the Fez Arab Summit Conference of November 1981. Even in countries that have been highly dependent on Saudi aid, such as North Yemen, the aid instrument has not always been successful in achieving Saudi goals. For instance, despite Saudi displeasure, Yemen has thus far refused to sever its military ties with the Soviet Union. In Yemen, in addition to aid, Saudi Arabia has used instruments ranging from the manipulation of internal divisions to perhaps even the removal of leaders not-sufficiently responsive to Saudi views and interests.[108]

Thus the other side of the picture has been that, while Saudi foreign assistance has provided some influence, it has rarely worked alone and then not when overriding national interests of recipients have dictated otherwise. Aid 'dependence', therefore, can be overrated.

On another front, Saudi Arabia's use of oil (together with its other financial assets) has been quite successful in enhancing its international prestige and standing. Yet even here, given Saudi Arabia's other shortcomings and vulnerabilities, it has not been able or perhaps willing to translate its enhanced prestige into real influence. For example, Saudi Arabia has generally been satisfied with being part of the international elite, and has rarely tried to use its position to bring about any particular changes or to promote particular policies.

In sum, therefore, Saudi Arabia has used foreign aid – both economic and military, through paying for arms – to try enhancing its security and to achieve national political goals. But concerns such as the developmental impact of aid or achievement of Third World goals have had a minimal impact on Saudi policies, in part because of its own relative lack of experience in dealing with developing countries very different from itself, and in part reflecting the deeply-political motives for its aid. This situation has also resulted from Saudi Arabia's military weakness, internal contradictions, and external dependencies, as discussed earlier.

PART THREE: CONCLUSIONS

This detailed study of the aid policies of Iran and Saudi Arabia has essentially confirmed the conclusions reached in Chapter 2's analysis of OPEC aid, both collective and national. Thus, the experiences of both Iran and Saudi Arabia have confirmed that:

(a) aid has essentially been a policy tool for OPEC members;
(b) principal motivations behind OPEC members' aid have been their security, political, and economic needs and objectives;
(c) regionalism rather than globalism has been the principal characteristic of OPEC aid. However, the geographical scope of OPEC members' aid has been directly related to the size of their financial assets. Thus Saudi aid has had a wider geographic scope than that of Iran;
(d) factors such as Third World solidarity have had a minor impact on the aid policies of OPEC members in general. Also, the degree of individual members' commitments to the achievement to Third World goals has essentially been a factor of their economic conditions and resource bases, including the relative size of their oil reserves; and
(e) leadership characteristics have had an important impact on the aid policies of OPEC donors. However, the relative impact of this factor has been less than that of security, political, and economic factors, as well as each country's historical experience.

Moreover, these case studies on Iran and Saudi Arabia have demonstrated that the relative importance of aid as an instrument of the defence and foreign policies of donors has depended on the size of their financial assets and on the availability of alternative and equally effective instruments, in turn reflecting each country's position in regard to other components of national power.

Notes

1. See, for example, the Shah's interview with *Blitz*, reprinted in *Keyhan International*, 21 July 1976, p. 4.

2. For a study of the impact of Iran's geostrategic conditions on its foreign policy see: Shahram Chubin and Sepehr Zabih: *The Foreign Relations of Iran*, Los Angeles: University of California Press, 1974.

3. In fact, some of the systemic changes created more uncertainties for Iran. For example, while the end of the Cold War and the onset of *detente* had somewhat eased Soviet pressure on Iran, it had also increased the danger of great power collusion at Iran's expense. The Shah had expressed the fear that the superpowers might interpret *detente* as a tacit agreement to choose their 'hunting grounds' elsewhere. For a detailed analysis of this aspect of Iran's security dilemma, see Shahram Chubin, 'Iran's Defense and Foreign Policy' in A. Amirie and H.H. Twitchel (eds.), *Iran in the 1980s*, Teheran: Institute for International Political and Economic Studies, 1978, pp. 309-27.

4. Among the systemic factors was the fact that policies such as 'peaceful coexistence' and '*detente*' had not eliminated ideological competition among the superpowers, although the competition was far less rigidly defined. Thus the broad divisions among countries which more-or-less favoured one or the other superpower also persisted. Within this broad division, Iran – despite its improved relations with the Soviet Union and its more autonomous foreign policy – remained on the side of the USSR's competitor. In addition, the Soviet Union's policies had become more pragmatic and less ideological, but it still supported those forces that were enemies of Iranian-type regimes. Also, the Soviet practice of distinguishing between relations at state level and those between the Soviet Communist Party and other like-minded parties – including the outlawed Iranian Communist Party, Tudeh – was not comforting to Iran. In fact, it was a constant cause of friction between the two countries.

5. Part of this phenomenon of diffused Soviet power was the result of the tremendous expansion of the Soviet's naval power that increased its capacity to project power in faraway places. Iran was concerned that one such place could become the Persian Gulf.

6. For a detailed treatment of Soviet and Iraqi involvement in the Baluchi separatist movement, see: R.M. Burrell and A.J. Cottrell, *Iran, Afghanistan, Pakistan: Tensions and Dilemmas*, California: Sage Publications, 1974, pp. 7-8.

7. For a study of Soviet-Iraqi cooperation in defence and Soviet arms delivery to Iraq, see: Shahram Chubin, *Security in the Persian Gulf: The Role of Outside Powers*, London: The International Institute for Strategic Studies, 1982, pp. 74-102.

8. Burrell and Cottrell, *Iran, Afghanistan, Pakistan*, pp. 3-4.

9. For an analysis of Iranian perceptions of growing Soviet threat and retrenching Western power – plus their policy implications for Iran – see Shahram Chubin, 'Iran's Foreign Policy 1960-1976: An Overview' in A. Amirsadeghi (ed.), *Twentieth Century Iran*, New York: Holmes & Meir, 1977, pp. 197-223. However, it is important to note that Iran's doubts regarding the value of its Western alliance ties go back as far as 1965 and were largely caused by US behaviour during the Indo-Pakistan war of the same year.

10. Frequent references by the Shah and other Iranian officials to 'Soviet pincer pressure' on Iran illustrate Iran's perception of the new nature of the Soviet threat and the depth of its preoccupation.

11. According to some reports, by 1973, 28 subversive movements had representatives in Bahgdad, and in fact Baghdad had replaced Egypt as the main centre for Soviet-sponsored fronts. See Burrell & Cottrell, *Iran, Afghanistan, Pakistan*, p. 7.

12. Needless to say, Iran was concerned about the impact of this subversion on its own internal security and about the link-up between regional subversive groups and Iran's dissident movements. For a study of Iran's dissident groups and their links with regional and international subversive groups see: Fred Halliday, *Iran: Dictatorship and Development*, Middlesex, England: Penguin Books, 1979, pp. 211-49, and Ervand Abrahamian, 'The Guerrilla Movement in Iran 1963-1977', MERIP Report no. 86, January 1980, pp. 3-21.

13. In modern times, Iran fought the Portuguese during the Safavid dynasty, liberating Bandar Abbas (named after the Safavid king) and Bandar Hormuz. Later, Nader Shah and Karim Khan Zand tried to develop a navy and re-establish Iran's traditional role in the Gulf. Even during the nineteenth century – the worst period of Iran's decline – there were a number of desperate efforts to create an Iranian navy and reassert Iran's rights. But all these efforts faced stiff British opposition. For detailed information, see the following works, among others: (in Persian), Fereydoun Adamiyat, *Amir-Kabir-va-Iran*, Teheran; Chapkhaneh Payam, 1323 (1945); and *Andisheh Taraghi va Hokumat Ghanoun, Asr-e-Seph-Salar*; (The Idea of Progress and the Rule of Law), Teheran: Kharazami Publishing Company, 1351 (1973); (in English) Fereydoun Adamiyat, *Bahrain Islands: A Legal and Diplomatic Study of British-Iranian Controversy*, New York: Praeger, 1955; and R.K.A. Ramazani, *The Persian Gulf: Iran's Role*, Charlottesville: University of Virginia Press, 1973.

14. The principal reason for lack of Iranian focus on the Persian Gulf prior to 1965 was British preponderance in the region. Also, as a result of this Pax Britannica, Iran did not face any immediate threat to its security from the Gulf. Nevertheless, as a result of the Egyptian and Iraqi revolutions during the 1950s, plus the growing focus of Arab nationalism on the Gulf, Iran began to feel increasingly threatened. Such Arab actions as calling the Persian Gulf the 'Arab Gulf' and claiming Khuzistan as 'part of the Arab homeland' increased Iran's sense of insecurity and shifted its attention to the Gulf. Iran's fears grew particularly after Egyptian interference in the Yemeni civil war, interpreted in Iran as the first step towards the radicalisation of the Persian Gulf and its dominance by Egypt. Closer to home, Iraq's attack on Kuwait sounded alarm bells in Iran; later in the 1960s the victory of radical forces in Aden and finally British withdrawal further increased Iran's fears. For detailed analysis of Egyptian-Iranian and Iran-Iraq relations, see Chubin and Zabih, *Foreign Relations*, pp. 140-63. For examples of anti-Iranian Arab propaganda and actions, see R.K.A. Ramazani, *The Persian Gulf*, pp. 33-49.

15. This apprehension was at the root of Iran's opposition to the creation of a Gulf federation that also included Qatar and Bahrain.

16. Continued US preoccupation with the war in Vietnam and growing American popular opposition to further US involvement overseas combined with increasing Soviet influence in Iraq, the PDRY and Somalia – plus growing Soviet naval power – justified such an assessment.

17. A.J. Cottrell, US Senate Committee on Foreign Relations, *Foreign Assistance Authorization: Arms Sales Issues*. Hearings before the Sub-Committee on Foreign Assistance, 94th Congress, 2nd session. Washington, DC: Government Printing Office, 1976, pp. 87-8.

18. In addition to improving Iran's military and economic prospects, this was the result of systemic changes. At the international level, the loosening of the bipolar system had increased the autonomy of regional actors such as Iran. At the regional level, growing strategic and political linkages between different regional sub-systems made it impossible for Iran to confine its security perimeter to its immediate neighbours. For example, as noted earlier, by the mid-1950s Iran increasingly felt the impact of developments in the Arab Middle East on its security, a phenomenon which became even more significant after the 1967 Six Day War and the greater involvement of Gulf Arab countries in the Arab-Israeli conflict. The Indo-Pakistani war of 1971 and following events brought home to Iran the interconnection between its own security and events in the Sub-continent. See Shahram Chubin, 'Iran Between the Arab West and the Asian East', *Survival*, vol. 16, no. 4, July-August 1974, pp. 172-82.

On Iran's policy towards the Indian Ocean, see also Mohammad Reza Djalili, 'Evolution de la Politique Iranienne de l'Ocean Indien', *Revue Iranienne des Relations Internationales*, no. 8, Autumn 1976, pp. 185-98.

19. Shahram Chubin, *Twentieth Century Iran*, p. 203.

20. In fact, some Iranian proposals for regional cooperation, such as that for an Indian Ocean common market, were inspired by functionalist thinking like that in Europe during the 1950s and 1960s. Moreover, Iran judged other countries essentially by their attitude towards it and its interests rather than by their ideology. In fact, to have friendly relations with countries with different social, economic, and political systems became a tenet of Iran's so-called National Independent Policy. Iran's extensive relations with socialist countries and its friendly relations with the PRC illustrate Iran's pragmatic and non-ideological foreign policy.

21. For example, unlike Arab members of OPEC – or even Venezuela and Nigeria, which were subject to pressures of Latin American and African solidarity – Iran's foreign policy did not have to respond to any special pressure deriving from ethnic or religious considerations. Even Islam – which is a potent force in Iran – under the secular regime of the Pahlavis did not play an important role, even though Iran had occasionally used it in its relations with Arab countries. However, Iran did not have any illusions about the impact of Islam. In fact, the Shah complained that the Arabs put more emphasis on their Arabism than Islam and say 'we Arabs' and not 'we Muslims'. See the Shah's interview with *Der Spiegel* reprinted in *Keyhan International*, 7 January 1974, p. 4.

22. For example, Iran's policy of expanding its relations eastward in Asia was prompted by a desire to break up this isolation, as the following statement illustrates: 'Bound by the USSR to the north and blocked by the Arab-Israeli conflict to the west, Iran is looking east in search of new friends, partners, and areas of economic and political activity.' Amir Taheri, 'Policies of Iran in the Persian Gulf Region' in Abbas Amirie (ed.), *The Persian Gulf and the Indian Ocean in International Politics*, Teheran: Institute for International Political and Economic Studies, 1975, p. 262. See also Shaul Bakhash, 'Iran is Looking Eastward', *Keyhan International*, 10 April 1974, p. 4.

23. R.K. Karanjia, *The Mind of a Monarch*, London: George Allen and Unwin, 1977, p. 236.

24. For example, unlike the Arab countries – which favoured intra-Arab organisations as channels of aid to developing countries – Iran proposed an international fund with OPEC, industrial, and developing country membership, based on the principle of one-country, one-vote, irrespective of the level of contribution. See the interview of Iran's Minister of Finance, Jamshid Amouzegar in *Keyhan International*, 3 April 1976, p. 4. Also see the editorial in *Keyhan International*, 11 April 1974, p. 4.

25. Over the centuries, memories of Iran's past have affected its policies. Given the close identification of the Shah with a glorious – perhaps unrealistically so – vision of the past, this factor became more important. Nevertheless it also does have solid popular roots. For the best examples of the impact that visions of the past have had on Iranian policy in the Persian Gulf, see R.K.A. Ramazani, *The Persian Gulf: Iran's Role*, pp. 8-27.

26. On the impact of Iran's economic needs on its foreign policy, see Burrell and Cottrell, *Iran, Afghanistan, Pakistan*, pp. 17-35.

27. According to Burrell, 'The Iranian planners know that Iran's economic development will require the importation of large supplies of raw materials, and therefore they are endeavouring to secure future deliveries at low and stable prices before these commodities begin to cost more.' Burrell & Cottrell, *Iran, Pakistan, Afghanistan*, p. 20. For example, the desire to secure reliable sources of food supply was the main reason behind the expansion of relations between Iran and Australia and New Zealand. In the case of India, access to the considerable pool of India's skilled manpower and certain types of technology was also a significant factor, as the following statement of the Shah to R.A. Karanjia illustrates: '. . .do not be surprised, however, if we drain you of nurses as England has done.' The Shah also said that 'India has undertaken to train Iranian cadets in the training ship Rajandra, and other facilities for maritime training have also been extended to Iran.' R.A. Karanjia, *The Mind of a Monarch*, pp. 232-3. See also 'Iran and India in Historic Agreement', *Keyhan International*, 23 February 1974, p. 19 and Nick Cumming Bruce, 'Need for Supply Sources Broadens World Outlook', *MEED*, vol. 9, no. 14, 4 April 1975, pp. 6-7.

28. In fact, given its development plans, 'The strategy of export promotion had become a no-choice policy for Iran's long-term development strategy.' Firouz Vakil, 'Iran's Basic Macroeconomic Problems: a 20-Year Horizon' in Jane W. Jacqz (ed.), *Iran: Past, Present and Future*, New York: Aspen Institute for Humanistic Studies, 1976, p. 84.

29. Mohsen Fardi, 'Iran's International Economic Outlook'. Ibid., p. 350.

30. For example, Iran's interests in issues such as the reform of the international economic system, trade liberalisation, transfer of technology, and the relationship between the price of raw materials and industrialised goods differed sharply from those of the industrial countries.

31. See R.K.A. Ramazani, 'The Instruments of Iran's Foreign Policy', *The Persian Gulf*, pp. 387-96.

32. For example, many observers ascribed Iran's defence build-up to the Shah's *folie de grandeur*. See Laurence Martin, 'The Future Strategic Role of Iran' in Amirsadeghi (ed.), *Twentieth Century Iran*, p. 225. However, the question of Iran's defence needs and thus the size of its military establishment has always been a bone of contention between Iran and its principal Western ally, the United States. See Chubin & Zabih, *Foreign Relations*, pp. 86-124.

33. In particular, Iran's historical experience had had a tremendous impact here. In the last 200 years, Iran's experience has been one of loss of territory and independence, and of the constant spectre of being partitioned (in the 1907 Russo-British plan; in the 1940 Molotov-Ribbentrop agreement; and in the 1945 Bevin-Molotov plan) as a result of great power collusion. Many Iranians had attributed these calamities to their military weakness, as the following statement by Iran's nineteenth century prime minister to its ambassador in the Court of Ottomans illustrates. In answer to the latter's complaints about Ottoman designs on Iran's interests in the Persian Gulf, the minister said: 'As I have told you before, the maintenance and restoration of rights depends on power and military and naval force. Knowing Iran's naval weakness, today, Medhat Pasha is infringing on our rights. Tomorrow the Sheikh of Kuwait or Amir of Muscat will have the

same designs.' Quoted in Fereydoun Adamiyat, *Andisheh Taraghi va Hokumat Ghanoun*, p. 419 (this is the author's translation).

In more recent times, the violation of Iran's neutrality during the First and Second World Wars demonstrated the need for a viable defence force. Thus as the Shah said on many occasions, Iran's defence build-up was an insurance policy, 'a lock on the door'. He also intimated that, if need be, Iran would fight a scorched-earth war. The ultimate purpose of this policy was to increase the political and opportunity costs for an aggressor and thus deter aggression. See Shahram Chubin, 'Iran's Defense & Foreign Policies' in A. Amirie (ed.), *The Persian Gulf and Indian Ocean*, pp. 309-22. Also, see the Shah's interview with M.H. Heikal, *Keyhan International*, 15 September 1975, p. 4.

34. For example, it is doubtful that Iran could have prevented Soviet aggression by offering it money, even if it had large surpluses. (Nor could this instrument have been used to placate Iraq, which itself had a large income from oil.)

35. The monolithic nature of Iran's decision-making process meant that the views of the Shah determined Iran's policies, and neither elite nor popular views had much impact. In turn, the Shah was essentially a military man who defined and analysed regional and global problems in strategic terms, and identified personally with Iran's past with its legendary Persian armies. Thus, he emphasised both the military dimensions of Iran's security problems, and military solutions to them. On Iran's decision-making apparatus, see Marvin Zonis, *Iran's Political Elite*, Princeton, New Jersey: Princeton University Press, 1971; and Khosrow Fatemi, 'Leadership by Distrust: The Shah's Modus Operandi' in *The Middle East Journal*, vol. 36, no. 1, Winter 1982, pp. 48-63. On the Shah's views, see M.R. Pahlavi, *Mission For My Country*, New York: McGraw Hill, 1961; R.A. Karanjia, *The Mind of a Monarch*, p. 265; and F.A. Bayne, *Persian Kingship in Transition: Conversations with a Monarch Whose Office is Traditional and Whose Aim is Modernization*, New York: American Universities Field Staff, 1968.

36. For example, Iran used diplomacy to resolve its disagreements with the Persian Gulf countries, the most important of which was the issue of Bahrain, where Iran also had recourse to multilateral diplomacy. Other disputes concerned the delineation of Iran's continental shelf in the Gulf. Iran also tried to resolve its dispute with Iraq and Afghanistan over the Shatt-al-Arab and the Helmand Rivers, respectively. Moreover, Iran tried to mediate the dispute between Pakistan and Afghanistan over Pushtunistan. And it also encouraged the improvement of Indo-Pakistan relations, particularly after the war of 1971.

Iran's call for the Gulf littoral states to assure the security of the Gulf, its proposition for a Gulf collective security system, its support for a 'peace zone' in the Indian Ocean, and its suggestion regarding a 'nuclear-free zone' in the Middle East illustrate its desire to reduce great-power influence in these regions.

In the economic sphere, too, Iran presented regional alternatives, such as the Shah's proposal to enlarge RCD (Regional Cooperation for Development) to include Iraq, Afghanistan, and India in addition to Iran, Turkey, and Pakistan. And he proposed an Asian common market to include first Iran and the countries of the Indian sub-continent, but possibly others as well. See R.K.A. Ramazani, 'The Instruments of Iran's Foreign Policy' in *Iran: Past, Present and Future*, pp. 387-96, and the Shah's interview with R.A. Karanjia 'On the Right Road to Peace and Affluence', reprinted in *Keyhan International*, 3 April 1974, p. 4.

37. See R.A. Karanjia, *The Mind of a Monarch*, pp. 235-40; and 'Iran's Position on Oil and AID', *Iran Economic News*, vol. I, no. 9, September 1975; p. 1, and the Shah's interview with the *Daily Telegraph*, reprinted in *Keyhan International*, 9 February 1974, p. 4.

38. For example, Iran used its military capacity to encourage Indo-Pakistan *rapprochement*, and to encourage India to distance itself from the Soviet Union.

Thus it offered its military support to Pakistan to deter India from attacking it, and yet refused to supply Pakistan with weapons, thus reassuring India. See Bhabhani SenGupta, 'The View From India' in A. Amiree (ed.), *The Persian Gulf and Indian Ocean*, p. 183. Iran's intervention in the war against the Dhofari rebellion was another example of the use of military power in support of Iran's anti-subversion policy.

39. For example, Iran agreed to provide Britain with 5 million tons of oil in exchange for £110 million worth of industrial goods. See *Keyhan International*, 22 January 1974, p. 1. Also, Iran wanted to prevent closer Indo-Soviet relations, and offered India credits for the purchase of Iranian oil. Some argue that Iran's decision was prompted by the fact that, in order to ease India's oil burden, the Soviet Union – during Brezhnev's visit to India (November 1973) – had agreed to provide India with crude oil and other petroleum products, which amounted to barter. See Burrell & Cottrell, *Iran, Afghanistan, Pakistan*, p. 2. Also see H. Mehraein, 'Iran and India Embark on Joint Oil Project', *Keyhan International*, 6 January 1974, p. 4.

40. To increase its investment in oil and oil-related activities abroad, and thus its ability to penetrate international markets, has been an important feature of Iran's investment policy. With increases in its oil revenues, Iran used aid to facilitate the achievement of this objective. For example, Iran and Senegal agreed to build an oil refinery in Senegal with Iran furnishing the crude oil. Iran also extended a $40 million loan to Senegal to cover its share of the capitalisation. See *Iran Economic News*, vol. II, no. 2, February 1976, p. 7.

41. Soviet-Iranian relations are a good example of the use of trade and economic cooperation to enhance security. In fact, the Shah was candid that his purpose was to involve the Soviet Union economically in Iran to such a degree – particularly in border areas – that any aggression against Iran would become extremely costly and almost self-defeating.

42. Iran signed massive, long-term trade and investment agreements with a number of industrialised countries. For example, Iran and Italy signed an agreement valued at over $3 billion, and signed similar agreements with France and West Germany. A US-Iranian agreement was valued at over $15 billion. Another major partner was Japan. Iran also explored long-term trade and investment agreements with Australia and New Zealand. It lent $1.2 billion to Britain to finance the latter's nationalised industries, and it bought a 25 per cent share in the German steel-making concern, Krupp. See: Burrell & Cottrell, *Iran, Afghanistan, Pakistan*, pp. 28-33. Also see *Keyhan International*, 17 and 24 January 1974, p. 2 and p. 3; and Shaul Bakhash, 'Matchmaking in Bonn', *Keyhan International*, 11 March 1974, p. 4. Iran signed trade agreements with Poland, Hungary, Czechoslavakia, Romania, and Yugoslavia. Most of these agreements led to an increase in Iran's exports to these countries. Iran even agreed to help Vietnam to develop its oil industry. See *Iran Economic News*, vol. II, nos. 1, 2, and 5, February, March and May 1975; and *Keyhan International*, 12 April 1974, p. 2. Principal Iranian trade agreements with the developing countries were with Egypt and India. Others included Syria, Tunisia, Senegal, and Morocco. See *Keyhan International*, 18 April 1974, p. 1; and *Iran Economic News*, vol. II, no. 1, pp. 6-7.

43. For example, discussing Indo–Iranian relations, *Keyhan International* said in an editorial, which reflected the official Iranian view, that both Iran and India believed in increased trade and cooperation rather than 'handouts'. 19 January 1974, p. 4.

44. See *Keyhan International*, 5 January 1974, p. 4.

45. For example, in an interview with the *Daily Telegraph*, the Shah said: 'Let's set up a completely neutral international board that will study the needs of

the developing countries and then put orders quite impartially to the industrialised countries.' Reprinted in *Keyhan International*, 9 February 1974, p. 4. See also Finance Minister Amouzegar's interview in *Keyhan International*, 'How the Fund Will Work', 12 March 1974, p. 4. On Arab opposition, see *Keyhan International*, 'Aid Fund Needs Arab Support', 11 April 1974, p. 4.

46. See *Financial Solidarity for Development, 1973-1976*, TD/B/C. 7/31, 1979, p. 33.

47. Personal interview.

48. For example, Iran extended a $47 million interest-free loan to Egypt for the purchase of Iran-made busses, *MEES*, vol. XXII, no. 23, 28 March 1979, p. 1. In addition, all or part of the products of those agricultural or industrial projects that Iran assisted were to be exported to Iran. For example, under the Iran-India agreement, India was to provide Iran with iron for its steel plants from the mines developed in part by Iranian aid.

49. Based on information gathered through personal interviews.

50. Moreover, given the changed circumstances in Egypt and the Gulf during the 1970s, the Shah had lost his earlier interest in Islamic solidarity.

51. UNCTAD figures of OPEC aid include contributions to the IMF Oil Facility, but those for OECD do not.

52. See *Financial Solidarity for Development*, p. 33, and *DAC Aid Review*, 1977, p. 88.

53. There is, however, some discrepancy between official Iranian estimates of the concessionality of Iranian ODA and those of the OECD. For example, Iranian sources put the overall grant element of Iran's ODA at 45 per cent and 76 per cent for the years 1975 and 1976. See *Financial Solidarity for Development*, p. 33.

54. For example, the interest charged on a $500 million Iranian oil credit to India was 2.5 per cent; and the $47 million loan to Egypt to purchase Iranian-made busses was interest free. See *DAC Review*, 1975, p. 136 and *MEES*, vol. XXII, no. 23, March 26, 1979, p. 1.

55. Based on information gathered through personal interview. The project was completed by India in 1981. By then, Iran had already disbursed $270 million of the $600 million that had been committed (India had to make up the shortfall from other sources). But the Islamic government of Iran has refused to honour the rest of the commitment, and as of this writing the fate of the whole agreement is unclear.

56. For example, India received the bulk of its aid from Western sources and multilateral organisations (and later from the Arab countries). Also, India received crude oil at concessional prices from some Arab countries, including Iraq and the UAE. See *MEES*, vol. XIX, no. 30, 17 March 1976, p. 3.

57. For example, Iran was utterly dismayed by Qaddaffi's visit to Pakistan during the Islamic Conference held in Lahore in 1974, and relations between the two countries cooled considerably. Yet Pakistan, knowing the problems Qaddaffi's participation would cause in relations with Iran (the Shah refused to go to Lahore), did not cancel the invitation.

58. Other OPEC countries have either terminated their aid programmes beyond a minimum, as in the case of Iran, or may have to do so in the future. Only Kuwait and the United Arab Emirates are other candidates for a sustained foreign aid programme in the future.

59. Saudi Arabia is believed to be rich in mineral resources beyond oil, but their exact amounts are not known. But even if they were present in quantities that made their exploitation economically profitable, other difficulties – such as lack of adequate indigenous manpower and water resources – make their full-scale development problematical. Prospects for agricultural development are even

less promising. For example, of a surface area of some 2.3 million square kilometers, only 0.2 per cent is cultivated. See, among others, Robert E. Looney, *Saudi Arabia's Development Potential*, Lexington, Massachusetts: D.C. Heath and Company, 1982; and Ragaei El-Mallakh and Dorothy El-Mallakh (eds.), *Saudi Arabia: Energy, Developmental Planning, and Industrialization*, Lexington, Mass.: D.C. Heath and Company, 1982.

60. For a study of the impact of Saudi wealth on regional and global balances of power, see Louis Turner and James Bedore, 'The Power of the Purse String', *International Affairs*, vol. 54, July 1978, pp. 405-21.

61. Adeed Dawisha, *Saudi Arabia's Search for Security*, Adelphi Paper no. 158, Winter 1979-80, p. 6.

62. Theoretically, however, at least two of Saudi Arabia's neighbours – Iran and Iraq – could launch a direct attack against it. Given its territorial contiguity, Iraq is in a better position to do so, whereas Iran would have to depend on amphibious operations, unless it first attacked through Iraq and Kuwait. In the past, Egypt's massive military intervention in North Yemen demonstrated its capacity to come very close indeed to Saudi borders, and of course there is the possibility that under certain circumstances Israel might attack Saudi Arabia. For example, Israel might want to punish Saudi Arabia for its financial assistance to the confrontation states and its role in the oil embargoes. Israel's past incursions into Saudi air space have demonstrated its capacity to do so. The impact of the American factor makes such an attack unlikely. See R.D. Tahtinen, *National Security Challenges to Saudi Arabia*, Washington, DC: American Enterprise Institute, 1978, pp. 4-5 and p. 24.

63. The foundations of Saudi-American relations are generally believed to have been laid at a meeting between President Franklin D. Roosevelt and King Abd-al-Aziz in 1943. But US interest in Saudi Arabia originated earlier in the Second World War when the United States came to appreciate the importance of oil for its future war-fighting capacity. The following statement by then US Secretary of Defense James Forrestal illustrated the depth of American interest in Saudi Arabia. Warning of American need for oil in the next 25 years, he said: 'I don't care which American companies develop the Arabian reserves, but I think most emphatically that it should be American.' See William B. Quandt, *Saudi Security in the 1980s*, Washington, DC: Brookings Institution, 1981, p. 48. Beginning at that time, Saudi and American interests grew closer together, and by the late 1960s, as one expert has put it, there developed 'a coincidence of interest between the U.S. and Saudi Arabia on almost every issue except on Israel'. Adeed Dawisha, *Saudi Arabia's Search*, p. 5.

64. For example, during the Yemeni civil war in 1963, the United States sent military aircraft to protect Saudi Arabia against possible Egyptian attack. More recently, after the outbreak of the Iran-Iraq war, the United States sent its Airborne Warning and Control System to Saudi Arabia.

65. As revolution, Soviet influence, and secular ideologies grew in the Arab world, many Saudis concluded that 'were it not for Israel . . . the Soviets never would have gained a foothold in Egypt, and without the Soviets in Egypt the Middle East would be a far safer place for conservative regimes such as Saudi Arabia'. William B. Quandt, *Saudi Security*, p. 4.

66. For a study of the strategic linkages among the Persian Gulf, Arabian Sea, and the Red Sea, see 'Gulf Security and the Linkage Process' in Enver M. Koury and Emile Nakleh (eds.), *The Arabian Peninsula, Red Sea and Gulf: Strategic Considerations*, Hyattsville, Maryland: Institute of Middle Eastern and North African Affairs, 1979, pp. 19-40.

67. The following statement by Prince Sultan – which is not limited to the Arab world – illustrated this Saudi awareness and the desire to deal with it: 'In the underdeveloped world we see the threat of radicalism and we can put

our money where the Communist mouth is.' *Newsweek*, 6 March 1978, p. 13.

68. A number of more-or-less significant border and other disputes have brought Saudi Arabia in opposition to some of the Gulf countries, as well as the Gulf countries in opposition to one another. For a fairly comprehensive list of intra-Gulf conflicts, see Robert Litwak, *Security in the Persian Gulf: Sources of Inter-State Conflict*, London: The International Institute for Strategic Studies, 1981.

69. For example, when he took office as Deputy Prime Minister in 1974, Crown Prince Fahd set the following priorities for Saudi Arabia: to get the Soviets out of Somalia, to support moderate forces in South Yemen, and to help Sudan in its efforts to resist communist subversion. See Adeed Dawisha, *Saudi Arabia's Search*, p. 20. Saudi Arabia also tried to encourage the United States to use its military aid potential to get the Russians out of Somalia. See *The New York Times*, 25 December 1977, pp. 10-11.

70. For example, the Saudis have had tremendous influence in Qatar and Bahrain – in the case of the former because of religious affinities; and in the latter, because of financial assistance and Bahrain's fear of Iranian designs. With the completion of a causeway to link Saudi Arabia and Bahrain, the former will gain considerable strategic advantages. In regard to the other Gulf countries, notably Kuwait and the UAE, in the past the Saudis were not able to establish their full influence, partly because of Iranian competition. But since the revolution in Iran and the formation of the Gulf Cooperation Council in 1981, Saudi influence has been enhanced in these countries, although misgivings still persist, especially in Kuwait. On the GCC, see 'Caution: Building in Progress', *The Middle East*, no. 78, April 1981, pp. 8-12.

71. For example, in the past Iran seemed to be the less-threatening state as compared with Iraq, but since the Islamic revolution in Iran Saudi perceptions have been reversed.

72. Some experts believe that the Saudis have wanted to turn the Red Sea into an Arab lake. See Enver M. Koury and Emile Nakhleh, 'Gulf Security', p. 23.

73. Djibouti has been of particular importance in the Arab scheme of turning the Red Sea into an Arab lake. See James Fitzgerald, 'Djibouti: Petrodollar Protectorate?', *Horn of Africa*, vol. 1, no. 4, October/November 1978, pp. 25-31.

74. For the purpose of this particular discussion, the Arab world is considered to consist of the Mashriq countries (Egypt, Syria, Lebanon, Jordan) and the North African or Maghreb countries (Morocco, Algeria, Tunisia, Libya, and Mauritania), North and South Yemen.

75. For a detailed analysis of this issue, See Chapter 1.

76. Of course, there are historical precedents for Egypt's interest in the Persian Gulf, as attested to by its massive propaganda during the Nasserite era. Moreover, Egypt's capacity to come very close to the Gulf, in particular to Saudi Arabia, was illustrated during the Yemeni civil war, which was viewed by Saudi Arabia – and other Gulf countries – as the first stage in an Egyptian policy of destabilising the Gulf and establishing its influence. Today, Egyptian fighter aircraft flying from the Ras Banas air base could reach the Saudi port of Yanbu on the Red Sea.

77. Since the late 1950s, the Arab world has seen half-a-dozen attempts starting with Egyptian-Syrian Union of 1958.

78. Saudi concern with developments in a number of African countries, such as Chad and Zaire, has derived from their possible impact on the balance of forces within the Red Sea region and the Arab world. That is why – according to some sources – Saudi Arabia financed the cost of the use of Moroccan paratroopers, Egyptian pilots, and French transport to combat the Shaba rebellion of 1977. See R.D. Tahtinen, *National Security Challenges*, p. 4.

79. This is why Saudi Arabia has assisted those countries that it has considered to be helping to preserve the present balance of global power, or even to improve it. Among these countries have been a number in southeast Asia that Saudi Arabia has seen 'as the second block of states resisting what they consider to be Soviet expansionism'. See Jamal Rasheed, 'Far East Wooing by the Saudis', *Eight Days/Middle East Business*, vol. 3, no. 14, April 1982, p. 23.

80. Among these policies have been those relating to the level of oil production, where Saudi policy has gone against the OPEC consensus. In fact, as one expert has put it: 'The Saudis have used oil as a political policy tool (or weapon) for several years – in general to push the policies they believe would help the West.' John Shaw and David Long, *Saudi Arabian Modernization: The Impact of Change on Stability*, Washington, DC: The Center for Strategic and International Studies, Georgetown University, 1982, p. 5. Also, 'Saudi Arabia's behavior within OPEC since 1973 has shown an obsessive concern with U.S. interests.' Adeed Dawisha, *Saudi Arabia's Search*, p. 28. A corollary of this policy has been that Saudi Arabia has not used its potential leverage to advance developing-country interests. See Chapter 1.

81. For example, Saudi diplomacy on the Arab-Israeli conflict focused on changing the attitude of the Arab countries, the Europeans, and the United States – encouraging the last-named to adopt a more pro-Arab posture, principally through use of financial leverage. Later, in November 1981, Saudi Arabia even presented a peace plan named after the then Crown Prince Fahd. Also, on several occasions the Saudis have tried to mediate in intra-Arab conflicts, including that between Morocco and Algeria over the Sahara.

82. See William B. Quandt, *Saudi Security*, p. 34. However, failing to become the centre of the Arab world, the Saudis would like to establish their uncontested influence in the Arabian Peninsula, the Persian Gulf, and the Red Sea approaches to Saudi Arabia.

83. For example, during the 1950s when the Hashemites were ascendant in the Middle East, the Saudis cooperated with Nasser's Egypt despite their disagreements. Later, the Saudis overcame their dislike for the Hashemites and supported Jordan against Egypt. They even joined Iran to fight Nasserism. The most recent reversal of alliances has been the friendly relations between Saudi Arabia and Ba'athist Iraq.

84. Pakistan is particularly important to the Saudis because of the military dimensions of their relations. For example, according to some reports 'Pakistani Air Force and Army units already are stationed in Saudi Arabia. The Air Force units are based toward the northern end of the Saudi Gulf coast, between the oil fields and the head of the Gulf . . . The Pakistani Army units reportedly are based on the Saudi Eastern province, site of the oil fields . . .' *Christian Science Monitor*, 20 February 1981, p. 14. It is interesting to note that Saudi-Pakistani relations became particularly close after the fall of Bhutto, to which the Saudis contributed. Rivalry with Iran – on whose support Bhutto relied – and the secular nature of his policies made him unpalatable to the Saudis. See Adeed Dawisha, *Saudi Arabia's Search*, p. 26. See also Helene Lackner, *A House Built on Sand: A Political Economy of Saudi Arabia*, London: Ithaca Press, 1978, pp. 129-30.

85. In fact, the Koran is Saudi Arabia's constitution.

86. This analysis implies that, should circumstances change, the Saudis might moderate their anti-Communist stance. For example, when in 1979 and 1980 the Saudis were feeling particularly vulnerable and insecure in their relations with the United States, there was some talk that they might decide to establish diplomatic relations with the Soviet Union. The Saudis have been encouraged to do so by Kuwait, which has relations not only with the USSR, but also with China and East European countries.

87. For example, among Saudi investment schemes in Egypt was the Arab Military Industries Organisation – an offshoot of the Arab Organisation for Industrialisation – that was dismantled after the Egyptian-Israeli peace treaty. See Jake Wien, *Saudi-Egyptian Relations: The Political and Military Dimensions of Saudi Financial Flows to Egypt*, Santa Monica, California: The RAND Corporation, 1978, pp. 52-6.

The following have been some other examples of Saudi investment in Arab countries:

Egypt: Despite problems, Egypt has still been the primary beneficiary of Saudi funds, where the latter has had an estimated $1 billion on deposit in Egypt's banking system. Saudi Arabia has also owned half of the Saudi-Egyptian Reconstruction Company, with an authorised capital of $50 million, and the Saudi-Egyptian Company for Investment and Finance, with an authorised capital of $100 million;

Syria: Saudi Arabia has been an equal partner with the Syrian government in the Syrian-Saudi Company for Industrial and Agricultural Investments, capitalised at $50 million;

Yemen: Saudi Arabia has controlled 49 per cent of Yemen Airways, the national airline of North Yemen;

Tunisia: Saudi Arabia has been a joint partner with Tunisia in the Saudi-Tunisian Investment Company, capitalised at $250 million. See John Law, *Arab Investors: Who They Are, What They Buy, and Where*, New York, Chase Trade Information Corporation, 1980, vol. II, pp. 63-5. For other details, see Ibid., vol. I, pp. 29-65.

Of an estimated $100 billion investable surplus funds managed by the Saudi Arabian Monetary Agency (SAMA), around $30 billion have been invested in US Treasury bills and notes and the bulk of the rest has been invested in short-term deposits in some 80 top Western banks. SAMA has also lent to private Western corporations, among which has been $650 million for AT & T, $300 million for IBM, and $200 million for US Steel. What has seemed to be important to the Saudis is the security of their investments, rather than the rate of return. However, recently it has seemed that the Saudis have shown more willingness to buy equity shares of Western and Japanese companies. See 'Squirreling Away $100 billion', *Time*, 13 July 1981, pp. 46-7; 'The Saudis Edge into Equities in Japan', *Business Week*, 13 April 1981; and 'The Right Road to OPEC Billions', *Fortune*, 17 November 1981, pp. 39-43. By contrast, Saudi investments in Third World countries – including Arab countries – have been minimal, as partly illustrated above, drawing criticism in particular from Arab nationalists. But, according to some sources, following the seizure of Iranian assets in the West, Saudi Arabia and other Arab countries might consider investing more in safer developing countries. See: 'The Arabs are Still Shy', *Far Eastern Economic Review*, 21 April 1982, p. 110.

88. Saudi Arabia's perception of the identity of its interests with those of the United States has been reflected in talk – in private circles – of 'our dollar'. See Shahram Chubin, *Security in the Persian Gulf*, p. 40.

89. Note this prognosis: 'Saudi Arabia is an advocate but not a champion of reducing the imbalance between the industrialised countries, OPEC countries, and those crippled by high bills for oil and capital goods imports.' *MEED Special Report on Saudi Arabia*, July 1980, p. 83. In 1981, Saudi Arabia agreed to lend $11 billion to the IMF.

90. Saudi leaders, who had seen other Middle Eastern monarchies toppled by military establishments, have consistently tried to minimise such risks to themselves by keeping a tight control over the military, and by taking a range of other steps. One such step has been the creation of several parallel military units, the

most important of which today are the regular army and the elite national guard. Senior officers have been drawn essentially from the Saud family, and loyalty rather than competence has been the principal yardstick for advancement. The combination of these and other factors have done little to enhance the capabilities of the Saudi military. See William B. Quandt, *Saudi Security*, p. 102. The damage done to the efficiency of Saudi armed forces was clearly illustrated during the Mecca incident when lack of coordination among different military and security forces was the principal reason for their poor showing. But even all these precautions have not totally shielded Saudi leaders from the potential danger of their military establishment, as illustrated the 1969 plot of Nasserite officers. In the future, with the recent growth of the Saudi military establishment, the frustration of the military could revive such dangers. For an account of the 1969 plot see Fred Halliday, *Arabia Without Sultans*, Harmondsworth, England: Penguin Books, 1974, pp. 67-78.

91. Unlike Iran, for example, Saudi Arabia has not been an arena of great-power rivalry. Nor has it suffered loss of territory or from Western colonialism or semi-colonialism. In fact, Saudi Arabia's physical isolation had 'reduced the danger of foreign intervention in internal Saudi affairs, thus allowing the Saud family to consolidate its power and to dominate its weak neighbors where possible'. William B. Quandt, *Saudi Security*, p. 3. Moreover, as noted earlier, Saudi Arabia has had a more positive experience with its Western ally than did Iran.

92. For example, 'Saudi development (as well as defense) is dependent principally on access to Western technology as well as to investment markets. As a large foreign investor, it has a vested interest in international stability.' Shahram Chubin, *Security in the Persian Gulf*. As a result, some Arab nationalists have felt that Saudi Arabia is 'a hostage of the West held by chains of gold'. *Time*, 13 July 1981, p. 67. Nor is this analysis totally wrong as the seizure of Iranian assets during the hostage crisis illustrated.

93. For example, when the Socialist party won the French presidential elections in 1981, the Saudis suspended their arms agreements with France. The reason for this was the declared policy of the Socialist party towards the Arab-Israeli conflict – a policy that was more pro-Israeli than that of the previous government. Thus the Saudis wanted to see what the new government's attitude would be towards the Arab world. When the Socialist government – despite improving relations with Israel – did not make any substantial changes in France's policy towards the Arab-Israeli conflict and in its relations with the Arab world, the Saudis resumed their arms and other commercial deals with France.

94. Information gathered through personal and confidential interviews.

95. Adeed Dawisha, *Saudi Arabia's Search*, p. 5.

96. President Sadat acknowledged this in a speech to the Central Committee of the Arab Socialist Union by saying: 'Saudi Arabia undertook to develop the armed forces . . . It undertook commitments for the next five years without our paying a mil to develop the armed forces.' *Foreign Broadcast Information Service (Middle East and Africa)*, 18 July 1977, p. D24.

97. *FBIS/MEA*, 2 May 1979, p. D13.

98. This aspect, however, was part of a pan-Arab scheme aimed at reducing Arab dependence on foreign sources of military supply. This relationship came to an end after the signing of the Egyptian-Israeli peace treaty.

99. This package was agreed upon after the border clashes between North and South Yemen in 1979. See Christopher Van Hollen, 'North Yemen: A Dangerous Pentagonal Game', *The Washington Quarterly*, vol. 5, no. 3, Summer 1982, pp. 139-40.

100. *The Washington Post*, 1 November 1979, p. 9.

101. The first Saudi military grant to Somalia was made in 1977 but its exact amount is not clear. *MEED Special Report on Saudi Arabia*, August 1978. The Saudis were prepared to finance larger purchases of US arms by Somalia, but for its own reasons the United States limited arms deliveries. However, since 1979 there has been a change in US policy and in the future Somalia might get more Saudi-financed US military supplies. On earlier US policy, See William E. Lewis, 'U.S. Debate in the Horn', *The Washington Quarterly*, vol. 2, no. 3, Summer 1979, p. 100. Saudi Arabia also paid the $75 to $80 million cost of F-5s sold to Sudan by the United States. See 'In Policy Shift U.S. is Willing to Sell F-5s to Sudan', *The New York Times*, 21 December 1979, p. 8.

102. For example, in August 1980 there were press reports that Saudi Arabia had discussed the possibility of providing as much as $1 billion in aid annually in exchange for large numbers of Pakistani ground forces and advisers. These were to be stationed primarily in the South Yemen border areas. According to one source: 'by early 1981 about 1,200 Pakistani noncombat forces and advisers were in Saudi Arabia with plans for an eventual total of as many as 10,000 military men, including some combat troops, half to be located at Tabuk and the rest in the South'. William B. Quandt, *Saudi Security*, p. 41. See also *Christian Science Monitor*, 20 February 1981, p. 14.

103. Prior to this period, Saudi aid (which began in 1967 following the Khartoum agreement) consisted of the following: Egypt, Jordan, and Syria (1967-74), $1,263 million; North Yemen (1970-3), $400 million; Sudan (1972-4), $52 million; Somalia, $29 million (interest-free loan), Niger, $2 million (grant); and Uganda, $15 million (interest-free loan). Source: *Annual DAC Review*, 1974.

104. Source: *Annual DAC Review*, 1981.

105. The limited degree of Saudi Arabia's leverage on some of its aid recipients has stemmed from the latter's capacity to create mischief for Saudi Arabia both internally and in the Arab world. In fact, as one Saudi source told the author: 'How could you impose conditions on aid you are giving a country in order to prevent it from taking subversive actions against you?' The significance of the lack of trained manpower for Saudi Arabia's capacity to influence the economic policies of recipient countries was also emphasised in all interviews.

106. Among infrastructure projects, the SFD has favoured transportation and power-generation.

107. J.E. Peterson, *Conflict in the Yemens and Superpower Involvement*, Washington, DC: Center for Contemporary Arab Studies, Georgetown University, 1981, p. 9.

108. Some observers have believed that the popular president of North Yemen, Ibrahim Muhammed, was murdered because he had become anti-Saudi. See: Christopher Van Hollen, 'North Yemen: A Dangerous Pentagonal Game', p. 139.

4 THE NATURE OF OPEC AID

Chapters 2 and 3 illustrated how the security, political and economic needs of OPEC members have affected the magnitude and direction of their aid programmes. Furthermore, the impact of these factors on the nature of OPEC aid was discussed briefly in the case of most OPEC members, and in more detail in the cases of Iran and Saudi Arabia.

Despite these earlier discussions, however, an analysis of the nature of OPEC aid as a donor group is in order, essentially for the following reasons: to permit (1) an analysis of the impact of common Third World objectives in determining the nature of OPEC aid; (2) an evaluation of OPEC's contribution to achievement of those objectives through the use of its aid; (3) an evaluation of the developmental impact of OPEC aid, based on such criteria as the level of concessionality, composition, attached conditions, and the development strategies favoured; and (4) a brief comparative study of OPEC aid with that from members of the Development Assistance Committee (DAC) of the OECD, as two distinct donor groups – to be included in the final chapter.

However, to do this analysis, a short introduction summarising expert opinion on some salient issues in aid giving and development is needed.

PART ONE: SALIENT AID ISSUES

I Definition

After almost three decades of development assistance, there is still no universally-accepted definition of aid. In fact, as one expert has put it, aid is very much 'what people say is aid', a situation that derives partly from the fact that there are two parties to any aid relationship, with often totally different perceptions of what constitutes aid.[1]

The donors have generally viewed as aid those transfers of goods and services that have entailed a cost to them, assuming that otherwise these resources would have been put to alternative uses. By contrast, recipients have viewed as aid only those transfers of goods and services that have contributed to their economic development and welfare and that would not otherwise have been available – at least not at affordable terms.

For practical purposes of computing aid flows, most experts have regarded as aid 'government-sponsored flows of resources made available on concessional terms to foreign governments, either directly on a bilateral basis or indirectly via multilateral organizations'.[2] The United Nations and the DAC have also applied similar criteria and have considered as aid all forms of grants and long-term loans (over five years) extended by governments and multilateral organisations.

II Types of Aid

Aid can be divided into several categories on the basis of the following factors: *motivations for aid*, such as development aid versus aid given for other purposes (including military); *conditions of aid*, whether it is tied or untied; *the contents of aid*, whether it is in the form of cash payment or in commodity or technical assistance; *the degree of concessionality*, whether aid is in the form of grants or loans and (if the latter) the degree of its softness or hardness; and *the channels of aid*, whether it is disbursed bilaterally or through multilateral channels.

A simpler way, however, would be to categorise aid – as some experts have done – solely on the basis of its concessionality and the conditions attached to it. This is a more logical approach and it will be used in this study. Based on these criteria, aid is given either as grants or loans. A grant is 'a transfer of resources with no obligation concerning its repayment'.[3] The grant could be in the form of commodities, technical assistance, and other services, or in convertible currencies. Also, conditions could be imposed on its use, or it could be totally unconditional. By contrast, a loan is 'a transfer of resources which has to be repaid'.[4] In turn, the degree to which a loan indeed qualifies as aid depends on its terms. The measurement of the aid component of loans is generally done according to a scale based upon a numerical comparison with the best terms available, which are those of grants.[5]

Although, in theory, grants are the best if not the only form of true 'aid', not all experts have agreed with this statement, and indeed some have preferred loans. Reasons for this preference have included the following: greater financial responsibility on the part of recipients; greater donor control over recipients' policies; and the generally higher level of aid provided when the proportion of loans is higher. Proponents of grants, however, have refuted these points in detail.[6]

Based on the conditions attached to aid, it is either tied or untied. The simplest form of aid would be 'the provision of convertible foreign exchange' without any restrictions attached to its use.[7] However, little aid has been given in this form and generally a variety of conditions relating either to the source of aid or to its end uses have been imposed.[8] Aid tying *by source* is essentially done to protect certain donor interests, but reduces the value of aid to recipients, sometimes to only 80 per cent of its total nominal value.[9] Another way of tying aid is by *end use*.

In general, when aid takes the form of capital, it can either be made available to finance certain items of expenditures in a particular sector, or, after an evaluation of the recipient's overall needs, it can be made available to finance a programme of activities over a period of time. The first method is called project aid; the second, a programme approach.[10]

There has been a long standing (and still continuing) debate among development experts regarding the merits and demerits of these two approaches. But the general consensus is that the choice of best method should depend on a variety of considerations, such as recipient's economic situation and its administrative and planning capacity, as well as the practical application of either of these approaches.[11]

III Commodity Aid and Technical Assistance

Commodity aid and most types of technical assistance are examples of the most tied of all aid, and as such they suffer from a number of disadvantages endemic to tying. However, some experts have attributed special ills to these two types of aid, whereas others have seen in them certain advantages. A detailed analysis of these issues is beyond the scope of this study. Yet because a very large proportion of DAC aid has consisted of commodity (particularly food) aid and technical assistance, because the share of this aid for OPEC has been minimal, and because this aid has been controversial, a brief evaluation is needed to permit both the evaluation of OPEC aid and its comparison to DAC aid.

Food aid started in 1954 when the United States began systematically to export food on concessional terms as part of its effort to cope with growing agricultural surpluses at home.[12] Today, food aid is provided for emergency relief purposes as well as for development.[13] It has been disbursed both bilaterally and through multilateral channels such as the World Food Programme and the European Community.[14] Moreover, different methods have been used to disburse food aid, including food for cash, food for nutrition, and food for wages. A number of criticisms have been voiced against each of these three forms of food aid, but the general criticism has come down to the following: the adverse effect of food aid on the agricultural development of recipient countries; and the creation of dependent populations.[15] Not everyone has agreed with this view.[16] However, most experts *would* agree with the following statement, to the effect that whether food aid could be beneficial to the recipients would depend on the circumstances under which it is disbursed and its relationship to other types of aid received by them:

> Food aid is unlikely to have a negative effect, and may have a positive impact if supplied in good time and in the form of locally acceptable commodities to a food deficit country with energetic agricultural development policies, and as part of a broader package of measures designed to assist a poverty oriented development strategy. It is likely to have a negative impact if supplied under the opposite circumstances. Since most recipients fall somewhere in between these two extremes, the decision whether or not to provide food aid will depend on a delicate judgment. In this food aid is no different from any other kind of aid.[17]

Evaluating *technical assistance* is even more difficult, since even today there is no universally accepted definition of what constitutes this form of aid.[18] Principal criticisms of technical assistance have related to its high cost; the large share of administrative expenses – such as high salaries; lack of coordination in view of the multiplicity of countries and agencies involved in this business; creation of technological bias and prevention of the development of an indigenous technological base by the recipients; and the perpetuation of political and other forms of dependence.[19] However, general expert consensus with regard to technical assistance, as in the cse of food aid, has been that it is neither inherently good or bad. Rather, its value would depend on the way it is given, its relationship with other forms of aid, and the conditions of the recipients.

IV Multilateral versus Bilateral Aid

The channel of disbursement can also affect the value and effectiveness of aid. Some development experts have attributed a number of advantages to aid disbursed multilaterally – advantages that correspond almost exactly to the disadvantages associated with bilateral aid. The most important are the following:

(i) freedom from prejudiced control by individual donors;
(ii) removal of aid from the vagaries of domestic political issues in donor countries;
(iii) increased acceptability to recipients;
(iv) sound, common, and well-known criteria for the allocation of aid; and
(v) efficient supervision.[20]

However, not all experts have agreed with this view. Some have challenged in particular the assumption that multilateral agencies are independent and free from the vagaries of the domestic politics of their contributors.[21] Thus, as the following statement illustrates, most experts have believed that the best way to evaluate multilateral agencies and their aid is to look into their actual operations rather than to make judgements on the basis of some hypothetical ideal that multilateral aid is inherently better than bilateral:

> In order to appraise the utility of multilateral agencies, what is required is not an answer to the question whether the hypothetical ideal of multilateral aid is in some indiscriminate and unqualified sense 'better' than bilateral aid, but rather a precise identification of the context in which particular institutions operate; the role which they are required, in that particular context, to perform; and their capabilities in relation to the tasks laid upon them.[22]

V Evolving Development Theories

A detailed discussion of development theories and their evolution is beyond the scope of this study. During the last decade, however, there has been growing criticism – by experts from the Third World and elsewhere – of the inadequacy of traditional development strategies to meet developing countries' needs, and these experts have suggested a number of reformist actions. Thus a brief discussion of the most salient aspects of this debate would be valuable. Such a discussion is also important to help in the evaluation, later in this study, of OPEC's contribution (or lack thereof) to the realisation of some of these suggestions.

Briefly, criticism of traditional development theories has related primarily to the following points:

(a) undue emphasis on the economic development experience of the industrialised countries, and efforts to repeat the same process of modernisation in the Third World;
(b) incorrect assumptions about the existence of a high degree of community of interest between the developed and developing worlds, and about the benign neutrality of the international economic system, reflected in such catchwords as 'one world' or 'interdependence';[23] and
(c) lack of due attention to the social, political, and humanistic dimensions of development.

In turn, those who have advocated change in both development strategies and the international system, as one expert has put it, could be divided into reformists and fundamentalists. With regard to the former:

> The Reformist position continues to be based essentially on conventional development thinking which assumes a conflict-free social framework for change. Further, even with the social justice tilt, it still considers the development process as mainly an economic exercise subject to allocation of scarce resources. Despite evidence to the contrary there is still an assumption of the 'Onc World' myth which will permit under existing conditions an orderly and continuous process of income transfers from rich countries to poor. Underlying all this is the further assumption that the problem of development is mainly in the developing countries and that a consistent set of 'policy packages' based on technocratic considerations can be evolved, ranging from structural changes to investment decisions to employment opportunities, which can be carried out from the top with the 'good will' of the international community.[24]

By contrast, the fundamentalists have not accepted any premise of past development strategies nor the reformist diagnosis of the international system.[25] They have recommended that individual developing countries adopt a principally self-reliant development strategy geared to meeting the basic needs of their populations, and particularly to eradicating abject poverty on the national level, coupled with a strategy of greater *collective* self-reliance on the part of developing countries, in general.[26] Their specific suggestions have included creating autonomous financial institutions in the Third World, a Third World monetary system, and Third World trade unions. Furthermore, the developing countries should improve their bargaining capacity through a number of cooperative measures, including the following:

(1) Creating data-flow units to identify price, quantity, and market potential independently of the multinational corporations (MNCs) and to provide a check on MNC intra-firm transaction prices.
(2) Identifying or creating adequate shipping, financial, and marketing channels.
(3) Finding new export markets, particularly among other Third World countries, and organising joint trading ventures.

Regarding the combined potential of Third World countries as importers, the most important step would be the creation of joint trading companies and the encouragement of intra-Third World trade.[27] Of course, the reformists have also advocated many of these measures, albeit in a less radical way. However, many obstacles in the path of achieving these objectives have related to the Third World countries themselves – including their divergent interests and rivalries – rather than to the industrialised countries or the international system. As noted in the last three chapters, this has been true of OPEC countries, although it has by no means been limited to them.[28]

VI Conclusions and Assessment Criteria

The most important and yet most disappointing conclusion to be drawn from the foregoing is that it is almost impossible to develop criteria for judging the value of aid that can be valid for all countries at all times. Nevertheless, in general there are certain basic criteria that have often been used to judge the *relative* value of aid:

1. Volume of aid. One of the standards used in judging the aid performance of a given country has been a target contribution at some percentage of national income. As early as the immediate post-Second World War years, the minimum percentage for capital flows to the developing countries was estimated at 1 per cent of the national income of capital surplus countries. This standard was adopted by the United Nations in 1960 – UNGA Resolution 1522 (XV); in 1961 – UNGA Resolution 1711 (XVI); and by the UNCTAD conference of 1964. However, since the target also included non-official – and thus non-concessional – transfers, in 1968 Third World countries tried at the second UNCTAD conference to formulate a target of 0.75 per cent of GNP for Official Development Assistance. This was not accepted by the developed countries, and later the Pearson Commission suggested the target of 0.7 per cent, which was also accepted by the UN in 1970. However, there is another factor to be taken into account: the balance of payments positions of donors. Thus, those countries with surpluses over an extended period of time have generally been expected to pay more in foreign aid.
2. Level of concessionality. In general, the higher the level of concessionality in aid, the higher its value. Thus grants as a form of aid are usually more valuable than loans.
3. Lack of restrictions. Aid free from restrictions like the need to buy in the donor country is better than aid tied to the purchase of specific items.
4. The lack of non-development motives. This condition perhaps obtains least frequently. To be sure, aid given for motives of self-interest can have a positive developmental impact, but it has generally been agreed that: 'Allocations of assistance heavily motivated by other than development purposes tend to be suboptimal.' One particularly negative impact of such aid is that it '. . . radically distorts the allocations of aggregate ODA away from what would be optimal were the development community free to maximise aid's development payoff more or less single-mindedly'.[29]
5. The allocation of a fair percentage of aid through multilateral agencies. This could reduce the danger of aid's being overly-motivated by non-developmental factors.
6. Continuity and predictability in aid flows to recipient countries.
7. Flexibility in combining project and non-project forms of assistance.
8. Flexibility in providing for local and recurrent cost financing.
9. Recognition of constraints arising from the limitations on recipients' administrative resources (which can be exacerbated by excessively-

burdensome aid procedures).
10. Harmonisation of aid procedures and other measures (to reduce the burden on recipients of having to meet the different requirements of many donors).[30]

In addition, there is value in aid designed to promote a development strategy that, although adapted to the needs of individual countries, could contribute to balanced development, increased self-sufficiency and the reduction of poverty.

PART TWO: OPEC RECORD

This part of Chapter 4 will evaluate OPEC aid based on the criteria discussed in the first part. It will also evaluate OPEC's use of aid as an instrument for achieving Third World goals, including that of collective self-reliance.

I Volume

One criterion to evaluate any aid programme is its volume. Needless to say, however, aggregate figures by themselves are not a sufficient yardstick and have to be complemented by other factors such as the level of concessionality, the conditions attached to aid, geographical distribution, as well as other considerations discussed earlier. In the case of OPEC, another criterion might also be useful: the degree to which OPEC aid has compensated for Third World losses from increased oil prices since 1973. The OPEC countries have objected to this type of analysis of OPEC's aid performance, denying that OPEC aid has had any 'compensatory' function.[31] Rather, they have liked to portray OPEC aid as determined solely by the imperatives of OPEC-Third World solidarity. However, not all have agreed with OPEC's interpretation, and in fact some experts have maintained that even the OPEC countries themselves – despite their official position – have appreciated problems created for the Third World countries by oil price increases and thus have 'made some partly compensatory capital donations'.[32] Some of these experts in turn have computed the impact of OPEC aid in offsetting oil price-induced Third World losses. Paul Hallwood and Stuart Sinclair are two economists who have analysed this relationship for the period 1974-7, and whose work will be examined here. Since the pattern of OPEC aid after the oil price increases that followed the Iranian revolution in 1978 has closely resembled that of the previous years, Hallwood and Sinclair's analysis also generally applies to the post-1978 period.

Between the period 1973-80, OPEC countries extended in concessional assistance the amounts as given in Table 4.1.

The volume of OPEC ODA is considerable, and its performance on the basis of percentage of GNP is also impressive.[33] However, the volume of OPEC aid *per se* is not sufficient to measure its value. It is, a good yardstick, however, to measure its efficacy as a compensatory mechanism for relieving the Third World's oil burden. In this regard, the Hallwood/Sinclair analysis is extremely useful and will be discussed here.

In order to calculate the extent of Third World losses because of oil price increases, Hallwood and Sinclair have estimated what, in the absence of OPEC actions, the normal increase of oil prices would have been. In their calculations, Hallwood and Sinclair have taken the end of 1960 posted price of $1.80 plus $0.27 ($2.07) as the base price, and have increased it according to the increase in the index of industrial countries' export prices. According to this calculation, by 1973 the crude oil posted price should have been about 62 per cent higher, and thus by January 1974 it would have stood at $3.30 per barrel. However, according to Hallwood and Sinclair, had the price of marker crude oil been index-linked to the price of other commodities – which between 1960 and 1973 increased by 77 per cent, then the price of oil would have stood at $3.66. Thus they have concluded that the $11.65 price of Arabian light marker crude in January 1974 was $8.29 higher than if oil prices had kept pace with prices in the industrial countries, and $7.99 higher if they had kept pace with prices in non-oil primary commodities. Therefore, according to Hallwood and Sinclair's calculations, OPEC's pricing policy had cost the consumers $8 more than would have been the case with an index-linked price.

Consequently, the non-OPEC developing states as a group between 1974 and 1977 spent an additional $38 billion on imported oil, with Asia suffering most ($16 billion extra), followed by South America ($12 billion), Central America and the Caribbean ($6 billion) and Africa ($0.4 billion extra). However, in their analysis Hallwood and Sinclair have illustrated that the volume of OPEC aid to different regions has not been commensurate with their extra oil cost. The situation becomes even worse once the relationship between the extra oil cost and volume of OPEC aid is looked at on a country-by-country basis.

Table 4.1: Volume of OPEC ODA

Donor Country	Total ODA Disbursements (in $US millions)									ODA as a percentage of GNP								
	1973	1974	1975	1976	1977	1978	1979	1980	1981	1973	1974	1975	1976	1977	1978	1979	1980	1981
Algeria	25.4	46.9	40.7	53.6	46.7	43.1	272	83	65	0.29	0.37	0.28	0.33	0.24	0.18	0.87	0.21	0.10
Iran	1.9	408.9	593.1	752.6	251.2	213.2	25	3	150	0.01	0.88	1.13	1.13	0.30	0.26	0.03	0.01	–
Iraq	11.9	422.9	218.4	231.7	56.0	144.2	1115	1062	143	0.21	3.98	1.65	1.44	0.29	0.66	2.53	2.12	0.37
Kuwait	345.2	622.5	976.3	615.3	1433.0	856.4	1055	1188	685	5.72	5.72	8.12	4.36	10.09	4.54	5.89	4.80	1.98
Libya	214.6	147.0	261.1	93.6	109.6	141.5	105	281	105	3.32	1.23	2.31	0.63	0.62	0.77	0.45	0.92	0.37
Nigeria	4.7	15.3	13.9	82.9	64.4	38.0	30	42	149	0.04	0.07	0.05	0.25	0.16	0.08	0.04	0.05	0.17
Qatar	93.7	185.2	338.9	195.0	194.3	100.8	277	319	175	15.62	9.26	15.62	7.95	7.83	3.48	5.89	4.80	2.64
Saudi Arabia	304.9	1029.1	1997.4	2407.1	2400.8	1455.3	2298	3040	5798	4.04	4.46	5.40	5.73	4.30	2.32	3.01	2.60	4.77
UAE	288.6	510.6	1046.1	1060.2	1229.4	616.5	1115	1062	799	15.96	7.57	14.12	11.02	10.67	5.37	5.87	3.96	2.88
Venezuela	17.7	58.8	31.0	102.8	51.5	94.6	83	130	62	0.11	0.20	0.11	0.33	6.14	0.23	0.17	0.23	0.10
Total	1307.8	3466.6	5516.9	5594.7	5846.9	3703.6	6106	6977	7836.0									

Source: *Annual DAC Reviews*, 1974-82.

For example, Africa as a region received more aid than it had to pay for oil. But because of the heavy concentration of OPEC aid on Egypt – followed by Sudan and Somalia – a large number of African countries (including some Arab) had to pay more for their oil than they received in aid. Among Asian countries as well, Pakistan, Bangladesh, and Afghanistan received the bulk of OPEC aid. India, by contrast – although a major recipient of OPEC aid – was a net loser regarding the ratio of its extra oil cost to the aid it received from OPEC.

The foregoing illustrates that the aggregate volume of OPEC aid or its measurement as a percentage of the donors' GNP – as the OPEC institutions have liked to do – cannot *per se* be an adequate yardstick for judging the value to recipients of OPEC aid. Moreover, oil price increases partly generated by OPEC contributed to a slowdown of the global economy – although there is no agreement as to OPEC's exact share of responsibility – leading to a cutback in the foreign aid programmes of most industrialised countries, as well as a reduction in developing countries' export earnings, thus imposing further losses on them. Also oil price increases led to an increase in the price of a whole range of oil-derived products such as fertilisers, for example. Furthermore, as noted earlier, another way of measuring the value of aid to the recipient is to evaluate its cost to the donor. In turn, a reasonable yardstick to measure the cost of aid to the donors would be to evaluate the profitability of the potential alternative uses of the aid funds. In the case of OPEC countries – particularly the financial surplus countries with a low absorptive capacity – highly profitable and risk-free alternatives for the use of their aid monies were not easily available. And, as discussed earlier, given the military and other limitations of major OPEC donors, aid was indeed a less costly way of achieving national interests, and as such its cost to them was not very high.[34]

II Concessionality

Another yardstick for evaluating aid is its level of concessionality. The level of concessionality of OPEC aid has followed an erratic curve since 1973 when its members first embarked on development assistance on a massive scale. However, judged in aggregate terms, OPEC aid has compared well with that of other donors, as Table 4.2 illustrates.

However, the overall rate of concessionality of OPEC ODA does not explain the whole picture, particularly as far as the LLDCs have been concerned. In fact, for them, the concessionality of OPEC aid has been

Table 4.2: Concessionality of OPEC ODA

	1973	1974	1975	1976	1977	1978	1979	1980	1981
Grants	76.7	60.4	47.5	69.3	62.4	59.2	41.4	59.7	57.7
Grant element of loans	49.3	44.1	46.9	46.9	45.9	51.9	50.2	49.2	52.4
Overall Grant element	84.8	77.8	72.1	83.7	79.6	80.4	70.8	79.5	79.9

Source: OECD, *Aid From OPEC Countries*, 1983.

Table 4.3: Terms of OPEC ODA For Different Income Groups

Group of Countries	1973	1975	1977	1978	1979	1980	1981
Least developed	75.2	78.8	70.2	65.3	68.3	67.4	71.5
Other low income	93.5	61.8	75.0	80.1	60.4	77.8	54.7
Middle income	97.4	80.6	81.5	93.8	74.0	90.9	87.0

Source: OECD, *Aid From OPEC Countries*, 1983.

much lower, as Table 4.3 illustrates. This has been so for the following reasons:

(a) although a large part of OPEC ODA has been in the form of grants, the LLDCs have not been the principal recipients of OPEC grants; in fact most of OPEC aid in grant form has gone to three Arab confrontation states and a very few Muslim countries, although some of these countries are among the LLDCs;
(b) OPEC aid to other countries has essentially been in the form of loans. The terms of these loans have been relatively hard and thus their grant element has been low.

Table 4.4: Geographical Distribution of OPEC ODA
(net disbursements as percentage of total, 1971-81)

Region	Percentage of Total
Arab countries	52.7
Non-Arab Asia	9.1
Non-Arab Africa	2.1
Europe (includes Turkey & Malta)	1.0
Latin America	0.2
Unspecified	34.9

Source: OECD, *Aid From OPEC Countries*, 1983.

Table 4.5: Geographical Distribution of OPEC ODA by Income Group, 1971-81

Income Group	Percentage of Total
Least developed	9.7
Low income	21.8
Middle income	32.7
Newly industrialised	0.9
Unspecified	34.9

Source: OECD, *Aid From OPEC Countries*, 1983.

However, most of the OPEC development institutions, in determining the conditions of their loans, have taken into account the economic conditions of the recipients. Still, the level of concessionality of their ODA, as far as this group of countries has been concerned, could have been greatly improved. In this respect, it is also important to note that the aid terms of some OPEC institutions have been better than others.

The details of this matter will be discussed in the next chapter dealing with the channels of OPEC aid. Suffice it to say here that the terms of collective OPEC aid disbursed through the OPEC Fund have been the best. However, the volume of this type of aid, as noted earlier, has not been much.

One way to improve the terms of aid would be if the OPEC countries committed themselves to extend aid to the LLDCs only in grant form. However, some other characteristics of OPEC aid have somewhat improved its value. For example, OPEC aid has been largely untied by source, which in turn has made competitive bidding for procurement possible. This characteristic sometimes could improve the value of aid to the recipient up to 20 per cent of the total value of aid.

III Share of Multilateral ODA

As noted earlier, another yardstick for evaluating aid is to measure the ratio of bilateral to multilateral aid, assuming that multilateral aid is less influenced by non-developmental motivations. But as discussed earlier, more often than not such an assumption has not been justified. Rather, multilateral institutions have generally been influenced by their major contributors either directly – proportionality of voting rights to the level of contribution – or indirectly. This situation in fact has for a long time been criticised by the Third World countries. One way of correcting this situation would be to give equal voting rights to both principal contributors and principal recipients. But as will be explained in the next chapter, despite Third World demand this approach has not yet been adopted, and of specialised international development institutions only IFAD has operated on this basis. The following is an examination of the share of multilateral aid in total OPEC aid.

Multilateral aid has constituted a small part of total OPEC ODA, particularly if the OPEC/Arab institutions are excluded. The bulk of multilateral assistance has been extended through OPEC/Arab institutions. Of total OPEC multilateral ODA, the share of Arab/OPEC institutions was 64 per cent in 1978, fell to 43 per cent in 1979, but increased again in 1980 as a result of the replenishment of the OPEC Fund. Another interesting feature of OPEC multilateral aid has been the small share of the UN agencies, particularly when contributions to IFAD are excluded. In 1981, however, the Arab countries of the Persian Gulf established the Arab Gulf Fund for United Nations

Development. Contributions to this fund have come mainly from Saudi Arabia. It is too early to judge the impact of this fund. The bulk of multilateral assistance – other than that extended through OPEC/Arab institutions – has been extended through the World Bank Group.

Moreover, the level of contributions made by individual OPEC members to different multilateral institutions has not been equal. For example, Saudi Arabia, Kuwait, and the UAE have been the only contributors to IDA, which has received the bulk of OPEC's contributions to traditional multilateral aid agencies.

What the foregoing illustrates, therefore, is that the bulk of OPEC aid has consisted of bilateral aid where considerations of national interest, rather than the developmental impact of aid, have been dominant. Moreover, OPEC's choice of multilateral channels has again tended to emphasise the achievement of specific Arab/OPEC interests, rather than Third World development. Also, this choice has not only not contributed to the achievement of such Third World objectives as gaining more say in both the operation of international institutions and the evolution of their development strategies, but rather it has tended to frustrate them.

IV Composition

The bulk of OPEC aid has been in the form of financial grants or loans. Commodity aid (such as food aid) and technical assistance has constituted an extremely small share of its aid.

However, the provision of oil on concessional terms by a number of OPEC countries has been somewhat comparable to traditional commodity aid.

This situation has been quite natural, and has reflected particular economic conditions of OPEC countries. For example, these countries have not had large agricultural surpluses and, in fact, they have been major importers of such commodities.

Similar factors have also accounted for the extremely small share of technical assistance in total OPEC aid, and what technical assistance that has been provided has been different from that of traditional donors. It has essentially consisted of financing feasibility studies and paying for the services of experts. On occasions some OPEC institutions (such as AFESD), as part of their technical assistance have paid for the cost of training of their members' nationals in the developed countries.

A certain amount of technical assistance has also been provided

Table 4.6: Sectoral Distribution of Bilateral OPEC ODA (percentage of total)

	1973	1975	1977	1978	1979	1980	1981
Non Project Assistance:	88.3	60.8	56.1	79.8	76.4	84.9	79.8
General Support	85.5	48.7	49.2	76.9	65.4	78.5	75.2
Emergency Relief	0.8	2.4	0.8	0.4	6.5	2.3	2.6
Oil Credits	—	9.5	1.8	1.9	4.4	3.1	0.2
Other	2.0	0.2	4.3	0.6	0.1	1.0	1.8
Project Assistance:	11.7	39.2	43.9	20.2	23.6	15.1	20.2
Agriculture	0.3	1.6	0.4	0.4	1.7	0.5	1.4
Extractive Industries	0.2	8.2	1.2	0.9	2.3	—	0.8
Manufacturing	2.6	2.0	8.7	3.4	2.7	1.1	0.8
Energy	1.1	1.6	10.5	1.4	5.1	1.9	4.6
Transport, Storage and Communications	0.2	4.9	14.5	8.1	4.1	7.2	6.2
Education	0.4	1.5	1.0	1.0	1.2	1.0	0.5
Health	0.4	0.4	1.3	0.3	0.5	0.6	1.2
Other	6.5	19.0	6.3	4.7	6.0	2.8	4.7

Source: OECD, *Aid From OPEC Countries*, 1983.

Table 4.7: Sectoral Distribution of Project Aid by OPEC Aid Institutions as of the end of 1980

Sector	Amount in $US millions	Percentage of total
Infrastructure	3,622	34.0
Energy	2,324	22.0
Agriculture	1,826	17.3
Industry and mining	1,778	16.6
Public utilities	995	9.4
Other	79	0.7

Source: OPEC Fund, *OPEC Aid and OPEC Aid Institutions, A Profile*, 1981.

through special arrangements between the OPEC Fund and the UNDP as well as through the Arab Fund for Technical Assistance to African and Arab countries. Thus the largest part of OPEC aid has still consisted of general balance of payment and budgetary support. Most of the non-project aid has gone to the Arab confrontation states and to a few other Arab and Muslim countries. Other Third World countries have received principally project aid, except for a certain amount of balance of payment support extended by the OPEC fund.

V Development Philosophy and Sectoral Distribution

All OPEC countries and institutions have claimed that they have favoured those development strategies most likely to reduce poverty, to meet the basic needs of populations, to increase the level of national and collective self-reliance among Third World countries, and to help bring about a new international economic order. In view of the ambiguities and disagreements regarding the definitions of these concepts – as well as regarding the strategies most likely to bring them about – it is very difficult to make a definite judgement as to the degree of OPEC's contribution to their realisation. Nevertheless, there have been some indicators that make a tentative evaluation of OPEC's performance possible.

One of these indicators has been the degree to which OPEC institutions and donors have worked out a strategy that has been poverty-oriented and has encouraged intra-developing country cooperation, and how they have systematically followed it.

The evidence thus far is that they have not done so. What is more, OPEC institutions have favoured sectors whose contributions to the welfare of the poorest sections of society – at least in short and medium terms – have not been very high as illustrated in Table 4.7.

The same has also been true of individual OPEC members and their national development institutions. Infrastructure has accounted for the bulk of OPEC aid. This pattern of distribution has had certain disadvantages. One disadvantage has related to the fact that OPEC aid, instead of being complementary to the aid of other international institutions, has almost duplicated it. Since the record shows that international institutions (and a number of other principal donors) have favoured this type of project, there has thus been more funding available for them, whereas other projects with a high social content and an almost immediate welfare effect have been harder to fund.

Moreover, this pattern of sectoral distribution has not contributed to any great extent to the level of economic self-sufficiency of the recipients, nor has it had a significant and immediate impact on the general welfare of recipient populations. For example, low levels of food producing capacity has been one of the principal problems of the developing countries, yet aid to agricultural sectors by OPEC institutions has amounted to only 17.3 per cent of the total aid of OPEC institutions. Aid to education has also been minimal, despite its vital importance for the developing-countries' prospects for developing an indigenous technological base. The same has been true of projects related to health, population control and other similar social programmes.

Several reasons have accounted for OPEC's attitude. First, the lack of adequate staff with the right kind of expertise has been a major problem that has prevented the development of a more integrated and poverty-oriented aid strategy. However, if OPEC countries had been more committed to such a strategy, the impact of this factor could have been reduced. For example, relevant OPEC institutions certainly could have afforded the services of development experts favouring this type of development strategy; they could have been more aggressive in training their own experts; or they could have entered into partnership and cooperation with those DAC countries – those in Scandinavia, for example, that have traditionally given their support to this type of development strategy.

Second, certain attitudes regarding particular aspects of project financing have also affected the sectoral distribution of OPEC aid. For example, most OPEC countries – particularly their development institutions – have preferred to finance the foreign exchange costs of projects and have had a rather inflexible approach to local cost financing. Basic-needs-oriented strategies have generally had a large local cost component, thus making them unattractive to these institutions.

Third – perhaps the most important reason – has been the extreme caution of OPEC aid donors. Consequently, except for cash grants made to the confrontation states and to a few other Arab and Islamic states, in choosing which projects to finance these countries have put considerable emphasis on the financial profitability of projects rather than on their social welfare yield. This attitude has also led OPEC donors, particularly Arab donors, to favour co-financing. Yet this practice has had certain disadvantages.[35] Given the technical deficiencies of the OPEC countries, this process has also meant that these countries have almost completely emulated the development strategies and priorities of principal DAC donors and the international organisations. The corollary of this situation has been that the OPEC countries have not tried to give enough consideration either to Third World needs or to other less-traditional strategies towards development.

VI Other Characteristics: Qualitative Implications

OPEC aid has had a number of other characteristics that have somewhat reduced its value. One of these characteristics has been the rather low ratio of disbursements to commitments, although some institutions have fared better than others. However, this has not been totally the fault of OPEC institutions, and to a great extent it has derived from infrastructural, administrative, and other deficiencies and bottlenecks in recipient countries.

A further characteristic has been the rather low degree of continuity and predictablity of OPEC aid, particularly aid extended to the non-Arab Third World countries. For example, OPEC countries – even the largest donors – have not yet had regular aid budgets or multi-year aid plans as some of the other donors have had. Some OPEC officials have recognised this flaw, as the following statement by the President of the Iraqi Fund for External Development illustrates:

> I believe it would be a very important development in OPEC's aid to try to plan and make more certain the aids you are extending. One of the major problems or weaknesses of various aids, whether international, OPEC collective or national, is that it still is unplanned, it is not long-term and is based on an ad hoc basis.[36]

This characteristic has also been blamed on the lack of adequate and expert staff. Important as this problem has been however, it would not have been insurmountable if there had been a stronger commitment to making aid more effective and to maximising its developmental impact.

Table 4.8: Commitments and Disbursements of OPEC Aid Organisations as of the end of 1982 (in $US millions)

Organisation	Commitments	Disbursements
OPEC Fund	2,905	1,723
IsBD	3,918	1,812
BADEA	728	449
AFESD	1,647	862
ABDF	1,667	802
KFAED	3,912	2,095
SFD	5,285	1,785
IFED	1,265	541

Note: a. The Venezuela Fund for Investment is not mentioned, because the bulk of its lending has been non-concessional.
Source: OPEC Fund, ***OPEC Aid and OPEC Aid Institutions, A Profile***, 1983.

Table 4.9: Comparative ODA Performance of OPEC, DAC and CMEA in Terms of Net Disbursements

	OPEC	DAC	CMEA
Total in $US billions			
1970	0.4	6.9	1.0
1975	6.2	13.8	9.4
1980	9.1	27.3	2.2
1981	7.7	25.6	2.1
Percentage of GNP			
1970	1.18	0.34	0.14
1975	2.92	0.36	0.07
1980	1.70	0.38	0.14
1981	1.40	0.35	0.14
Percentage of total ODA			
1970	5	83	12
1975	30	67	3
1980	23	71	6
1981	22	72	6

Source: OECD, *Aid From OPEC Countries*, 1983.

Another problem has been the inadequate degree of coordination of OPEC aid efforts, at national, collective OPEC and international levels.

However, inadequacy of coordination among aid donors has not been peculiar to OPEC countries and, despite efforts made by traditional donors, they too have still been faced with this problem. The fact has been that, given the variety of donors with a host of varying and sometimes even conflicting objectives, there have been severe limits as to how far aid efforts could be coordinated.

In fact, the OPEC countries have made some effort at coordination. For example, on many occasions the OPEC Fund has acted on behalf of all OPEC members. The Arab aid institutions have also made efforts to harmonise project appraisal methods, loan allocations, and rules on disbursement and procurement.

Moreover, the officials of Arab and OPEC institutions have regularly met with each other and with officials of other donor countries and aid agencies. In turn, these efforts have been recognised by other traditional donors.

However, there could have been a more efficient use of resources, both financial and human. For example, the smaller countries of the Persian Gulf, such as the UAE and Qatar, instead of each engaging in

Table 4.10: Comparative Terms of ODA for OPEC, DAC and CMEA

	Share of Grants			Grant Elements of Loans			Overall Grant Element		
	1975	1980	1981	1975	1980	1981	1975	1980	1981
OPEC	48	60	58	47	49	52	72	80	80
DAC	69	75	75	63	59	58	89	90	90
CMEA	20	28	31	50	52	57	52	65	90

Source: OECD, *Aid From OPEC Countries*, 1983.

Table 4.11: Composition of Aid Commitments for OPEC, DAC and CMEA as Percentage of Total Aid

	OPEC			DAC			CMEA		
	1975	1980	1981	1975	1980	1981	1975	1980	1981
Bilateral aid	93	88	74	76	72	70	99	99	99
General support assistance	45	69	56	34	53	5	12	21	24
Other non-project	11	6	3	24	14	14	4	5	8
Project assistance	37	13	15	55	51	51	83	73	67
Multilateral	7	12	26	24	28	30	1	1	1

Source: OECD, *Aid From OPEC Countries*, 1983.

independent aid efforts could have combined their resources in a Gulf development institution. Even Kuwait, the most experienced Arab country in the aid business, could have joined in this effort. In fact, a Gulf development institution could have been established using the Kuwait Fund – the oldest and most experienced of OPEC institutions – as its core unit. Such a pooling of resources would have permitted the development of a larger pool of indigenous expertise. This in turn would have permitted OPEC institutions to stop looking almost exclusively to the traditional development establishment for guidance and inspiration. It would have become possible for them to engage both in independent thinking and in reaching out to, and making use of, other development experts and institutions with valuable insights into problems of development, but which have essentially remained at the periphery of the establishment.

Another negative aspect of OPEC aid has been the overwhelming dominance of security and political motives. This situation has led particularly to severe distortion in the pattern of OPEC aid's geographical distribution. In fact, a few Arab countries (for example, Egypt, Syria, Jordan, Sudan, Yemen, plus a few other Muslim countries) have received the bulk of OPEC aid.

This situation has been particularly unjustifiable in view of the criticism made by the OPEC countries – and rightly so – of other donors, to the effect that the latter have concentrated their aid on a few countries for political reasons. There has also been the criticism that some DAC donors have included in their ODA figures aid such as that to their overseas dependencies. This has been fair criticism. But by the same token, the OPEC countries should not have included purely politically-motivated contributions – such as those to the Arab confrontation states – in their ODA figures, just as French aid to its overseas territories should not have been included in French ODA figures.[37]

VII Impact on Third World Goals

Another criterion for evaluating OPEC aid is the extent to which it has contributed to the achievement of Third World objectives. This criterion is necessary since OPEC countries have portrayed both their development aid efforts and their role in the global North-South debate as being part and parcel (and even perhaps the prime mover) of Third World efforts to create a New International Economic Order

(NIEO). OPEC's role in North-South negotiations was discussed in Chapter 1, dealing with the historical context of OPEC aid. Chapter 5 will analyse to what extent (if at all) OPEC's choice of channels of aid has contributed to the achievement of Third World objectives, including those of systemic reform.

The rest of this chapter, therefore, will evaluate the impact of OPEC aid in advancing those objectives which, in the view of many experts, would improve the developing countries' position within the present system and could lead to its significant structural reform.

Alternative Development Institutions

As noted earlier, many non-establishment Third World experts have believed in the importance of breaking the monopoly of the existing international financial institutions. Thus they have suggested creating a Third World Development Bank and a Third World monetary organisation. The OPEC countries – or at least some of them – had the money and the opportunity to do so, but they failed. It is true that they finally established an OPEC Fund, but its resources and mode of operations have not qualified it as an institution committed to an innovative and different type of development. Also, it is true that at least the Arab countries created an Arab Monetary Fund, but its resources have not been sufficient to deal with the financial problems of its members. Quite the contrary, the principal surplus OPEC countries – through concessional contributions and other dealings such as purchase of World Bank bonds and substantial loans to the IMF – have tended to strengthen these institutions which are part and parcel of the present system. A good example of this OPEC practice is Saudi Arabia's $11 billion loan to the IMF.

OPEC Investments and Third World Self-reliance

Another way in which OPEC could have helped increase the level of collective Third World self-reliance would have been by investing in the industrial and other sectors of the developing countries. However, OPEC's record in this respect has not been satisfactory. For example, only 5 per cent of Kuwait's foreign investment has been in the developing – including Arab – countries. Excluding the Arab countries, the share of the developing countries has been only 1 per cent. Other OPEC surplus countries, including Saudi Arabia, have not fared better (see Chapter 3 regarding Saudi investments). Ironically, the same has been true of the so-called radical OPEC states.[38] It has of course been true that a number of infrastructural (including administrative and technical) deficiencies in the developing countries have created an unfavourable investment situation. But it has also been true that there has not been any coherent OPEC strategy to use its aid to rectify these deficiencies, although initially some experts in OPEC nations made a connection between aid and investment opportunities in the developing countries.

Another excuse of OPEC countries for not investing in the Third World has been that risks have been higher there. However, risks involved in investing in the industrialised countries have also been high. For example, most of OPEC investment in the industrialised countries has been in monetary assets whose value has been eroding as a result of high rates of inflation and sometimes currency devaluations. Moreover, as the seizure of the Iranian assets illustrated, in times of political crisis OPEC investments have been highly vulnerable to the retaliatory actions of the industrialised countries.

In sum, therefore, OPEC's investment policies, as was amply demonstrated in Chapters 2 and 3, have reflected their inherent weaknesses, contradictions and deficiencies, rather than any specific economic logic.

Economic and Trade Relations

Another way the OPEC countries could have contributed to the achievement of Third World objectives – including that of collective self-reliance – would have been through increased trade and other economic relations. Indeed, economic and trade relations between OPEC and certain Third World countries have expanded. The important question within the context of this study, however, is to what extent this expansion was the result of conscious OPEC strategy, and to what extent it reflected the price differences and the comparative advantage of some Third World countries in certain fields of economic activity. Another relevant question is to what extent did OPEC countries use aid to encourage trade.

One especially important aspect of this expanded relationship has been the export of large labour forces from the developing countries to the OPEC countries.

The bulk of this expatriate labour force has consisted of the nationals of Arab countries, but there have also been large numbers of Indians, Pakistanis, Turks, and East Asians – particularly Koreans – working in the OPEC countries. For example, 700,000 Indians, ranging from highly-skilled technicians and engineers to unskilled labourers, have been working in the OPEC countries. Remittances of these workers have constituted a major source of foreign exchange earnings for a number of Third World countries, but the developmental impact has been a matter of controversy.[39]

Between 1973 and 1980, an estimated $20-25 billion was transferred from OPEC countries to other Third World countries in worker remittances. Among recipients were Egypt, Pakistan, India, the YAR, South Korea, the Philippines, Sudan, Jordan, Bangladesh, Sri Lanka and Afghanistan. However, the volume of these remittances has fallen sharply since 1981 because of the oil glut and economic slowdown in OPEC countries.

As far as trade relations have been concerned, exports of a number of Third World countries to OPEC members have increased substantially: in the case of one country, South Korea, at a phenomenal rate of 7,558 per cent between 1972 and 1978. However, the countries that have fared well in their trade relations have been the most advanced of Third World countries, which had already achieved considerable growth in their manufacturing capacities. Moreover, trade between these countries and OPEC has reflected the comparative advantage of these countries in certain fields, translated into lower prices, rather than a conscious trade strategy on the part of OPEC countries.[40]

The Third World economic sector that has benefited most from the development boom in the OPEC countries has been that of the construction industries. However, these benefits have not been equally shared. One East Asian country – Korea – captured the bulk of OPEC's construction markets, particularly that of Saudi Arabia. Other Third World countries that have also fared well have been India, Pakistan, and Turkey. For example, in 1981 53 Turkish companies were handling work valued at an estimated $2,943 million, with Libya being their largest market, followed by Saudi Arabia and Iraq.[41]

But the least-developed Third World countries have not benefited from this trade boom. Concerning the specific use of aid for the expansion of trade – through procurement policies, for instance – there has been no evidence of a clear OPEC strategy to link aid and trade. There have been some exceptions, however. For example, the procurement provisions of BADEA have given priority to Third World bidders, provided that the difference in cost has not been higher than 10 per cent (see Chapter 5). In November 1981, the OPEC Fund for International Development also decided to give a preferential margin to Third World bidders.[42] And some OPEC countries (for example, Iran) have used aid to help develop certain extractive and manufacturing industries in some Third World countries whose products were to be exported, in this case to Iran.

With the end of the construction boom in OPEC countries, coupled with an increased level of industrialisation in these countries, the outlook for the expansion of OPEC-Third World trade has become even less promising. Thus, not only will those Third World countries that did well in trade with OPEC lose some of their export opportunities, but also OPEC-Third World economic relations will become more competitive rather than complementary in a number of fields.[43]

Table 4.12: OPEC Trade with Developed (Market) Countries

Year	OPEC Exports	OPEC Imports
1970	13,541	7,736
1972	20,871	11,686
1973	31,940	16,259
1974	96,547	29,044
1975	83,884	47,455
1976	100,711	54,769
1977	112,010	67,720
1978	110,432	79,647
1979	164,023	77,634
1980	226,990	110,880

Source: *United Nations Yearbook of International Trade Statistics*, 1980.

Table 4.13: OPEC Trade with Developing Countries[a]
(in $US millions, FOB)

Year	OPEC Exports	OPEC Imports
1970	3,465	1,065
1972	4,955	1,696
1973	8,329	2,690
1974	24,630	5,256
1975	24,291	6,611
1976	29,825	7,828
1977	33,529	10,698
1978	31,454	12,156
1979	49,262	15,537
1980	68,047	21,681

Note: a. Includes intra-OPEC trade.

Source: *United Nations Yearbook of International Trade Statistics*, 1980.

Improvement of Third World's Negotiating Position

As noted earlier, closer cooperation between OPEC and the Third World has been highly recommended by Third World and other experts in order to improve the Third World's bargaining position *vis-à-vis* the developed countries. Thus it is legitimate to ask whether OPEC has followed this advice and, in particular, whether it has used aid to achieve this purpose. Yet this aspect of OPEC-Third World relations is least amenable to accurate quantitative measurement and fair qualitative judgement, largely because of the difficulty in choosing the right measuring criteria.

For example, should the evaluation of OPEC's contributions be based on the number of concrete, positive results achieved by the Third World in negotiations with the developed countries? Or should it be based on the fact that, without OPEC, there might not have been any ongoing Third World-developed country negotiations at all? Furthermore, any fair assessment of OPEC's contributions should take into account the serious limitations on OPEC's power.

The fact is that OPEC's power has been 'too narrowly based on a single and exhaustible commodity – namely natural crude – and that this power is not readily fungible into other forms of power'. By contrast, the developed countries have

> a broader and deeper power base, insofar as their relative economic superiority derives from diversified economies and control of several key commodities, their sophisticated manpower, their superior technical knowledge in the military and civilian domains, including their capacity to develop alternative sources of energy.[44]

In addition, as demonstrated in Chapters 2 and 3, key OPEC members have had serious problems of internal and external security, making them vulnerable to a wide range of outside pressures. Therefore, the enormous task of coping with these pressures has both sapped a large part of their energies and resources, and has limited their freedom of action concerning the conduct of their international relations.

Likewise, these problems and the nature of means required to deal with them have made key OPEC members highly dependent on some developed countries, thus seriously limiting OPEC's capacity to extract concessions from them on issues of interest to the Third World.

Moreover, beyond a certain point pressure could only have a negative impact, in that it could provoke extreme reactions on the part of the developed countries. For example, at the height of the oil crisis in 1973-4, there was some consideration of the military option to deal with a possible cut-off of oil supplies.

Also, divergences of economic interests between key OPEC members and the Third World have compounded the negative impact of the above-mentioned factors. However, despite these limitations, OPEC could have done more to improve the Third World's bargaining position, particularly during the crucial period between 1974 and 1976 when the developed countries felt economically and emotionally vulnerable to OPEC actions. But the preoccupation of key OPEC members with other issues, plus their internal divisions and rivalries, has prevented them from doing so.

The OPEC countries have also failed to use aid to improve the Third World's position. For example, they have shied away from creating a credible alternative to the existing international development institutions. They have also refused, in the absence of equal financing from the developed countries, to finance schemes favoured by the Third World. Nor have they used aid to increase the level of the Third World's collective self-reliance. Of course, there was no guarantee that such measures would have led to a greater willingness on the part of the developed countries to make compromises. Yet such measures certainly would have improved the Third World's position and made such a development more likely.

VIII Conclusions

The most important conclusion to be drawn from the foregoing is the following: OPEC aid has fared well if it is judged in the aggregate and on the basis of such criteria as ODA as a percentage of GNP, the level of concessionality, and conditions attached to aid packages. Judging OPEC as a donor group, its aid as a percentage of its members' GNP has been very respectable and, indeed, has been much higher in these terms than that of the DAC countries. The level of concessionality of OPEC ODA has also been quite high; moreover, the bulk of OPEC aid has been in the form of cash grants or loans and has not been tied by source. A large part of it has also not been tied by end use.

However, the picture changes when OPEC aid is looked upon and judged from the perspective of individual recipients. This type of analysis reveals a number of characteristics that have reduced the value of OPEC aid. First has been its geographical distribution, which has been highly distorted in favour of a few countries, based on their political and security significance to OPEC countries. Second, the best aid terms have been extended to a few countries politically or otherwise important to OPEC members. Third, both the volume and the conditions of OPEC aid to other Third World countries – including the least-developed ones – have not been as satisfactory as they should have been.

A final conclusion is that, although OPEC has tried to place its aid within the context of the NIEO and other efforts by Third World countries to increase their level of collective self-reliance, its record does not support its claims. Nor, with few exceptions, have there been conscious OPEC efforts to use aid to increase trade and other economic relations between OPEC and the Third World, or intra-Third World trade in general. Rather, a number of OPEC practices have tended to strengthen the present international economic system. One of the most important of those practices has been the choice of channels for OPEC aid, their organisation, and their modes of operation, which are the subject of Chapter 5.

Notes

1. E.K. Hawkins, *The Principles of Development Aid*, Harmondsworth, England: Penguin Books, 1970, p. 25.
2. David Wall, *The Charity of Nations: The Political Economy of Foreign Aid*, New York: Basic Books, 1973, p. 3.
3. Robert E. Asher, *Grants, Loans and Local Currencies*, Washington, DC: The Brookings Institution, 1961, p. 6.
4. Ibid.
5. For details, see E.K. Hawkins, *Development Aid*, p. 30.
6. For a detailed discussion of these points, see David Wall, *The Charity of Nations*, pp. 100-3.
7. I.M.D. Little and J.M. Clifford, *International Aid*, Chicago: Aldine Publishing Company, 1966, p. 160.
8. For details, see J. Bhagwati, 'The Tying of Aid' in J. Bhagwati and R.S. Eckhaus (eds.), *Foreign Aid*, Harmondsworth, England: Penguin Books, p. 236-50.
9. Donor interests include: prevention of any deterioration of balance of payments, general support for exports, and the boosting of failing industries, that is, prevention of any real loss to the donor. The cost to the recipient of tied aid derives from higher prices of commodities, equipment, and services provided by an aid package. This in turn is the result of the fact that the suppliers in the donor country require a monopolistic advantage through procurement restrictions. For examples, see Ibid., p. 257; David Wall, *The Charity of Nations*, p. 21; and I.M.D. Little and J.M. Clifford, *International Aid*, p. 27.
10. E.K. Hawkins, *Development Aid*, pp. 84-6.

11. Most development assistance thus far has been tied to specific projects. For explanations of this situation, plus the merits and disadvantages of either approach, see Alan Carlin, *Project Versus Program Aid: From the Donor's Viewpoint*, Santa Monica: The RAND Corporation, 1965, p. 4; David Wall, *The Charity of Nations*, p. 106; and E.K. Hawkins, *Development Aid*, p. 88.

12. Food aid, however, since then 'has undergone considerable changes and has become an instrument of development agencies. For instance, it is no longer restricted to food in surplus supply, rather it uses exotic concoctions that have been developed especially for food aid, and do not exist outside its domain. Thus, the general trend had been to shift the emphasis from surplus disposal to development.' Christopher Stevens, *Food and the Developing World*, London: Croom Helm/ODI, 1979, p. 23.

13. For a description of methods, see Hartmuth Schneider, *Food Aid for Development*, Paris: OECD Development Center, 1978, pp. 23-4.

14. The World Food Programme was founded in 1963 under the umbrella of the UN and the FAO, partly as a US device to encourage burden-sharing. Following the 1974 World Food Conference, the WFP's governing body was reconstituted as the Committee on Food Aid Policies and Programmes with a mandate 'to evolve and coordinate short-term and long-term food aid policies'. Christopher Stevens, *Food and the Developing World*, p. 398.

15. Some experts go as far as to suggest that: 'Dumping of large quantities of low-priced American grain on under-developed countries makes it economically impossible for the small domestic producer to compete.' See F.M. Lappe and J. Collins, *Food First: Beyond the Myth of Scarcity*, Boston: Houghton Mifflin, 1977, p. 335.

16. For instance, a former executive director of the World Food Programme has argued that 'Food aid is not second class aid when people need food, only food will serve their needs, and direct distribution of the food is often the most effective way of meeting these needs.' *WFP News*, Rome, Oct.-Dec. 1977, p. 3.

17. Christopher Stevens, *Food and the Developing World*, p. 209.

18. Jahangir Amuzegar, *Technical Assistance in Theory and Practice: The Case of Iran*, New York: Praeger, 1966, pp. 30-5.

19. On the cost of technical assistance, the following statement is illuminating: 'Some countries [in Africa] have paid $50,000 for surveys which a good economic journalist could have written in less than a month.' I.M.D. Little, *Aid to Africa: An Appraisal of UK Policy to Aid Africa South of the Sahara*, New York: Macmillan, 1966, p. 55. On the appropriate nature of most technical assistance, political and economic dependence, and general issues, see also G.K. Helleiner, 'International Technology Issues: Southern Needs and Northern Responses' in J. Ramesh and Charles Weiss, Jr (eds.), *Mobilizing Technology for World Development*, New York: Praeger, 1979, pp. 84-98; and 'France's Role in Africa: The Colonial Master Who Didn't Go Home', *The Wall Street Journal*, 22 July 1981, pp. 1 & 26.

20. David Wall, *The Charity of Nations*, p. 132.

21. They argue that, for this to be true, multilateral agencies 'would require an elected authority with supra-national power to raise resources [for example, through an international taxation system] and to distribute them'. John White, *Regional Development Banks*, London: Overseas Development Institute, 1970, p. 12.

22. Ibid., p. 16.

23. Needless to say, many Third World experts have not accepted this premise, as the following illustrates: 'Much of what goes on in the name of international cooperation and interdependence is heavily loaded in favor of the North. If the world community desires to promote genuine interdependence there will

have to be a deliberate tilt toward developing nations. Such a tilting would require: (a) removal of those aspects of international economic relations which act as restraints on the development of the South and (b) willingness on the part of the North to make the "interdependence" concept not a mere cover for projecting its own interests but rather a means to bring about a genuine complementarity of Northern and Southern interests.' Samuel L. Parmar, 'Self-Reliant Development in an Interdependent World' in Guy Erb and Valeriana Kallab (eds.), *Beyond Dependency*, Washington, DC: Overseas Development Council, 1975, p. 17.

24. Ponna Wignaraja, 'An Annotated Agenda for the Discussion on New Development Strategies,' in 'The Development of Development Thinking', *Liaison Bulletin*, no. 1, Paris: Development Center of the OECD, 1977, p. 38.

25. Rather, they have maintained that 'The international crisis is that of a system of unequal relations between a few dominant countries and the majority of dominated. The crisis in institutions results from their maladjustment to a world undergoing rapid change. The situation cannot be properly understood, much less transformed, unless it is seen as a whole: in the final analysis the crises are the result of a system of exploitation which profits a power structure based largely in the industrialised world although not without annexes in the Third World.' 'Another Development', the 1975 Dag Hammarskjöld Foundation's Report on Development and International Cooperation, pp. 38-9. See also Ibid., pp. 65-6.

26. Ibid. p. 14. The importance of increased collective self-reliance was officially recognised by the Third World countries, and indeed was made one of the principal steps towards the establishment of the NIEO. Following that decision, the Group of 77 convened a conference in Mexico City in 1976 on Economic Cooperation (ECDC) among Developing Countries. Later, at the request of the Group of 77, a new main committee on ECDC was established within UNCTAD in 1978.

The next step in this direction was the ministerial meeting of the Group of 77 in 1979 in Arusha, Tanzania. This conference adopted the Arusha Program for Collective Self-Reliance, which included a First Short/Medium-Term Action Plan for Global Priorities on Economic Cooperation among Developing Countries. For more detail, see: 'Assessment of the Progress Made in the Establishment of the New International Economic Order and Appropriate Action for the Promotion of the Economic Development of the Developing Countries and International Economic Cooperation', Document A/S-11/6, 25 July 1980; and 'Arusha Programme for Collective Self-Reliance and Framework for Negotiation', 1979, TD/236.

27. 'Another Development', pp. 67-87.

28. See, for instance, George Corm, 'Gestes Symboliques et Refus Persistant', *Le Monde Diplomatique*, September 1981, p. 3. In addition: 'Although everybody at G-77 did their best to overlook the issue, it was apparent that some Middle Eastern OPEC countries were reluctant participants in the Conference. Even before Caracas there was grumbling about the venue. Middle Eastern delegates could not understand why the meeting did not take place in New York. These complaints, however, hid a deeper source of resentment: the feeling of OPEC members that other Third World countries would attempt to place too heavy a burden on their financial surpluses.' 'South-South: A Necessary Alliance', *South: the Third World Magazine*, no. 9, July 1981, p. 17.

29. 'The Important but Elusive Issue of Aid Effectiveness', *DAC Aid Review 1980*, pp. 56-7. Among the criticisms of aid provided on this basis have been the following: 'Such allocations may overtax the absorptive capacity of the recipients, thereby entailing waste and inviting corruption. The concentration of very large

quantities of aid on small populations may entrench levels of per capita income so that it would be very hard for the recipients, unassisted, to sustain any time soon. Thus, despite efforts and intent to build self-reliance, over-concentration can prolong dependency.' Ibid., p. 56.

30. These principles are included in the Aid Implementation Guidelines adopted by the DAC High Level Meeting of November 1979. *Annual DAC Review 1980*, pp. 58-9.

31. Some experts – with links to OPEC member countries – have argued that 'OPEC aid should not be related to oil price increases', since 'the increase in the price of a commodity is due to supply and demand developments'. See Hossein G. Askari, 'OPEC and International Aid: An Appraisal', *SAIS Review*, Winter 1981-2, No. 3, p. 137. The important point to emphasise is that this argument runs against the logic used by the Third World that demands the protection of Third World countries from sharp fluctuations in their terms of trade – logic which, ironically, OPEC had earlier used in trying to protect its members against unilateral actions of the oil companies in setting the price of oil.

32. Paul Hallwood and Stuart Sinclair, *Oil, Debt & Development: OPEC in the Third World*, London: George Allen & Unwin, 1981, p. 107.

33. OPEC countries have believed that the percentage of GNP is not an appropriate standard for judging their aid performance, since a large portion of their national product – oil – is not derived from a sustainable source. Moreover, they have argued that they face the uncertain future of transforming their oil wealth into productive assets that could sustain their economies in the future. Thus they have argued that a measure of OPEC national product – comparable to that of the DAC – could be derived by 'estimating the highest value of long-run consumption that can be maintained when oil runs out'. Hossein G. Askari, 'OPEC and International Aid'. See also Ibrahim F.I. Shihata and Robert Mabro, *The OPEC Aid Record*, Vienna: The OPEC Special Fund, 1978, p. 5.

34. Even in the case of countries with a high absorptive capacity (such as Iran) with large military forces, foreign aid sometimes was a cheaper way of achieving national objectives. Note the Shah's expression that Iran either had to give aid to Pakistan or maintain a new armoured division in Baluchistan at the cost of $2 billion (see Chapter 3).

35. For example, between 1974 and 1981, co-financing amounted to 35 per cent of total OPEC commitments. Among the disadvantages of co-financing have been the 'danger of encouraging or participating in excessively-ambitious projects. . .' and imposing significant administrative burdens on recipient countries. 'The Growing Importance of Co-financing in Funding Development Projects', *The OECD Observer*, no. 117, July 1982, pp. 31-3.

36. 'Iraqi Fund President Gives Views on OPEC and the Third World', *OPEC Bulletin*, vol. X, no. 18, September 1980, p. 19.

37. Perhaps for this reason Kuwait has decided not to include in its ODA figures its contributions to the confrontation states. *DAC Review*, 1982, p. 157.

38. Libya's most significant foreign investment was the purchase of 9 per cent of Fiat with an option to increase its ownership up to 15 per cent. Libya's financial exposure in Italy has been around $1.2 billion. Libya has also made term loans to Spain and Greece. For a detailed study of Arab investment, see John Law, *Arab Investors*.

39. For a detailed study of this issue, see J. Birks and S. Sinclair, *International Migration and Development in the Arab Region*, Geneva: International Labour Office, 1980.

40. Paul Hallwood and Stuart Sinclair, *Oil, Debt & Development*, pp. 130-6. In fact, one reason OPEC countries turned to Third World countries in the field of construction, for instance, was because they became frustrated by the high prices charged by the industrialised countries. Ibid., pp. 140-3.

41. *MEED*, vol. 25, no. 6, 6 February 1981, pp. 2-3.

42. *MEES*, vol. XXVI, no. 7, 29 November 1982, p. B5 and OPEC Fund Annual Report 1981, p. 24. Certain practices of the OPEC Fund also have marginally contributed to an increased intra-Third World trade. For instance, in 1980 the Fund contributed $25 million to the International Emergency Food Reserve (IEFR) for the period 1981-2 for the purpose of purchasing foodstuffs from food surplus developing countries (principally Argentina) which offer concessional terms.

43. Hallwood and Sinclair, *Oil, Debt and Development*.

44. Zuhayr Mikdashi, *OPEC States and Third World Solidarity*, Vienna: OPEC Fund, 1980, p. 15.

5 CHANNELS OF OPEC AID

The last four chapters demonstrated how intra-OPEC divisions and rivalries, coupled with the serious shortcomings and internal contradictions of its members, have prevented them from establishing a sizeable collective OPEC aid institution. They also demonstrated how the imperatives of intra-Arab politics – and in particular the requirements of Arab unity – have led to the creation of a number of multilateral Arab institutions, and how the requirements of Islamic solidarity have resulted in the creation of a multilateral Islamic institution. Beyond these efforts, however, OPEC aid has essentially been disbursed bilaterally, either directly by ministeries of finance or through special development institutions.

In addition, OPEC countries have contributed to existing international development and financial institutions. They have also contributed to other channels of a temporary nature that were created immediately after the 1973 oil crisis in order to meet certain urgent needs. At the time, other schemes of a more permanent nature were suggested; however, they did not materialise because of a cool reception by key OPEC countries.

The purpose of this chapter is therefore to analyse these diverse channels of OPEC aid, focusing not on their organisational aspects – since organisationally they have closely resembled one another – but rather on such issues as whether they have been political and have principally served donor interests, and what sort of development strategies they have promoted. This chapter will also evaluate the implications of OPEC's choices of channels of aid in terms of its commitment to the achievement of Third World goals, including that of establishing a New International Economic Order.

PART ONE: MULTILATERAL CHANNELS

I International Emergency Organisations

One consequence of OPEC's actions in 1973 was the development of a number of emergency mechanisms to deal with the immediate financial problem of the non-oil developing countries. The following are the most important of these mechanisms.

The United Nations Special Fund

On 1 May 1974, the UN General Assembly adopted resolution 3202 (S.VI), establishing a Special Fund to provide emergency relief and development assistance to those countries most seriously affected (MSAs) by the global economic crisis prompted by the oil revolution. Initially, however, the problems of the MSAs were a matter of controversy between developing and developed countries, and only after much debate did the developing countries succeed in including this subject among the issues to be discussed in the context of efforts to establish a New International Economic Order.[1]

Later, when the creation of a special fund was suggested in the UN, it was not received with enthusiasm by the industrialised countries. They argued that the existing international institutions could achieve the purposes of the Special Fund.[2] When they finally agreed to the creation of such a fund, they insisted that it should be financed through voluntary contributions by the industrialised countries and other potential donors – meaning the OPEC countries.[3]

However, for lack of resources, the UN Special Fund never really got off the ground, since during the four years of its existence only two countries, Norway and Venezuela, made contributions to it.[4] Lack of resources finally forced the Fund's Board of Governors to suspend operations in 1978, and they made the following recommendation to the General Assembly:

> The activities of the United Nations' Special Fund should be suspended *ad-interim* since the Fund cannot carry out its main function of providing assistance to the most seriously affected countries because the situation in regard to contributions to the Fund continues to be unfavourable and does not seem to improve in the foreseeable future.[5]

The immediate reason behind the UNSF's failure was thus the lack of contributions, resulting from disagreements both between OPEC and industrialised countries and among OPEC members themselves, regarding the best and most equitable way to assist developing countries. For example, the OPEC countries were determined to resist efforts by industrialised countries to attribute the global economic crisis to OPEC's actions and to impose on it the sole responsibility for assisting the developing countries. For their part, the industrialised countries refused to increase their aid efforts significantly, for a variety of reasons (for example, some genuine domestic economic problems and a belief that OPEC countries, with their monetary surplus, should provide the bulk of aid). Moreover, the industrialised countries were not well-disposed to the idea of yet another UN agency.

The preference of OPEC's Arab members for giving aid bilaterally or through collective Arab institutions also contributed to the UNSF's failure since, with both Arab and industrialised countries' being cool to the idea of an international institution, other OPEC countries joined in opting for a bilateral approach to aid.

It is difficult to judge what the response of the OPEC countries might have been had the industrialised countries responded positively. As noted in earlier chapters, there were strong impulses within OPEC countries moving them towards a bilateral and regional approach to aid. Nevertheless, they might have reacted more positively to the UNSF had the industrialised countries also been so inclined.

The United Nations Special Account

As part of the UN's special programme for Emergency Relief and Development Assistance, the General Assembly in resolution 3202 (S.VI) asked the Secretary General as a first step to launch an emergency operation to provide 'timely and urgent relief to the most seriously affected developing countries with the aim of maintaining unimpaired their essential imports during the coming 12 months'.[6] The account was to be used principally for high priority requirements, such as supplying food to countries facing grave shortages and fertilisers to the most seriously affected countries.[7]

The response to the Secretary General's call for contributions to the emergency operation was more positive. But even here most countries preferred to give aid bilaterally or through other agencies rather than through the UN Special Account.

The IMF Oil Facility

Another emergency financing mechanism created to deal with the problems caused by sharp oil price increases was the IMF Oil Facility.[8] The idea of an oil facility to help both the industrialised and the developing countries cope with their balance of payments problems was first introduced at a meeting of the IMF's Committee of 20 in Rome in 1974 by its Director General.[9] Following a number of studies and visits by the Directors General of the IMF and the World Bank, the idea of an oil facility was approved at the June 1974 meeting of the Committee of 20, and became operational shortly after that.[10]

The IMF Oil Facility was a temporary instrument intended to deal with the unusual emergency situation of the time. In turn, the temporary nature of the facility affected its rules of operations to varying degrees during its life span. For example, in general the conditions of access to the facility's resources were easier than those of the regular IMF loans, but they varied from one year to another depending on circumstances.

Thus, in 1974 the Oil Facility was principally viewed as an anticyclical operation, and therefore its conditions of access were more relaxed. In 1975, the facility was viewed more as a medium-term device and – while all its conditions of access were still more relaxed than were those for regular IMF loans – the borrowing countries had to satisfy the IMF that they had taken necessary measures to deal with their balance of payments problems.

The Oil Facility was originally designed to be financed by borrowing from the OPEC countries, but some industrialised countries have also lent to it.[11] Interest was to be paid by the Fund at an annual rate of 7 per cent, and repayment was to be completed within an outside period of three to seven years from the date of borrowing. Provision was also made for early repayment under certain circumstances.

In order for a country to borrow from the Oil Facility, the Fund had to be satisfied that it needed assistance because of increases in the cost of petroleum and petroleum products and because it had a balance of payments need. Also, a borrower had 'to cooperate with the Fund to find appropriate solutions for its balance of payments problems'.[12]

Also, the total amount of a member's purchases (borrowing) was not to be in excess of the increase in the cost of the member's net imports of petroleum and petroleum products over the similar cost in 1972, minus an amount equivalent to 10 per cent of the member's reserves at the end of 1973 adjusted for variability of exports, and subject to the limitation that the amount outstanding under the Oil Facility did not exceed 75 per cent of the quotas.

Conditions of the 1975 Oil Facility differed in a number of ways from the Oil Facility for 1974. For example, in 1975 more weight was given to a member's quota in calculating its access to the facility and less weight to the increase in its oil import costs. Furthermore, stricter conditionality was applied to the 1975 facility. For instance, unlike the 1974 facility where a member was required only to consult with the Fund on its balance of payments prospects and policies – including the effect of policies adopted in relation to the oil problem – the use of the 1975 facility required the purchasing member to describe its policies to achieve medium-term solutions to its balance of payments problems and entailed an assessment by the Fund of these policies.[13]

In general, loans were to be repaid – or in IMF parlance, 'repurchased' – as soon as the problem for which the purchase had been made was overcome or in 16 equal quarterly instalments, to be completed not later than seven years after the purchase.

The IMF Oil Facility was discontinued once its resources were exhausted.

The IMF Subsidy Account

In view of the non-concessionary nature of loans made by the Oil Facility, the IMF decided to establish a subsidy account to help reduce the burden of the Fund's most seriously affected members. A proposal to this effect was endorsed at the January 1975 meeting of the Fund's Interim Committee in the following terms:

> In connection with the oil facility, the committee fully endorsed the recommendation of the Managing Director that a special account should be established with appropriate contributions by oil exporting and industrial countries, and possibly by other members capable of contributing, and that the Fund should administer this account in order to reduce for the most seriously affected members the burden of interest payable by them under the oil facility.[14]

Following this recommendation, the account was established on 1 August 1975, by a decision of the Fund's Executive Directors.

Later, the Fund solicited contributions from all members not included in the UN list of most seriously affected countries. Finally, 24 countries contributed to the subsidy account, of which only three – Iran, Saudi Arabia and Venezuela – were members of OPEC.[15]

The objective of the Subsidy Account was to reduce the effective rate of annual charges payable on drawings under the 1975 Oil Facility by about 5 per cent per annum, thus reducing the average cost of using that facility by the MSA members from 7.71 per cent to 2.71 per cent per annum, and implying a grant element on Oil Facility purchases for these countries of 28 per cent.

The Executive Board in 1978 proposed to the contributors that the list of beneficiaries be expanded to include Grenada, Malawi, Morocco, Papua New Guinea, the Philippines, Zaire, and Zambia. However, the

Table 5.1: Use of IMF Oil Facility in 1974

	Number of Purchases	Amount Purchased (million SDRs)
Industrialised countries		675.000
Italy	2	675.000
Other developed countries		802.700
Cyprus	2	8.100
Greece	3	103.500
Iceland	2	17.200
New Zealand	2	109.300
Spain	1	296.200
Turkey	1	113.200
Yugoslavia	3	155.200
Developing countries		1,021.551
Bangladesh	3	51.500
Burundi	1	1.200
Cameroon	1	4.620
Central African Republic	3	3.300
Chad	2	2.205
Chile	2	118.500
Costa Rica	2	18.837
El Salvador	2	17.890
Fiji	1	0.340
Guinea	1	3.510
Haiti	3	4.800
Honduras	1	16.785
India	1	200.000
Israel	1	62.000
Ivory Coast	1	11.170
Kenya	3	36.000
Korea	4	100.000
Malagasy Republic	3	14,300
Mali	2	5.000
Nicaragua	2	15.500
Pakistan	3	125.000
Panama	1	7.370
Senegal	1	15.525
Sierra Leone	2	4.914
Sri Lanka	3	43.500
Sudan	2	28.710
Tanzania	3	31.500
Uganda	2	19.200
Uruguay	2	46.575
Yemen, People's Democratic Republic	2	11.800
TOTAL		2,499.251

Source: *The IMF Survey*, 14 April 1975, p. 98.

Table 5.2: IMF Subsidy Account Contributions (in millions of SDRs)

Contributors	Anticipated Total Contributions	Contributions Received as of 30 April 1980
Australia	5.700	5.700
Austria	2.300	2.300
Belgium	5.600	4.200
Brazil	1.850	1.850
Canada	9.500	9.500
Denmark	2.200	1.270
Finland	1.600	1.200
France	12.900	9.773
Germany, Fed Rep of	13.700	13.720
Greece	0.600	0.597
Iran	6.000	6.000
Italy	8.600	8.600
Japan	10.300	8.054
Luxembourg	0.110	0.108
Netherlands	6.000	6.000
New Zealand	1.700	1.187
Norway	2.100	2.100
Saudi Arabia	40.000	40.000
South Africa	1.350	1.350
Spain	3.400	2.450
Sweden	2.800	2.800
Switzerland	3.285	3.285
United Kingdom	12.050	10.573
Venezuela	6.000	6.000
Yugoslavia	0.900	0.900
Total	160.545	149.517

Source: *IMF Annual Report*, 1980.

use by these countries of the Subsidy Account's funds was made conditional on the account's having any surplus.

The account registered a surplus of SDR 44 million, which normally should have been disbursed to the seven members which became eligible after the November 1978 decision of the Executive Board. But since this amount was not sufficient to pay the additional beneficiaries at the full 5 per cent rate over the life of the subsidy account (1976-83), the Executive Board decided to retain the bulk of the surplus in the account to earn investment income, and to begin payments to the additional beneficiaries by subsidising the cost to those members

Table 5.3: IMF Subsidy Account: Total Use of 1975 Oil Facility by Beneficiaries, and Subsidy Payments in the Financial Year Ended 30 April 1980 (in millions of SDRs)

	Total Use of 1975 Oil Facility	Subsidy at 5 per cent Amount	Cumulative to date
Original Beneficiaries:			
Subsidy for financial year ended 30 April 1980			
Bangladesh	40.47	1.68	8.36
Cameroon	11.79	0.50	2.40
Central African Republic	2.66	0.11	0.56
Egypt	31.68	1.40	6.30
Haiti	4.14	0.17	0.86
India	201.34	–	26.95
Ivory Coast	10.35	–	1.42
Kenya	27.93	1.10	5.93
Mali	3.99	0.18	0.79
Mauritania	5.32	0.23	1.08
Pakistan	111.01	1.38	23.48
Senegal	9.91	0.38	2.15
Sierra Leone	4.97	0.22	0.99
Sri Lanka	34.13	1.43	7.01
Sudan	18.30	0.75	3.85
Tanzania	20.61	0.76	4.50
Western Samoa	0.42	0.02	0.09
Yemen, People's Democratic Republic of	12.02	0.50	2.47
Total	551.03	13.79	99.17
Additional Beneficiaries:			
Subsidy for financial years ended 30 April, 1975/6 and 1976/7			
Grenada	0.49	0.03	0.03
Malawi	3.73	0.24	0.24
Morocco	18.00	0.89	0.89
Papua New Guinea	14.80	0.80	0.80
Philippines	152.03	10.44	10.44
Zaïre	32.53	1.59	1.59
Total	221.58	13.98	13.98

Source: *IMF Annual Report*, 1980.

of using the 1975 Oil Facility for the financial years 1975/6 and 1976/7. Thus, SDR 14 million was paid to six of the seven additional beneficiaries.[16]

The IMF Trust Fund

The idea of creating a special trust fund that could provide additional highly-concessional resources to assist the developing countries in dealing with their balance of payments problems was first discussed at the Joint Development Committee of IMF-IBRD at its January 1975 meeting, and the Trust Fund was finally established on 5 May 1976.[17]

The primary objective of the Trust Fund is to provide special balance of payments assistance to the developing countries that are members of the IMF.

The resources of the Trust Fund have been provided by the profits accruing from the sale of gold, and by any other financing which might be available from voluntary contributions or from loans.[18] Thus far, the bulk of the Trust Fund's resources has come from the profits from the sale, in public auction, of 25 million ounces of gold, after the deduction of a proportion of the profits or surplus value of the gold corresponding to the share of developing countries in Fund quotas on 31 August 1975.[19] The amounts deducted have been directly transferred to each developing country in proportion to its quota.

The operations of the Trust Fund were to be divided into two separate periods of two years each.[20] Total profits from the sale of 25 million ounces of gold during the two periods amounted to US $4.6 billion, of which US $1.3 billion was distributed directly to the 106 developing-country members. The remainder of the profits, together with interest income and other transfers to the trust, amounted to SDR 2.9 billion at the end of July 1980. A total of over SDR 2.1 billion has already been used to make loan disbursements to eligible low income members that have qualified for balance of payments assistance.[21]

The eight eligible OPEC countries – Iran, Iraq, Saudi Arabia, Kuwait, Libya, the UAE and Venezuela – decided to make irrevocable transfer to the Trust Fund of their share of profits from the gold sale. However, only six of these eight countries have fully transferred their shares. Libya has transferred only one-fourth of its profit share. And Iran in June 1980 advised the Trust Fund that it wished to receive its profit share in full. The total value of irrevocable transfers by the OPEC members amounted to $US 122 million.[22]

The terms of loans from the Trust Fund have been highly concessional,

Table 5.4: IMF Trust Fund: Loan Disbursements and Distributions of Profits from Gold Sales, by Region, 1977-80 (in millions of SDRs)

	Financial Years Ended April 30				
	1977	1978	1979	1980	Total
Africa	20.0	130.0	286.5	660.5	1,097.0
Asia	9.1	199.0	322.0	635.3	1,165.4
Europe	–	16.7	8.6	61.3	86.6
Middle East	1.6	61.5	87.4	185.1	335.6
Western Hemisphere	1.0	83.6	36.1	288.7	409.4
Total	31.7	490.8	740.6	1,830.9	3,094.0

Source: *IMF Annual Report*, 1980.

Table 5.5: Transfers of Profits from IMF Gold Sales to the Trust Fund by OPEC Members (in thousands of $US)

	First Period	Second Period	TOTAL
Iraq	4,871	12,438	17,309
Kuwait	2,912	7,436	10,348
S.P. Libyan A.J.	964	2,842	3,805
Qatar	888	2,268	3,155
Saudi Arabia	5,994	15,306	21,300
United Arab Emirates	666	1,700	2,367
Venezuela	14,756	37,681	52,437
Total	31,049	79,671	110,721

Source: *OPEC Fund Annual Report*, 1980.

and have carried an interest rate of one half of one per cent annually. The loans have been required to be repaid in ten equal semiannual instalments after a five-year grace period. In order to qualify for loans from the Trust Fund, the members have had to satisfy the trustee (IMF) that they have had a need for balance of payments assistance and have been making reasonable efforts to strengthen their balance of payments positions.

World Bank Third Window

Another emergency instrument designed to assist the poor countries in coping with the problems of oil price increases was the World Bank's Third Window, which started operations in July 1975 but lasted only one year. The Third Window was in fact an interest-subsidy account similar to those which had been proposed in the past.[23] It was financed by voluntary contributions, including those by the following OPEC countries: Qatar, Kuwait, Saudi Arabia, the UAE and Venezuela. Its resources amounted to $447.8 million, much less than the $1 billion that the Bank had hoped to raise.

The Third Window functioned as an intermediate financing facility with terms softer than bank loans but harder than IDA credits. Its interest rates were 4 to 4.5 per cent below those of bank loans, with a maturity of 25 years and a seven-year grace period – implying a grant element of about 40 per cent, accounting for inflation. The primary beneficiaries of Third Window loans were India, 30 per cent; Pakistan, 10 per cent; and Egypt, 10 per cent. Other recipients were Korea, Sudan, El Salvador, the Philippines and Botswana. The very poorest countries could not afford Third Window loans but benefited from it indirectly since it released some IDA funds for lending to them. In fact, 10 per cent of all IDA funds released as a result of the Third Window went to the poorest countries.

II The United Nations and Other International Organisations

The United Nations Development Programme (UNDP)

UNDP was established in 1965 by General Assembly Resolution 2020 (XX) and resulted from the merging of the Expanded Programme for Technical Assistance and the UN Special Fund. It has been the principal UN development agency.

UNDP's internal organisation during the past 25 years has undergone considerable expansion and change, reflecting its enlarged scope of operations. Its activities have grown to encompass the complete spectrum of needs for resource management and utilisation. The main areas of UNDP's activities have been locating and assessing development resources, activating resources, and allocating resources wisely. Within this general scope of operations, principal UNDP objectives have been to increase available supplies of nourishing food, pure water, and energy; to foster basic health, literacy and employment; to help establish a New International Economic Order (NIEO); and to strengthen technical and economic cooperation among developing countries.

Given the importance attached by developing countries to the establishment of an NIEO, a summary follows of UNDP activities in this regard, prepared by the organisation itself:

> . . . In May 1974, the UN General Assembly called for establishment of a New International Economic Order designed to remove some of

the external barriers to development progress that were making an already difficult climb into an obstacle race as well. By 1977, UNDP had become directly involved in 13 priority areas of the NIEO Programme of Action. And, by mid-1979, UNDP had approved 3,037 projects with a total value on completion of $2,610 million in four spearhead NIEO fields – industrialisation, international trade, the transfer of science and technology, and transport and communications. In fact, as the material immediately following indicates, most of the new tasks assumed and new directions taken by UNDP since 1974 are contributing at the operational level to accomplishing key NIEO goals.

A major component of NIEO is *technical cooperation among developing countries* – and here UNDP has been acting as a bellwether virtually throughout the past decade. Major initiatives included establishment of a computerised referral and exchange service covering facilities and expertise at the disposal of developing countries and UNDP's organisation of a global TCDC conference which produced a major Plan of Action for implementing this crucial concept. During 1979, the Governing Council authorised use of up to $1 million from the Programme Reserve to stimulate additional TCDC activities, and some 2.8 million to expand and strengthen UNDP's Special Unit for TCDC. A high-level governmental meeting on UN system efforts to foster TCDC is scheduled for May 1980. Meanwhile, UNDP is expanding its support for projects with a TCDC content – such as, for example, the cooperative effort among 33 African countries to improve sugar production, processing and marketing.

Closely allied with TCDC is ECDC – *economic cooperation among developing countries*, a field of increasing concentration throughout the decade for UNDP-assisted intercountry and interregional activities. Particularly illustrative is the Programme's collaboration with UNCTAD in formulating a wide-ranging network of proposals to strengthen the basic position of the developing countries on world markets. Projects envisioned for UNDP backing would aim at helping these countries to reduce tariff and non-tariff barriers among their own ranks, promote multi-national production facilities and marketing enterprises, carry out joint research on increased earnings from commodities exports, build up shipping and other transport networks and stimulate capital flows for trade expansion.

Mobilisation of Resources and Programming of Projects for Large Scale New Cooperative Efforts. These include the international Drinking Water Supply and Sanitation Decade whose goal is to make safe, clean water available to everyone on *earth by 1990 – and the Interim Fund for Science and Technology* to which 35 countries have thus far pledged $45.7 million toward a target of $250 million for projects that will help strengthen Third World capabilities for research and development.[24]

UNDP's operating methods have also undergone a number of changes, to create a more coherent process for identifying and meeting the needs of developing countries. These changes have also led to more planning at the regional level and greater emphasis on the poorer countries.[25]

The contributions of OPEC countries to UNDP Associated Programmes have not been significant. In fact, even in 1980 the bulk of voluntary contributions to UNDP was made by a 'rather small minority of the industrialised countries'.[26]

OPEC member countries' contributions to UNDP have also been small compared to their contributions to other multilateral institutions. For example, total OPEC members' contributions to UNDP amounted to $12.5 million in 1977 and $19.4 million in 1978, falling to $9.2 million in 1980 and $9.7 million in 1981. But this low level of OPEC members' contributions has been somewhat remedied by the OPEC Fund's contributions, within the context of the latter's arrangements with UNDP in the field of technical assistance.

Under these arrangements, the OPEC Fund contributed $40 million to UNDP between 1977 and 1980. Another agreement was reached between the two organisations, according to which the OPEC Fund contributed a further $50 million to UNDP for 1980-2. But given the fact that the policies of UNDP have been geared more towards an NIEO, plus the fact that its operational system has been more representative of the Third World, OPEC's total contributions could have been higher. In turn, this situation illustrates the discrepancy between OPEC's rhetoric and its actions.

The United Nations Capital Development Fund (UNCDF)

Neither the resources, range of operation, nor the extremely meagre level of OPEC contributions justifies the inclusion of the UNCDF as a channel of OPEC aid. Yet its inclusion is still necessary, given the history of the Fund and the reasons behind its failure to become the

Table 5.6: UNDP Expenditures by Region in 1980 (in $US millions)

Region	Amount	%
Latin America	115.3	17
Africa	222.3	33.5
Europe	22.2	3
Asia/Pacific	207.1	31.5
Arab States	81.5	12
Interregional/Global	21.5	3

Source: *UNDP At A Glance*, 1981.

Table 5.7: UNDP Expenditures by Sector in 1980 (in $US millions)

Sector	Amount	%
Natural Resources	76.9	11
Transport & Communications	89.8	13.5
Trade & Development Finance	15.5	2
Human Settlements	14.4	2
Health	29.5	4
Employment	40.5	6
Science & Technology	25.7	4
Social Conditions & Equity	5.3	1
Education	47.1	7
Industry	66.4	10
Agriculture, Forestry & Fisheries	170.8	25.5
Development Policies	78.8	12.5
Culture	6.1	1
Others	2.0	0.5

Source: *UNDP At A Glance*, 1981.

primary multilateral institution to provide concessional capital to the developing countries. Moreover the fact that OPEC countries – with their tremendous financial resources – did nothing to give new life to the Fund further illustrates the discrepancies between OPEC's rhetoric and its actions.

Historical Background. UNCDF is almost as old as the United Nations itself. In fact, the idea of an UNCDF can be traced to the Third Session of the Sub-commission on Economic Development (March-April 1949). At that meeting, the Sub-commission's chairman from India suggested that a United Nations economic agency be established with the objective of providing financing for those schemes that would not be financed from the country's own resources and for which loans could not be obtained on strict business principles.[27] However, that proposal and a host of others were defeated by the persistent opposition of the developed countries, and it was not until 1966 that the General Assembly passed a resolution establishing the Fund.

In the meantime, a number of institutions, within both the UN and Bretton Woods systems, were established in partial response to developing-country demands and pressures which grew increasingly strong during the decades of the 1950s and 1960s.

Among these institutions were the UN Special Fund and the UN Expanded Programme for Technical Assistance – which later were merged to form UNDP – and the International Development Agency and International Finance Corporation, affiliated with the World Bank. However, even after having been legally established, UNCDF did not become operational for almost another ten years for lack of financial resources.

This situation also led to subtle but important changes in the legal and administrative status of the Fund. For example, according to UNGA Resolution 1186 (XXI) which established the Fund, UNCDF was an independent UN organ, and its Executive Board – through its managing director – reported directly to ECOSOC and through it to the General Assembly. In 1967, the Fund's management was entrusted to the UNDP Administrator on a provisional basis. However, the dependence of UNDCF on UNDP has continued until now. Although technically independent, UNCDF has been under UNDP's supervision. Thus, the UNDP administrator has performed the functions of the UNCDF's managing director, and the governing council has performed the functions of the Fund's executive board. In 1973, the General Assembly appraised the decision of the UNDP governing council – which itself was based on UNCTAD Resolution G2 (III) of 19 May 1972 – that the UNCDF be used to serve the least developed countries and those countries for which the General Assembly in its relevant resolutions had requested the granting of similar treatment in terms of development assistance.

Activities. In 1980, after five years of operations, the Fund had committed a total of $165.2 million to development projects. Cumulative disbursements of the Fund, however, were only $143.9 million.[28]

Most of UNCDF's resources are allocated to the rural sector with emphasis on:

1. *Basic Social Infrastructure*, such as provision of drinking water, schools and training institutions, health clinics, and low-cost housing and slum rehabilitation.
2. *Economic Infrastructure and Production Inputs*, such as feeder roads, water resources development and irrigation schemes, crop storage and distribution facilities, small scale agro-based and agricultural-related industries.[29]

Table 5.8: Distribution of UNCDF Commitments in 1980 as Percentage of Total (in $US millions)

Water Resource Development	42
Feeder Road Construction	14
Crop Storage and Food Distribution	10

Source: *UNCDF Annual Report*, 1981.

Reasons for Failure. The most obvious and immediate reason for the failure of UNCDF – at least in the form initially envisaged – was the lack of resources. But lack of resources was itself the result of much deeper causes. The underlying reason for the Fund's failure was indeed 'an inability on the part of the developed and the developing nations to reconcile their fundamental differences in perspectives'.[30]

By establishing UNCDF, the developing nations wanted to go beyond the need for additional capital. The purpose of the Fund was to be both economic – providing scarce capital – and political, enabling the developing countries to share in the decision-making process regarding development issues.

More profoundly, what was implied in the notion of UNCDF was 'a change in the *status quo* – i.e., freeing capital assistance from political entanglements'.[31] Yet this was precisely what the countries possessing capital did not want. Scarcity of resources was just an excuse, since there was always the possibility of shifting funds from one programme to another.

Precisely for this reason, the capital-endowed countries preferred to channel their multilateral aid through organisations in which they held the overwhelming voting power and influence over the bureaucracy. That is why they created IDA, affiliated with the World Bank. The following statement about the US attitude also illustrates the view of other capital rich countries:

Table 5.9: UNCDF Approved Projects by Main Field of Activity as of the end of 1980

Fields of activity	1980 No. of projects	1980 Amount ($US millions)	1980 Per Cent of amount	Cumulative 1975-80 No. of projects	Cumulative 1975-80 Amount ($US millions)	Cumulative 1975-80 Per cent of amount
Agriculture, fisheries and livestock						
Crop production and improvement	1	2.0	4	6	7.4	4
Crop storage and market infrastructure	6	5.2	10	12	7.7	5
Land conservation and rehabilitation	2	2.0	4	2	2.0	1
Water resources development (Irrigation)	7	13.1	25	21	24.7	15
Training and extension services	2	0.7	1	5	1.6	1
Credit	1	–	–	8	5.6	3
Co-operatives	2	2.3	4	5	3.5	2
Integrated rural development	–	–	–	4	0.9	–
Fisheries	–	–	–	4	1.2	1
Livestock	3	1.6	3	11	7.3	4
Sub-total	24	26.9	51	78	61.9	36
Small industry and handicrafts	2	3.9	7	14	10.0	6
Rural and feeder roads	3	7.1	14	17	22.0	13
Rural electrifications	–	–	–	4	8.0	5
Low-cost housing	1	2.0	4	11	15.5	9
Potable water supply	7	9.1	17	23	24.5	15
Rural health facilities	1	2.7	5	11	12.3	8
Rural schools	–	0.2	–	8	9.5	6
Social welfare	1	0.9	2	2	1.5	1
Total	39	52.8	100	168	165.2	100

Source: *UNCDF Annual Report*, 1980.

In the United States the acceptability of the multilateral alternative is based largely on the vision of a well-proportioned pyramid with the World Bank Group, headed by the weighted voting, at the apex. The rest of the development machinery is assumed to fall neatly into place somewhere below.[32]

Given the OPEC countries' claims of solidarity with the developing countries, plus their commitment to the establishment of the NIEO and to meeting the basic needs of the poorest countries, it would have been logical for them to contribute to the UNCDF. However, as a result of factors amply discussed in the first three chapters, the OPEC countries also chose bilateralism and favoured such multilateral organisations as the World Bank.

The International Fund for Agricultural Development (IFAD)

The idea of establishing a new fund to mobilise resources for increasing agricultural production in developing countries emerged at the United Nation's World Food Conference held in Rome in November 1974. Intensive negotiations were held during 1975 and 1976 which culminated in a United Nation's conference of plenipotentiaries. This conference produced an intergovernmental agreement establishing IFAD on 13 June 1976. The agreement was opened for signature on 20 December of the same year when the target of one billion dollars in total pledges was reached. The agreement entered into force on 30 November 1977, when it was ratified by countries pledging a total of $750 million, and it began its operations on 13 December 1977 by holding the first meeting of its governing council.

IFAD has 125 members, of which 90 are original members. Almost all Western industrialised countries, OPEC countries, and a large majority of the developing countries have been members of IFAD. The Soviet Union and other East European countries have not joined, which is understandable in view of the fact that IFAD's establishment was seen as a manifestation of a new partnership that some OPEC countries and the Western industrialised countries were trying to forge and to use to win over the developing countries.

One organisational aspect of IFAD needs stressing: the distribution of the voting power among its members. This has reflected the developing countries' long-held position that the workings of international organisations should be democratised and that influence should not be based solely on the level of each member's financial contribution.

Objectives. Article 2 of IFAD's constituent agreement spells out the Fund's objectives in the following terms:

> Objectives of the Fund shall be to mobilise additional resources to be made available on concessional terms for agricultural development in developing member states. In fulfilling this objective, the Fund shall provide financing primarily for projects and programmes specifically designed to introduce, expand or improve food production systems and to strengthen related policies and institutions within the framework of national priorities and strategies, taking into consideration: the need to increase food production in the poorest food deficit countries; the potential for increasing food production in other developing countries; and the importance of improving the nutritional level of the poorest populations in developing countries and the conditions of their lives.[33]
>
> Article 7 of the agreement requires that the Fund, in allocating its resources, should be guided by the following priorities:
>
> (i) the need to increase food production and to improve the nutritional level of the poorest populations in the poorest food deficit countries;
> (ii) the potential for increasing food production in other developing countries. Likewise emphasis shall be placed on improving the nutritional level of the poorest populations in these countries and the conditions of their lives.
>
> Within the framework of the above-mentioned priorities, eligibility for assistance shall be on the basis of objective economic and social criteria with special emphasis on the needs of the low income countries and their potential for increasing food production as well as due regard to a fair geographic distribution in the use of such resources.[34]

Based on the above framework, IFAD's strategy has been built on the assumption that supply shortfalls of the food-deficit countries cannot be met adequately by increased output in the developed parts of the world, and thus it has emphasised production rather than distribution.[35]

To increase production, IFAD has tried to diminish shortages of inputs such as fertilisers, pesticides, or reliable water from existing wells and canals; and to reduce institutional or other barriers to the dissemination of new technologies, through an essentially flexible and multifaceted approach.[36]

Moreover, IFAD has been aware that reducing rural poverty would only be possible within a policy of agrarian reform and a strategy geared to increasing rural employment.[37]

Lending Criteria. IFAD has based its lending criteria on the following factors:

1. Flexibility of approach. As it has expected to learn from experience, IFAD has intended to bring new interpretations to the broad criteria laid down by its constituent agreement.
2. Country requirements, focusing on the poorest countries with serious food problems.
3. A project appraisal standard. While taking into account the principle of economic viability of projects, the Fund has been supposed to give special consideration to those activities that could lead to an increase in food output; that could essentially benefit small farmers, that could promote domestic and international trade in food; and that promote other forms of cooperation among the developing countries. IFAD has also been supposed to favour projects that can strengthen the technological and administrative bases of recipients.[38]

Terms and Conditions. IFAD has provided three types of loans:

1. Special loans on highly concessional terms, carrying a service charge of 1 per cent annually and a maturity period of 50 years, including a grace period of ten years.
2. Loans on intermediate terms, with an interest rate of 4 per cent annually and a maturity period of 20 years, including a grace period of five years.
3. Loans on ordinary terms, with an interest rate of 8 per cent and a maturity period of 15 to 18 years, including a grace period of three years.[39]

Needless to say, the terms of IFAD loans have generally depended on the economic and financial positions of recipients and the nature of projects. Technical assistance has been provided on a grant basis, except for feasibility studies leading to a loan provided by the Fund, in which case the cost of such technical assistance would be included in the loan. Assistance to the absolute-poorest food-deficit countries could also be in grant form. The Fund's attitude towards local-cost financing has also been quite flexible.

The OPEC countries have contributed heavily to IFAD, and they played an important role in its creation. In view of the foregoing, regarding IFAD's objectives and priorities, this has been one of the few cases where, through its aid, OPEC has contributed to the achievement of developing country objectives.

IFAD's future, however, seems uncertain, principally because of the change in US policy towards international aid institutions, aimed at cutting the level of US contributions. However, this attitude on the part of the present US administration has been criticised by some Americans who have seen IFAD as the only working example of OPEC, industrial – country, and Third World cooperation.[40]

Table 5.10: Cumulative Payments by OPEC Member Countries to IFAD as of the end of 1979 (in $US millions)

Country	In cash	In Promissory Notes	Total
Algeria	6.67	–	6.67
Gabon	0.50	–	0.50
Indonesia	1.25	–	1.25
Iran	12.22	29.36	41.58
Iraq	1.96	18.04	20.00
Kuwait	3.53	32.47	36.00
S.P. Libyan A.J.	8.63	4.71	13.34
Nigeria	17.33	–	17.33
Qatar	3.00	3.00	6.00
Saudi Arabia	70.33	–	70.33
United Arab Emirates	1.62	9.38	11.00
Venezuela	22.00	44.00	66.00
Total	149.04	140.96	290.00

Source: *OPEC Fund Annual Report* 1979.

Table 5.11: Regional Distribution of IFAD Loans, 1978-80

Region	1978 No.	1978 $US (millions)	1979 No.	1979 $US (millions)	1980 No.	1980 $US (millions)	Total No.	Total $US (millions)
Africa	2	15.8	10	122.2	12	160.9	24	298.9
Asia & Near East	5	82.5	8	204.8	10	149.7	23	437.0
Latin America	3	19.3	5	45.1	5	69.9	13	134.3
Total	10	117.6	23	372.1	27	380.5	60	870.2

Table 5.12: Distribution of IFAD Loans by Region and by Lending Terms, 1978-80

Region	Highly Concessional $US (millions)	Intermediate $US (millions)	Ordinary $US (millions)	Total $US (millions)
Africa	255.1	43.8	–	298.9
Asia & Near East	368.5	68.5	–	437.0
Latin America	26.7	65.4	42.2	134.3

Table 5.13: Regional Distribution of Projects by Source, 1978-80

	Co-financed		IFAD Initiated		Total	
Region	No.	$US (millions)	No.	$US (millions)	No.	$US (millions)
Africa	15	180.8	9	118.1	24	298.9
Asia & Near East	13	201.5	10	235.5	23	437.0
Latin America	8	74.5	5	59.8	13	134.3
Total	36	456.8	24	413.4	60	870.2
% of Total	(52)		(48)		(100)	

Source: Tables 5.11, 5.12, 5.13, *IFAD, Annual Report*, 1980.

The World Bank Group

The International Bank for Reconstruction and Development (IBRD) was one of the principal institutions created after the Second World War within the context of the Bretton Woods system, to bring order to global financial and economic relations. Since then, the World Bank has undergone tremendous changes in its objectives, organisation and outlook. For example, from being an institution principally geared to the reconstruction of war-damaged economies of Western Europe it has become the most influential and authoritative organisation in the field of development.

Yet the World Bank, its policies, and in general its central role within the present international economic system have been controversial subjects. In particular, a large number of Third World scholars have believed that the World Bank, as presently organised and with its present underlying objectives, simply cannot contribute either to the Third World's development or – more importantly – to its economic emancipation. These scholars have maintained that if the IBRD were to follow policies in the true interests of developing countries, it would both become unacceptable to the industrialised countries and lose its credibility in international financial markets. Analysis of the IBRD's structure, objectives and policies, as well as their evaluation, is beyond the scope of this study, as are judgements about the validity of charges made against it.

However, it is important to indicate here some of the inherent limitations of the World Bank to act purely as an agent of development; and in the light of that assessment to make a tentative judgement as to whether the World Bank (including IDA) has been the best development institution from the perspective of developing countries. Depending on that verdict, it is important to explore whether the extensive links between OPEC countries and the World Bank have been justified, and – more important – have been consistent with OPEC's claims that it has been an instrument of international reform and that its actions have been conducive to the establishment of an NIEO.

Principal Criticisms. Those observers who have questioned the World Bank's suitability as the principal instrument of international development refer to two of its most salient characteristics, namely that it is first and foremost a bank, although at times there have been tensions between its function as a bank and its function as a development institution; and that its main function is promoting '. . . capitalist development in the Third World countries, and promoting it in such a way as to make those countries as receptive, as safe, and as profitable as possible for foreign capital'.[41]

In turn, the critics have maintained, this has deeply affected the Bank's philosophy, lending criteria, development strategy, and modes of operation. For example, the lending criteria of the World Bank as an instrument of the present international economic system have still been based on the principles of the creditworthiness of borrowers and the financial viability of projects; and on whether borrowers' policies and projects themselves facilitate the investment of capital for productive purposes and create a satisfactory climate for private investment.[42]

Regarding the Bank's development strategy, concentration of lending on infrastructural projects – even after initiation of the new poverty-oriented strategy in the late 1960s – has been explained by some experts by the fact that these projects have been calculated to open up countries to foreign trade, rather than to integrate their different regions and sectors, and to make it easier for foreign capital to enter special, export-oriented fields without incurring the attendant costs of necessary preliminary infrastructure. Moreover, these critics have maintained that changes in the Bank's philosophy and strategy have largely been only adjustments to new circumstances and forces, in order to limit their potential damage to the system and as far as possible to control and direct the new forces into directions most beneficial to the preservation of the system.[43]

These criticisms – particularly the last one – have also been applied to IDA, since it was essentially created to prevent the establishment of a sizeable UN Development Fund that could have undermined the control of the World Bank and thus its major contributors. In turn, this has affected IDA's nature and modes of operations. Thus IDA became an appendage of the World Bank, as the following statement illustrates:

> As an international organisation affiliated with the World Bank, IDA is an elaborate fiction. Called an 'association' and possessed of Articles of Agreement, officers, governmental members galore, and all the trapping of other international agencies, it is as yet simply a *fund administered by the World Bank.*[44]

In light of the foregoing, the development of extensive links between the World Bank and the OPEC countries – particularly the surplus countries – plus the latter's development institutions, could not be viewed as an OPEC effort to achieve Third World goals, including that of creating development institutions more responsive to Third World needs. The only way this could have been the case would have been if the OPEC countries had tried to change the structure and working methods of the World Bank. But there is no evidence that they have done so. Indeed, the only time the OPEC countries have tried to use their financial clout in the international development and financial institution has been when they have tried to gain observer status for the PLO in the IMF.[45] Thus, even in this respect, narrow political interests rather than Third World solidarity and the desire to reform the international system have guided OPEC's actions – although rhetorically, at least, some OPEC members have called for the reform of the international financial system. Moreover, the extensive dependence of OPEC institutions on World Bank expertise has meant that they have followed its methods and philosophy rather than trying to find alternative ways that could be more suitable to developing-country needs.

PART TWO: MULTILATERAL OPEC/ARAB ORGANISATIONS

I The OPEC Fund for International Development (OFID)

OPEC's collective aid organisation was first established under the name of The OPEC Special Fund on 28 January 1976, by a decision of its Ministerial Committee on Cooperation and Consultation in Financial Matters held in Paris, and it became operational in August of the same year. In 1980, OSF was turned into a full-fledged development institution. Yet since, thus far, the Fund has not undergone organisational or other major changes, discussion here will be principally based on the nature and operations of the OSF, and recent changes will only be stressed when necessary.[46]

Legal Status

OPEC's collective aid institution was initially an international account collectively owned by the contributing parties, all members of OPEC, which thus made it different from similar institutions. Yet the OSF was also different from other special accounts in that it was not owned by the institution whose name it carried.

After the changes made in 1980, the OPEC aid institution has evolved into 'an international agency for financial cooperation and assistance' endorsed by OPEC countries with an international legal personality of its own.[47]

Organisation

Initially, OSF was viewed as a temporary institution, and thus it was not given an elaborate administrative structure. In fact, its administrative structure had been 'designed in a way that satisfies both the objective of simplicity and that of efficiency'.[48] OSF's administrative structure initially consisted of a Governing Committee and a Director General. After the changes made in 1980, the administrative structure of the Fund has consisted of a Ministerial Council, a Governing Board and a Director General.

The most important departure from the Fund's previous mode of operation after the 1980 changes has been 'the authorisation of the Fund to directly appraise the projects and programmes submitted to it for financing and to administer its loans'.[49] This departure would have far-reaching implications as far as the internal organisation of the Fund and its staffing policies are concerned. For example, the Fund was to increase the number of technical staff and reduce its heavy reliance on international and OPEC institutions for project appraisal and loan executing functions.[50] This development may thus affect the Fund's development strategy.

Development Philosophy

The OPEC Fund was the symbol of the OPEC countries' collective solidarity with other developing countries. It was conceived at the Algiers conference of OPEC heads of state and government in 1975, and thus its philosophy was affected by the tenets of the Algiers Solemn Declaration. The Fund's aims have been to promote economic development as affirmed in the Solomn Declaration, thus facilitating the establishment of a New International Economic Order.[51]

Nevertheless, the Fund was not conceived 'as an instrument of compensation for the difference – or part of the difference – between the new and the old price of petroleum'.[52] Rather, the Fund's 'preferred approach has been to consider the resource gap for development in the totality of its causes, and to contribute to its closing, especially in the most seriously affected countries, irrespective of the way in which the gap arises'.[53]

The Fund's philosophy has been based on universal application, and thus no developing country affected by economic and financial problems has been excluded from its assistance on the basis of geographic location or political orientation.

According to its official documents, the Fund has had:

> a particular concern for projects which meet the basic needs of the population, which alleviate income and regional disparities, and those which lessen the dependence of recipient countries on imported energy. Projects which involve cooperation with other OPEC aid agencies as co-financers, or which in a more substantial manner lead to an increase in the volume of trade or in the mobility of factors of production among developing countries, are given clear preference.[54]

Lending Operations

The OPEC Fund has offered balance of payments support, project aid, and programme loans. Its first lending programme was in the form of balance of payments support loans. This programme started shortly after the Fund's establishment in 1976 and was essentially designed to alleviate the effects of oil price increases on developing countries.

Among the early recipients were 43 of the 45 most seriously affected countries as defined by the UN. By 1979, the Fund had disbursed the bulk of $200 million allocated for this purpose.

Balance of payments support loans have been interest free with only a 0.5 per cent service charge on amounts withdrawn and outstanding, with a maturity of 25 years and a grace period of five years. The Fund has required that the loans be used either for the importation of capital goods and spare parts, or the importation of other agricultural and industrial inputs for civilian production. Loans have been disbursed in two stages: the first half upon the taking effect of the loan agreement, and the second half upon receipt of a satisfactory statement from the borrower regarding the use of amounts previously transferred.

In order to enhance the developmental impact of its balance of payments support programme, the Fund has required its borrowers to set aside in local currency an amount equivalent to the Fund's balance of payments loan for the purpose of financing local development projects. This should be done within 180 days of withdrawal of each portion of the proceeds from the balance of payments loan, followed by the submission of proposals for their use to the OPEC Fund. The specific use of counterpart funds has then been mutually agreed upon within one year of the date of transfer of the first half of the loan, thereby ensuring that the decision on their use would not be unduly delayed. The borrower can withdraw the counterpart funds if no agreement has been reached, or if it has decided not to use them, in which case the maturity of the balance of payments support loans would be reduced by five years.

The Fund's project lending started in 1977 and its experience thus far has reflected the Fund's project lending philosophy as well as its limitations.

Eligibility Criteria. In extending assistance, the Fund has demonstrated a considerable degree of political and ideological impartiality, and has chosen recipient countries on the basis of internationally-set economic and financial criteria. The Fund has generally used four main variables to determine the eligibility of applicants: per capita income as an index of relative poverty; population as a proxy for size; deficits in current account as a measure of liquidity and financial problems; and net oil imports of 1973 as a sign of energy import dependence. Using these criteria, the OPEC Fund has succeeded in extending assistance to a large number of least-developed as well as most seriously affected countries.

Criteria for Project Selection. In selecting projects, the Fund has thus far given particular weight to the following considerations: economic priorities of recipient countries; opportunities for co-financing; and the compatibility of projects with the Fund's philosophy.

Several reasons explain the Fund's emphasis on these considerations. For example, the Fund has not wanted in any way to be seen as influencing the economic policies of other countries or, as a Fund staffer put it, to be accused of economic interference.

The Fund's preference for co-financing has derived from its limited resources – both material and human – and its cautious approach. In the past, the Fund's limited financial resources imposed the choice of either co-financing or limiting the geographical scope of its operations. Wanting to keep the geographical base as broad as possible, the Fund has opted for co-financing and has seen its role principally as a gap filler. Moreover, staff limitations and the desire to avoid the risk of over-committing the Fund's resources, and thus to limit its margin of error in appraising projects, have argued for co-financing.

Regarding choice of projects, the Fund's stated preferences have been similar to its overall philosophy.[55] In practice, however, the Fund has favoured energy and transportation sectors, followed by agriculture and agro-industry.

However, it is important to note that the above have been the practices of the Fund in the past, and if the 1980 change in its legal status were followed by other organisational changes (for example, a larger professional staff) – and particularly by increased financial resources, some of the Fund's lending policies might also change.

Table 5.14: OPEC Fund Commitments and Disbursements as of 31 December 1980 (in $US millions)

Type of aid	Commitment	Disbursement
Lending operations	904.29	480.11
Technical assistance grants	38.00	14.37
Other grants	0.38	0.28
IFAD	435.50	201.71
IMF Trust Fund	110.72	110.72
Total	1,488.89	807.19

Source: *OPEC Fund Annual Report*, 1980.

Table 5.15: OPEC Fund Cumulative Balance of Payments Support Loans as of 31 December 1980 (in $US millions)

Country/Region	Amount	Country/Region	Amount
Benin	6.50	Afghanistan	3.75
Botswana	3.00	Bangladesh	13.90
Burundi	6.20	Burma	2.25
Cameroon	4.95	India	21.80
Cape Verde	5.05	Lao, PDR	7.15
Central African Rep.	1.75	Maldives	2.30
Chad	2.40	Nepal	4.15
Comoros	2.00	Pakistan	21.45
Congo	4.00	Solomon Islands	1.00
Djibouti	1.50	Sri Lanka	8.10
Egypt	14.45	Turkey	15.00
Equatorial Guinea	1.50	Western Samoa	3.35
Ethiopia	4.80	Yemen, AR	2.25
Gambia	6.15	Yemen, PDR	8.40
Ghana	7.80	ASIA	114.85
Guinea	8.85		
Guinea-Bissau	5.65		
Kenya	5.00	Barbados	3.00
Lesotho	3.40	Dominica	0.50
Madagascar	8.10	Dominican Rep.	5.00
Mali	13.05	El Salvador	1.75
Mauritania	7.10	Grenada	2.35
Mauritius	2.00	Guatemala	1.75
Mozambique	15.05	Guyana	8.60
Niger	10.75	Haiti	3.15
Rwanda	9.20	Honduras	1.75
Sao Tomé & Principe	0.35	Jamaica	14.00
Senegal	11.90	Nicaragua	20.00
Seychelles	1.30	LATIN AMERICA	61.85
Sierra Leone	3.05		
Somalia	7.05		
Sudan	7.45	TOTAL	399.25
Tanzania	10.45		
Togo	3.50		
Uganda	4.55		
Upper Volta	12.75		
AFRICA	222.55		

Source: *OPEC Fund Annual Report*, 1980.

Table 5.16: Imports Financed through Balance of Payments Support Loans, Cumulative through the end of 1980

Imports	(%)
Foodstuffs	32.4
Crude oil and oil products	23.6
Equipment and space	32.7
Ports	
Other commodities	11.3

Source: *OPEC Fund Annual Report*, 1980.

Table 5.17: OPEC Fund Project Lending Sectoral Distribution

Type of project	Cumulative to the end of 1980 (%)	1980 (%)
Energy	44.4	63.7
Agriculture and Agro-Industry	14.0	4.9
Transportation	20.6	20.3
Industry including Development Banks	14.8	6.5
Public Utilities	5.0	4.6
Communications	13.0	

Source: *The OPEC Fund Annual Report*, 1980.

II The Islamic Development Bank (IsDB)

Creation of the Islamic Development Bank resulted from long efforts to increase cooperation among the Islamic countries – efforts that were accelerated after the oil revolution and ensuing problems. The first step towards establishing the Bank was taken in December 1973 at the Jeddah conference of finance ministers of Islamic countries, which created a preparatory committee to prepare necessary documents. That committee presented draft articles for the Bank to the August 1974 conference of finance ministers, which adopted them. The inaugural meeting of the Islamic Development Bank was held in July 1975, and it began work officially on 20 October 1975.

Legal Status

The IsDB is an independent international institution possessing a judicial personality. It has had relations with other regional and international development institutions, as well as the UN's specialised agencies. The IsDB has also had observer status with UNCTAD. The IsDB has 32

Table 5.18: OPEC Fund Cumulative Project Lending Operations, Geographical and Sectoral Distribution of All Loans Committed as of 31 December 1980 (in $US millions)

Country/ Region	Energy	Agriculture & Agro-Industry[a]	Transport-ation	Industry incl. Develop-ment Banks	Public Utilities	Com-munica-tions	Total
Angola			3.00				3.00
Benin			1.60	4.50			6.10
Botswana			1.00				1.00
Burundi		2.00			3.00		5.00
Cameroon				4.50			4.50
Chad		2.45					2.45
Comoros			1.00				1.00
Congo			8.00				8.00
Egypt				8.75			8.75
Ghana	9.70			1.50			11.20
Kenya				5.30	3.00		8.30
Lesotho			3.00				3.00
Liberia	5.00		3.00				8.00
Madagascar	6.50						6.50
Malawi			1.80				1.80
Mali			7.00				7.00
Mauritania				5.00			5.00
Morocco	3.00	5.00		2.00			10.00
Rwanda	2.35						2.35
Senegal				5.00			5.00
Sierra Leone	1.60						1.60
Somalia		5.50			2.66		8.16
Sudan	9.50		10.95				20.45
Tanzania	5.00			5.00			10.00
Tunisia	6.00		6.00				12.00
Upper Volta			4.50				4.50
Zaïre		1.50	7.00	3.50			12.00
Zambia			4.50				4.50
AFRICA	48.65	16.45	62.35	45.05	8.66	–	181.16
Afghanistan			3.55				3.55
Bangladesh	39.50	17.00	3.50				60.00
Burma	2.00		6.32	6.50	1.28	3.14	19.24
India	54.00						54.00
Jordan		1.65		7.00			8.65
Maldives			1.00				1.00
Nepal	1.30	3.00	5.00				9.30
Pakistan	28.70			11.00			39.70
Philippines		8.00	8.25				16.25

Table 5.18 (Cont.)

Country/ Region	Energy	Agriculture & Agro-Industry[a]	Transport-ation	Industry incl. Develop-ment Banks	Public Utilities	Com-munica-tions	Total
Sri Lanka	9.15						9.15
Syria					2.00		2.00
Thailand	22.00						22.00
Vietnam		17.00					17.00
Yemen, AR			8.70				8.70
Yemen, PDR					4.00		4.00
ASIA	156.65	46.65	36.32	24.50	7.28	3.14	274.54
Bolivia					5.00		5.00
Costa Rica			3.00				3.00
Dom. Rep.	1.00	1.935					2.935
Guyana		4.00					4.00
Haïti				3.50	4.00		7.50
Honduras	10.20						10.20
Jamaica	3.30						3.30
Paraguay					2.90		2.90
LATIN AMERICA	14.50	5.935	3.00	3.50	11.90	–	38.835
Total	219.80	69.035	101.67	73.05	27.84	3.14	494.535
(in per cent)	44.4	14.0	20.6	14.8	5.6	0.6	100.0

Note: a. Not including part of the credits to local development banks which are earmarked for the agricultural sector, but appear in this table under the heading 'Industry including development banks'.

Source: *The OPEC Fund Annual Report*, 1980.

members, including a large number of African countries. Its headquarters are in Jeddah, but it has been authorised to establish other agencies or branch offices.

Objectives and Development Strategy

The principal purpose of the Islamic Development Bank has been to foster the economic development and social progress of its members and of other Muslim communities, in accordance with the principles of the Shari'a and through intensified cooperation among Muslim countries. The Bank has also been designed to encourage research in Islamic economics and to assist member states to organise their economic structure and planning on essentially Islamic principles.

Thus the IsDB's objectives and indeed its whole philosophy have been influenced by Islam. In turn, this has led to its adoption of a flexible and multifaceted development and operational strategy, and – in contrast to Arab institutions – a lesser degree of adherence to the traditional strategy of international institutions, such as the World Bank. As a result, the scope of the Bank's operations has been quite wide. For instance, it has participated in equity capital of productive projects and enterprises in member countries, and has invested in their economic and social infrastructure projects through financial participation or other financial arrangements. The Bank has also been charged with responsibility for assisting in the promotion of foreign trade among member countries, especially in capital goods, as well as with providing technical assistance and training facilities for personnel engaged in the development activities of member countries.

In addition, the Bank was permitted to establish and operate special funds, including a fund for assistance to Muslim communities in non-member countries, and also to operate trust funds. Further, it was authorised to accept deposits and to raise funds in any other manner, as well as to invest funds not needed in its operations.

In fact, the IsDB has not been a development bank in a strict sense; rather it has been a financial institution engaged in a number of activities on behalf of Islamic countries, including development financing, with the ultimate objective of promoting an Islamic economic and financial system among its member countries.

Lending and other Financing Operations

Major financing operations in which the IsDB has been involved during its existence are set out below.

Equity Participation. This has had an important place in the Bank's financing operations. In fact, the Bank has been required to maintain a suitable ratio between equity investments made in, and loans granted to, member countries, preferably with this balance being in favour of equity investments. This preference has derived from the Islamic nature of the institution. Since the Bank cannot charge any interest on its loans, it has had to look to other means of safeguarding its financial credibility. The Bank's equity participation has been subject to the following conditions:

1. It has been required to satisfy itself that the project or enterprise is currently or potentially revenue-yielding and that it is and will be properly managed.

2. It has retained the option to sell its equity with the proviso that it shall not sell any part to a non-national of the member country, without consent.
3. It has been prohibited from acquiring a majority or controlling interest in the share capital of the projects or enterprises in which they participated, except when necessary to protect the Bank's interest or to ensure the success of such projects or enterprises.
4. It could not assume responsibility for managing any project or enterprise in which it has invested except when necessary to safeguard its investment.

Loans. In addition to equity participation, the Bank has extended project and programme loans. The Bank could only levy a service fee to cover its administrative expenses. The amount of the fee and the manner of applying it has been determined by the Bank.

Regarding project loans, the Bank has been required to take into account each project's potential return and importance in the scheme of priorities of the recipient country. In regard to programme lending, whether to member countries or to development institutions and agencies, the Bank has been required to satisfy itself that the purpose has been to promote the well-being of the people through economic and social development. The Bank has also provided technical assistance. In the past, this has been mostly in the form of financing feasibility studies. Recently, according to the Bank's 1981 Annual Report, it has decided to increase its technical assistance programme and to raise the grant ceiling for technical assistance.

Foreign Trade Financing. In addition, the IsDB has engaged in foreign trade financing, principally 'to utilise the short term funds for developmental purposes within the member countries'.[56] In addition to this general objective, the Bank has used this instrument to promote trade among its member countries. Thus the Bank's policy on trade financing has been 'to accord priority to such transactions as have the effect of promoting trade among member countries'.[57]

Most trade financing operations of the Bank have involved the import of crude oil and other petroleum products. In project financing and equity participation, the Bank has favoured infrastructure projects. Projects with a high social content have not accounted for a large share of its total operations.

III The Arab Bank for Economic Development in Africa (BADEA)

BADEA has been the most significant institutional symbol of Afro-Arab cooperation and was the outcome of lengthy and intense diplomatic efforts to promote closer Arab-African cooperation following the events of 1973.

The decision to establish BADEA was reached at the Arab Summit Conference held in Algiers on November 1973, and it became operational in 1975. Only Arab countries are members of BADEA, despite the fact that the purpose of the bank has been to provide assistance to African countries. The capital of the bank has also been provided by Arab countries, with Saudi Arabia the largest contributor. The size of each member's vote has been determined by the level of its contribution. Thus, currently, the voting power of the conservative Arab countries outweighs that of the rest of the bank's members.

Objectives and Development Strategy

BADEA's underlying objective has been to win African friendship for the Arabs by contributing to African economic development and thus, as such, has been essentially political.[58] At an operational level, BADEA has wanted to achieve this objective by strengthening economic and technical cooperation between Arab and African countries; by providing concessional financing to African countries; by encouraging Arab and international investment in Africa; and by providing technical assistance. In addition BADEA has acted as the coordinator of Arab-African cooperation in the field of economic development.

Concerning BADEA's development strategy, it has not yet seemed to have developed one in the real sense of the term. Nevertheless, the Bank's operations thus far have been influenced by traditional strategies and by the World Bank.

However, BADEA has claimed that its development strategy has been flexible and non-normative, and that it has tried to follow a policy that is 'the most effective and best suited possible'.[59] The Bank has justified this attitude on the grounds of the complexity of planning a development strategy, the failure of past strategies and the enormity of Africa's development needs.[60] After only eight years of operation, it is difficult to judge the extent to which the Bank has applied its declared principle of flexibility to its operations, but there has been some evidence that the Bank has been responsive to the emergency requirements of African countries.[61] Nevertheless, thus far the Bank's

Table 5.19: IsDB Operations, 1976-81 (1396H-1401H) (in ID millions)[a]

Type of Operations	1396H 1976			1397H 1977			1398H 1978			1399H 1979			1400H 1980			1401H 1981			Total		
	No.	Amount	%	No.	Amount	%	No.	Amount	%	No.	Amount	%	No.	Amount	%	No.	Amount	%	No.	Amount	%
Loan	1	6.00	44.60	11	55.41	55.6	6	31.96	39.3	6	33.74	30.7	9	52.68	40.1	5	31.12	27.1	38	210.91	38.3
Equity	1	7.45	55.40	8	38.23	38.4	6	34.36	42.2	9	44.78	40.8	8	38.94	29.6	9	45.98	40.0	41	209.74	38.1
Leasing	—	—	—	1	5.22	5.2	1	10.00	12.3	4	29.60	27.0	5	36.47	27.7	3	30.69	26.7	14	111.98	20.3
Profit-sharing	—	—	—	—	—	—	1	4.27	5.3	—	—	—	—	—	—	—	—	—	1	4.27	0.8
Technical Assistance	—	—	—	3	0.84	0.8	3	0.82	1.0	6	1.68	1.5	3	3.38	2.6	11	7.06	6.2	26	13.78	2.5
Total Projects	2	13.45	100	23	99.70	100	17	81.41	100	25	109.80	100	25	131.47	100	28	114.85	100	120	550.68	100
Foreign Trade Financing Operations	—	—	—	5	43.61	30.4	15	127.14	61.0	24	262.43	70.5	36	365.06	73.5	34	392.22	77.4	114	1190.46	68.4
Total Operations	2	13.45	100	28	143.31	100	32	208.55	100	49	372.23	100	61	496.53	100	62	507.07	100	234	1741.14	100

Note: a. One Islamic Dinar is equivalent to one IMF Special Drawing Right.

Source: *Islamic Development Bank Annual Reports*, 1980/81.

Table 5.20: Types of Financing

Type of Financing	Cumulative 1976-81	1981
Equity	209.75	45.98
Loan	210.91	31.12
Leasing	111.98	30.69
Technical assistance	13.77	7.06
Profit sharing	4.27	—

Source: *Islamic Development Bank, Annual Report*, 1980-1.

Table 5.21: Sectoral Distribution of Financing (in ID millions)

Sector	Amount Cumulative 1976-81	1981
Transportation and Communication	138.02	22.32
Industry & Mining	240.42	60.31
Agriculture and agro-based industry	79.15	27.10
Public utility	62.43	5.12
Social services	23.34	—
Others	7.32	—

Source: *Islamic Development Bank, Annual Report*, 1980-1.

Table 5.22: Sectoral Distribution of Financing as Percentage of Total

Sector	Cumulative till end 1979	1979
Industry & Mining	45.1	52.1
Transport & Communications	27.7	25.2
Agriculture	10.4	7.9
Utilities	11.2	8.0

Source: *Islamic Development Bank Annual Reports*, 1978-9.

operations have shown a certain bias in favour of infrastructure projects, but agricultural sectors have been rapidly catching up.[62]

Within this general framework, the Bank has taken into account a number of other considerations, principally regarding economic priorities set for the continent's development either by the UN, by other international organisations, or by African countries themselves.[63] The encouragement of regional cooperation has been another BADEA

Table 5.23: Foreign Trade Financing Operations in IsDB Member Countries in 1979 (1399H) (in millions)

Commodity involved	Amount ID	Amount $US	Name of Importing Member Country	Name of Exporting Member Country	Date of approval
Importation of Refined Petroleum Products	10.73	14.00	Sudan	Kuwait	24.1.1979
Urea Fertilisers	3.80	4.88	Pakistan	Kuwait	10.4.1979
Urea Fertilisers	1.64	2.12	Pakistan	Saudi Arabia	10.4.1979
Crude Oil	15.54	20.00	Somalia	Iraq	10.4.1979
Crude Oil	7.77	10.00	Bangladesh	Saudi Arabia	10.4.1979
Crude Oil	7.77	10.00	Bangladesh	Abu Dhabi	10.4.1979
Refined Petroleum Products	12.43	16.00	Sudan	Kuwait	10.4.1979
Crude Oil	11.65	15.00	Morocco	Iraq	28.5.1979
Crude Oil	23.31	30.00	Turkey	Iraq	28.5.1979
Crude Oil	10.00	13.00	PDR Yemen	Libya	28.5.1979
Refined Petroleum Products	7.68	10.00	Guinea Bissau	Algeria	14.7.1979
Crude Oil	15.77	20.00	Pakistan	Saudi Arabia	14.7.1979
Refined Petroleum Products	15.77	20.00	Niger	Libya	14.7.1979
Cotton Yarn	4.00	5.30	Somalia	Pakistan	4.9.1979
Refined Petroleum Products	9.15	11.71	Sudan	Kuwait	4.9.1979
Crude Oil	3.07	4.00	Bangladesh	Saudi Arabia	11.11.1979
Crude Oil	12.26	16.00	Bangladesh	Abu Dhabi	11.11.1979
Crude Oil	11.15	15.00	Morocco	Iraq	11.11.1979
Jute Finished Goods	12.73	16.50	Sudan	Bangladesh	11.11.1979
Fuel Oil	11.62	15.00	Turkey	Pakistan	11.11.1979
Total:	207.84	268.51			

Source: *Islamic Development Bank Annual Reports*, 1978-9.

objective, and BADEA could give preference to projects involving two or more countries.

Lending and Other Assistance Operations

BADEA's principal activity has entailed project lending, and the Bank has not had any programme lending operations. In financing projects, in addition to the foregoing considerations the Bank has applied a number of other rules. For instance, BADEA has had a marked preference for co-financing. Most of BADEA's partners in co-financing operations have been other Arab development funds as well as the OPEC Fund and the Islamic Development Bank; but BADEA has also had co-financing arrangements with the African Development Bank, the European Development Bank, and, of course, the World Bank.[64] The Bank's preference for co-financing has derived from the same considerations as with other Arab and OPEC development institutions.

In selecting projects, BADEA has respected recipients' priorities, and has not tried to impose its views; but it has reserved the right to refuse applications for financing. However, on occasion the Bank has tried to induce some changes that would make possible the financing of a given project.[65]

The Bank has made no loans without the approval of the country in which a project has been located. Loan agreements have generally been made with governments but earmarked for a particular project, either in the public or private sector. When the project has been in the private sector, it has had to be under the majority control of local entrepreneurs and to have had a government guarantee. The Bank has preferred to make its loans no more than $10 million, but it could make exceptions. Loans could cover anywhere from 5 per cent to 90 per cent of a project's costs.

In its lending operations, the Bank has tried to keep a balance between East and West African countries, while favouring those countries with lowest per capita income. The concessionality of BADEA's loans has been quite high. The highest rate of interest thus far charged by the Bank has not exceeded 7 per cent. In deciding the rate of interest, BADEA has taken into account a country's economic and financial situation and the sectors for which loan applications have been made. Thus the poorest countries and the agricultural sector have received the lowest rate. BADEA's loans have had a grace period of up to five years and a maturity period of between 15 to 25 years.

In addition to project lending, in order to promote investment in Africa BADEA has issued guarantees for the benefit of African and Arab institutions, whether or not it has been involved in a project. Furthermore, BADEA has tried to help Arab and African enterprises through its procurement policy. For instance, it has given preference to Arab, African, or mixed enterprises whenever the service quality and performance ability have been comparable, provided that the difference in cost has not exceeded 10 per cent (see Tables 5.24-5.28).

Table 5.24: Subscriptions and Voting Power of BADEA Members

Member States	Subscription			Voting Power	
	Amounts (in $US)	Shares	Percentage	Number of votes	Percentage
Hashemite Kingdom of Jordan	1,500,000	15	0.20	215	1.96
State of the United Arab Emirates	90,000,000	900	12.19	1100	10.01
State of Bahrain	1,500,000	15	0.20	215	1.96
Republic of Tunisia	6,250,000	62.5	0.85	262.5	2.39
Democratic and Popular Republic of Algeria	30,000,000	300	4.07	500	4.55
Kingdom of Saudi Arabia	180,000,000	1800	24.38	2000	18.21
Democratic Republic of the Sudan	1,500,000	15	0.20	215	1.96
Arab Republic of Syria	1,000,000	10	0.14	210	1.96
Republic of Iraq	105,000,000	1050	14.23	1250	11.38
Sultanate of Oman	11,000,000	110	1.49	310	2.82
Palestine	1,500,000	15	0.20	215	1.96
State of Qatar	60,000,000	600	8.13	800	7.28
State of Kuwait	110,000,000	1100	14.90	1300	11.84
Republic of Lebanon	5,000,000	50	0.67	250	2.28
Arab Libyan People's Socialist Jamahiriya	120,000,000	1200	16.26	1400	12.75
Arab Republic of Egypt	1,500,000	15	0.20	215	1.96
Kingdom of Morocco	11,000,000	110	1.49	310	2.82
Islamic Republic of Mauritania	1,500,000	15	0.20	215	1.96
Total	738,250,000	7382.5	100.00	10,982.5	100.00

Source: *BADEA Annual Report*, 1980.

IV Special Arab Fund for Africa

In addition to BADEA, in 1974 the Arab countries set up a special fund to help African countries cope with the consequences of oil price increases. Once BADEA became operational, the administration of the Fund was entrusted to it. Later in 1977, SAFA's capital was transferred to BADEA.

The objectives of SAFA were to alleviate balance of payments difficulties; to compensate partly for the increase in the price of oil; to meet some of the most urgent needs of the sub-Saharan countries;

Table 5.25: Paid-up Ordinary Capital as of 31 December 1980 (in $US)

Member States	Amount of subscription to capital stock as at 31.12.1980	Paid-up capital as at 31.12.1980	Amounts outstanding as at 31.12.1980
Hashemite Kingdom of Jordan	1,500,000	1,500,000.00	–
State of the United Arab Emirates	90,000,000	80,000,000.00	10,000,000.00
State of Bahrain	1,500,000	1,500,000.00	–
Republic of Tunisia	6,250,000	6,250,000.00	–
Democratic and Popular Republic of Algeria	30,000,000	30,000,000.00	–
Kingdom of Saudi Arabia	180,000,000	180,000,000.00	–
Democratic Republic of the Sudan	1,500,000	1,334,000.00	166,000.00
Arab Republic of Syria	1,000,000	1,000,000.00	–
Republic of Iraq	105,000,000	105,000,000.00	–
Sultanate of Oman	11,000,000	9,000,000.00	2,000,000.00
Palestine	1,500,000	1,500,000.00	–
State of Qatar	60,000,000	60,000,000.00	–
State of Kuwait	110,000,000	110,000,000.00	–
Republic of Lebanon	5,000,000	5,000,000.00	–
Arab Libyan People's Socialist Ja,ahiriya	120,000,000	113,334,000.00	6,666,000.00
Arab Republic of Egypt	1,500,000	1,166,667.00	333,333.00
Kingdom of Morocco	11,000,000	11,000,000.00	–
Islamic Republic of Mauritania	1,500,000	1,067,507.53	432,492.47
Total	738,250,000	718,652,174.53	19,597,825.47

Source: *BADEA Annual Report*, 1980.

to support the purchase of oil by African countries; and to develop oil resources in Africa. But since the transfer of SAFA's capital to BADEA, it was used according to the same criteria as the rest of BADEA's capital. However, loans made out of SAFA's capital had a higher rate of concessionality. By 1978, all the commitments made of SAFA's capital had been disbursed.

Table 5.26: Weighted Average Terms of BADEA Loans

Year	Amounts of Loans (in $US millions)	Interest Rate (%)	Maturity Period (in years)	Grace Period (in years)	Grant Element (%)
1975	71.6	3.7	23.5	5	41.08
1976	61.9	2.6	23	5	47.42
1977	66.24	5	18	4.5	28.97
1978	67.87	4.3	16	4.2	40.97
1979	44.07	4.3	17.1	4	36.86
1980	71.95	5.5	16.3	3.8	25.07
Total Averages	383.63	4.2	19	4.4	36.50

Source: *BADEA Annual Report*, 1980.

V The Arab Fund for Economic and Social Development (AFESD)

The establishment of the AFESD was the culmination of lengthy efforts within the Arab League to create an intra-Arab development institution.

AFESD's Articles of Agreement were adopted on 16 May 1968, but it did not become operational until February 1972. Since then, the Fund's financial resources and the scope of its operations have been expanded. The underlying goal of AFESD has been to assist the development of Arab economies in ways that would facilitate the achievement of the Arab League's objectives and ultimately that of Arab economic unity. To a large extent, this guiding philosophy of the Fund has also determined its priorities. However, in practice, the Fund has been forced to compromise on these priorities and to fashion its programme to the realities of intra-Arab politics rather than to the vague ideal of Arab unity.

AFESD has two kinds of members: the founding members and those who joined the Fund later. Those states, members of the Arab League that subscribed to the capital of the Fund before 1 July 1968, have been considered as founding members.

Objectives

The overriding objective of the Fund has been to encourage Arab economic cooperation and to assist Arab countries in their socio-economic development, in ways that would facilitate greater Arab economic integration and ultimately Arab economic unity.

Table 5.27: Sectoral Breakdown of Total BADEA Commitments, 1975-80

	In $US millions						%						1975-1980	
	1975	1976	1977	1978	1979	1980	1975	1976	1977	1978	1979	1980	In $ m.	%
Infrastructure	42.0	29.1	13.20	17.60	36.67	32.25	58.7	47.0	19.9	25.9	83.2	44.8	170.82	44.5
Agriculture	11.6	17.8	12.20	14.65	2.40	18.50	16.2	28.8	18.4	21.6	5.5	25.7	77.15	20.1
Industry	18.0	–	24.84	9.70	5.00	20.00	25.1	–	37.5	14.3	11.3	27.8	77.54	20.2
Power	–	15.0	16.00	10.92	–	1.20	–	24.2	24.2	16.1	–	1.7	43.12	11.3
Emergency Aid	–	–	–	15.00	–	–	–	–	–	22.1	–	–	15.0	3.9
Totals	71.6	61.9	66.24	67.87	44.07	71.95	100	100	100	100	100	100	383.63	100

Source: *BADEA Annual Report*, 1980.

Table 5.28: BADEA Aid Beneficiary Countries

1975	1976	1977	1978	1979	1980
Benin	Burundi	Cameroon	Benin	Angola	Botswana
Cameroon	Gambia	Ghana	Botswana	Cape Verde	Burundi
Congo	Kenya	Guinea	Burundi	Comoros	Cameroon
Ghana	Mali	Liberia	Chad	Gambia	Comoros
Madagascar	Mauritius	Madagascar	Guinea Bissau	Guinea	Mozambique
Niger	Rwanda	Mali	Lesotho	Kenya	Senegal
Senegal	Sierra Leone	Rwanda	Liberia	Lesotho	Seychelles
Tanzania	Upper Volta	Senegal	Niger	Mali	Sierra Leone
Togo	Zambia	Tanzania	Uganda		Tanzania
Ivory Coast			Zaïre		
Zaïre					

Source: *BADEA Annual Report*, 1980

In operational terms, this basic objective logically would mean that the AFESD would principally finance those projects involving several Arab countries and contributing to regional development and integration. Indeed, both the Fund's reports and statements by its officials have confirmed this assumption.[66] Yet, in practice, thus far the Fund has not financed any regional development schemes of any significance. In fact, most of the Fund's projects which have had any significant regional impact have been in the form of 'studies', and the Fund has spent considerable sums of money for either organising symposiums and seminars or participating in them. However, some of the studies commissioned by the Fund could prove useful for the future planning of intra-Arab projects.

Another major objective of AFESD has been to develop the infrastructure of Arab countries. But the Fund has had a broad conception of infrastructure, one that has entailed human as well as physical dimensions. Thus, AFESD has undertaken a number of studies regarding the problem of manpower shortage in the Arab world. One major Fund study sought to 'identify areas of critical manpower shortages in the major production sectors and to determine possible remedies, among which may be the establishing of a center or centers for the training of trainers to meet the member countries' requirements in technical and professional cadres.'[67] In the meantime, the Fund has granted considerable numbers of scholarships and has financed the advisory services of consultants for its members.

Another major objective of the Fund has been to seek opportunities in the Arab region for the investment of surplus Arab funds with a bias, however, in favour of productive outlets. Thus, part of the Fund's project for the development of Sudan's agricultural development has been supposed to serve this purpose. Although thus far the Fund has not been too successful in attracting Arab capital – public and private – to productive investments, it has on occasion played an important role in generating additional financing for certain projects.[68]

To achieve this objective, the Fund has an Investment Servicing and Promotion Programme, as well as a special administrative unit for this purpose. Under this programme, the Fund has conducted field surveys in Arab countries, aimed at the identification of commercially viable projects and providing for the promotional services needed to attract capital for their implementation.

A further objective of the Fund has been to attract Arab professionals living abroad to participate in the development of Arab regions. Thus, the Fund has tried to use Arab experts both in staffing the Fund and in its projects. But there is no information pointing to the existence of a coherent long-term policy in this regard.

Politics

Unlike national Arab aid organisations which have first and foremost been instruments of national foreign policy and because of its composition and its ambitions as the principal vehicle for Arab economic integration, AFESD has been basically a non-political institution. However, this basic assumption has not meant that the Fund has been insensitive to political pressures and considerations. But the Fund's major preoccupation has been with balancing various interests, taking particularly into consideration the attitudes of major capital contributors and major recipients.[69] The distribution of votes within the Fund has been in proportion to the capital contribution of member states, thus further intensifying this tendency.

The combination of these factors has thus meant that the Fund's lending policies, as well as its development strategy, have been influenced by views and aspirations of conservative Arab regimes, since they have provided the bulk of the Fund's finances. Despite this fact, the Fund has tried to maintain a certain degree of neutrality in its lending policies. For instance, the internal socio-political system of a country has not been a factor ruling it out from the Fund's assistance; and radical countries, such as the PDRY, have received considerable assistance from the Fund.

In general, however, it is difficult to measure the impact of political factors in the Fund's lending policies. Since the Fund's main objective – namely, promotion of intra-Arab economic cooperation and integration – has been thus far frustrated because of political and ideological divisions, the Fund has not followed a very coherent lending policy.

Lending Strategy and Terms

External realities, rather than any particular preferences, have determined AFESD's lending strategy. The Fund's overriding objective has been tc promote intra-Arab projects. However, it has not found achieving this goal to be easy. Consequently, the Fund has opted for country project-financing with a strong bias in favour of infrastructure development. The reasons for the Fund's preference for project rather than programme financing have been the traditional ones in favour of project financing. In the case of AFESD, lack of sufficient expertise in development financing and the shortage of qualified manpower have also argued in favour of project financing, since most of the projects to which the Fund has contributed had already secured an external financier – such as the World Bank – to provide technical assistance.

In general, AFESD has shown a preference for joint financing, rather than for assuming the full cost of a project. Interest rates charged by AFESD have varied between 4 per cent and 6 per cent. The Fund has tried to keep uniform the interest rate for two types of project: 6 per cent for standard loans and 4 per cent for special concessionary loans. The interest rate has depended on the state of the economy of the borrowing country and the sector in which the project has fallen. Given AFESD's infrastructural bias, most concessionary loans have been given to infrastructure projects (see Tables 5.29-5.35).

Table 5.29: AFESD: Technical Assistance Allocations by Activity, 1974-9[a]

Activities	Allocations (KD thousands)[b]	Per cent
Technical Assistance for Countries		
Support of development institutions	420	23
Feasibility studies of projects	475	26
Sub Total	895	49
Technical Assistance for the Region		
Support of regional training institutions	242	13
Support of research and studies	360	20
Support of professional unions	42	2
Sub Total	644	35
Special Programmes	299	16
Total	1838	100

Note: a. Figures exclude KD 145,000 approved in 1979 and not yet allocated and also exclude savings; b. KD is equivalent to $US 3.42.
Source: *AFESD Annual Report*, 1979.

VI The Arab Monetary Fund (AMF)

The idea of creating some kind of Arab monetary institution went back to the late 1950s and early 1960s. For example, when the Arab Economic Unity Council passed a resolution relating to the establishment of the Arab Common Market, it also alluded to the establishment of an Arab Monetary Fund and an Arab Payments Union.[70] However, as was the case with a number of other Arab economic cooperation

Table 5.30: AFESD: Technical Assistance Allocations by Country, 1974-9

Country	Allocations (KD thousands)	Per cent
Egypt	300	29
Palestine	190	19
North Yemen	250	24
Sudan	125	12
Somalia	100	10
South Yemen	26	3
Mauritania	29	3
Total	1020	100

Source: *AFESD Annual Report*, 1979.

Table 5.31: AFESD: Loans Extended to Recipient Countries, 1974-9

Country	Total Loans (KD millions)	Percent of Total Loans	Per Capita of AF Loans (KD)	Average Per Capita Income in 1977 (KD)
Egypt	67.9	21	1.8	91.4
Sudan	38.4	12	2.3	82.9
Morocco	28.0	9	1.5	157.1
North Yemen	27.8	9	5.6	122.9
Mauritania	22.2	7	14.8	77.1
Syria	22.0	7	2.8	260.0
South Yemen	20.2	6	11.9	97.1
Jordan	19.0	6	6.6	202.9
Algeria	18.3	6	1.1	317.1
Tunisia	16.3	5	2.8	245.7
Somalia	16.0	5	4.3	31.4
Lebanon	11.0	3	3.8	260.0
Oman	6.0	2	7.5	725.7
Bahrain	5.0	2	16.7	1082.9
Total	318.1	100	2.6	171.1
Least Developed Countries' Share	124.6	39.2	4.3	84.4
Other Countries' Share	193.5	60.8	2.0	189.4

Source: *AFESD Annual Report*, 1979.

schemes, its realisation had to wait until after the oil revolution of 1973.

In 1975, Governors of Arab Central Banks met in Baghdad and approved the general principles for the creation of an Arab Monetary Fund, and their decisions – after several other meetings – were finalised at the meeting of the Arab Ministers of Finance and Economy in Rabat in April 1976.[71]

Membership, Capital, and Organisation

According to Article 12 of the Articles of Agreement of the Fund, its capital was to be equivalent to 250 million Arab Dinar Units of Account.[72]

The table on page 244 shows the countries that are members of the Fund.

The organisational structure of the Fund has resembled that of similar institutions and has consisted of a Board of Governors, a Board of Executive Directors, a Director General, and several committees.[73] The voting system of the Fund, however, has been more democratic, since each member has had 75 votes irrespective of the number of shares it has held.[74]

Objectives

Article 4 of the Fund's Articles of Agreement spelled out its objectives in the following way:

(1) Correcting disequilibria in the balances of payments of member States.
(2) Promoting the stability of exchange rates among Arab currencies, rendering them mutually convertible, and striving for the removal of restrictions on current payments between member States.
(3) Establishing such policies and modes of Arab monetary cooperation as will achieve the quickest pace of Arab economic integration and speed the process of economic development in the member States.
(4) Rendering advice, whenever called upon to do so, with regard to policies related to the investment of the financial resources of member States in foreign markets, so as to ensure the preservation of the real value of these resources and to promote their growth.
(5) Promoting the development of Arab financial markets.
(6) Studying ways to promote the use of the Arab dinar unit of account and paving the way for the creation of a unified Arab currency.

Table 5.32: General Features of AFESD Activities, 1974-9 (KD millions)

	1972	1973	1974	1975	1976	1977	1978	1979	Situation as at 31/12/1979
Loans									
Number of Loans	–	–	8	11	14	15	–	6	54
Total Amount	–	–	33.700	56.100	98.200	103.900	–	26.200	318.100
Average Amount/Loan	–	–	4.200	5.100	7.000	6.900	–	4.400	5.900
Total Disbursements	–	–	1.809	11.753	18.285	24.681	61.822	36.967	155.317
Technical Assistance									
Total Amount	–	–	0.125	0.115	0.628	0.805	0.366	0.200[a]	2.239[b]
Total Disbursements	–	–	0.125	0.112	0.159	0.623	0.278	0.169	1.466
UN Joint Programme[c]									
Fund Allocations	–	–	–	–	1.700	–	–	–	1.700
Amounts Disbursed	–	–	–	–	0.115	0.093	0.122	0.051[d]	0.381
UN Allocations	–	–	–	–	2.200	–	–	–	2.200
Amounts Disbursed	–	–	–	–	0.099	0.179	0.189	0.094	0.561
Authorised Capital	100.000	–	102.500	400.000	–	–	–	–	400.000
Subscribed Capital	81.010	–	18.850	2.190	87.460	180.930	–	14.700	385.140
Paid-up Capital	15.440	6.291	14.219	16.079	47.618	32.227	33.001	37.775	202.650
Total Income	0.593	0.984	2.924	3.706	5.929	10.277	11.331	14.696	50.440
Total Expenditure	0.045	0.562	0.831	0.928	1.449	2.107	2.199	1.997	10.118

Table 5.32 (Cont.)

	1972	1973	1974	1975	1976	1977	1978	1979	Situation as at 31/12/1979
Income Surplus	0.548	0.422	2.093	2.778	4.480	8.170	9.132	12.700	40.322
General Reserve	0.055	0.042	0.197	0.266	0.448	0.817	0.913	1.270	4.008
Additional Reserve	0.493	0.380	1.536	2.397	3.011	4.211	6.526	10.602	29.156
Foreign Currencies and Investments Reserve	–	–	0.235	–	0.278	2.244	1.204	0.625	4.586
Technical Aid	–	–	0.125	0.115	0.743	0.898	0.488	0.203	2.572
Number of Member Countries	17	17	17	20	21	21	21	21	21
Number of Recipient Countries		–	7	8	10	11	–	6	14
Professional Staff	–	16	24	28	39	53	45	30	30

Notes: a. Figures include KD 145,000 approved during 1979 but not yet allocated; b. includes KD 258,000 savings of which KD 28,000 were reallocated to the Arab Institute for Statistics; c. The Fund provides in kind technical assistance which is worth one million KD; d. Includes KD 48,000 administrative expenses of the Joint Programme.

Source: *AFESD Annual Report*, 1979.

Table 5.33: AFESD: Loans Approved in 1979

Country/Project	Loans Amount (KD millions)	Date of Approval
Jordan/Aqaba Water Supply	2.10	May 1979
Mauritania/Guelbs Iron Ore	10.00	May 1979
PDRY/ Hadramout Electricity	4.00	June 1979
Tunisia/Gabis Water Supply	3.30	Oct. 1979
Sudan/Gedaref-Kassala Road	5.20	Dec. 1979
Somalia/Tse-Tse Control	1.60	Dec. 1979

Source: *AFESD Annual Report*, 1979.

Table 5.34: AFESD: Lending by Sector and Country in 1979

Sectors	Amount (KD millions) Arab Least Developed Countries	Other Arab Countries	Total	Per cent
Transport	5.2	–	5.2	20
Electricity	4.0		4.0	15
Water Supply		5.4	5.4	21
Sub total	9.2	5.4	14.6	56
Mining	10.0	–	10.0	38
Agriculture	1.6	–	1.6	6
Sub total	11.6	–	11.6	44
Total	20.8	5.4	26.2	
Per cent	79%	21%		100%

Source: *AFESD Annual Report*, 1979.

(7) Coordinating the position of member States in dealing with international monetary and economic problems with the aim of realising their common interests while, at the same time, contributing to the settlement of world monetary problems.
(8) Settling current payments between member States in order to promote trade among them.[75]

Operational Methods and Lending Terms

Article 5 spelled out how the Fund would go about achieving its objectives:

(1) Providing short-term and medium-term credit facilities to member States with a view to assisting in financing their overall balance

Table 5.35: Projects Implemented by the AFESD/UNDP Joint Programme, 1976-9 and Expected Investments

Project	Beneficiary	Cost (KD 1000)	Joint Programme (KD 1000)	Expected Investment (KD millions)
Determination of Requirements for a Natural Resources Survey	YAR and PDRY	19	19	Not decided
Advanced Medical Training Programme	All Arab countries	13	13	0.650
Inter-Arab Tele-communications Link: Sub-region III	Iraq, Syria, Jordan, Egypt, Saudi Arabia and Kuwait	82	82	22.000
Pan-Arab Shipping Company (PASCO): Fleet Expansion Study	Egypt, Iraq, Jordan, Sudan, Kuwait and Syria	29[a]	22	10.000
Arab Passenger Air-lines Reservation System (APARS)	11 Arab airline companies	23	23	8.000
Preliminary Study on the Status and Prospects of Agricultural Machinery and Equipment in the Arab Countries	All Arab countries	35[a]	16	Not decided
Educational Tele-vision Programme for Children (Pan-Arabised Version of Sesame Street)	All Arab countries	280[a]	80	1.800
Management Information System for the Arab Maritime Transport Academy (AMTA)	16 Arab countries	19	19	0.150
Equipment Study for the Arab Maritime Transport Academy (AMTA)	16 Arab countries	22	22	1.500
Arab Long-Term Regional Model	All Arab countries	18	10	Not decided
Total		540	306	

Note: a. Including contributions from other sources.

Source: *AFESD Annual Report*, 1979.

Table 5.36: Details of AMF Membership

Country	Capital Share	Subscribed	Shares Number	% of total	Number of votes	Date of Ratification of Agreement
1. The Hashemite Kingdom of Jordan	4	1,080	80	1.60	155	28.10.1976
2. The United Arab Emirates	15	4,050	300	6.00	375	4. 4.1977
3. The State of Bahrain	4	1,080	80	1.60	155	18.11.1976
4. The Republic of Tunisia	5	1,350	100	2.00	175	15.11.1976
5. The People's Democratic Republic of Algeria	38	10,260	760	15.20	835	23. 8.1976
6. The Kingdom of Saudi Arabia	38	10,260	760	15.20	835	19. 2.1977
7. The Democratic Republic of the Sudan	10	2,700	200	4.00	275	14. 4.1977
8. The Syrian Arab Republic	4	1,080	80	1.60	155	30. 3.1977
9. The Somali Democratic Republic	4	1,080	80	1.60	155	19. 8.1976
10. The Republic of Iraq	25	6,750	500	10.00	575	16.11.1976
11. The Sultanate of Oman	4	1,080	80	1.60	155	29. 9.1976
12. The State of Qatar	10	2,700	200	4.00	275	15. 2.1977
13. The State of Kuwait	25	6,750	500	10.00	575	20.11.1976
14. The Republic of Lebanon	5	1,350	100	2.00	175	14. 4.1977
15. The Socialist People's Libyan Arab Jamahiriya	9.3	2,511	186	3.72	261	16.10.1976
16. The Arab Republic of Egypt	25	6,750	500	10.00	575	3.10.1976
17. The Kingdom of Morocco	10	2,700	200	4.00	275	18. 4.1977
18. The Islamic Republic of Mauritania	4	1,080	80	1.60	155	12. 1.1977
19. The Yemen Arab Republic	5	1,350	100	2.00	175	23. 1.1977
20. The People's Democratic Republic of Yemen	4	1,080	80	1.60	155	9.11.1976
21. Palestine	1.7	425	34	0.68	109	26. 3.1977
Total	250	67,466	5,000	100.00	6,575	

Source: *The Arab Monetary Fund Annual Report*, 1977.

of payments deficits with the rest of the world, resulting from trade in goods and services, transfers, and capital movements.

(2) Issuing guarantees in favour of member States to strengthen their borrowing capabilities from other financial sources for the purpose of financing the overall deficits in their balances of payment.

(3) Acting as intermediary in the issuance of loans in Arab and international financial markets for the account of member States and under their guarantees.

(4) Coordinating the monetary policies of member States and promoting cooperation between the monetary authorities in these States.

(5) Liberalising and promoting trade and the resulting current payments and encouraging capital movements between member States.

(6) Allocating from its resources, paid in the currencies of the member States, sufficient funds to provide the necessary credits to settle their current payments among them, in accordance with the rules and regulations to be laid down by the Board of Governors and within the framework of a special account to be opened by the Fund for that purpose.[76]

In accordance with these principles, the Fund has extended four types of loan to its members:

1. Automatic loans. Under this provision a member has been entitled to borrow up to 75 per cent of its subscription paid in convertible currencies, without the total, however, exceeding the member's overall balance of payments deficit.
2. Ordinary loans. Where a member's balance of payments need has exceeded the limit stipulated in the automatic loan, it has been granted an ordinary loan in support of a financial programme to be agreed upon by the Fund and the borrower. The amount of this type of loan could not exceed 225 per cent of a member's subscription paid in convertible currencies.
3. Extended loans. This type of assistance has been granted after the full use of automatic and ordinary loans, in cases of chronic balance of payments deficits, and in support of corrective policies. Its amount must not exceed 225 per cent of a member's subscriptions paid in convertible currencies.
4. Compulsory loans. This type of loan has been granted to deal with an unexpected balance of payments problem, and its amount should

not exceed 100 per cent of a member's subscription paid in convertible currencies.[77]

Interest rates charged on ordinary, extended, and compulsory loans have been 5.2 per cent, with an annual increase of 0.3 per cent to a maximum of 7 per cent in the seventh year. The Fund has also charged a commitment fee of one-quarter of 1 per cent on the total amount of these loans, payable on signing of the loan agreement. A further charge of the same amount has been payable on each disbursement.[78]

In many respects, the Arab Monetary Fund has emulated the IMF, as Arab development agencies have emulated the World Bank.[79] As a result, the Arab Monetary Fund has not exactly been the kind of Third World monetary institution recommended by a number of experts, aimed at breaking the monopoly of existing institutions and contributing to the collective self-reliance of the Third World.

Table 5.37: AMF: Disbursed Loans as of 31 December 1979

	Automatic Loans	Extended Loans	Total
	AAD	AAD	AAD[a]
Arab Republic of Egypt	4,687,500	–	4,687,500
Democratic Republic of Sudan	3,750,000	6,250,000	10,000,000
Islamic Republic of Mauritania	750,000	–	750,000
Kingdom of Morocco	1,875,000	–	1,875,000
Syrian Arab Republic	750,000	–	750,000
	11,812,500	6,250,000	18,062,500

Source: *The Arab Monetary Fund Annual Report*, 1979, p. 47.
Note: a. AAD is Arab Accounting Dinar. Each AAD is equivalent to one SDR.

PART THREE: NATIONAL ARAB ORGANISATIONS

I The Kuwait Fund for Arab Economic Development (KFAED)

Kuwait was the first Arab country to use economic assistance systematically to advance its national security and political goals. It also was the first country to choose a development fund as the main instrument to implement this policy. The Kuwait Fund thus was established the same year that Kuwait gained its independence. The motives behind the establishment of the Fund were discussed in some detail in Chapter 2.

Thus, suffice it to note here that the underlying factor was Kuwait's desire to project the image of being a responsible member of the Arab world and the international community, hoping that this would enhance its security and preserve its independence. Until 1974, the focus of the Kuwait Fund's activities was solely on Arab countries, but since that time the Fund has enlarged the scope of its operations to include all developing countries and has increased its capital accordingly.

Development Strategy and Lending Policy

KFAED officially has not advocated any particular development strategy. But two factors, namely the innate conservatism of the Fund – which has been a reflection of Kuwaiti society and in particular its business community – and those forces which influenced its formative years have deeply affected the Fund's development philosophy and strategy. For instance, the Fund has demonstrated a marked preference for project financing with a strong bias in favour of infrastructure and, in general, has shunned financing social projects in education, health, or population. This approach illustrates the impact of the World Bank strategy on the Fund.[80] Recently, the Fund has shown more willingness to finance agricultural projects and possibly to extend programme loans.

Another factor which has affected the Fund's strategy to some extent has been its avowed desire to contribute towards Arab economic cooperation by devising a coherent regional development strategy. But thus far the Fund has not been very successful, despite the fact that it has been instrumental in establishing a number of intra-Arab development, economic and financial institutions.

In addition, KFAED has also taken into account the following factors:

(a) the degree of importance of the project or prorgramme for which the loan has been requested and its priority in relation to other projects or programmes;
(b) the completeness and accuracy of the cost estimates for the project or programme;
(c) the adequacy of the economic technical evaluation of the project;
(d) ascertainment of the availability of other funds necessary, in addition to Fund financing, for the execution and completion of the project or programme; and

(e) the solvency of the applicant or the guarantor. The Fund's loans have been either interest free with only a service change of 0.5 per cent, or have had interest rates up to 5 per cent.

Politics

As noted earlier, KFAED was established almost immediately after Kuwait's independence in order to enhance its security and newly-won independence. As such, the creation of the Fund was thus a political act and its objectives were ultimately political. Even today, the Fund is first and foremost an instrument of Kuwait's foreign policy. In its operations, the Fund has tried to contribute to the achievement of Kuwait's political ambitions. For instance, the Fund's activities in regard to the establishment or strengthening of diverse intra-Arab organisations has fit within Kuwait's strategy in regard to the Arab world and Kuwait's role in it. But beyond this, KFAED has tried to limit the impact of political considerations on its lending operations. However, this attitude has also been a reflection of Kuwait's approach to intra-Arab politics, which fundamentally has been neutralist. Moreover, it has been politically important for Kuwait to preserve the image of the Fund as a non-political aid institution, since only in this way could it use the Fund to gain some influence with those countries which have normally been suspicious of Kuwait. But perhaps the most important factor which has preserved the relatively non-political character of the Fund has been the fact that KFAED has not been the only source of Kuwaiti aid. Thus, through other channels, the Kuwaiti government has used its financial assets for political purposes while preserving the Fund's image.[81]

As far as the impact of political considerations in the Fund's management is concerned, the following points should be stressed. For example, for reasons discussed earlier, the Fund has emphasised professional and technical expertise in its management. As a result, and in view of the importance of technical considerations in the Fund's lending policies, its management has enjoyed a high degree of independence in making its lending decisions. However, despite these factors the Fund has not been totally immune from the impact of politics because of its structure. For example, the Fund's Board of Directors and particularly its Chairman have had responsibility for the Fund's policies. Thus the fact that the Chairman of the Board is either the Prime Minister – or the Minister of Finance acting on his behalf – has ensured that the Fund's management would comply with the government's political and economic objectives.

Table 5.38: Concessionality of KFAED Loans

Year	Grant Element ($US)
1976	49
1978	44
1979	47
1980	41

Source: OECD: *Annual DAC Reviews*, 1979, 1981.

Table 5.39: Sectoral Distribution of KFAED Loans in Terms of Percentage of Total

Sector	Cumulative 1962-1980	Cumulative 1975-1980
Industry & Services	23.8	24.0
Agriculture & Primary Sector	18.8	17.6
Transport & Communications & Storage	30.5	29.6
Electricity	26.9	28.8

Source: KFAED, *Annual Report*, 1980.

Table 5.40: Sectoral and Geographical Distribution of KFAED Loans, 1 July 1979-30 June 1980 (KD millions)

	Sectors					
Countries	Agriculture & Primary Sector	Transport, Communications & Storage	Electricity	Industry & Services	Total	Percentage
Arab Countries	2.00	5.30	–	22.56	29.86	41.5
African Countries	–	5.60	4.50	5.00	15.10	21.0
Asian Countries	2.90	9.50	11.50	0.57	24.47	34.0
Other Countries	2.50	–	–	–	2.50	3.5
Total	7.40	20.40	16.00	28.13	71.93	100.0
Percentage	10.3	28.3	22.3	39.1	100.0	

Source: *KFAED Annual Report*, 1980.

Table 5.41: Sectoral and Geographical Distribution of KFAED Loans, 1 January 1962 - 30 June 1980 (KD millions)

	Sectors					
Countries	Agri-culture & Primary Sector	Transport, Com-munications & Storage	Electricity	Industry & Services	Total	Per-centage
Arab Countries	85.715	148.033	64.902	131.085	429.735	64.9
African Countries	14.910	33.600	20.870	9.500	79.880	11.9
Asian Countries	20.100	18.300	92.350	16.915	147.665	22.3
Other Countries	3.700	2.130	–	–	5.830	0.9
Total	124.42	202.063	178.122	157.500	662.110	100.0
Percentage	18.8	30.5	26.9	23.8	100.0	

Source: *KFAED Annual Report*, 1980.

Table 5.42: Sectoral and Geographical Distribution of KFAED Loans, 1 January 1975 - 30 June 1980 (KD millions)

	Sectors					
Countries	Agri-culture & Primary Sector	Transport, Com-munications & Storage	Electricity	Industry & Services	Total	Per-centage
Arab Countries	49.970	95.400	31.750	94.290	271.410	53.8
African Countries	14.910	33.600	20.870	9.500	79.880	15.7
Asian Countries	20.100	18.300	92.350	16.915	147.665	29.3
Other Countries	3.700	2.130	–	–	5.830	1.2
Total	88.680	149.430	144.970	120.705	503.785	100.0
Percentage	17.6	29.6	28.8	24.0	100.0	

Source: *KFAED Annual Report*, 1980.

II The Abu Dhabi Fund for Arab Economic Development (ADFAED)

The Abu Dhabi Fund was established in July 1971. The motives behind its creation were principally political, and even now the Fund is an instrument of UAE foreign policy.

When the Abu Dhabi Fund was established, the Federation of the United Arab Emirates had just come into being, and it was still facing regional opposition (for example, Saudi Arabia did not recognise the UAE until 1974). Under these circumstances, the newly established state's principal concern was to gain regional and Arab acceptance and to become a legitimate member of the Arab world. In order to achieve this aim, the UAE had to rely on its most important asset, namely its financial resources. Thus Abu Dhabi, the richest and the core member of the Federation, took the lead in organising an aid institution. In making its choice, Abu Dhabi was greatly influenced by Kuwait's experience ten years before. Furthermore the Kuwaitis actively encouraged Abu Dhabi in this direction.

At the beginning, the main function of the Fund was to extend economic assistance to Arab countries; but after the 1973 oil price increases, both the capital and the scope of the Fund's operations were expanded. Presently, the Fund extends aid to all developing countries.

Politics

As noted above, the Abu Dhabi Fund's organisation and operations have been greatly influenced by political considerations. The underlying reason has been that the Fund, being a national aid agency, has in fact been an instrument of Abu Dhabi's foreign policy. However, it seems that the Fund has been realising that, in order to establish itself as a viable development aid organisation, it must take into account more technical rather than political considerations. Such an attitude would, for instance, facilitate the Fund's cooperation with other regional and international aid organisations, which within a certain political and ideological framework have given more weight to technical considerations. A change in this direction could very well occur in the Fund, particularly as it develops an indigenous professional staff. Moreover, the Fund is not the only channel of Abu Dhabi's aid. In fact, large sums of aid – in some cases on better terms – have been given through the Ministries of Finance and Foreign Affairs. Thus, while somewhat depoliticising the Fund, the UAE has been able to use aid for political and other purposes.

Development Strategy and Lending Policy

The Abu Dhabi Fund's operation thus far has not indicated adherence to any particular development strategy, although in its lending policies there has been a significant bias in favour of infrastructure. As in the case of the Kuwait Fund, this emphasis has largely resulted from World Bank influence.

At the operational level, the Abu Dhabi Fund has had certain characteristics which have distinguished it from other Arab development funds. For instance, unlike other funds the Abu Dhabi Fund has undertaken equity participation in certain projects. Beyond this, however, the Abu Dhabi Fund has also favoured project rather than programme financing. In addition, it has followed the following guidelines:

(a) the Fund's contribution to any single project should not exceed 10 per cent of the Fund's capital;
(b) the Fund's contribution to any single project should not exceed 50 per cent of the total cost of the project; and
(c) the project to which the Fund has given assistance should not be in conflict with the economic interests of Abu Dhabi or of any other Arab country.

These conditions have been aimed principally at ensuring the financial soundness of the Fund. The third condition could also be construed as trying to prevent industrial duplication in the Arab region and to promote at least a semblance of regional development strategy.

The loans granted by the Fund have carried an interest rate of 3-5 per cent. Loans for agricultural development and infrastructure have carried a 3 per cent interest rate, whereas loans to industrial sectors and tourism have carried a 5 per cent interest rate. In addition to interest, the Fund's loans have carried a 1½ per cent service charge. The grace period of the Fund's loans has varied between 3.5 to 8 years, and the maturity period from 8 to 22.5 years. The length of the maturity period has depended on the sector of the economy to which the project loan has been given and the general economic conditions of the borrowing country.

III The Saudi Fund for Development

Unlike Kuwait and Abu Dhabi, Saudi Arabia did not establish an aid organisation until very late, despite the fact that since the late 1960s it had used financial assistance as an instrument of its foreign policy. This was so partly because Saudi Arabia did not have the same problems of legitimacy and did not face similar threats from its stronger neighbours. But it was also the consequence of a marked preference on the part of the Saudi leadership for less institutionalised and more informal channels of aid.

Table 5.43(a): Geographical Distribution of ADFAED Loans, 1974-80, Arab Countries (dirhams millions)[a]

Country	1974	1975	1976	1977	1978	1979	1980	Totals
Jordan	21.5	5	–	100	–	–	19	145.5
Bahrain	40	–	160	20	–	–	–	220.0
Tunisia	51.2	–	–	47	–	321.7	10	429.9
Sudan	–	–	96.5	40	4	–	–	140.5
Syria	51.5	–	–	56	–	–	–	107.5
Oman	–	–	60	–	663	–	–	723.0
Lebanon	–	–	–	67.8	–	–	–	67.8
Egypt	50	138	18.4	60	–	–	–	266.4
Morocco	–	–	110	–	–	40	–	150.0
Mauritania	–	–	–	16	–	120	24	160.0
Yemen AR	4	40	–	–	45	–	37.5	126.5
PDR Yemen	–	–	35.7	–	–	–	172.5	208.2
Totals	218.2	183	480.6	406.8	712	481.7	263	2,745.3

Note: a. The UAE dirham is equivalent to $0.3085.
Source: *Abu Dhabi Fund Annual Report*, 1980

However, international developments following the 1973 oil revolution, which put new pressures on Saudi Arabia to expand both the volume and the geographical scope of its aid, made a development fund a useful instrument. Thus the Saudi Fund for Development was established in 1974 and began its operations in mid-1975.

The SFD has also been first and foremost an arm of the Saudi government, and thus one of the state's foreign policy intruments. The capital of the Fund has been provided by the government; once depleted, it has had to be replenished by the government since the Fund has not had any borrowing power.

Table 5.43(b): Geographical Distribution of ADFAED Loans, 1974-80, African Countries

Country	1976	1977	1978	1979	1980	Total
Burundi	4	–	–	–	–	4
Mali	16	–	–	–	–	16
Gambia	–	5.2	–	–	2.7	7.9
Tanzania	–	24	–	–	–	24
Guinea	–	16	–	–	–	16
Uganda	–	–	25	–	–	25
Lesotho	–	–	3	–	4	7
Madagascar	–	–	–	16	–	16
Senegal	–	–	4	–	–	4
Seychelles	–	–	–	4	–	4
Comoro Islands	–	–	–	4	–	4
Cape Verde	–	–	–	–	4	4
Guinea Bissau	–	–	–	–	12	12
Totals	20	45.2	32	24	22.7	143.9

Source: *Abu Dhabi Fund Annual Report*, 1980.

The political nature of the Fund has also been reflected in the composition of its Board of Directors. The Chairman of the Board since its establishment has been the Minister of Finance and Economy.

Development Strategy and Lending Policy

The underlying objective of SFD – although not spelled out in these terms – has been to win the goodwill of developing countries towards Saudi Arabia through extension of economic assistance. In addition, there has been the genuine desire, inspired by Islamic teachings, to share the wealth with which God has blessed Saudi Arabia. Beyond this, the Saudis have not seemed to want to encourage any particular development strategy. This has been so partly because they have not had either the skilled manpower or sufficient experience in the field of development financing. However, despite the lack of any pronounced bias in favour of, or against, a particular development strategy, SFD's lending operations thus far have shown a marked preference for infrastructure development. As with the Kuwait and Abu Dhabi Funds, this situation resulted from SFD's efforts to emulate the World Bank, as well as from the caution of Saudi authorities.

As far as SFD's lending operations have been concerned, it has shown an absolute preference for project lending and has not been

Table 5.44: Distribution of ADFAED Loans and Equity Participation by Sector, 1974-80 (dirhams millions)

	1974		1975		1976		1977		1978		1979		1980		Totals	
Sector	No.	Value	No.	Value	No.	Value	No.	Value	No.	Value	No.	Value	No.	Value	No.	Value
Agriculture, Fisheries & Rural Development	1	21.8	1	40	7	118.7	–	–	2	9	1	40	4	125.5	16	354.6
Transport, Communications & Storage	1	13.5	1	5	1	60	5	192.9	3	39	2	44	3	16.7	16	371.1
Water & Electricity	3	95.5	1	130	2	168	4	160.1	2	100	2	19.2	1	112.5	15	785.3
Housing	–	–	–	–	1	40	–	–	–	–	–	–	–	–	1	40
Tourism & Hotels	2	41.7	1	8	–	–	–	–	–	–	–	–	1	10	4	59.7
Manufacturing & Extractive Industry	2	46	–	–	5	275	5	186	3	692	3	402.5	3	121	21	1722.5
Gross Total	9	218.2	4	183	16	661.6	14	539	10	840	8	505.7	12	385.7	73	3333.2

Source: *Abu Dhabi Fund Annual Report*, 1980.

Table 5.45: Concessionality of ADFAED Loans

Year	Grant Element (%)
1978	29
1979	26
1980	35

Source: *Annual DAC Reviews*, 1979, 1981.

involved in any programme lending or balance of payments support programme. SFD's preference for project lending has derived from the obvious advantages which this type of financing has had for the donor country, as well as from the fact that the Saudi government has extended other types of assistance through other channels.

Like other development funds and for the same reasons, SFD has also preferred co-financing. SFD's aid programme has not been limited to any particular region and all developing countries have been eligible for its aid. But, understandably, SFD has extended assistance only to countries friendly towards Saudi Arabia. Despite this fact, however, the bulk of SFD's assistance has gone to Arab and Islamic countries. But following the Afro-Arab summit conference of 1977, the African countries have also become major recipients.

SFD's loans carry interest rates ranging between 2 and 4 per cent. They have a maturity period of 20 to 30 years with a grace period of five to ten years. The rate of concessionality of SFD loans has been determined by the economic and financial situations of recipient countries and by the sector for which the loans have been granted.[82]

IV Iraqi Fund for External Development (IFED)

The Iraqi Fund for External Development was established in 1975 with a capital of 50 million Iraqi dinars. However, its capital has quadrupled since then and, according to its President, was 20 million ID in September 1980. Moreover, according to the Fund's President, it could make commitments beyond its capital because 'we know that the government would in time of disbursement increase the capital of the Fund'.[83]

Development Strategy and Lending Policy

According to the Fund's president, IFED extends aid to 'all developing countries whose policies are consistant with the general policies of

OPEC member countries and Iraq's interests, and their attitude to the relationship between industrialised countries and developing countries, and their attitude to the non-aligned movement. . .'[84] What the foregoing illustrates is that the lending criteria of the Fund, like most of the national funds, has been basically political. According to its President, accumulated commitments of the Fund by September 1980 were $1.25 billion, spread over 27 countries.

According to the Fund's president, IFED's lending has not been limited 'to the so-called development projects but extends to services, particularly health and education'. Furthermore, the Iraqi Fund has been considering the possibility of trying to plan its aid to various friendly countries, 'namely to make its commitments for a number of years ahead, either for a three year or five year period with various projects annually financed from such aggregate loans allocated to that particular country'.[85]

Moreover, on instructions from the Iraqi government, the Fund has since 1979 been making interest-free loans to those developing countries which lift Iraqi oil, in order to compensate them for the oil price increases. By September 1980, the Fund had made loan commitments amounting to $220 million.[86] However, in view of the war with Iran and the financial problems ensuing from it, the future of IFED's lending is unclear.

PART FOUR: CONCLUSIONS

This analysis of the choices made by OPEC members regarding channels of aid, development strategies, and lending policies has also confirmed the central thrust of this study: that little role has been played in OPEC-country decisions by considerations of the developmental impact of aid on recipients, or of its contribution to the achievement of Third World objectives.

For example, choices made by OPEC countries have not contributed to the achievement of two principal objectives of the Third World countries – namely, to increase their influence in the international development and financial institutions and to strengthen those institutions in which they have been better represented. For instance, OPEC's contributions to UNDP could have been much more substantial. Nor have the OPEC countries tried to resurrect the UNCDF, which historically symbolised the developing countries' efforts to break the monopoly of the World Bank. The only exception has been the creation of IFAD, whose voting process has been more egalitarian.

Moreover, there has been no evidence that the OPEC countries, through their monetary contributions and other close links to the international institutions, have tried to make them more responsive to the needs and demands of the Third World. In fact, quite the opposite has happened, and the international institutions and their experts have come to shape the structures, development philosophies, and lending operations of the OPEC institutions. Thus, partly as a result of this factor, the OPEC countries have failed to develop a coherent aid strategy, sufficiently meshed with other aspects of their relations with Third World countries, that could facilitate the achievement of their declared common objectives.

To be sure, lack of adequate expertise and knowledge on the part of OPEC members has been an important factor in their total emulation of the practices of the dominant international institutions. However, this factor alone has not accounted for the above phenomenon, since the OPEC countries could have acquired the services of independent development experts – as they have done in many other fields – or they could have been more aggressive in training their own collective pool of experts. As with so many other aspects of OPEC aid, the principal reasons have lain in its members' internal contradictions and external dependencies, as well as in certain basic divergences of interest between key OPEC members and a large number of Third World countries.

Notes

1. Disagreements on this issue were part of broader discord between developing and developed countries regarding the roots of the economic crisis at the time. The developed countries attributed the crisis to the oil price increases, and thus held OPEC responsible for meeting the needs of the MSAs. By contrast, the developing countries claimed that systemic deficiencies were responsible for the crisis and thus the plight of the MSAs, and argued that their problems should be dealt with in the context of global discussions regarding the NIEO.

2. In order somewhat to assuage the misgivings of the industrialised countries, the Ad Hoc committee established to study the special programme to help the MSAs made some effort to find ways of using existing institutions. For example, it prepared a report entitled 'Considerations Relating to the Possibility of Merging the UN's Capital Development Fund with the Operations of the Special Fund'. *Secretary General's Report on the UN's Special Program* Document A/10201, 21 August 1975.

3. The UNSF's structure, purposes, and modes of operation were embodied in UNGA Resolution 3356 (XXIX).

4. *Report of Board of Governors of the UNSF*, Fifth Session SF/13, 22 June 1978, p. 3. In 1976, Venezuela made a contribution of $11,629,440 and Norway $9,981,851, which they later transferred to IFAD.

5. Ibid.

6. *UN Yearbook*, 1974, p. 358.

7. By November 1974, $223 million had been committed to the Special Account. The first recipients of assistance were countries whose projected deficits exceeded 75 per cent of their imports. Among them were Bangladesh. $12,245,000; the Central African Republic, $1 million; Chad, $500,000; Honduras, $2 million; India, $7 million; Kenya, $1.75 million; Madagascar, $1 million; Mali, $2.5 million; Sierra Leone, $750,000; Sri Lanka, $2 million, and Tanzania, $4.5 million.

8. The inclusion of the IMF Oil Facility among the channels of OPEC aid has been done with some hesitation, since (1) industrialised as well as developing countries have benefited from it; and (2) contributions to the Oil Facility have been considered in some quarters to be investment and not aid, since they have been in the form of loans to the IMF and have earned interest. Thus, for example, OECD figures on OPEC aid have not included these contributions, while those of UNCTAD have done so. But since the feeling of the OPEC countries has been that contributions to the Oil Facility should be included in the aid figures, it has been treated in this study as a channel for OPEC aid.

9. *Finance and Development*, vol. II, no. 3, September 1974, p. 17.

10. During the winter and spring of 1974, the Director General of the IMF visited Iran, Algeria, Saudi Arabia, Kuwait, the UAE, Venezuela and Nigeria. Among the OPEC countries, Iran was an early supporter of the facility and one of its largest contributors. *IMF Survey*, 13 May 1974, p. 129.

11. In August 1974, the Fund concluded borrowing agreements with seven oil exporting countries for a total of about SDR 2.8 billion; Canada, SDR 258 million; Iran, SDR 580 million; Kuwait, SDR 400 million; Oman, SDR 20 million; Abu Dhabi, SDR 100 million; and Venezuela, SDR 450 million. In November and December, the Fund concluded borrowing agreements with the Netherlands for SDR 150 million, and Nigeria for SDR 100 million. In connection with the oil facility for 1975, the Fund concluded borrowing agreements with twelve lenders for a total amount of SDR 2.9 billion. The lenders were the Austrian National Bank, SDR 50 million; the National Bank of Belgium, SDR 100 million; The Deutsche Bundesbank, SDR 300 million; the Central Bank of Iran, SDR 410 million; the Central Bank of Kuwait, SDR 200 million; the Kingdom of the Netherlands, SDR 300 million; the Government of Nigeria, SDR 200 million; the Bank of Norway, SDR 50 million; the Saudi Arabian Monetary Agency, SDR 1,000 million; the Swiss National Bank, SDR 150 million; the Central Bank of Trinidad & Tobago, SDR 10 million; and the Central Bank of Venezuela, SDR 200 million. *IMF Annual Report*, 1975, pp. 55-6.

12. *IMF Annual Report*, 1974, p. 53.

13. *IMF Annual Report*, 1975, pp. 53-4. The members were also required under the 1975 facility to describe measures that they had taken or were going to take to conserve oil or to develop alternative sources of energy in the light of their economic situation. These measures, however, were not subject to the Fund's assessment. Ibid., p. 54.

14. *IMF Annual Report*, 1976, p. 58.

15. *IMF Annual Report*, 1980, pp. 89-90.

16. *IMF Annual Reports*, 1978-9, 1980.

17. *IMF Annual Report*, 1975, p. 43 and 1976, p. 60.

18. *IMF Annual Report*, 1975, p. 60.

19. 'The Operation of the Trust Fund', *Finance & Development*, vol. 15, no. 3, September 1978, p. 37. 'The agreement to sell part of the IMF's gold was part of a highly complicated understanding concerning the problem of gold, including the disposition of the IMF's holdings, in the context of the second

amendment to the Articles of Agreement. The Interim Committee agreed that the IMF should sell one-third of its gold holdings (50 million ounces). Half that amount was to be sold directly to all members in proportion of their quotas, in so-called restitution operations. The other half would be sold for the benefit of developing countries, of which a proportion of the profits corresponding to the share of quotas of the developing countries would be transferred directly to each country in proportion to its quota – the so-called indirect restitution to the developing countries. The remainder of the profits would provide the resources of the Trust Fund.' Ibid.

20. In view of the fact that the Interim Committee had decided that the amount of gold available for sale should be disposed of over a four-year period, the IMF decided to divide the operation of the Trust Fund into two periods.

21. *IMF Annual Report*, 1980, pp. 86-8.

22. Ibid., p. 88. Despite the rather insignificant contribution of OPEC to the Trust Fund, it is mentioned here as a channel for OPEC aid because the OPEC members have emphasised, in their aid record, the irrevocable transfer of their share of profits from the gold sale.

23. Several suggestions had been made to make access to bank loans easier for the poor countries. One of these suggestions was for the creation of an interest-subsidy facility in the World Bank. The Third Window was in fact a variation on this proposal. See: Bettina Hurni, *The Lending Policy of the World Bank in the 1970s*, Boulder, Colorado: Westview Press, 1980, p. 93.

24. *The United Nations Development Programme in 1979: Report and Review*, pp. 14-15.

25. Information largely based on *UNDP At a Glance*, published by UNDP Information Services, 1981.

26. *UNDP in 1979*, p. 22.

27. For a detailed study of the history of UNCDF, see M.V. Kamara and J.C. Plano, *United Nations Capital Development Fund: Poor and Rich Worlds in Collision*, Kalamazoo, Michigan: New Issues Press, 1974, pp. 8-22.

28. *UNCDP Annual Report*, 1981, DP/536, 12 March 1981, p. 1.

29. Ibid., pp. 3-4.

30. M.V. Kamara and J.C. Plano, *United Nations Capital Development Fund*, p. 76.

31. Ibid.

32. Robert Asher, 'Development Assistance in DD II', *International Organisation*, vol. 25, no. 2, Spring 1971, p. 107.

33. *Lending Policies and Criteria*, IFAD/I Rev. I, December, 1978, p. 1.

34. Ibid.

35. Ibid., p. 2.

36. Ibid., p. 3.

37. Ibid., p. 4.

38. For more detail, see Ibid., pp. 6-7.

39. Ibid., pp. 7-8.

40. See George Dorsey, 'Fulfill America's Pledge to the Hungry', *Christian Science Monitor*, 30 November 1982, p. 23.

41. Mansour F. Fawzi, 'Restructuring the World Bank' in Khadija Haq (ed.), *Dialogue for a New Order*, New York: Pergamon Press, 1980, p. 109.

42. Over the years, the Bank has developed an elaborate machinery to ascertain the creditworthiness of its applicants and the soundness of their projects. For a detailed study see: Bettina Hurni, *Lending Policy*. Moreover, according to some experts, the Bank has not done this through a real dialogue with recipients; rather it has frequently given the impression of having made up its own mind on the issues with little prior discussion with the governments concerned, and then of

having determined to persuade governments to adopt its solutions. Teresa Hayter, *Aid as Imperialism*, Harmondsworth, England: Penguin Books, 1971, p. 71.

43. According to one expert, examples of such changes are 'the periodical tendency of developing countries to alternate between a liberal and a bureaucratic form of capitalism, the *cooptation of third world capital surplus countries*, the financing of new types of projects previously shunned by the Bank and the advocacy of certain countries for a development strategy based primarily on the satisfaction of basic needs and the alleviation of poverty'. Mansour F. Fawzi, 'Restructuring the World Bank', p. 115, emphasis added. See also: Walden Bello and David Kinley, 'La Politique de la Banque Mondiale a l'Heure de l'Ortodoxie Liberale', *Le Monde Diplomatique*, September 1981, p. 3; and Betsy Hartman, 'McNamara's Legacy: Basic Needs Without Basic Reforms', *South: The Third World Magazine*, August 1981, pp. 31-5.

44. Robert E. Asher and Edward S. Mason, *The World Bank Since Bretton Woods*, Washington, DC: Brookings Institution, 1973, p. 381. Consequently, IDA's aim has been 'to finance the same types of projects as does the Bank, selected according to the same standards but on terms that place a lighter burden on the balance of payments of the borrowing country'. Ibid.

45. The issue of the PLO's observer status was a problem at the 1981 IMF-Bank meeting, but it was not raised at the 1982 meeting. Among OPEC countries, Kuwait, at least rhetorically, has been more openly supportive of the developing countries' position. See: *MEED*, vol. 26, no. 37, 10-16 September 1982, pp. 9-10.

46. The extent of the impact of the new changes is not clear yet. The Assistant Secretary General of the Fund has said in an interview that 'The Fund might undergo cosmetic or even substantial change.' *Saudi Business and Arab Economic Report*, vol. IV, no. 26, 3 October 1980, p. 18.

47. *The OPEC Fund for International Development*, Annual Report 1980, p. 14. For details of the legal and organisational aspects of the Fund, see Ibrahim F.I. Shihata, *The OPEC Fund*.

48. *The OPEC Special Fund*, Annual Report, 1976, p. 13.

49. *The OPEC Fund*, Annual Report, 1980, p. 15. 'In conformity with the revision of the agreement establishing the Fund, its administration will be reorganized to handle the demands of a permanent international agency. The strengthening of the Fund's staff and the buildup of its capacity to undertake project appraisal will take place progressively in order to ensure a smooth transition.' Ibid.

50. However, for a time 'reliance on other agencies will continue concurrently with the strengthening of the Fund's technical capabilities'. Ibid.

51. *The OPEC Special Fund*, Annual Report, 1976, p. 12.

52. Ibid.

53. Ibid.

54. *The OPEC Special Fund*, Annual Report 1977, p. 9. OSF has tried to promote cooperation among developing countries on a number of initiatives of which the following have been the most important: the OSF provided a grant of $US 40 million (in two $20 million instalments) to the United Nations Development Programme (UNDP) to be used for specific projects carried out with UNDP support by a number of countries in different regions of the world. All these projects have been designed to increase either energy, minerals, or food production, and they have all been regional, involving close cooperation among developing countries.

55. Ibid.

56. *Islamic Development Bank*, Second Annual Report 1976/7, p. 35.

57. Ibid., p. 36.

58. BADEA's officials have admitted that the Bank's underlying objective has

been political. One official has defined BADEA as a 'political fund through which the Arab League hopes to win friends in black Africa'. Quoted in John Law, *Arab Aid: Who Gets It, Why, and For What*, New York: Chase World Information Corporation, 1978, p. 121.

59. *BADEA Annual Report*, 1978, p. 8.

60. '. . . It is quite a complex task to plan a strategy for development and more particularly to guarantee its rationality. The Bank does not ignore in this respect the complexity and limitations inherent in any conception that is purely normative . . . Some sectoral priorities which for years had prevailed in the Third World eventually proved to be misguided . . . It should be added that after the break with various development norms of the past, the problem of choice and priorities remains unsolved in a most dramatic way. For in a continent like Africa there is urgency and priority for practically everything.' Ibid.

61. In 1978, in response to the appeal made by the OAU, BADEA set up an Emergency Aid Programme to a number of African countries. Most of the aid under this programme has gone to projects involving irrigation and crop protection schemes. Ibid., p. 25.

62. In 1975, $52 million was lent to infrastructure projects and only $11.6 million to agriculture. In 1978, infrastructure claimed only $24.1 million and agriculture $27 million. Ibid., p. 29.

63. For example, in financing infrastructure projects, BADEA has tried to follow the guidelines laid down by UN resolution A/32/160. recommending the development of Africa's road, sea, river, air and railway transport, as well as telecommunications systems. In respect to agriculture, BADEA has tried to finance those projects which would help improve Africa's food producing capacity. In regard to industrial development, BADEA has tried to observe the guidelines set in the Lima Declaration which among other things recommended the promotion of such industries as can foster the development of other industries and thus create a chain of industrial growth. Ibid., pp. 24 and 26.

64. 'BADEA's Washington office, located across the street from the World Bank complex of buildings, keeps in touch with World Bank officers who identify possible projects for BADEA lending. Particularly those in which the World Bank (including its affiliates, the IFC and the IDA) has an interest and for which it would like to find co-financing.' John Law, *Arab Aid*, p. 123.

65. 'The Bank has succeeded in getting borrowers to revise a project. For example, Guinea had wanted to borrow to build a cement plant that the Bank thought was too ambitious in scale. After the Bank convinced the Guinean Government that a 250,000 ton per year plant would be big enough, Guinea then got the loan.' Ibid.

66. Based on a personal interview.

67. *AFESD Annual Report*, 1976, p. 2.

68. Ibid.

69. 'Politics in the Arab Fund's activities is manifested in the need to balance the interests of the various members. This process of balancing various interests requires attention to the attitudes of major capital contributors (such as Kuwait and Saudi Arabia) and of major recipients whose attitudes are politically significant for the viability of the Fund (such as Sudan and Egypt).' Soliman Demir, *Arab Development Funds in the Middle East*, New York: Published for UNITAR by Pergamon Press, 1979, p. 47.

70. *The Arab Monetary Fund Annual Report*, 1977, p. 2.

71. Ibid., p. 3.

72. *The Articles of Agreement of the Arab Monetary Fund*, November 1977, p. 11.

73. Articles 32-34, Ibid., pp. 23-6.

74. Article 31, Ibid., p. 23.
75. Ibid., p. 6.
76. Ibid., p. 7.
77. *The Arab Monetary Fund Annual Report*, 1978, pp. 14-15.
78. Ibid.
79. For example, according to the Fund's first Annual Report: 'Several objectives of the AMF parallel those of the International Monetary Fund (IMF). Therefore, the AMF initiated steps aimed at establishing a close relationship with that institution and utilising both its expertise and information to help draw appropriate policies suited to conditions of member countries who are also members of IMF.' *Arab Monetary Fund Annual Report*, 1977, p. 5.
80. In general, the World Bank has had a determining influence on the Kuwait Fund – as on other Arab funds – as the following statement illustrates: 'Since it started its operations, the Kuwait Fund has had very close contacts with the World Bank. For the first few crucial years of its operations, it depended on World Bank experts to help in designing its operational methods. This was achieved by having one or two resident Bank experts as consultants. The loan agreements with the borrowers are still modelled after World Bank agreements. It is evident that the cautious policy of the Fund in lending has been at least encouraged (if not designed) through the influence of the World Bank.' Soliman Demir, *The Kuwait Fund: The Political Economy of Arab Regional Development*, New York: Praeger, 1976, p. 47.
81. Most experts who have studied the operations of the Fund have noted that it has had a relative lack of discrimination on political grounds. However, most have also argued that keeping KFAED non-political has been itself a political decision. According to one expert '. . . From an interview with a Fund expert and long-time associate of Al-Hamad (the Director General of the Fund) we learn that it is political for the Fund not to be "political"; the leaders realised that by maintaining integrity of the Fund's operations and decisions regarding loans, a good image of Kuwait and its independence could be more enhanced. . .' Ibid., p. 27. Another expert has noted that 'although the Fund has given in project loans less than half the amount given by the Kuwait government in "political loans" there is growing recognition that the Fund's money has been more effectively spent, even from the point of view of political prestige.' Robert Stephens, *The Arabs New Frontier*, p. 55.
82. For details of Saudi Fund loans, see Chapter 4.
83. 'Iraq Fund's President for External Development Gives Views on OPEC and the Third World', *OPEC Bulletin*, vol. XI, no. 18, September 1980, p. 18.
84. Ibid., p. 19.
85. Ibid.
86. Ibid.

6 CONCLUSIONS

The preceding chapters have attempted to analyse the nature of OPEC-Third World relations since the oil revolution of 1973, by focusing on one aspect of these relations – namely, that concerning aid.

In doing so, the underlying purpose of this study has been to investigate whether the OPEC countries – as members of the Third World – have succeeded in advancing principal Third World objectives, including those concerning the reform of the international economic system, crystalised in the call for a New International Economic Order (NIEO). And if the answer is negative, what have been the root causes of this failure?

The principal yardstick used in this study to measure OPEC's contribution to advancing Third World objectives has been the use of aid by OPEC members as an instrument for both reform of the global economic system and realisation of other Third World goals. Thus special attention has been paid to determining whether OPEC's use of aid has been different from that of the traditional donors.

The central thesis that emerges from this study is that the OPEC countries have failed to act vigorously and with determination to advance Third World objectives. Moreover, the OPEC countries' use of aid has generally followed the established pattern of the traditional donors, and consequently they have failed to use aid in any systematic manner to achieve Third World goals.

However, the other – and equally important – thesis of this study is that OPEC's failure has not been due to its members' conscious deception in representing their goals and aspirations as being essentially the same as those of the rest of the Third World. Rather, this failure has been the almost inevitable outcome of basic contradictions relating both to intra-OPEC relations and to those between OPEC and the rest of the Third World – contradictions that came to the fore after the events of 1973. Moreover, the negative impact of these contradictions on OPEC-Third World relations has been further compounded by the serious internal deficiencies of OPEC countries, their external dependencies, and the highly unstable and permeated nature of the security and political environments within which key OPEC members had to operate. Also, pressures emanating from the nature of the international political system have tended to strengthen the impact of the abovementioned factors.

I OPEC and the NIEO

Following the events of 1973, early statements by OPEC countries emphasised the themes of OPEC-Third World solidarity and of the community of interests between them. These statements created expectations that the OPEC countries, together with the rest of the Third World, would press for significant structural reforms in the international economic system. Third World countries also expected that OPEC would forge a new form of economic partnership with them that in turn would contribute further to the reform of the system.

OPEC's early actions also supported its statements. Thus, for example, largely as a result of OPEC efforts a special session of the United Nations was convened in 1974. By consensus, it adopted a declaration and a programme of action for the establishment of a New International Economic Order, although the industrialised countries expressed reservations. The next year, OPEC heads of state and governments met in Algiers and, in a Solemn Declaration, reiterated their commitment to establishing an NIEO and set guidelines for OPEC's future actions.

Yet beyond these steps, OPEC as a whole has failed either to pressure the industrialised countries into making concessions or to take independent actions conducive to reforming the global system. Quite the contrary, a number of OPEC countries have adopted policies – particularly in regard to the supply and price of oil – that have weakened their bargaining position, and thus that of the Third World in general, *vis-à-vis* the industrialised countries.

Actions of certain key OPEC members in the field of development aid (for example, their choice of channels for disbursement) have also run counter to the aspirations of Third World countries. For example, not only have OPEC countries failed to create alternative development and financial institutions geared to the particular needs of the Third World and more responsive to its demands, but also a number of their practices have tended to strengthen the existing dominant aid institutions.

Moreover, OPEC has failed to reform the existing institutions by increasing the Third World's capacity to affect their development and other operational policies, through such measures as creating more equitable voting systems. At the same time, OPEC has failed to use financial contributions to strengthen those development institutions in which Third World countries have had greater influence, such as those of the United Nations. These failures have occurred despite the fact that all these steps have been deemed necessary for the eventual establishment of an NIEO.

Intra-OPEC Divisions and Institutional Limitations

Among reasons for OPEC's failure to contribute effectively to the establishment of an NIEO have been its own internal divisions and institutional limitations. In the former category, divisions among OPEC countries have reflected differences among them in terms of resource bases – including oil reserves – developmental needs, political and ideological orientations, ethnic origins, and national rivalries and aspirations. These differences have affected the perceptions of individual OPEC members about their interests in regard to a wide range of issues, including reform of the international economic system. Thus, for example, those OPEC members with relatively low oil reserves, high absorptive capacities, and in general better prospects for creating diversified economic bases have also tended to be more committed to the goal of establishing an NIEO.

However, even among this group, other factors (such as political orientation) have tended either to enhance or to mitigate the impact of economic ones. Thus, for example, Iran's pro-Western orientation prior to the revolution somewhat reduced its militancy on reform of the international economic system. By contrast, Algeria's non-aligned posture has made it one of the most outspoken proponents of reform in the international system.

The divisive impact of economic difference has been compounded by other elements, particularly intra-OPEC ethnic and national rivalries, such as those between Iran and some of OPEC's Arab members, especially Saudi Arabia. The industrialised countries, in turn, have manipulated these rivalries in order to prevent the emergence of a solid OPEC-Third World front.

OPEC's institutional characteristics have also limited its ability to coordinate its members' policies towards the Third World, the reform of the international system, and triangular relations among OPEC, Third World, and industrialised countries. For example, OPEC has not been a supranational organisation with authority to set policies for its member states. Moreover, its rule of consensus has meant that even majority views could not be imposed on reluctant members. Nor have even OPEC decisions reached by consensus been binding on individual member states.

These institutional rules have reflected the realistic approach of OPEC members, and in fact for most of the institution's life they have contributed to OPEC's success and even its survival, despite serious divisions and strains. Yet they have also been a serious hindrance to the development of coherent and binding OPEC strategies towards a whole range of issues.

Diverging OPEC/Third World Interests

While, as developing countries, OPEC members have shared many problems of other Third World countries – and thus have shared interests in some aspects of reforming the international economic system – there have also been significant and growing divergences of interests between these two groups of states. The most significant has concerned the price of oil and the vigour and speed with which alternative sources of energy should be developed.

Strains in OPEC-Third World relations had appeared as early as 1971, after the Teheran and Tripoli agreements between OPEC members and the oil companies, leading to oil price increases. These strains were further sharpened following the price increases of 1973-4 and of the late 1970s. Consequently, by 1974, Third World interests would have been best served by moderate oil prices and a vigorous energy development programme; but OPEC's interests required the maximisation of revenues through higher oil prices and energy development programmes that would not dramatically erode oil's competitive advantage.

Noteworthily, the divergence of OPEC-Third World interests in regard to these two issues has not been the same for all OPEC countries, nor has the divergence applied equally to both issues. For example, OPEC members with high absorptive capacities and relatively low oil reserves have, up to a point, shared the Third World's interests in a speedy development of alternative sources of energy, while they have sharply differed from it in regard to oil prices, since they have wanted to maximise their own oil revenues in a short period of time through higher prices. By contrast, almost the exact opposite of this situation has prevailed in the cases of low absorptive, financial surplus OPEC members with large oil reserves.

These differences have also affected the evaluation by OPEC members of the importance of reforms in the international economic system in order to advance their individual interests. Consequently, those OPEC members with better prospects for industrialisation have been more committed than the rest of OPEC to those reforms that could both facilitate their internal development and create a better competitive environment in the future.

Another source of strain has been the very high OPEC economic dependence on the industrialised countries – a dependence that became more rather than less serious after the oil revolution and the ensuing development boom in OPEC countries. A particularly important result of the 1973 oil revolution was the accumulation of large monetary surpluses by a number of OPEC countries. Most of these assets were invested in the industrialised countries and thus became highly vulnerable to economic developments there, in two ways: adverse developments have affected the level of OPEC exports and thus revenues; and such developments have affected OPEC monetary assets invested in the industrialised countries.

Logically, therefore, OPEC could not have been expected to press for reforms in the international economic system that, at least in the short term, could have had major adverse effects on the economies of the developed countries and, by extension, on those of the OPEC countries, themselves.

However, as important as these economic divergences have been, they could still have been bridged, especially since, as developing countries, OPEC states have had at least a long-term stake in the reform of the international system. In fact, had it not been for other reasons (for example, intra-OPEC rivalries, OPEC members' internal weaknesses and contradictions, and pressures emanating from the nature of the international political system and regional sub-systems), formulas reconciling essential interests of OPEC members with those of the Third World countries could probably have been worked out. Having done so, together they could then have approached the developed world with a more unified front; and OPEC could have made a more direct and sustained link between the willingness of the developed world to make concessions on the reform of the international system and its own willingness to be more cooperative concerning the supply and price of oil. Of course, even if OPEC had achieved this objective, there would have been no guarantee that it could have extracted the necessary concessions from the developed countries.

Having missed that opportunity, the OPEC countries have found it increasingly difficult to extract concessions from the developed countries. Yet there has been nothing surprising or unexpected in this situation since, once the OPEC countries lost their initial edge over the developed countries, their inherent weaknessses reasserted themselves, intensifying their vulnerability to developed-country counter-measures, and thus at least partly reversing the relative shift of power that had taken place in OPEC's favour – a development that has greatly diminished OPEC's capacity to act as an agent of reform of the international system and promoter of Third World interests.

Internal Weaknesses and External Dependencies

Among factors behind OPEC's inability to be an effective agent of reform, perhaps the most significant have been those related to its members' inherent military, economic and technological weaknesses, plus their external dependencies. Moreover, these factors have been even more consequential because they have applied to key OPEC members in terms of their oil reserves, production capacities, and monetary surpluses – those areas potentially providing them with the greatest leverage over the industrialised countries. Thus, for example, the fact that Saudi Arabia and the small Persian Gulf oil producers have not had viable military forces to ensure their security has contributed significantly to their unwillingness to use their leverage over the industrialised countries, fearing that this might provoke military reprisals. Likewise, their technological deficiencies have contributed to their inability to utilise their leverage fully, by making them highly dependent on foreign experts – primarily from industrialised countries – even to run their oil industries.

In addition, the leadership characteristics of many OPEC states and the underdeveloped state of their social and political institutions, have further diminished their ability to use their potential leverage over the industrialised countries. For example, the conservative nature of this leadership – coupled with other factors such as envy generated by oil wealth – has made them prime targets for regional radical forces. In turn, these countries to a great extent have depended on key industrialised countries for protection through the supply of needed military hardware and advisers, and for efforts to improve their immediate and peripheral security environments, thus giving the latter considerable leverage that they have consistently used to the full.

It is interesting that even such OPEC members as Iran, with sizeable indigenous military forces, have had high levels of military and technological dependence on the key industrialised countries, particularly in terms of military supply.

Furthermore, the underdeveloped state of these countries' social and political institutions, particularly the lack of well-established processes for the orderly transfer of political power, have made their leaderships highly vulnerable to a wide range of pressures, including the possibility of foreign-inspired and sudden political change. Here, too, these vulnerabilities have been manipulated effectively by the industrialised countries through, for example, offers of protection and support against internal and external challenges to existing leaders in exchange for moderation on oil prices or on the reform of the international economic system.

Regional Factors

The characteristics of regional sub-systems to which key OPEC members have belonged have played an important role in determining their behaviour towards a number of important issues, including that of reforming the international economic system. The key OPEC members are located in the strategically important region of the Middle East, which for decades has been a zone of great power rivalry, and thus has been highly unstable and permeated by outside forces. In addition, this region has been bedevilled by deep and long-standing conflicts and rivalries that, on many occasions, have been manipulated by outside powers for the latter's own interests.

The combination of these factors has both created special security problems for the Middle Eastern countries and has imposed special demands on them in terms of their policy choices. For reasons elaborated earlier, key OPEC members have been particularly vulnerable to these pressures.

The most pressing demand that the Middle East's regional factors have generated for most of its countries – namely the Arab states – has related to the question of Israel, and especially to the means for dealing with the Israeli enemy and for restoring Arab rights. The paramountcy of the Israeli question for the Arabs has meant that no other issue could be allowed to distract Arab attention and energy from the goal of dealing with Israel. For the Arab members of OPEC, this situation has meant that their newly-gained wealth and influence should be used first and foremost to resolve the Israeli problem, even if this were to mean compromising on other objectives and relegating them to second or third place.

In addition, the Israeli question has caused special problems for some Arab members of OPEC, because of the linkage – especially since the 1967 Arab defeat – between the legitimacy of Arab governments and their stand on the Arab-Israeli conflict. The conservative and pro-Western Arab regimes, including those of the Persian Gulf, have thus faced even greater pressure to prove their commitment to restore Arab rights. This pressure has been intensified at a more practical level, given their vulnerability to Palestinian-inspired subversion.

However, there has been no inherent or logical contradiction between the goal of restoring Arab rights in Palestine and the goal of advancing Third World objectives, in general. In fact, some Arab members of OPEC have felt that both goals should be pursued vigorously and in parallel, thus forcing the developed countries to make concessions on both fronts. Yet key OPEC members, especially Saudi Arabia, have not agreed with this view. While they have concurred that the problem of Israel could only be resolved after a change in the policies of the developed countries – particularly those of the United States and West European countries – they have believed that such a change could only be produced through persuasion and through concessions on other issues, including the reform of the international system. Saudi Arabia's attitude on this point has also been affected by strained Arab-Iranian relations, plus intense rivalry between Iran and Saudi Arabia for leadership in the Persian Gulf. Thus, in order to enhance its leadership potential, Saudi Arabia has been anxious to replace Iran as the favoured US ally in the Gulf and to gain the latter's support for its own position.

Finally, those Arab countries that, for a variety of reasons, have favoured a more conciliatory approach toward the industrialised countries over the Arab-Israeli conflict, have also had the largest share of OPEC's oil, financial assets, and thus influence. Therefore, their view and their stategy have so far prevailed. As a result, achieving Third World objectives has been subordinated to the more immediate objective of persuading developed countries to change their policies on the Arab-Israeli conflict more in favour of the Arab position. Of course, the choice of the best strategy to deal with Israel that has been made by OPEC's Arab members has reflected their particular weaknesses and problems, and has been largely determined by their perception of what would best serve their own narrow national interests and advance their regional aspirations for influence.

International Factors

The ability of OPEC countries to be effective agents of change in favour of the Third World has also been affected by the characteristics of the international political system, by the perceptions of OPEC members of their own positions within that system, and by the possible changes that might adversely affect them.

When the oil revolution occurred in 1973, the international political system was no longer the tight bipolar system of the 1950s and the early 1960s. On the contrary, a number of military, political, and other developments had led to a considerable diffusion of power and to the emergence of new power centres. On the ideological level as well, the rigid East-West division had become blurred, especially after the onset of *détente*. All of these developments led to an even greater demand for economic and political autonomy on the part of many Third World countries.

Yet despite this erosion of bipolarity and easing of the ideological rigidities of the Cold War, the basic international divide along the lines of the East-West conflict remained. Moreover, despite the quest of most Third World countries for greater autonomy and their desire not to be overly-identified with either camp, they nevertheless have held strong preferences. At any rate, this has been true of the ruling elites in these countries. OPEC countries have been no exception. The majority – particularly key countries such as Saudi Arabia and the other Persian Gulf states – have generally favoured the Western camp. This is not to say that OPEC's relations with the West have been free from strains and contradictions. In fact, there have been considerable strains between certain OPEC members and Western countries. This has been particularly true of those OPEC members with broader economic and military power bases and regional ambitions for leadership, such as Iran and Venezuela.

Still, most OPEC members have perceived that serious erosion of the Western position within the global balance of power would be detrimental to their own vital interests. As a result, they could not insist on reform that, at least in the short run, could have a negative impact on Western economies with implications of political problems – at least in some countries – that could lead to a general erosion of the Western position.

In brief, considerations of the East-West balance in OPEC calculations and choices of strategy (for example, in dealing with the triangular relations among OPEC, the Third World, and the developed countries) have competed with those of North-South. More often than not, the former considerations have prevailed.

However, it should be stressed that, important as they have been, none of the foregoing factors alone could have led to the situation that developed. Rather, it has been their interaction that in most cases has intensified the divisive and conflictual aspects of intra-OPEC and OPEC-Third World relations, and has led to OPEC's failure as an agent of reform. Thus, for example, economic divergences between two key OPEC members – namely, Iran and Saudi Arabia – have been aggravated by their interactions with regional factors such as Saudi-Iranian rivalry for Gulf leadership. Likewise, the impact of key OPEC members' economic dependence on the industrial countries has been further intensified by their military and security dependence on the same countries. Yet another example has been the way in which considerations of the East-West balance have eroded OPEC solidarity with the Third World on issues that oppose North and South to one another.

Nevertheless, it should be emphasised that OPEC has not been alone responsible for the Third World's failure to bring about a reform of the international economic system, even though it has certainly failed to use the largely psychological edge it had over the industrialised countries in 1974 and perhaps also in 1975. In fact, both intra-OPEC divisions and OPEC-Third World divergences have been a partial reflection of deeper political and economic divisions within the Third World in general.

In the last decade, economic differences among Third World countries have become particularly significant. This has been the result of considerable industrial development in a number of Third World countries. Although these so-called Newly-Industrialising Countries (NICs) still have a number of important interests in common with the rest of the Third World, they have become more rather than less dependent on the industrialised countries for export markets and for sources of capital. Moreover, as new – albeit fledgling – industrialised powers, these countries have benefited from certain aspects of the current international economic system. As a result, their approach to reform of the international system has become increasingly more selective and far less militant. In addition, political differences with other Third World nations, as well as their still-persisting military and political vulnerabilities and dependencies, have increasingly reduced their capacity for unified action and thus their collective bargaining power *vis-à-vis* the industrialised world.

In sum, therefore, OPEC's failure to be an effective agent of reform, plus the reasons behind it, have only reflected the essentially fragmented nature of the Third World and the latter's weak position within the current international system, despite considerable improvement in the relative economic and political power of some of its members in the last two decades.

II OPEC Aid and Third World Development Prospects

Evaluating OPEC's contribution to improving Third World development prospects has been the most difficult aspect of OPEC-Third World relations, essentially because of the problems involved in evaluating any aid programme. Three problems stand out.

Appropriate Criteria and OPEC's Record

The thorniest problem in evaluating the contribution of any foreign aid to development relates to the lack of clear and widely-accepted criteria defining what constitutes development. For instance, should a country's development performance be judged in terms of increases in overall GNP? Should it be measured in terms of success in reducing the level of poverty, providing for basic needs, and closing glaring income gaps? Or should it be measured in terms of success in achieving reasonable economic self-sufficiency, and ability to generate self-sustained growth?

The second problem relates to the difficulty in evaluating the relative role of different factors – economic, technological, social, and political – in the process of development. Thus, for example, there is as yet no agreement on which factors play the most important role in advancing the process of development: economic factors, such as the availability of capital and proper and adequate technology, or factors such as social attitudes and the nature of social and political institutions.

The third problem relates to uncertainties regarding the impact of the international economic system. Hence the question: Can the developing countries achieve a level of development enabling them to eliminate mass poverty and sustain a steady and reasonable rate of economic growth within a highly-discriminatory international economic system?

As yet, there have been no settled answers to any of these questions. Nor is it firmly settled what kinds of development strategies are most likely to achieve the goals implied in these questions. Within these limits, however, there is still a general inclination that an adequate development strategy should do the following in a developing country, in general:

(a) reduce the level of poverty, close income gaps, and provide for basic needs;

(b) increase the level of economic self-sufficiency, particularly in such vital sectors as agriculture; and

(c) improve the technological base and employment prospects.

There is also a general inclination that the best foreign aid programmes are those that encourage such strategies and help in their implementation. Moreover, during the last decade a certain consensus – at least at the declaratory level – has emerged among Third World countries regarding the elements of an effective development strategy that includes all of the above factors, plus a contribution to an increase in the industrial capacity of the Third World.

In addition, the enhancement of the Third World's collective self-reliance – through increased intra-Third World trade, economic, and technological cooperation, and the development of Third World monetary, development, and other joint economic schemes – has become an important common Third World objective.

Within the Solemn Declaration of 1975, the OPEC countries committed themselves to the achievement of many of these objectives. Thus a fair basis for judging the effectiveness of OPEC aid from the point of view of development would be to measure its contribution to their achievement.

Judged on this basis, OPEC aid has not been very effective. OPEC's failure either to develop viable alternatives to existing development institutions – or at least to reform them – or to strengthen those institutions in which the Third World has been better represented was discussed earlier.

Concerning trade and other economic relations, as well, there has been no clear evidence of a systematic use of aid by OPEC to increase trade and other economic relations with the Third World, although some exceptions have existed. Rather, the increase in both the volume of OPEC-Third World trade and other economic interactions – such as an increased movement of labour – has been due to certain economic and demographic characteristics of OPEC members and to the comparative advantage of a number of Third World countries that has been translated into lower prices. Further, these increases have been limited to a very few economic sectors (for example, construction) and to a few Third World countries; they might even prove to have been of a temporary nature. For example, as the OPEC countries' development boom subsides due both to reduced oil revenues and to the satisfaction of initial needs – gains to a number of Third World countries from construction business in the OPEC countries will also be reduced.

Nor has there been any clear evidence that OPEC has used aid to improve the Third World's collective technological base, or to increase intra-Third World cooperation in the field of technology, although the OPEC fund, through UNDP, has made some financial contributions to such schemes.

Also, there has been no evidence that the OPEC countries have used their aid systematically to encourage development strategies that would increase the Third World's economic and technological self-sufficiency, alleviate poverty, and meet basic needs. For example, despite the acute nature of Third World food problems, aid to agricultural sectors has constituted a relatively-low percentage of total OPEC aid, particularly if OPEC's contributions to IFAD are excluded. Likewise, education, health, and other social welfare projects have accounted for a small share of total OPEC aid.

In addition to the above, there is general agreement that certain characteristics of aid could improve its positive developmental impact. Thus, for example aid is generally judged most effective that (1) is in the form of financial grants and is largely untied either by source or by end use; (2) is not motivated by non-developmental considerations; (3) is extended over a long period of time with a predictable flow; and (4) is sufficiently meshed with the broad development needs and possibilities of the recipient country.

Judged on the basis of these criteria, OPEC's aid performance has been mixed. On the one hand, OPEC aid has essentially consisted of financial grants or loans and has been untied by source and in many cases also by end use. On the other hand, however, non-developmental considerations have been the primary motive for OPEC aid and have led to a serious distortion of its geographical distribution, content, and terms. Thus a few countries – judged by OPEC members to be politically and strategically important – have received the bulk of OPEC's untied financial grants. By contrast, other developing countries have received aid mostly in the form of project loans and in much smaller volume. Further, aid to these countries has essentially been *ad hoc*, unpredictable, and not sufficiently meshed with the recipient countries' development needs and plans – a combination of factors that have reduced the positive development impact of OPEC's aid.

Finally, in evaluating the developmental impact of OPEC aid, Third World financial losses from oil price increases should be taken into account. In many instances, these financial losses have led to lower rates of economic growth and in some cases to total stagnation or a negative rate of growth. Since, as far as most Third World countries have been concerned, OPEC's aid has not compensated for financial losses – at least partly induced by oil price increases – the inevitable conclusion has been that the positive developmental impact of OPEC aid has been minimal.

Reasons for Ineffectiveness

Many factors that have contributed to OPEC's failure to achieve a structural reform of the international economic system have also been at the root of its aid's ineffectiveness. Here, too, the interaction of these factors, rather than any single one, has been the principal culprit. Thus, for example, economic differences among OPEC members have contributed to their failure to establish a sizeable Third World development institution, since those OPEC members with the largest monetary surpluses have also had the severest skilled-manpower problems. Therefore, they have understandably been unwilling to contribute heavily to an institution that would essentially have been run by experts from other OPEC or Third World countries and in which they would have had minimal influence.

Regional factors have tended to strengthen the impact of economic considerations. For instance, the requirements of intra-Arab politics have led the Arab members of OPEC to neglect broader Third World objectives. Therefore, in order to demonstrate their commitment to common Arab goals and to the enhancement of Arab prestige, these countries have developed a number of development institutions to which the words 'Arab' or 'Islamic' – given the Arabs' tendency wrongly to equate Islam with Arabism – have been attached.

This situation has led to waste and has hampered a more vigorous harnessing of OPEC-Third World human and technical resources within a development institution with the potential perhaps to become a viable alternative to the World Bank. It has also led to the World Bank's domination of OPEC aid institutions, since the former has been the primary – if not sole – source of technical advice through, among other things, providing key staff members, particularly during the institutions' formative years.

Furthermore, the impact of regional factors has been strengthened by the inherent weaknesses of the key OPEC members and the vulnerability of their ruling elites, factors that have made them extremely susceptible to pressures from the developed countries, with highly-threatening implications. For instance, important roles have been played by the over-dependence of Saudi Arabia on the United States for its security and – given the dominant US position within the World Bank – US desire to maintain the Bank's paramount role.

Concerning the quality of OPEC aid, again the same factors and their interaction have been the problems. Thus, for example, various factors have had a very negative impact on motivations for OPEC aid, and consequently on its geographical distribution (for example, the military weaknesses of key OPEC members, the highly unstable nature of their regional environments, and the requirements both of intra-Arab politics and of the global balance of power), since these factors have meant that political and strategic rather than developmental considerations have decided the direction of OPEC aid.

The technological deficiencies of OPEC countries have also had a negative impact on the quality of their aid. In particular, because of their lack of expertise, these countries have not been able to develop innovative development and aid strategies that might have been better suited to meet Third World requirements. As a result, they essentially have tended to emulate the developed countries and the existing aid institutions.

With regard to increased trade and other OPEC-Third World economic relations, once again the factors discussed earlier have had a limiting impact. Thus, for example, the desire of key OPEC members to influence the attitudes of industrialised countries towards the Arab-Israeli conflict has led them to offer economic incentives: essentially increased trade, loans and investments. In turn, this step has reduced the available OPEC financial surpluses to be invested in the Third World or to be used for purchases from the Third World.

Nevertheless, it must be stressed that both the low developmental quality of OPEC aid and OPEC's failure to use aid to advance Third World objectives have to a considerable extent been due to the general economic and political problems of the Third World. For instance, the low level of OPEC-Third World trade has essentially been due to the underdeveloped nature of Third World economies which simply have not produced the goods that OPEC members have needed. Likewise, the absolute economic and trade dependence of many Third World countries on the industrialised world has created serious barriers in the way of closer economic relations between these Third World countries and OPEC. For example, Nigeria's efforts to forge closer relations with other West African countries have thus far been frustrated by the intricate links between the French-speaking African countries and France, rooted in their colonial past. In the Arab world, similar links between the North African countries and France have hampered intra-Arab trade.

Deficiencies in the infrastructure of Third World countries have also led to a low level of OPEC investments, resulting in a less-than-optimal use of available aid and investment. In the same vein, manifestations of excessive nationalism, regionalism, or ethnic- and religious-centredness by OPEC members have essentially reflected the fragmented state of the Third World, which still lacks a developed sense of collective identity.

III Comparison of OPEC and DAC Aid

Comparison of OPEC and DAC aid should be done at three levels: motives, terms and content, and developmental impact.

Motives

Once the OPEC countries failed to develop a unified and global strategy for the use of their newly-acquired financial assets as a vehicle to advance long-held Third World objectives, they have used these assets almost exclusively as instruments of their national policies. This is not to suggest that, at some level, no OPEC countries have viewed the advancement of Third World objectives as a valid goal of their own. Rather, it is to emphasise that this goal has not been among their principal concerns.

In their use of aid as an instrument of national policy, the OPEC countries have behaved very much like the traditional donors. In fact, any differences in the behaviour of the two groups have resulted from special circumstances rather than from conscious policy choices. For instance, with both OPEC and DAC donors, security and political needs and interests have been primary motivations for aid and have largely determined its direction. However, the two groups have been somewhat different in that, while OPEC members have been preoccupied with direct threats to their security within their immediate regions, DAC donors have been primarily concerned with calculations of global strategic balances of power and the stability of economically-important areas. At any rate, for both groups the paramount character of security and political motivations has resulted in a distorted pattern in the geographical distribution of aid.

Likewise, special links – ethnic and religious in the case of OPEC countries and colonial connections in the case of some DAC countries – have affected the direction of both donor groups' aid. Similarly, both groups have tended to use aid to propagate their own political, ideological, cultural and, in the case of OPEC, religious values.

By contrast, traditional economic motives, such as access to raw materials and export markets, have in general been much less important for OPEC than for DAC countries in determining the direction of aid, although these motives have been quite important for a few OPEC countries, notably Iran. To be sure, the traditional motive of using aid to improve the investment environment in recipient countries has played some role in the case of low-absorptive OPEC countries. But because of an increasing concentration of OPEC investments in the developed countries, no clear OPEC strategy to link aid and increased investment in the Third World has been developed.

The aid extended by the socialist countries (CMEA) has also been influenced by the above factors, especially ideological affinity and the desire to propagate ideology – indeed, to an even greater extent than in the case of OPEC and DAC.

Terms and Content

Concerning the terms of aid, the weighted-average concessionality of DAC and OPEC aid has been quite similar. However, the terms of DAC aid to the least-developed countries has been more favourable, since the largest share of OPEC's grants and soft loans has gone to the Arab confrontation states and to other Arab countries. Still, OPEC aid has essentially been untied by source, which has somewhat improved its terms, whereas most DAC aid has been tied – although not to the same extent by all DAC donors. However, the terms of OPEC aid have been far superior to those of CMEA.

Regarding the content of aid, differences between OPEC and DAC have been more pronounced than has been true concerning motivations for aid. Thus, while DAC aid has primarily consisted of commodity aid and technical assistance, most of OPEC's aid has been financial, reflecting the economic and technological deficiencies of its members. For example, they have not even had the technological expertise needed to appraise projects and to determine technical requirements, let alone to provide that assistance. In fact, OPEC members themselves have been importers of technology. Nor have their industrial and agricultural capacities allowed them to provide commodity aid. However, some OPEC countries have tied their aid to the purchase of oil (Iraq) or to certain industrial products (Iran) in order to promote domestic industries.

Turning to other aspects of aid, again there have been more similarities than differences. For example, although DAC has provided a greater share of its aid through multilateral rather than bilateral channels – particularly if OPEC/Arab aid institutions are excluded from the comparison – this fact has essentially reflected a tendency common to all donors to channel their aid through those institutions in which they have had more influence, rather than a basic philosophical difference.

Even regarding development strategies, similarities have far outnumbered differences. In general, despite rhetoric emphasising such popular Third World themes as 'satisfying basic needs', 'poverty-oriented development strategy', and 'collective self-reliance', OPEC donors have followed the strategies favoured by principal DAC donors and by such institutions as the World Bank. This development has resulted in part from increased co-financing arrangements between OPEC and the World Bank and OPEC and DAC countries, including some of the latter's development institutions such as the European Development Fund. It has also resulted from the inherent deficiencies of OPEC countries – including their lack of adequate technical expertise; from an innate financial caution on the part of key OPEC donors in situations where there has been no compelling security or political motive for aid; and from the underlying similarity of security and economic interests as between key OPEC donors and principal DAC countries. In consequence, there has been the irony that the Scandinavian members of DAC – even more than OPEC countries – have encouraged development strategies aimed at satisfying basic needs and alleviating poverty.

Developmental Impact

Comparing the developmental impact of DAC and OPEC aid is most difficult of all, both because there are inherent problems in evaluating any aid programme in these terms, and because the DAC group has been in the aid business longer than has OPEC. In general, however, it can be argued that most aid from both groups has not been used in ways designed to maximise its positive developmental impact. Most important has been the primacy of non-developmental motivations. Thus, for example, DAC aid has tended to perpetuate the economic and technological dependence of the recipients on the donors. In fact, the technical assistance programmes of DAC countries have been used to ease their own unemployment problems rather than to help aid recipients to create indigenous technological bases. In like manner, food aid has been used by a number of DAC countries to dispose of large agricultural surpluses generated by artificially-high and subsidised agricultural prices.

By contrast, OPEC aid has had certain characteristics (for example, untied aid in the form of financial grants or loans) that could have improved its developmental impact. But these advantages have been nullified by OPEC's failure to develop a proper institutional framework and its own technical base for aid – together with other Third World countries and using independent experts – plus its practice of emulating the DAC donors and cooperating with them.

In fact, the experience of both DAC and OPEC have demonstrated the complexity of the whole development process and the inadequacy of aid to resolve the problems of the Third World, in the absence of both domestic social and political reforms among the recipients and reforms in the international economic system.

IV Outlook for OPEC-Third World Relations

What, therefore, is likely to be the future of relations between OPEC and the Third World? Will their interests coalesce or diverge? Will the gap between their perceptions widen or is there a possibility of a real *entente*?

At least in the short and medium terms, all indications are that a rekindling of OPEC-Third World solidarity, even to the level of 1974, is unlikely. Likewise, it is unlikely that the OPEC countries will do anything significant to advance Third World objectives or that they will change their approach towards the specific issue of aid.

This prediction is founded in part on awareness that intra-OPEC divisions and contradictions not only persist, but are actually intensifying, even endangering the survival of the organisation itself. For example, two principal OPEC members – Iran and Iraq – have been engaged in a bloody war for more than three years, a war that has been sapping their energies and depleting their resources. In addition, tensions and conflicts in regions of vital interest to key OPEC members (such as the Persian Gulf and the Arab Middle East) have been heightened, demanding the full attention of these countries and the use of all their resources, thus reducing their ability to allocate time and money to broader Third World problems. Furthermore, regional tensions have intensified the sense of insecurity and vulnerability of key OPEC members, thus increasing their dependence on developed-country allies. Under these circumstances, OPEC members cannot afford to challenge the developed countries on issues related to the Third World.

Essential economic, political, and other characteristics of the OPEC countries have also remained the same, as have basic contradictions in OPEC-Third World relations – thus barring significant changes in the nature of those relations. The same basic lack of change is also true of factors in the international political system, such as the East-West division. The combination of these factors points to the persistence of previous patterns of OPEC-Third World relations in the future.

In addition, as a result of changed economic conditions, OPEC's dominant position in oil markets has been eroded, thus diminishing its influence in international affairs. This development has also dimmed the prospects of the OPEC countries to continue securing large revenues, at least while the global oil glut lasts. In fact, a number of OPEC members are already in considerable financial trouble.

The important question is whether this is a temporary situation – caused by recession in the industrialised countries and by overproduction of oil by some OPEC countries – or whether it reflects structural change prompted by conservation and more efficient use of energy by the industrialised countries, plus the availability of non-OPEC sources of oil such as the North Sea, Mexico, and Alaska. If the latter proves to be the case, it would mean a permanent erosion of OPEC power.

In the long run, such a development might again bring OPEC and the rest of the Third World close together, but it would also mean a reduction of their bargaining capacity towards the developed world. However, this possibility of greater OPEC-Third World solidarity is unlikely to come about, since the financial and political interdependence of key OPEC members and the industrialised world has increased so significantly in the last decade.

With regard to the specific issue of OPEC aid, recent developments will have a negative impact on its volume and nature. In the immediate future, therefore, any increase in the volume of OPEC aid is unlikely, and in fact it may well be reduced. Moreover, in the future perhaps even more than in the past, the OPEC countries will use aid to meet their urgent security and other needs; and issues such as the general development of the Third World will at best be secondary objectives. Likewise, with their prospects for large revenues having deteriorated, most OPEC countries will become even more cautious in the use of their aid money, and therefore will not depart from the past practice of following the policies of established international development organisations.

Thus the wheel may be coming full circle: from a time when the OPEC countries had no potential as aid donors, to one in which their economic fortunes reduce the opportunity for them to consider this role. In between these two periods, meanwhile, their record as aid donors has fallen far short of what it could have been.

APPENDIX

'SOLEMN DECLARATION' OF OPEC SUMMIT CONFERENCE

Issued 6 March 1975

The Kings and Presidents of the OPEC member countries convened in Algiers at the invitation of President of the Revolution Council and Prime Minister of the Democratic and Popular Republic of Algeria.

1. They discussed the current world economic crisis. They exchanged views on the causes of this crisis, which has been in progress for many years, and studied the measures to be taken to safeguard the rights and legitimate interests of their peoples within the framework of international solidarity and co-operation.

The Kings and Presidents affirm that international peace and progress depend on the mutual respect for the sovereignty of the member countries of the world community and on equality among them in accordance with the UN Charter. They also affirm that the basic statements embodied in this declaration are in line with the resolutions of the special sixth session of the UN General Assembly on the questions of raw materials and development.

The Kings and Presidents reaffirm the importance of an exchange of views among their countries to unite them in a bid to safeguard the rights and legitimate interests of their peoples and they once more proclaim their countries' right to develop their natural resources, to exploit them and fix their prices. The right is one of the rights of their sovereignty which brooks no argument. The Kings and Presidents reject any idea or attempt to infringe these basic rights – ideas and attempts which constitute a challenge to their countries' sovereignty.

They stress anew that OPEC member states work for the higher interest and progress of the entire world community, through a firm and cohesive collective defence of the legitimate rights of its peoples. They are thus promoting the interests of the raw material producing developing countries in defence of their peoples' legitimate rights. They believe that the nations' joint responsibilities with regard to the international economic situation demand that more importance be attached to international co-operation.

They declare that they are prepared to contribute to the development and stability of the world's economy, as has been stated in the declaration and the special action programme to establish a new international economic system, a document approved by the UN General Assembly at its sixth special session.

Economic Differences

2. The Kings and Presidents observe that the current international economic crisis is due basically to the great differences in the economic and social progress of the various peoples: that these differences, of which the backwardness of the developing countries is one feature, is basically the result of foreign exploitation, which perpetuates these differences. It has become more acute with the passing of time in the absence of adequate international co-operation for development. This situation has led to the accelerated exhaustion of the developing countries' natural resources, and this in itself hinders the effective transfer of capital and technology and greatly disturbs the balance of economic relations.

They point out that this disturbance which besets the current international economic situation has been aggravated through a widespread inflation. The latter has reduced economic growth in general and has contributed to the instability of the world monetary system in the absence of adequate controls.

They reaffirm that the reasons for this disturbance must be sought in the chronic and deep-seated defects which have been accumulating for years, such as the advanced countries' general tendency to overconsumption and waste of limited resources and to the inappropriate, short-sighted economic policies pursued by the industrialised world.

The Kings and Presidents reject all allegations which attribute the responsibility for the present instability in the world's economy to the price of oil. The fact is that oil, which has made a considerable contribution to the progress and prosperity of the industrialised countries in the last quarter of this century, is not only the cheapest energy source, but the cost of imported oil accounts for only a minute portion of the advanced countries' GNP. The latest adjustment in the price of oil has contributed only slightly to their high average inflation, which is basically due to other causes, whose roots are within the economies of the advanced countries.

This inflation, which is consistently being exported to the developing countries, has resulted in obstructing their efforts in the sphere of development.

Propaganda Campaign

3. The Kings and Presidents also condemn the threats that have been made, the propaganda campaign and other measures taken, culminating in the accusation levelled at the OPEC member countries that they wish to undermine the economy of the developed countries. These campaigns and measures, which may lead to a confrontation, have precluded a clear understanding of the existing problems, and have created an atmosphere of tension hardly conducive to consultations or co-operation in the international sphere. They denounce any attempts by the consuming countries to form cartels with a view to a confrontation: they condemn any plan of strategy aimed at economic or military acts of aggression by these or other cartels against any member countries of OPEC.

In view of these threats, the Kings and Presidents once more emphasise the solidarity which unites their ranks in defence of their peoples' legitimate rights. They declare their readiness, within the framework of that solidarity, to take immediate and effective measures to oppose these threats by adopting a united policy whenever this is called for, particularly in the event of aggression.

4. While the Kings and Presidents are careful to respond to the legitimate aspirations of their peoples for development and progress, they are fully aware of the close links that exist between the national development of their respective countries and the economic prosperity of the world as a whole. The increasing co-operation between nations has made the Kings and Presidents more aware of the difficulties which other peoples have had to face and which may affect world stability. In view of this, they once more emphasise their support for dialogue, co-operation and joint action for finding solutions to the major problems facing the world's economy.

Prompted by this spirit, the OPEC member countries, thanks to the increasing financial resources which have been accruing to them for a relatively short period, have contributed – both through bilateral and multilateral arrangements – to the efforts made for development and for stabilising the balance of payments of other developing countries as well as the industrially advanced states. The financial aid given by these countries to other developing countries during 1974 was, in proportion to their GNP many times the volume of the annual average of the assistance given by the industrially advanced countries to the developing countries in the last development decade.

In addition to this, the OPEC member countries have offered credit facilities to the developed countries to help them meet their balance of payment deficit. Furthermore, the measures taken by the OPEC member countries to speed up their economic development and encourage trade among themselves have contributed to the expansion of international trade and to establishing an equilibrium in the balance of payments of the developed countries.

Oil Vital for Development

5. The Kings and Presidents agree in principle to the holding of an international conference between the developing and the advanced countries. They believe that the aim of such a conference should be to make concrete progress towards alleviating the existing major difficulties in the world's economy. That conference should therefore pay equal attention to the problems facing the advanced and the developing countries. Consequently, the agenda of that conference should under no circumstances be confined to a study of the problem of energy: it should clearly cover the questions of the raw materials of the developing countries: reform of the international monetary system and co-operation for development, with a view to achieving world stability. Furthermore, the conference could take place on a limited scale so that it can work efficiently, provided that all countries concerned with the problems under discussion are suitably and genuinely represented.

6. The Kings and Presidents emphasise that the exploitation of the oil resources of their respective countries – which are liable to run out – should be so conducted as to serve primarily and above all the interests of their peoples in the best possible manner, proceeding from the fact that oil, which represents the major source of income, is a factor vital for the development of their countries.

While they realise the crucial role which oil supplies play in the world's economy, they believe that to conserve the resources of oil is a basic requirement for the prosperity of the generations to come. Consequently, they urge the pursuit of policies aimed at the optimum utilisation of this essential resource, which is both finite and non-renewable.

7. The Kings and Presidents point out that the artificially low prices of oil have in the past led to continuous exploitation of this limited and exhaustible resource. To persevere with that policy would lead to disaster, both as regards the conservation of this resource and for the

world's economy. They are of the opinion that the interests of the OPEC member countries, as well as those of the rest of the world, require that the price of oil, being the basic source of national income of the member countries, should be determined by taking into consideration the following:

(a) The need to conserve oil, the fact that it is a finite resource and its increasing rarity in the future;
(b) The value of oil, having regard to its utilisation for other than energy purposes,
(c) The facts with regard to alternative energy sources, from the point of view of their availability, use and cost.

The price of oil should, moreover, be stabilised by linking it with certain objective criteria, including the price of industrial products, the rate of inflation, and the conditions of transfer of commodities and technology for the development of the OPEC member countries.

8. The Kings and Presidents declare that their countries are ready to continue to offer positive facilities for the solution of the major problems affecting the world's economy, and to encourage the consistent co-operation, which is the key to the establishment of a new international economic system. They propose, with a view to advancing this international co-operation, that a number of measures should be taken *vis-à-vis* the other developing and the industrialised countries. In this context, they would like to emphasise that the measures proposed in this declaration constitute a comprehensive programme whose provisions must be implemented in full if the goals of justice and efficiency are to be achieved.

Aid to Developing Countries

9. Once again the Kings and Presidents stress the natural solidarity which unites their countries with the other developing countries in their struggle to overcome their backwardness. They express their deep appreciation of the strong support given by all the developing countries to the member countries of OPEC at the developing countries' conference on raw materials held in Dakar from 3rd to 8th February 1975. They realise that the developing countries suffer worst from the world economic crisis. Consequently they stress anew their determination to implement measures to strengthen their co-operation with these

countries. They are also prepared to participate within the limit of their resources, in implementing the special international programme drawn up by the UN and to give additional special allocations, loans and grants to the developing countries. In this connection they have agreed to co-ordinate their special programme for financial co-operation to aid the worst-hit developing countries in the best possible manner, especially to help them overcome their balance-of-payments difficulties. They have also agreed to co-ordinate these financial measures with long-term loans for the development of the economies of these countries.

To help improve the use of the agricultural potentials of the developing countries, the Kings and Presidents have decided to encourage the production of fertilisers and to provide the latter at favourable terms to the countries which have been badly affected by the economic crisis. They stress their readiness to co-operate with the other raw material exporting developing countries in their efforts to obtain a fair price for their exports.

10. As a contribution to alleviating the difficulties affecting the economies of the advanced countries, the Kings and Presidents declare that the OPEC member countries will continue to make special efforts in respect of the needs of the advanced countries.

As for oil supplies, they reiterate their countries' readiness to guarantee sufficient supplies to meet the vital needs of the economies of the advanced countries, provided that the consumer countries do not erect artificial barriers to distort the natural functioning of the laws of supply and demand. In furtherance of this aim [of guaranteeing supplies], the OPEC member countries will establish close co-operation and co-ordination among themselves so as to preserve a balance between oil production and the needs of the world's market.

As to oil prices, the Kings and Presidents point out that despite the apparent huge increase in these prices, the high rate of inflation and the deterioration of the value of currency have wiped out a large part of the real value of the prices following their adjustment. The current price falls noticeably below that which would have resulted from the development of alternative sources of energy.

However, they are ready to discuss conditions for the stabilisation of oil prices – a matter which will help the consumer countries introduce the necessary changes in their economies.

The Kings and Heads of State, motivated by a spirit of dialogue and co-operation, stress that the OPEC member states are prepared to negotiate with the advanced countries which have suffered most, bilaterally or through international organisation, with a view to the provision of financial facilities that would enable the economies of these countries to develop while guaranteeing the value of the deposits of the OPEC member states as well as their co-operation.

UN Programme of Action

11. The Kings and Presidents, while maintaining that any genuine international co-operation must benefit all the developing and advanced countries alike, declare that in return for the efforts, guarantees and commitments that the OPEC member states are willing to undertake, the advanced countries must contribute to the progress and development of the developing countries by taking specific steps, particularly with a view to achieving economic and monetary stability and giving appropriate attention to the interests of the developing countries.

In this connection, they underline the need for the full implementation of the programme of action approved by the UN General Assembly at its sixth special session. Accordingly, they stress the following prerequisites:

(a) The advanced countries should support the measures adopted by the developing countries with the aim of stabilising the prices of their exports of raw materials and other essential commodities at fair and satisfactory levels.
(b) The advanced countries should honour their international commitments arising out of the second UN development decade as a minimum contribution which could be increased, in particular by the most advanced states, for the benefit of the developing states which have suffered most.
(c) To draw up and implement an effective food programme under which the advanced states, particularly the major food-producing and exporting states, will give grants and aid to the most needy developing states in relation to their foodstuff and agricultural requirements.
(d) To speed up operations to effect the development of developing states, particularly by using modern technology efficiently and quickly and by eliminating obstacles in the way of the application and development of technology in the service of the economy of our countries.

In view of the fact that in several instances obstacles to development arise from the inadequate and unsuitable transmission of technology, the Kings and Presidents attach the greatest importance to the transmission of technology, which they regard as a big test of the degree of commitment on the part of the advanced countries to the principle of international co-operation in the interest of development.

The transmission of technology should not be based on a division of labour whereby the developing states would produce commodities of inferior technological standard. All efficient transmission of technology should help the developing countries to overcome the technological backwardness characterising their economies by means of manufacturing products of high technological standard themselves, particularly in relation to the development and processing of their natural resources.

As regards exhaustible natural resources, such as the oil of the OPEC member states, it is vital that the rate of the transmission of technology should keep pace as far as possible with the mean rate of exploitation, which is now being stepped up in the interest of the economy and progress of the advanced countries.

A large proportion of the planned or new petrochemical complexes, oil refineries and fertiliser factories should be built in the territory of the OPEC member states in co-operation with the industrial states for the purpose of exporting to the advanced countries and guaranteeing that these products will reach the markets of these countries.

There should be sufficient protection against reduction in the value of the external reserves of the OPEC member states as well as guarantees of the security of their investments in the advanced countries.

Furthermore, the Kings and Presidents consider it essential for the advanced countries to open their markets not only to oil and other primary products, but also to goods manufactured by the developing countries and to regard the discriminatory methods adopted against the developing countries, including the members of OPEC, as being in conflict with the spirit of co-operation and partnership.

Monetary Reform

12. The Kings and Presidents note the current disruption of the international monetary system and the absence of norms and documents needed to protect trade exchanges and the value of the financial assets of the developing countries. They stress in particular the constant need for the adoption of measures to safeguard the legitimate interests of the developing countries.

They also stress that the mobilisation of the financial resources of the OPEC member countries and the advanced countries and the technical capabilities of these countries for aiding the developing countries will greatly help in solving the international economic crisis. They stress the need for fundamental and urgent measures to remedy the international monetary system, with a view to strengthening the mechanisms for expanding trade, developing production resources and ensuring a balanced growth of the world economy.

They note that the steps taken so far to redress the international monetary system have failed because these initiatives did not aim at removing the injustice inherent in the structure of that system.

The power of taking decisions which affect the value of currency reserves and of the Special Drawing Rights, the price of gold and the role of gold in the international monetary system must not continue to rest with one side and must not be negotiated by the advanced countries alone. It is essential that the advanced countries contribute to a genuine reform of the world monetary and international financial systems and that they ensure fair representation for all developing countries and safeguard their interests.

The reform of the currency and financial systems should allow for an ample increase in the share of the developing countries in the making of decisions, and in controlling and participating in the spririt of community of interest in world development and on an equal footing. The Kings and Presidents have therefore decided to set up machinery for consultation and co-ordination among their countries within the framework of their solidarity in order to promote a true reform of the international currency and financial systems.

OPEC Coordination

13. The Kings and Presidents attach the utmost importance to the strengthening of OPEC, especially in coordinating the activities of the national oil companies within the framework of the Organisation and the Organisation's role in the world's economy. They consider that there are specific tasks of the utmost importance to be implemented. These require co-ordinated planning among their countries and the co-ordination of their policies in the sphere of oil production, conservation, pricing and marketing – as well as in all financial matters of common interest. Coordinated planning and economic cooperation among the member countries would aid the world's development and stability.

14. The Kings and Presidents wish to voice their deep anxiety about the current world economic crisis, which is a threat to stability and peace. At the same time they realise that the crisis has generated an awareness of problems, the solution of which will contribute to the security and prosperity of all mankind.

Aware of the aspirations of the peoples of the whole world and anxious to promote the settlement of the major problems affecting their life, the Kings and Presidents declare that they have agreed that their states shall implement measures designed to usher in a new chapter in international cooperation.

The advanced countries, which possess most of the instruments of progress, prosperity, and peace, as well as most of the instruments of destruction, should respond to the initiatives of the developing countries with similar initiatives, seizing the historic opportunity made available as a result of this critical situation to open a new chapter in the relations among peoples. This would alleviate the distress resulting from the disturbance in the relations of those who possess the elements of power and the accompanying atmosphere of instability resulting from the prevailing chaos in the world economies. It would open the door to confidence and peace and promote an atmosphere of true international cooperation which would be most advantageous to the developing countries and to which these countries would contribute with their gigantic resources.

Whereas man's genius has provided people with scientific and technological progress and great means of overcoming the hazards of nature and effecting significant changes for the better, the future of mankind ultimately depends exclusively on mankind's ability to mobilise its creative power and work for the good of all and in the interest of all human beings.

The Kings and Presidents of the OPEC member states express their deep faith in the ability of all peoples to set up a new economic system based on justice and fraternity to enable the world of tomorrow to assure progress for everyone on an equal footing in a spirit of co-operation, stability and peace. They therefore address this warm appeal to the governments of the world's other states and officially pledge to provide the full support of their peoples towards achieving this objective.

BIBLIOGRAPHY

I Official Sources

OPEC and OPEC-Related Multilateral Organisations

1. *Organisation of Petroleum Exporting Countries* (OPEC).

Statute, Vienna, OPEC Secretariat, Information Dept., Vienna, 1971; 25 p.

Annual Review and Record, 1962-80.

OPEC Official Resolutions and Press Releases, 1960-80, published for OPEC by Pergamon Press, New York, 1980; 214 p.

Annual Statistical Bulletin, 1968-80.

OPEC Member Country Profiles, Vienna, 1980; 85 p.

OPEC Bulletins, Vienna, various issues.

OPEC Review, Vienna, various issues.

OPEC Chronological Events: September 1960-December 1977. Supplement to *OPEC Bulletin*, vol. IX, no. 33, 14 August 1978.

'Concessional Assistance by OPEC Members, 1973-1976'. *OPEC Bulletin*, vol. IX, no. 35, 23 August 1978; pp. 1-8.

'An Economic Analysis of OPEC Aid' by John T. Cummings, Hossein Askari, Mehdi Salehizadeh, supplement to *OPEC Bulletin*, vol. IX, no. 39, 25 September 1978; 40 p.

'OPEC Aid to the Developing Countries'. *OPEC Bulletin*, vol. IX, no. 50, 11 December 1978; pp. 1-29.

'Text of Speech Delivered by Mr Fuad Rouhani, Secretary General, at the II Consultative Meeting in Geneva', Geneva: OPEC Public Relations Department, 1963, 8 p.

2. *OPEC Fund for International Development* (OFID) (OPEC Special Fund prior to 1980).

OPEC Special Fund. Text of agreement establishing the Fund.

Basic facts about the OPEC Special Fund, Vienna 1976.

Annual Reports, 1976-81.

Press Releases, various issues.

'The OPEC Aid Record', by Ibrahim F.I. Shihata and Robert Mabro, January 1978; 17 p.

'Reactivating the North-South Dialogue', by Mahbub ul Haq, September 1978; 7 p.

'The OPEC Special Fund and the North-South Dialogue', by Ibrahim F.I. Shihata, April 1979; 11 p.

'OPEC As A Donor Group', by Ibrahim F.I. Shihata, December 1980; 21 p.

'OPEC States and Third World Solidarity', by Zuhayr Mikdashi, December 1980; 25 p.

'OPEC Aid and OPEC Aid Institutions: A Profile', January 1981; 30 p.

3. *Organisation of Arab Petroleum Exporting Countries* (OAPEC).

Basic Facts about the OAPEC Kuwait 1976.

OAPEC Bulletin, various issues.

Oil and Arab Cooperation, various issues.

Oil in the Seventh Special Session of the United Nations, Kuwait, 1976, 77 p.
Petroleum and Arab Economic Development, Kuwait, 1978.

4. *Arab Bank for Economic Development in Africa* (BADEA).
Text of agreement setting up the Bank, Khartoum, 1974.
Annual Reports, 1975-80.

5. *Arab Fund for Economic and Social Development* (AFESD).
Text of agreement establishing the Fund, Kuwait, 1968.
Annual Reports, 1974-80.

6. *Arab Monetary Fund* (AMF).
The Articles of Agreement, 1977.
Annual Reports, 1977-9.

7. *Islamic Development Bank (IsDB).*
Annual Reports, 1976-9.

The United Nations Organisation and Affiliated Agencies

1. *The United Nations Yearbook*, 1948-80.

2. *Assessment of the Progress Made In the Establishment of the New International Economic Order and Appropriate Action for the Promotion of the Economic Development of the Developing Countries and International Economic Cooperation*, A/S/11, 25 July 1980.

3. *United Nations Capital Development Fund (UNCDF) Annual Report of the Administrator for 1980*, DP/536 12 March 1981.

4. *United Nations Conference on Trade and Development* (UNCTAD).
Proceedings of UNCTAD Santiago TD/180 1972.
Proceedings of UNCTAD Nairobi TD/218 1976.
Proceedings of UNCTAD Manila TD/269 1979.
Arusha Programme For Collective Self-Reliance and Framework For Negotiation, TD/236 1979.
Committee on the Economic Cooperation Among Developing Countries: Report of the Second Session TD/B/C 7/10, 1978 and *Report of the First Special Session* TD/B/818, 1980.
Financial Solidarity Among Developing Countries, TD/B/627 1975.
Financial Solidarity For Development: Efforts and Institutions of the Members of OPEC, 1973-1976, TD/B/AC 7/31.
Joint Ventures Among Arab Countries, TD/B/AC 19 Rev. 5, 1975.

5. *United Nations Development Programme* (UNDP).
Programme Implementation, Ten Year Record. The Record in 1981 DP/1 (add 1-6).
UNDP At A Glance, 1981.
UNDP Report and Review, 1979.
The United Nations Development Programme, Activities and Achievements and the World in 1990, 1981.
Promises To Keep, 1982.

6. *United Nations Institute for Research and Training* (UNITAR).
A New International Economic Order: Selected Documents compiled by A.G. Mass and Harry N.M. Weirton. doc. series no. 1, 1978.

Arab Development Funds In the Middle East, by Soliman Demir, published for UNITAR by Pergamon Press, New York, 1979.

7. *UN Secretary General's Report on the UN's Special Programme*, A/10201, 21 August 1975.

8. *United Nations Special Fund* (UNSF).
Report of the Board of Governors, fifth session, SF/13, 22 June 1978.

9. *International Fund for Agriculture Development* (IFAD).
Report of the Governing Council, first session, GC/1, 1978.
Annual Reports, 1978-80.
Lending Policies and Criteria, IFAD/I REV I, December 1978.

International Development and Financial Institutions

1. *International Bank for Reconstruction and Development (IBRD).*
Annual Report, 1973-80.
World Development Report, 1973-80.

2. *International Development Association* (IDA).
Annual Report, 1973-80.

3. *International Monetary Fund (IMF)*
Annual Reports, 1974-80.

4. *The Organisation for Economic Cooperation & Development (OECD).*
Development Assistance Committee, *Annual Review of the Chairman on the Efforts and Policies of the Members of the Development Assistance Committee*, 1974-82.
DAC Review of Canada's Aid Press /A/(80) 78, December 1980.
DAC Review of French Aid Press /A/(80), March 1980.
DAC Review of Netherland's Aid Press /A/(80) 70 December 1980 and Press /A/(82) 71 December 1982.
DAC Review of Switzerland's Aid Press /A/(80) 3 January 1980.
DAC Review of United Kingdom's Aid Press /A/(81) 5 February 1981.
DAC Review of United States Aid Press /A/(81) May 1981.
The Co-financing of Development Projects by DAC and OPEC Members and International Financial Institutions. Development Cooperation Directorate, working document DD/481 – Rev. II, 1977.
Triangular Arrangements Designed to Encourage OPEC Investment in Developing Countries, DD/477, 1975.
Development Center of the OECD.
The Development of Development Thinking, Liaison Bulletin no. 1, 1977, 151 p.
Food Aid and Development, by Hartmuth Schneider 1978, 130 p.
Pour Une Autre Developement, by Alain Briou and Paul-Marc Henry, published by Presse Universitaire de Paris (collection Tiers Monde) 1976.
Oil Reserves in the Gulf, by Y.L. Ahmad, 1974.
Prospects for Industrial Joint Ventures in the Oil Exporting Countries of the Middle East and North Africa, by Laurence G. Franko, occasional paper no. 8 CD/T, 1975.
Triangular Arrangements Designed to Encourage OPEC Investment in Developing Countries, working document DD/477, 1975.

Trilateral Cooperation: vol. I, 271 p., *Arab Development Funds and Banks,* vol. II, 241 p., *Approaches to Trilateral Cooperation*, by Traute Schaf, 1978.
Geographical Distribution of Financial Flows to Developing Countries, 1976-9, 1980.
OECD Observer, various issues.

Regional Development Banks

1. *African Development Bank (ADB).*
Annual Reports, 1975-80.

2. *The Inter-American Development Bank (IDB).*
Annual Report, 1974-80.

Summit Conference of Developing Countries

1. *Islamic Conference.*
Report on Islamic Summit, 1974 Pakistan-Lahore. 22-24 February 1974. Ministry of Information and Broadcasting, Augaf and Haj. A compilation of speeches, declarations and resolutions of the conference.

2. *Conference of the Heads of States or Governments of the Non-Aligned Countries.*
Fourth Conference of Heads of States and Governments of the Non-aligned Countries, Algiers, 5-9 September 1973. Fundamental Texts, declarations, resolutions, Action Programme for Economic Cooperation. Algiers – 1973 – The Secretariat of the Fourth Conference.
Fifth Conference of NAC Columbo, August 1976.
Documents:
NAC/CONF/5/Resolutions 1-32.
NAC/CONF/5/FM/15.
NAC/CONF/5/FM/15 Add. 1.
NAC/CONF/5/S.2.

OPEC Members' Governments

1. *Iran*
Bank Markazi (Central Bank), *Annual Report and Balance Sheet*, 1974-8.
Collection of the Writings, Speeches, Messages and Interviews of H.I.M. The Shah of Iran, vols. I-XI. Teheran, Ministry of Education, 1976 (Persian).
The Sayings of H.I.M. The Shah on Oil, July 1953-July 1975 (Tir 1331-Tir 1353) Teheran, Ministry of Information and Tourism, August 1975 (Persian), 138 p.
Iran's Relations With the West Asian Countries and Egypt, Teheran, Ministry of Foreign Affairs, December 1976 (Persian).
Iran's Relations With the African Countries in the Last 50 Years, Teheran, Ministry of Foreign Affairs (Persian).
Summary of the Fifth National Development Plan, 1973-1978, Teheran, Plan and Budget Organisation (English).

2. *Kuwait.*
The Kuwait Fund for Arab Economic Development (KFAED), Annual Report, 1974-80.

3. *Libya*.

On Arab-American Relations, Libyan Paper no. 1, prepared by Mousur R. Kikhia, New York, Permanent Mission of Libya to the United Nations, 1977.

On Libya and Foreign Aid, Libyan Paper no. 3, prepared by Ibrahim S. Dharat, New York, Permanent Mission of Libya to the United Nations, 1978.

On Libya and the United Nations Development Programme, Libyan Paper no. 4, prepared by Ibrahim S. Dharat, New York, Permanent Mission of Libya to the United Nations, 1978.

On the New International Economic Order and the Role of OPEC Countries, Libyan Paper no. 15, prepared by Mausur R. Kikhia, New York, Permanent Mission of Libya to the office of the United Nations, 1979.

4. *Saudi Arabia*.

Saudi Arabian Monetary Fund (SAMA) Annual Report, 1974-80.

Saudi Fund for Development (SFD) Annual Report, 1975-9.

Saudi Arabian Development Plan, 1975-1980 (1395-1400), Saudi Arabian central planning organisation.

5. *United Arab Emirates*.

A Report on the United Arab Emirates, 1971-1977, Abu Dhabi Ministry of Information and Culture.

Abu Dhabi Fund for Arab Economic Development (ADFAED), Annual Report, 1975-80.

6. *Venezuela*.

Documents, Speeches and Venezuelan and World Views Relating to the Antecedents and Creation of OPEC, Venezuelan Ministry of Mines and Hydrocarbons. Division of Petroleum Economics, General Secretariat of the Presidency, 1961; 144 p.

Text of the Trust Agreement between the Fondo de Inversiones de Venezuela and the Inter-American Development Bank, 1975.

Venezuela Up To Date, Washington, DC. Venezuelan Embassy, various issues.

Governments of DAC Members

1. *Canada*.

Canadian International Development Agency (CIDA).

Annual Report, 1974-80.

Taking Stock: A Review of CIDA Activities, 1974.

Strategy for International Development Cooperation, 1975-80, 1980.

2. *Denmark*.

Danish International Development Agency.

Annual Report, 1973-80.

3. *Federal Republic of Germany*.

The Federal Republic of Germany and the Third World: Cooperation in Development, Bonn, Press and Information Office of the Federal Government, May 1979.

4. *Netherlands*.

Netherlands' Development Cooperation Policy and Aid Budget, The Hague, 1981.

5. *Norway*.

Norwegian Agency for International Development (NORAD).

Annual Report, 1974-80.

6. *The United Kingdom.*

British Aid Statistics 1975-1979, Overseas Development Administration, London (ODA), 1980.

Britain's Aid Programme, Opportunities for Exporters, London, ODA, 1980.

UK Memorandum to the Development Assistance Committee of the OECD, London, ODA, 1979.

New Perspectives in North-South Relations, Overseas Development Paper no. 7, Ministry of Overseas Development, London, 1975.

The Priority of Rural Development Overseas, Ministry of Overseas Development, London, 1975.

7. *The United States.*

The United States Senate Committee on Foreign Relations.

United States Economic and Foreign Assistance Programs.

Compilation of General Accounting Office, Report, Findings and Recommendations.

Report to the Committee on Foreign Relations, Washington, DC, Government Printing Office, 1971; vii-62 p.

Sub-Committee on Foreign Assistance.

Hearings on U.S. Contributions to IDA, 93rd Congress, Washington, DC, Government Printing Office, 1974; iv-13 p.

Hearings on Proposed Sales of Arms to Iran and Saudi Arabia, 94th Congress, Washington, DC, Government Printing Office, 1977; 55 p.

Sale of AWACS to Iran, 94th Congress, Washington, DC, Government Printing Office, 1977; iii-107 p.

U.S. Military Sales to Iran, a staff report by Robert Mantel and Geoffry Kemp, 1976; xiv-59 p.

Sub-Committee on Foreign Economic Policy.

The Witteveen Facility and the OPEC Financial Surpluses, 95th Congress, Washington, DC, Government Printing Office, 1978; iii-196 p.

International Debt, the Banks and U.S. Foreign Policy, staff report by Karin Lissaker, Washington, DC, Government Printing Office, 1977; vi-68 p.

The Future of Saudi-Arabian Oil Production, staff report, Washington, DC, Government Printing Office, 1979; v-37 p.

Library of Congress. Foreign Affairs Division.

Alternatives to Bilateral Aid, Washington, DC, Government Printing Office, 1973; v-53 p.

United States-OPEC Relations, selected materials prepared by the Congressional Research Center, Washington, DC, Government Printing Office, 1976; ix-646 p.

Works

Books Written by One or Several Authors

Abir, Mordechai, *Oil, Power and Politics: Conflict in Arabia, the Red Sea and the Gulf,* London, F. Cass, 1974; 221 p.

Abujaber, Kamel S., *The Arab Ba'ath Socialist Party: History, Ideology and Organization*, Syracuse, NY, Syracuse University Press, 1966; 218 p.

Adamiyat, F., *Amirkabir-va-Iran*, Teheran, Chapkhaneh Payam, 1323 (1944); 499 p.

Adamiyat, *Andisha-Taraghi-va-Hokumat Ghanoum: Asr Sephsallar* (The Idea of Progress and the Rule of Law), Teheran, Entesharat Kharazmi, 1351 (1973); 514 p.

Adamiyat, F., *Bahrain Islands: A Legal and Diplomatic Study of the British-Iranian Controversy*, New York, Praeger, 1955; x-268 p.

Addona, Angela F., *The Organization of African Unity*, Cleveland, World Publishing Co., 1969; 224 p.

Ali, Sheikh Rustm, *Saudi Arabia and Oil Diplomacy*, New York, Praeger, 1976; 197 p.

Alkuwari, Ali-Khalifa, *Oil Revenues in the Gulf Emirates: Patterns of Allocation and Impact on Economic Development*, Epping, England, Bowker Centre for Middle Eastern and Islamic Studies of the University of Durham, 1978; 218 p.

Allber, Robert Z., *Policies Towards the OPEC Oil and Wealth*, Tubingen Mahr, 1975; 14 p.

Al-Otaiba, Mana Saeed, *OPEC and the Petroleum Industry*, London, Croom Helm, 1975; 182 p.

Al-Otaiba, Mana Saeed, *Petroleum and the Economy of the United Arab Emirates*, London, Croom Helm, 1978; 181 p.

Amin, Samir, *Imperialism and Unequal Development*, New York, Monthly Review Press, 1977; 267 p.

Amin, Samir, *Unequal Development: An Essay on the Social Formation of Peripheral Capitalism*, New York, Monthly Review Press, 1976, 441 p.

Amuzegar, Jahangir, *Technical Assistance in Theory and Practice: The Case of Iran*, New York, Praeger, 1966; 275 p.

Amuzegar, Jahangir & Fekrat, Ali M., *Iran: Economic Development under Dualistic Conditions*, Chicago, University of Chicago Press, 1971; 177 p.

Amuzegar, Jahangir, *Iran: An Economic Profile*, Washington, DC, Middle East Institute, 1977; 280 p.

Anthony, John Duke, *Arab States of the Lower Gulf: People, Politics, Petroleum*, Washington, DC, Middle East Institute, 1975; 261 p.

Antonius, George, *The Arab Awakening: The Story of the Arab National Movement*, London, H. Hamilton, 1938; 470 p.

Asher, Robert E., *Grants, Loans, and Local Currencies: Their Role in Foreign Aid*, Washington, DC, Brookings Institution, 1966; 142 p.

Asher, Robert E., *Development Assistance in the 1970s: Alternatives for the United States*, Washington, DC, Brookings Institution, 1970; 248 p.

Asher, Robert E. & Mason, Edward S., *The World Bank Since Bretton Woods*, Washington, DC, Brookings Institution, 1973; 913 p.

Askari, Hossein & Cummings, John T., *Oil, OECD, and the Third World: A Vicious Triangle?*, Austin, Texas, Center for Middle East Studies, University of Texas, 1978; 135 p.

Bahrampour, Firouz, *Iran: Emergence of a Middle Eastern Power*, Brooklyn, New York, Theo Gan's Son, 1970; 125 p.

Balogh, Thomas, *The Economics of Poverty*, London, Weidenfeld and Nicholson, 1974; 291 p.

Bauer, Peter, *Dissent on Development: Studies and Debates in Development Economics*, London, Weidenfeld and Nicholson, 1971; 550 p.

Bayne, E., *Persian Kingship in Transition: Conversations with a Monarch Whose Office is Traditional and Whose Goal is Modernization*, New York, American Universities Field Staff, 1968; 288 p.

Bayne, E. & Collin, Richard O., *Arms and Advisers: Views from Saudi Arabia and Iran*, New York, American Universities Field Staff, 1976, 31 p.

Bhagwati, Jagdish N., *Amount and Sharing of Aid*, Washington, DC, Overseas Development Council, 1970; 197 p.

Bhagwati, Jagdish N., *The New International Economic Order: The North-South Debate*, Cambridge, Mass., MIT Press, 1977; 390 p.
Bhattacharya, Amindya K., *The Myth of Petropower*, Lexington, Mass., Lexington Books, 1977; 108 p.
Birks, J.S. & Sinclair, C.A., *Arab Man-Power: the Crisis of Development*, London, Croom Helm, 1980; 391 p.
Black, Eugene R., *The Diplomacy of Economic Development*, Cambridge, Mass., Harvard University Press, 1960; 74 p.
Black, Lloyd, *The Strategy of Foreign Aid*, Princeton, NJ, D. Van Nostrand, 1968; 168 p.
Blake, David H. & Walters, Robert S., *The Politics of Global Economic Relations*, Englewood Cliffs, NJ, Prentice Hall, 1976; 240 p.
Burrell, R.M. & Cottrell, Alvin J., *Iran, Afghanistan, Pakistan: Tensions and Dilemmas*, Washington, DC, The Center for Strategic and International Studies, Georgetown University, 1974; 68 p.
Bustani, Emile, *Marche Arabesque*, London, Robert Hale Ltd, 1961; 216 p.
Cable, Vincent, *British Interests and Third World Development*, London, Overseas Development Institute, 1980; 85 p.
Carlin, Alan, *Project Versus Program Aid: From the Donor's Point of View*, Santa Monica, The Rand Corporation, 1965; 15 p.
Casadio, J.P., *The Economic Challenge of the Arabs*, Farnborough, Hampshire, Westmead, 1976; xi-216 p.
Chevalier, Jean-Marie, *Le Nouvel Enjeu Petrolier*, Paris, Calman-Levy, 1973; 305 p.
Chibwe, Ephraim Chimpampe, *Arab Dollars for Africa*, London, Croom Helm, 1976; 147 p.
Chibwe, Ephraim Chimpampe, *Afro-Arab Relations in the New World Order*, London, S. Friedman, 1977; 150 p.
Choucri, Nazli, *International Politics of Energy Interdependence*, Lexington, Mass., D.C. Heath, 1976; 250 p.
Chubin, Shahram, *Security in the Persian Gulf: The Role of Outside Powers*, London, The International Institute for Strategic Studies, 1982; 180 p.
Chubin, Shahram & Zabih, Sepehr, *The Foreign Relations of Iran: A Developing State in a Zone of Great Power Conflict*, Berkeley, University of California Press, 1974; xiii-362 p.
Clark, Paul Gordon, *American Aid for Development*, New York, Praeger, 1972; 231 p.
Clarkson, Stephen, *The Soviet Theory of Development: India and the Third World in Marxist-Leninist Scholarship*, Toronto, University of Toronto Press, 1978; 322 p.
Cooley, John K., *Libyan Sandstorm*, New York, Holt, Reinhart and Winston, 1982; 320 p.
Cooper, John Franklin, *China's Foreign Aid: An Instrument of Peking's Foreign Policy*, Lexington, Mass., Lexington Books, 1976; xiii-197 p.
Cottrell, Alvin J. & Dougherty, James E., *Iran's Quest for Security: U.S. Arms Transfers and the Nuclear Option*, Cambridge, Mass., Institute for Foreign Policy Analysis, 1977; 59 p.
Cunningham, George, *The Management of Aid Agencies: Donor Structures and Procedures for the Administration of Aid to Developing Countries*, London, Croom Helm, 1974; 181 p.
Demir, Soliman, *The Kuwait Fund and the Political Economy of Arab Regional Development*, New York, Praeger, 1976; xvi-138 p.
Dinwiddy, Bruce, *Aid Performance and Development Policies of Western Countries*, New York, Praeger, 1973; vii-139 p.

Domergue, Maurice, *Technical Assistance: Theory, Practice, and Policies*, New York, Praeger 1968; 196 p.
El-Mallakh, Ragaei, *Economic Development and Regional Cooperation: Kuwait*, Chicago, University of Chicago Press, 1968; xxi-256 p.
El-Mallakh, Ragaei, *Capital Investment in the Middle East: The Use of Surplus Funds for Regional Development*, New York, Praeger, 1977; 195 p.
El-Mallakh, Ragaei, *Kuwait: Trade and Investment*, Boulder, Colorado, Westview Press, 1979; 262 p.
El-Mallakh, Ragaei, *Qatar: Development of an Oil Economy*, London, Croom Helm, 1979; 183 p.
El-Mallakh, Ragaei, *The Economic Development of the United Arab Emirates*, London, Croom Helm, 1981; 215 p.
Elwell-Sutton, Laurence P., *Persian Oil: A Study in Power Politics*, London, Lawrence and Wishart, 1955; 343 p.
Ezzati, Ali, *World Energy Markets and OPEC Stability*, Lexington, Mass., Lexington Books, 1978; xvi-205 p.
Fallon, Nicholas, *Middle East Oil Money and Its Future Expenditure*, New York, Crane Russak, 1975; 230 p.
Feis, Herbert, *Foreign Aid and Foreign Policy*, New York, St Martin's Press, 1964, 246 p.
Field, Michael, *A Hundred Million Dollars a Day*, London, Sidgwick and Jackson, 1975; 239 p.
First, Ruth, *Libya: The Elusive Revolution*, Harmondsworth/Baltimore, Penguin Books, 1974; 204 p.
Friedman, Wolfgang Gaston, *International Financial Aid*, New York, Columbia University Press, 1966; xiv-498 p.
Fuchs, Yves, *La Cooperation: aide ou neo-colonialisme?*, Paris, Editions Sociales, 1973; 190 p.
Ghadar, Fariborz, *The Evolution of OPEC Strategy*, Lexington, Mass., Lexington Books, 1978; 205 p.
Goldman, Marshall, Irwin, *Soviet Foreign Aid*, New York, Praeger, 1967; 265 p.
Grunwald, Kurt & Ronall, J.O., *Industrialization in the Middle East*, New York, Council on Middle Eastern Affairs Press, 1960; xxi-367 p.
Habib, Henry P., *Politics and Government of Revolutionary Libya*, Montreal, Circle de Livre de France, 1979; 358 p.
Haim, Sylvia A., *Arab Nationalism, an Anthology*, Berkeley, University of California Press, 1962; 225 p.
Halliday, Fred, *Arabia Without Sultans*, Harmondsworth, England, Penguin Books, 1976; 527 p.
Halliday, Fred, *Iran: Dictatorship and Development*, Harmondsworth, England, Penguin Books, 1979; 348 p.
Hallwood, Paul & Sinclair, R. Stuart, *Oil, Debt, and Development: OPEC in the Third World*, London, Allen & Unwin, 1981; 206 p.
Hansen, Roger D., *Beyond the North South Stalemate*, New York, McGraw Hill, 1979; 329 p.
Hart, Judith, *Aid and Liberation: a Socialist Study of Aid Policies*, London, V. Gollancz, 1973; 287 p.
Hawkins, E.K., *The Principles of Development Aid*, Harmondsworth, England, Penguin Books, 1970; 147 p.
Hayter, Teresa, *French Aid*, London, Overseas Development Institute, 1960; 220 p.
Hayter, Teresa, *Aid as Imperialism*, Harmondsworth, England, Penguin Books, 1971; 221 p.
Hayter, Teresa, *The Creation of World Poverty*, London, Pluto Press, 1981; 128 p.

Heineback, B., *Oil and Security*, New York, Humanities Press, 1974; 197 p.
Hensman, C., *Rich Against Poor; The Reality of Aid*, London, A. Lane, Penguin Press, 1971; 293 p.
Hirst, David, *Oil and Public Opinion in the Middle East*, London, Faber & Faber, 1966; 125 p.
Holden, David, *Farewell to Arabia*, London, Faber & Faber, 1966; 268 p.
Hopwood, Derek, *The Arabian Peninsula: Society and Politics*, London, Allen & Unwin, 1972; 320 p.
Huang, Po-Wen, *The Asian Development Bank: Diplomacy and Development in Asia*, New York, Vantage Press, 1975; 210 p.
Hudson, Michael C., *Arab Politics: The Search for Legitimacy*, New Haven, Yale University Press, 1977; xi-422 p.
Hurewitz, J.C., *Changing Military Perspectives in the Middle East*, Santa Monica, Calif., Rand Corporation, 1970; ix-51 p.
Hurewitz, J.C., *The Persian Gulf: Prospects for Stability*, New York, Foreign Policy Association, 1974; 63 p.
Hurni, Bettina, *Lending Policies of the World Bank in the 1970s*, Boulder, Colorado, Westview Press, 1980; 173 p.
Issawi, Charles, *Oil, the Middle East and the World*, New York, Library Press, 1972; 86 p.
Kamara, M.V. & Plano, J.C., *United Nations Capital Development Fund: Poor and Rich Worlds in Collision*, Kalamazoo, Michigan, New Issues Press, 1977; 98 p.
Kapur, Harish, *Soviet Russia and Asia 1917-1927: A Study of Soviet Policy Towards Turkey, Iran and Afghanistan*, Geneva, Michael Joseph Ltd., 1965; 265 p.
Kapur, Harish, *China and the Afro-Asian World*, New Delhi, Publications Division, India International Centre, 1966; 66 p.
Kerr, Malcom H., *The Arab Cold War*: 3rd edn, London/Oxford/New York, Oxford University Press, 1971; 153 p.
Khaduri, Majid, *Political Trends in the Arab World: the Role of Ideas and Ideals in Politics*, Baltimore, Johns Hopkins University Press, 1970; 298 p.
Khaduri, Majid, *Socialist Iraq: a Study in Iraqi Politics Since 1968*, Washington, DC, Middle East Institute, 1978; 481 p.
Khaduri, Majid, *Arab Personalities in Politics*, Washington, DC, Middle East Institute, 1981; 353 p.
Khalifa, Ali Mohammed, *The United Arab Emirates: Unity in Fragmentation*, London, Ithaca Press, 1978; 224 p.
Kiernan, Thomas, *The Arabs: Their History, Aims and Challenge to the Industrialized World*, Boston, Little Brown, 1975; 449 p.
Kindleberger, Charles P., *Economic Development*, New York, McGraw Hill, 1958 & 1965; xx-410 p.
Knauerhase, Ramon, *The Saudi Arabian Economy*, New York, Praeger, 1975; 359 p.
Koury, Evver M., *The United Arab Emirates: Its Political System and Politics*, Hyattsville, Maryland, Institute of Middle Eastern & North African Affairs, 1980; 146 p.
Kubbah, Abdle Amir, *OPEC, Past and Present*, Vienna, Petro-Economic Research Centre, 1974; 170 p.
Lackner, Helene, *A House Built on Sand: a Political Economy of Saudi Arabia*, London, Ithaca Press, 1978; 224 p.
Lappe, F.A.M. & Collins, J., *Food First: Beyond the Myth of Scarcity*, Boston, Houghton Mifflin, 1977; 446 p.
Law, John D., *Arab Aid: Who Gets It, for What, and How*, New York, Chase World Information Corporation, 1978; 256 p.

Law, John D., *Arab Investors, Who They Are, What They Buy, and Where*, New York, Chase World Information Corporation, 1980; vol. I, 311 p., vol. II, 271 p.

Leifer, Michael, *The Foreign Relations of the New States*, Camberwell, England, Longman, 1974; 114 p.

Lenczowski, George, *The Middle East in World Affairs*, Ithaca, NY, Cornell University Press, 1958; xx-576 p.

Lenczowski, George, *Oil and State in the Middle East*, Ithaca, NY, Cornell University Press, 1960; xiv-379 p.

Levine, Victor T. & Luke, Timothy W., *The Arab-African Connection: Political and Economic Realities*, Boulder, Colorado, Westview Press, 1979; 155 p.

Little, I.M.D., *Aid to Africa: An Appraisal of UK Policy for Aid to Africa South of the Sahara*, New York, Macmillan, 1964; 76 p.

Little, I.M.D. & Clifford, J., *International Aid: A Discussion of the Flow of Public Resources from Rich to Poor Countries with Special Reference to British Policy*, London, Allen & Unwin, 1965; 360 p.

Litwak, Robert, *Security in the Persian Gulf: Sources of Interstate Conflict*, London, The International Institute for Strategic Studies, 1982; 105 p.

Long, David D., *Saudi Arabia*, Beverly Hills, California, Sage Publications, 1976, 70 p.

Looney, Robert E., *A Development Strategy for Iran Through the 1980s*, New York, Praeger, 1977; xiv-207 p.

Looney, Robert E., *Saudi Arabia's Development Potential: Application of an Islamic Growth Model*, Lexington, Mass., Lexington Books, 1981; 358 p.

Lutfi, Ashraf, *OPEC Oil*, Beirut, The Middle East Research & Publishing Centre, 1968; 115 p.

Lutfi, Ashraf, *Arab Oil: A Plan for the Future*, Beirut, the Middle East Research & Publishing Centre, 1960; 95 p.

Lyon, Peyton V. & Ismail, Tareg, *Canada and the Third World*, Toronto, Macmillan, 1976; 307 p.

MacDonald, Robert W., *The League of Arab States: A Study in the Dynamics of Regional Organization*, Princeton, NJ, Princeton University Press, 1965; xiii-407 p.

Malone, Joseph, *Saudi Arabia: The Pace of Growth and Spreading Influence*, Washington, DC, Middle East Institute, 1973; 11 p.

Mason, Edward S., *Foreign Aid and Foreign Policy*, New York, Harper & Row, 1964; vi-113 p.

Mazrui, Ali, *Africa's International Relations: the Diplomacy of Dependency and Change*, Boulder, Colorado, Westview Press, 1977; 310 p.

Meier, Gerald, *Problems of Cooperation for Development*, New York, Oxford University Press, 1974; xvi-240 p.

Mikdashi, Zuhayr, *The Community of Oil Exporting Countries: A Study in Governmental Cooperation*, London, Allen & Unwin, 1972; 239 p.

Mikessell, Raymond F., *Public International Lending for Development*, New York, Random House, 1966; 239 p.

Montgomery, John D., *Foreign Aid in International Politics*, Englewood Cliffs, NJ, Prentice Hall, 1967; 114 p.

Montgomery, John D., *The Politics of Foreign Aid*, New York, Praeger, 1962; 322 p.

Musrey, Alfred G., *An Arab Common Market: A Study in Inter-Arab Trade Relations*, New York, Praeger, 1969; xiii-247 p.

Nakleh, Emile, *Arab-American Relations with the Persian Gulf*, Washington, DC, American Enterprise Institute for Public Policy Research, 1978; 82 p.

Nelson, Joan Marie, *Aid, Influence and Foreign Policy*, New York, Macmillan, 1968; ix-149 p.

Odell, Peter Rardam, *Oil and World Power: Background to the Oil Crisis*, Harmondsworth/Baltimore, Penguin, 1974; 245 p.

O'Kelly, Elisabeth, *Aid and Self-help: A General Guide to Overseas Aid*, London, C. Knight, 1973; x-140 p.

O'Leary, Michael Kent, *The Politics of American Foreign Aid*, New York, Atherton Press, 1967; xiv-172 p.

Ostheimer, John M., *Nigerian Politics*, New York, Harper & Row, 1973; viii-200 p.

Pahlavi, Mohammad Reza, *Mission for My Country*, New York, McGraw Hill, 1961, 336 p.

Perera, Phillip, *Development Finance Institutions; Problems and Prospects*, New York, Praeger, 1968; xxii-440 p.

Peterson, J.E., *Conflict in the Yemen and Superpower Involvement*, Washington, DC, Center For Contemporary Arab Studies, Georgetown University, 1981; 38 p.

Pincus, John, *Trade, Aid and Development*, New York, McGraw Hill, 1967; 400 p.

Quandt, William B., *Saudi Arabia in the 1980s, Foreign Policy, Security and Oil*, Washington, DC, Brookings Institution, 1981; 190 p.

Rabe, Stephen G., *The Road to OPEC: United States Relations with Venezuela 1919-1976*, Austin, University of Texas Press, 1982; 262 p.

Ramati, Yohannan, *Economic Growth in Developing Countries*, New York, Praeger, 1975; xv-501 p.

Ramazani, Rouhollah K., *Iran's Foreign Policy, 1941-73: A Study of Foreign Policy in Modernizing Nations*, Charlottesville, University Press of Virginia, 1975; xiv-507 p.

Ramazani, Rouhollah K., *The Persian Gulf: Iran's Role*, Charlottesville, University Press of Virginia 1972; xiv-157 p.

Rix, Allen, *Japan's Economic Aid*, London, Croom Helm, 1980; 280 p.

Roberts, Stephen, *The Arabs' New Frontier*, London, M. Temple Smith, 1973; 256 p.

Rouhani, Fuad, *A History of OPEC*, New York, Praeger, 1971; xvi-281 p.

Rubin, Seymour J., *The Conscience of The Rich Nations, The Development Assistance Committee and the Common Aid Effort*, New York/London, Harper & Row Publisher, 1966; 164 p.

Rustow, Dankwart A. & Ugno, John F., *OPEC, Success and Prospects*, New York, New York University Press, 1976; 179 p.

Safran, Nadav, *From War to War*, New York, Western Publishing Company, 1969; 445 p.

Sarkis, Nicholas, *Le Petrole a L'heure Arabe*, Paris, Stock, 1975; 317 p.

Sauvant, Karl P. & Hasenpflug, Haj, *The New International Economic Order: Confrontation or Cooperation Between North and South*, Boulder, Colorado, Westview Press, 1977; 447 p.

Sayegh, Kamal Salim, *Oil and Arab Regional Development*, New York, Praeger, 1968; xiv-357 p.

Sayigh, Yusif A., *The Economies of the Arab World: Development Since 1945*, London, Croom Helm, 1978; 726 p.

Sayigh, Yusif, *The Determinants of Arab Economic Development*, New York, St Martin's Press, 1978; 181 p.

Shaw, John M. & Long, David E., *Saudi Arabian Modernization, The Impact of Change on Stability*, Washington, DC, Center for Strategic and International Studies, Georgetown University, 1982; 110 p.

Shihata, Ibrahim F.I., *The Other Face of OPEC: Financial Assistance to the Third World*, London/New York, Longman, 1982; 281 p.

Shihata, Ibrahim F.I., *The OPEC Fund for International Development*, London, Croom Helm, 1983; 289 p.

Simmons, Andre, *Arab Foreign Aid*, London, Fairleigh Dickinson University Press, 1981; 196 p.

Stevens, Christopher, *Food Aid and the Developing World: Four African Case Studies*, London, Croom Helm, 1979; 224 p.

Stone, Russell A., *OPEC and the Middle East: The Impact of Oil on Societal Development*, New York, Praeger, 1977; xviii-264 p.

Stork, Joe, *Middle East Oil and the Energy Crisis*, New York/London, Monthly Review Press, 1975; 315 p.

Sylvester, Anthony, *Arabs and Africans*, London, Bodley Head, 1981; 252 p.

Tahtinen, Dale R., *National Security Challenges to Saudi Arabia*, Washington, DC, American Enterprise Institute For Public Policy Research, 1978; 45 p.

Tanzer, Michael, *The Political Economy of International Oil and the Underdeveloped Countries*, Boston, Beacon Press, 1969; 367 p.

Tendler, Judith, *Inside Foreign Aid*, Baltimore, Johns Hopkins University Press, 1975; 140 p.

Tetrault, Mary Ann, *The Organization of the Arab Petroleum Exporting Countries: History, Policies, and Prospects*, London, Greenwood Press, 1981; 215 p.

Tugwell, Franklin, *The Politics of Oil in Venezuela*, Stanford, Calif., Stanford University Press, 1975; xv-210 p.

Ul Haq, Mahbub, *The Poverty Curtain: Choices for the Third World*, New York, Columbia University Press, 1976; 247 p.

Uri, Pierre, *Development Without Dependence*, New York, Praeger, 1976; 166 p.

Vallenilla, Luis, *Oil, The Making of New Economic Order: Venezuelan Oil and OPEC*, New York, McGraw Hill, 1975; 302 p.

Vernon, Raymond, *The Oil Crisis*, New York, Norton, 1976; vii-310 p.

Vicker, Ray, *The Kingdom of Oil, the Middle East, Its People and Its Power*, Great Britain, Law & Brydone (printers) Ltd, 1975; 242 p.

Wall, David, *The Charity of Nations: The Political Economy of Foreign Aid*, New York, Basic Books, 1973; vii-181 p.

Waterbury, John, *The Middle East in the Coming Decade: from Well-Head to Well-Being?*, New York/London, McGraw Hill, 1978; xvi-219 p.

Wells, Donald, *Saudi Arabian Development Strategy*, Washington, DC, American Enterprise Institute for Public Policy Research, 1976; 76 p.

White, John, *The German Aid*, London, Overseas Development Institute, 1963; 221 p.

White, John, *Japanese Aid*, London, Overseas Development Institute, 1964, 78 p.

White, John, *Regional Development Banks: a Study of International Style*, London, Overseas Development Institute, 1970; 204 p.

Wien, Jake, *Saudi-Egyptian Relations: The Political and Military Implications of Saudi Financial Flows to Egypt*, Santa Monica, the Rand Corporation, 1980; 91 p.

Wilson, Rodney, *Trade and Investment in the Middle East*, New York, Holmes & Meir, 1977; xii-152 p.

Zeylstra, William Gustoff, *Aid or Development; The Relevance of Development Aid to Problems of Developing Countries*, Leyden, A.W. Sijthoff, 1975; 257 p.

Zonis, Marvin, *Iran's Political Elite*, Princeton, New Jersey, Princeton University Press, 1971, 381 p.

Books Edited by One or Several Authors

Beyond Dependency: the Developing World Speaks Out, ed. by Guy F. Erb & Valleriana Kallab, Washington, DC, Overseas Development Council, 1975; 238 p.

Contemporary Venezuela and its Role in International Affairs, ed. by Robert D. Bond, New York, New York University Press, 1977, 267 p.

Development Today: a New Look at US Relations with the Poor Countries, ed. by Robert E. Hunter & John E. Rielly, New York, Praeger, 1972; x-286 p.

Dialogue for a New Order, ed. by Khadija Haq, New York, Pergamon Press, 1980; 312 p.

Foreign Aid, ed. by Jagdish N. Bhagawati & R.S. Eckhous, Harmondsworth, Middlesex, Penguin Books, 1970; 351 p.

Iran Faces The Seventies, ed. by Ehsan Yarshater, New York, Praeger, 1970; xx-309 p.

Iran in the 1980s, ed. by Abbas Amirie & H. Twitchel, Teheran, Institute for International Political and Economic Studies, 1978; 477 p.

Iran: Past, Present and Future, ed. by Jane W. Jacqz, New York, Aspen Institute for Humanistic Studies, 1976; 481 p.

Israel in the Third World, ed. by Michael Curtis & Susan Gitelson, New Brunswick, New Jersey, Transaction Books, 1976; 410 p.

Mobilizing Technology for World Development, ed. by Jairam Ramesh & Charles Weiss, Jr, New York, Praeger, 1979; 233 p.

Nigerian Government and Politics Under Military Rule, ed. by Oyeleye Oyediran, New York, St Martin's Press, 1979; xii-319 p.

Oil, the Arab-Israeli Dispute and the Industrial World: Horizons of Crisis, ed. by J.C. Hurewitz, Boulder, Colorado, Westview Press, 1976; xiii-331 p.

Saudi-Arabia, Energy Developmental Planning and Industrialization, ed. by Ragaei & Dorothea El-Mallakh, Lexington, Mass., Lexington Books, 1982; 204 p.

Security in the Persian Gulf: Domestic Political Factors, ed. by Shahram Chubin, London, The International Institute for Strategic Studies, 1982; 90 p.

The Arabian Peninsula, Red Sea and Gulf: Strategic Considerations, ed. by Enver M. Koury & Emile Nakleh, Hyattsville, Maryland, Institute of Middle Eastern & North African Affairs, 1979; 100 p.

The Arab Oil Producing States of the Gulf, Political and Economic Development, ed. by Richard Erb, Washington DC, The American Enterprise Institute for Public Policy Research, 1980; 88 p.

The Middle East: A Political and Economic Survey, ed. by Peter Mansfield, London, Oxford University Press, 1973; 573 p.

The Persian Gulf and Indian Ocean in International Politics, ed. by Abbas Amirie, Teheran, Institute for International Political and Economic Studies, 1975; 417 p.

The Soviet Union & The Developing Nations, ed. by Roger E. Kanet, Baltimore, Johns Hopkins University Press, 1974; xii-302 p.

Trilateralism: The Trilateral Commission and Elite Planning for World Management, ed. by Holly Sklar, Boston, Southend Press, 1980; 604 p.

Twentieth Century Iran, ed. by Hossein Amirsadeghi, New York, Holmes & Meir Publishers, 1979; 299 p.

Articles by One or Several Authors

Abrahamian, Ervand 'The Guerrilla Movement in Iran 1963-1977', *MERIP Report*, no. 86, March/April 1980, pp. 3-21.

Abu Khadra, Y. 'The Role of Arab Institutions in the Recycling of the Surplus Funds', *The Arab Economist*, vol. VII, no. 72, January 1975, pp. 29-30.

Akins, James E. 'The Oil Crisis: This Time the Wolf Is Here', *Foreign Affairs*, vol. 5, no. 11, April 1973, pp. 462-90.

Al-Hamad, Abdlatif Y. 'Arab Capital and International Finance', *The Banker*, vol. 124, no. 575, January 1974, pp. 25-9.

Al-Hamad, Abdlatif Y. 'Fifteen Years of International Development Assistance: The Kuwait Fund for Arab Economic Development', *Oil and Arab Cooperation*, vol. 3, no. 1, 1977, pp. 228-9.

Al-Hamad, Abdlatif Y. 'Surplus Oil Funds and Arab Capital Market', *Euromoney*, February 1975, pp. 17-21.

Al-Khalaf, Nazar 'OPEC Members and the New International Economic Order', *The Journal of Energy and Development*, vol. 2, no. 2, Spring 1977, pp. 239-52.

Allen, Loring 'OPEC's Amazing Rise to World Power', *Harvard Magazine*, vol. 8, no. 5, May/June 1978, pp. 22-8.

Amirsadeghi, H. 'Iran's New Outward Look – An Authoritative Report from Tehran', *The New Middle East*, no. 35, August 1971, pp. 9-10.

Amuzegar, Jahangir 'The Oil Story: Facts, Fiction and Fair Play', *Foreign Affairs*, vol. 51, no. IV, July 1973.

Amuzegar, Jahangir 'The North-South Dialogue: from Conflict to Compromise', *Foreign Affairs*, vol. 54, no. III, April 1976, pp. 547-62.

Amuzegar, Jahangir 'International Growth, Equity and Efficiency', *Finance and Development*, vol. 15, no. 1, March 1978, pp. 24-7.

Amuzegar, Jahangir 'World Economic Co-operation: Not Enough', *OPEC Review*, vol. II, no. 4, September 1978, pp. 8-15.

Asher, Robert E. 'Development Assistance in DDII', *International Organizations*, vol. 25, no. 2, Spring 1971, pp. 97-119.

Askari, Hossein 'OPEC and International Aid', *SAIS Review*, no. 3, Winter 1981/2, pp. 133-48.

Atigha, A. 'Development Options of the Arab Oil Exporting Countries', *OAPEC Bulletin*, vol. 8, no. 3, March 1982, pp. 13-24.

Aubert de la Rue, Phillipe 'Le Recyclage Des Excedents Petroliers', *Politique Etrangere*, 40e anne, no. 4, 1975, pp. 405-16.

Ayari, Chadly 'Un Banquier Arab et Africain Pour l'Afrique', *Jeune Afrique*, no. 741, 21 Mars 1975, p. 21.

Bakhash, Shaul 'Hoveyda: Iran Will Hear Regional Pleas for Help', *Keyhan International*, October 30, 1975, p. 1.

Bakhash, Shaul 'Iran is Looking Eastward', *Keyhan International*, 10 April 1974, p. 4.

Bakhash, Shaul 'Matchmaking in Bonn', *Keyhan International*, 11 March 1974, p. 4.

Beauce de, Thiery 'Trois Fonds Arabes de Cooperation', *Politique Etrangere*, 41e anne, no. 1, 1976, pp. 43-56.

Bedore, James & Turner, Louis 'The Industrialization of the Mid-Eastern Oil Producers', *The World Today*, September 1977, pp. 326-34.

Bell, Geoffrey 'The OPEC recycling problem in perspective', *The Columbia University Journal of Business*, vol. XI, no. 3, Fall 1976, pp. 28-33.

Bello, Walden & Kingley, David 'La Politique de la Banque Mondiale a l'heure de l'ortodoxie liberale', *Le Monde Diplomatic*, September 1981, p. 3.

Bergsten, Fred 'The Threat From the Third World', *Foreign Policy*, no. XI, Summer 1973, pp. 90-107.

Bergsten, Fred 'The Response to the Third World', *Foreign Policy*, no. XVII Winter 1974, pp. 3-35.

Bruzonsky, Mark 'Are the Arabs Buying America', *The Middle East*, no. 52, February 1979, pp. 25-32.

Buckley, Robin 'Sudan Backs Development Through Foreign Loans', *African Development*, January 1975, pp. 513-14.
Burrell, R.M. 'Iranian Foreign Policy: Strategic Location, Economic Ambition, and Dynastic Determination', *Journal of International Affairs*, vol. 29, no. 2, Fall 1975, pp. 129-38.
Cambell, John C. 'The Mediterranean Crisis: OPEC and the Industrialized Countries: The Next Ten Years', *Foreign Affairs*, vol. 53, no. IV, July 1975, pp. 605-24.
Caplan, Basil 'Sudan – Acid Test for Arab Money', *The Banker*, vol. 128, no. 623, January 1978, pp. 33-7.
Caplow, Theodore 'Are the Poor Countries Getting Poorer', *Foreign Policy*, no. III, Summer 1971, pp. 90-108.
Chandavarkar, Anand G. 'Use of Migrants' Remittances in Labor-Exporting Countries', *Finance & Development*, vol. 17, no. 2, June 1980, pp. 36-9.
Chanderly, A. 'Infra-structural Development Requirements in the Arab World with Special Reference to the Arab Fund', *Oil and Arab Cooperation*, vol. 3, no. III, 1977, pp. 190-1.
Chubin, Shahram 'Iran Between the Arab West and the Asian East', *Survival*, vol. 16, no. 4, July/August 1974, pp. 172-82.
Cohen, Jean Allen & Park, Choon-Ho 'The Politics of the Oil Weapon', *Foreign Policy*, no. XX, Fall 1975, pp. 28-49.
Cooley, John K. 'The Libyan Menace', *Foreign Policy*, no. 42, Spring 1981, pp. 74-93.
Cooper, Richard N. 'A New International Economic Order', *Foreign Policy*, no. XXVI, Spring 1977, pp. 65-139.
Corm, George 'Gestes symboliques et refus persistants', *Le Monde Diplomatique*, September 1981, p. 3.
Cumming Bruce, Nick 'Need for Supply Sources Broadens World Outlook', *The Middle East Economic Digest*, vol. 19, no. 14, 4 April 1975, pp. 6-8.
Dergham, Raghide 'South Clutches at Straws to Save Dialogue', *The Middle East*, no. 70, August 1980, pp. 58-9.
Djalili, Mohammad Reza 'Evolution de la Politique Iranienne de l'Ocean Indien', *Revue Iranienne des Relations Internationalles*, no. 8, Autumn 1976, pp. 185-9.
El-Belawi, Hazem 'Petro Surpluses and the Structure of the World Economy', *Oil and Arab Cooperation*, vol. 4, no. 4, 1978, pp. 252-3.
El-Mallakh, Ragaei 'Kuwait's Economic Development and Her Foreign Aid Programmes', *World Today*, vol. 22, no. 1, January 1966, pp. 13-22.
El-Negar, Said 'The Common Commodity Fund and the Role of Arab Oil Counties in its Financing', *Oil and Arab Cooperation*, vol. 2, no. 4, 1976, pp. 97-8.
El-Zein, Y. 'The Economies of the Gulf: a Look at the Future', *The Arab Economist*, vol. 7, no. 13, February 1975, pp. 14-17.
Farmanfarmaian, K. 'How Can the World Afford OPEC Oil', *Foreign Affairs*, vol. 53, no. II, January 1975, pp. 201-22.
Fatemi, Khosrow 'Leadership by Distrust: The Shah's Modus Operandi', *The Middle East Journal*, vol. 36, no. 1, Winter 1982, pp. 48-63.
Fellowes, Peregrine 'OPEC's Aid Performance', *Middle East International*, no. 89, November 1978, pp. 17-20.
Fitzgerald, James 'Djibouti: A Petrodollar Protectorate?', *Horn of Africa*, vol. I, no. 4, October/November 1978, pp. 25-31.
Fried, Edward R. 'International Liquidity and Foreign Aid', *Foreign Affairs*, vol. 48, no. 1, October 1969, pp. 139-49.
Gail, Norman 'The Challenge of Venezuelan Oil', *Foreign Policy*, no. XX, Fall 1975, pp. 46-67.

Galbraith, John Kenneth 'A Positive Approach to Economic Aid', *Foreign Affairs*, vol. 40, no. 111, April 1961, pp. 444-57.
Ghadimipour, Fatemeh 'Les relations regionales de l'Iran avec les pays non-Arabes', *Politique Etrangere,* 41^e^ anne, no. 2, 1976, pp. 149-68.
Gonensay, Emir 'Regional Economic Cooperation as a Strategy of Development and the Middle East', *The RCD Magazine*, vol. 3, no. 2, 1976, pp. 14-37.
Grant, James P. 'Development, The End of the Trickle Down', *Foreign Policy*, no. XII, Fall 1973, pp. 43-65.
Habiby, Raymond N. 'Muamar Qadhafi's New Islamic Scientific Socialist Society', *Middle East Review*, vol. XI, no. 4, Summer 1979, pp. 32-9.
Hallwood, Paul & Sinclair, Stuart 'An Interpretation of the Economic Relationship Between OPEC And Non-oil LDCs During The 1970s', *OPEC Review*, vol. V, no. 3, Autumn 1981, pp. 98-111.
Hartman, Betsy 'McNamara's Legacy: Basic Needs Without Basic Reforms', *South, the Third World Magazine*, no. 10, August 1981, pp. 31-5.
Hellyer, Peter 'Somalia Learns How to Keep Aid Flowing from All Sides', *African Development*, September 1974, p. 37.
Herskowitz, Jean 'Democracy in Nigeria', *Foreign Affairs*, vol. 58, no. 2, pp. 314-35.
Holden, David 'The Persian Gulf: After the British Raj', *Foreign Affairs*, vol. 40, no. IV, July 1971, pp. 721-35.
Hunter, Robert E. 'Power and Peace', *Foreign Policy*, no. 9, Winter 1972-3, pp. 37-54.
Huntington, Samuel P. 'Does Foreign Aid Have a Future?', *Foreign Policy*, no. II, Spring 1971, pp. 114-34.
Huntington, Samuel P. 'Foreign Aid, for What and for Whom?', *Foreign Policy*, no. 1, Winter 1970-1, pp. 161-89.
Jakubiak, Henry E. & Dajani, M.T. 'Oil Income and Financial Policies in Iran and Saudi Arabia', *Finance and Development*, vol. 13, no. 4, December 1976, pp. 12-15.
Kasver, Stephen D. 'The Great Oil Sheikh Down', *Foreign Policy*, no. XII, Winter 1973-4, pp. 139-53.
Kelidar, Abbas 'Iraq: The Search For Stability', *Middle East Review*, vol. XI, no. 4, Summer 1979, pp. 21-6.
Khalid, Tahsin Ali 'Food Security and the Joint Arab Effort', *Oil and Arab Co-operation*, vol. 4, no. 1, 1978, pp. 258-9.
Kleinman, David 'Oil Money and the Third World', *The Banker*, vol. 124, no. 583, September 1975, pp. 1061-5.
Kucznski, Pedro Pablo 'Recycling Petro-Dollars to the Third World', *Euromoney*, November 1974, pp. 40-3.
Lambertini, Adrian 'Energy Problems of Non-OPEC Developing Countries', *Finance and Development*, vol. 13, no. 3, September 1976, pp. 24-9.
Laulan, Yves 'Recycling Oil Surpluses: Can the Banks Do It This Time?', *The Banker*, vol. 130, no. 5, 650 & 651, April/May 1980, pp. 43-8.
Lavernic, Karl 'Sudan Economic Survey: The Arab Connection', *African Development*, January 1976, pp. S11-S13.
Lavernic, Karl 'KFAED Still Sticks Close to Home', *The Middle East*, no. 67, May 1980, p. 75.
Levy, Walter J, 'World Oil Co-operation or International Chaos', *Foreign Affairs*, vol. 52, no. IV, July 1974, pp. 690-713.
Lewis, William H. 'US Debate in the Horn', *Washington Quarterly*, vol. 2, no. 3, Summer 1979, pp. 97-102.

Lycett, Andrew 'Libyans in Chad: Guests or Hosts?', *The Middle East,* no. 77, March 1981, pp. 26-8.

Mabro, Robert 'OPEC After the Oil Revolution', *Journal of International Studies,* vol. 4, no. 3, Winter 1975-6, pp. 191-9.

Mazrui, Ali A. 'Black Africa and the Arabs', *Foreign Affairs,* vol. 53, no. 4, July 1975, pp. 725-42.

McNoun, Robert &Wallace, Myles 'International Reserve Flows of OPEC States: A Monetary Approach', *The Journal of Energy and Development,* vol. II, no. 2, Spring 1977, pp. 267-79.

Mehraein, H. 'Iran and India Embark on Joint Oil Project', *Keyhan International,* 6 January 1974, p. 4.

Merklein, A. 'Mid-East Petro-dollars: Enough to Buy Corporate America?', *The Arab Economist,* vol. 7, no. 72, January 1975, pp. 36-9.

Mikdashi, Zuhayr 'Commodity Agreements and International Economic Co-operation', *OPEC Review,* vol. II, no. 4, September 1978, pp. 70-6.

Moorstein, Richard 'OPEC Can Wait, We Can't', *Foreign Policy,* no. XVIII, Spring 1975, pp. 3-11.

Mossavar-Rahmani, Bijan 'OPEC and the Indian Ocean in the 1980s', *OPEC Review,* vol. III, no. 3, Autumn 1979, pp. 66-76.

Mozafari, Mehdi 'Les Nouvelles Dimensions de la Politique Etrangere de l'Iran', *Politique Etrangere,* 40^{e} anne, no. 2, 1975, pp. 141-60.

Nahavandi, Houshang 'La politique d'independence de l'Iran', *Revue Iranienne des Relations Internationales,* no. 7, Printemps, 1976, pp. 5-18.

Nan-Guema, Marc 'Twenty-One Years of OPEC', *OPEC Bulletin,* vol. XI, no. 10, October 1981, pp. 16-26.

Nashashibi, Hikmat 'Regional Involvement for Arab Money', *The Banker,* vol. 127, no. 615, May 1977, pp. 33-7.

Nashashibi, Hikmat 'Other Ways to Recycle Oil Surpluses', *Euromoney,* August 1976, pp. 49-52.

Nashashibi, Hikmat 'Needs and Requirements for Directing Oil Financial Surpluses into Regional Arab Investments', *Oil and Arab Cooperation,* vol. 2, no. 1, Winter 1976, pp. 148-9.

Olorumfeni, M.A. 'Cooperation between OPEC and Oil Consuming Countries in Africa', *OPEC Review,* vol. I, no. 4, April 1977, pp. 20-7.

Oppenheim, V.H. 'Arab Tankers Move Downstream', *Foreign Policy,* no. XXIII, Summer 1976, pp. 117-30.

Ortiz, Rene G. 'International Relations: OPEC as a Moderating Political Force', *OPEC Review,* vol. IV, no. 2, Summer 1980, pp. 1-7.

Oweiss, Ibrahim M. 'Strategies for Arab Economic Development', *The Journal of Energy and Development,* vol. III, no. 2, Autumn 1977, pp. 103-15.

Peck, Malcolm 'Saudi Arabia's Wealth: a Two-Edged Sword', *New Middle East,* no. 40, January 1972, pp. 5-7.

Peek, Gail L. 'A New Twist to Afro-Arab Relations', *Middle East Review,* vol. XI, no. 3, Spring 1979, pp. 34-8.

Perera, Judith 'Together Against the Red Peril: Iran and Saudi Arabia, Rivals for Super-Power Role', *The Middle East,* no. 43, May 1978, pp. 16-25.

Pindyck, Robert S. 'OPEC's Threat to the West', *Foreign Policy,* no. XXX, Spring 1978, pp. 36-52.

Quandt, William B. 'Saudi Arabia: Security and Foreign Policy in the 1980s', *Middle East Insight,* vol. II, no. 2, January/February 1982, pp. 25-30.

Qudsi, al Hursam 'OPEC, LDCs Back in Tune at Money Talks', *The Middle East,* no. 72, October 1980, pp. 65-6.

Rake, Allan 'Arab League and Africa Special', *African Development,* July 1975, pp. AL4-AL14.

Ramazani, Rouhallah 'Iran's Search for Regional Cooperation', *The Middle East Journal*, vol. Spring 1976, pp. 173-86.
Raphael, Arnold 'Arab Aid to Africa: Arab Oil Wealth Starts to Flow in Africa', *African Development,* May 1975, pp. 24-8.
Rasheed, Jamal 'Far-East Wooing by the Saudis', *8 Days, Middle East Business,* vol. 3, no. 14, 11 April 1981, pp. 22-3.
Regard, J. 'L'Iran et ses Petro-dollars', *Notes et Etudes Documantaires,* nos. 4188-4189, Mai 1975, pp. 6-78.
Robinson, Nicholas 'The Role of Oil Funds Recycling in International Payments and Adjustment Problems', *OPEC Review,* vol. IV, no. 2, Summer 1980, pp. 98-109.
Rondot, Philippe 'L'Iraq: une Puissance Regionale en Devenir', *Politique Etrangere,* 45^{e} anne, no. 3, September 1980, pp. 637-52.
Roque, Germain 'The Non-aligned Summit: Collective Self-Reliance', *Development Dialogue,* 1976, no. 1, pp. 61-6.
Sakr, Naomi 'OPEC Donors may Rethink Piggyback Approach', *The Middle East,* no. 52, February 1979, pp. 90-1.
Sami, C. 'The Energy Crisis and After: an OPEC View', *Petroleum Review,* no. 28, May 1974, pp. 323-35.
Sarkis, Nicholas 'Oil, Europe and the Arab World', *Arab Oil and Gas Journal,* vol. 6, no. 145, January 1977, pp. 21-4.
Serageldin, Ismail & Socknat, James 'Migration and Manpower Needs in the Middle East', *Finance and Development,* vol. 17, no. 4, December 1980, pp. 32-6.
Shihata, Ibrahim F.I. 'The Working Relationship Between the OPEC Special Fund and Other Development Finance Institutions', *OPEC Review,* vol. II, no. 3, Autumn 1978, pp. 5-14.
Shihata, Ibrahim F.I. 'The OPEC Fund for International Development – The First Five Years', *OPEC Review,* vol. V, no. 3, Autumn 1981, pp. 1-8.
Shihata, Ibrahim F.I. 'Aid Strategy for Sub-Saharan Africa', *OPEC Bulletin,* vol. XIII, no. 3, April 1982, pp. 1-6.
Singer, Fred S. 'Limits to Arabs' Oil Power', *Foreign Policy,* no. XXX, Spring 1978, pp. 53-67.
Sing, Shasher 'The Aftermath of 1974: A World Bank View', *OPEC Review,* vol. II, no. 2, April 1978, pp. 21-31.
Spence, Allen 'The Middle East and the New International Economic Order', *The Middle East,* no. 44, June 1978, pp. 125-8.
Soulie, G.J.L. & Champenois, L. 'La Politique Exterieure de l'Arabie Saoudite', *Politique Etrangere,* 42^{e} anne, no. 6, 1977, pp. 601-23.
Stewart, Frances 'Country Experience in Providing for Basic Needs', *Finance and Development,* vol. 17, no. 3, September 1980, pp. 11-14.
Sturg, Ernest 'The Trust Fund', *Finance & Development,* vol. 13, no. 4, December 1977, pp. 30-2.
Sultan, Ataf 'OPEC is Backing Brandt', *The Middle East,* no. 83, September 1981, p. 7.
Terzian 'Les surplus petroliers des pays de l'OPEP: Bilan et perspective', *Le Petrole et le Gaz Arabe,* no. 9, lre Mais 1977, pp. 20-3.
Thorn, Phillip 'IMF Policy: Medicine Now Better Than Surgery Later', *The Middle East,* no. 45, July 1978, p. 71.
Thorp, Willard L. 'Foreign Aid: A Report on the Reports', *Foreign Affairs,* vol. 48, no. III, April 1970, pp. 561-73.
Tomeh, George 'OPEC; its Growing Role in Arab and World Affairs', *The Journal of Energy and Development,* vol. III, no. 1, Autumn 1978, pp. 26-37.
Tran, Mark 'Saudi Arabia Enters the Real World', *The Middle East,* no. 79, May 1981, pp. 48-9.

Truell, Peter 'Scoring Points over Aid', *The Middle East,* no. 79, pp. 47-8.
Turner, Louis & Bedore, James 'The Power of the Purse String', *International Affairs,* vol. 54, July 1978, pp. 405-21.
Ul-Haq, Mahbub 'Changing Emphasis on the Bank's Lending Policies'. *Finance & Development,* vol. 15, no. 2, June 1978, pp. 12-14.
Ul-Haq, Mahbub 'An International Perspective on Basic Needs', *Finance & Development,* vol. 17, no. 3, September 1980, pp. 11-14.
Van Hollen, Christopher 'North Yemen: A Dangerous Pentagonal Game', *Washington Quarterly,* vol. 5, no. 3, Summer 1982, pp. 137-42.
Wassa-Wassef, Ceres 'L'Arabie Saoudite et le Conflit Israelo-Arabe', *Politique Etrangere,* 39[e] anne, no. 2, 1976, pp. 185-200.
Watt, Donald C. 'Can the Union of Arab Emirates Survive?', *The World Today,* vol. XXVII, no. 4, April 1974, pp. 144-7.
Weintraub, Sidney 'Saudi Arabia's Role in the International Markets', *Middle East Review,* vol. X, no. 4, Summer 1978, pp. 16-20.
Williams, Maurice J. 'The Aid Programs of the OPEC Countries', *Foreign Affairs,* vol. 54, no. 1, January 1976, pp. 308-24.
Williams, Maurice J. 'The Development Challenge of Today: Meeting the Basic Needs of the Poorest People', *The OECD Observer,* no. 89, November 1977, pp. 17-22.
Wright, Claudia 'Iraq – New Power in the Middle East', *Foreign Affairs,* vol. 58, no. II, Winter 1979-80, pp. 257-77.
Yamani, Zaki 'Oil and the World Economy', *Middle East Economic Survey,* vol. XIX, no. 8, 12 December 1975, pp. 6-7.
Yamani, Zaki 'Legitimate Interests of Oil Exporting Countries', *MEES*, vol. XIX, no. 8, 12 December 1975, pp. 2-6.
Yamani, Zaki 'Changing Patterns of World Oil Supplies', *MEES*, vol. XXI, no. 39, July 1978.
Yeganeh, Mohammad 'OPEC Special Fund: An Illustration of Solidarity with the Third World', *OPEC Review,* vol. I, no. 4, April 1977, pp. 3-10.
Zabih, Sepher 'Iran's International Posture: De Facto Non-Alignment within a Por-Western Alliance', *The Middle East Journal,* vol. 24, no. 3, Summer 1970, pp. 302-18.
Zaki, Abbas Hassan 'Arab Financial Institutions and a New Financial Market', *Euromoney,* July 1974, pp. 52-4.

Special Reports, Surveys and Other Miscellaneous Works

1. *MEED Special Reports*

Iran	February 1977
Libya	February 1977
Iraq	June 1977
Sudan	August 1977
Egypt	May 1978
Saudi Arabia	August 1978
UAE	December 1978
Banking & Finance	March 1979
Construction	April 1979
Saudi Arabia	June 1979
Bahrain	July 1979
Qatar	November 1979
Kuwait	February 1980
Arab Banking	May 1980
Malta	May 1980

UAE	October 1980
Oman	November 1980
Saudi Arabia	July 1981
Qatar	August 1981
UAE	November 1981

2. *Financial Times Surveys.*

Kuwait	25 February 1980
Saudi Arabia	28 April 1980

3. *Commonwealth Secretariat.*

Towards a New International Economic Order, a final report by a Commonwealth experts' group, London, 1977; 104 p.

4. *Dag Hammarskjöld Foundation.*

Another Development. The 1975 Hammarskjöld Report on Development and International Cooperation, 128 p.

5. *The International Institute for Strategic Studies.*

Military Balance. 1974-80 issues.

Soviet Dilemma in the Middle East: Part II. *Oil and the Persian Gulf,* by Robert E. Hunter, Adelphi Paper, no. 60, October 1969, 18 p.

The Middle East and the International System. I *The Impact of the 1973 War,* Adelphi Paper, no. 114, September 1974; 40 p.

The Middle East and the International System. II. *Security and the Energy Crisis,* Adelphi Paper, no. 115, September 1974; 41 p.

Saudi-Arabia's Search for Security, by Adeed Dawisha, Adelphi Paper no. 158, Winter 1979-80, 36 p.

6. *Institute for the Study of Conflict.*

Libya's Foreign Adventures, by Brian Crozier, Conflict Studies no. 41, 1973; 16 p.

7. *Trilateral Commission.*

OPEC, the Trilateral World and the Developing Countries: New Arrangements for Cooperation, 1976-1980, a report of the trilateral task force on relations with developing countries to the Executive Committee by: R.N. Gardner, Saburo Okita, and B.J. Udnik, 1975; 32p.

8. *Area Handbooks of the American University Foreign Area Studies.*

Algeria, Washington, DC, Government Printing Office, 1972, 330 p.

Iran, Washington, DC, Government Printing Office, 1978; xxviii-442 p.

Algeria, Washington, DC, Government Printing Office, 1979; xxi-320 p.

Libya, Washington, DC, Government Printing Office, 1979; xxviii-250 p.

Persian Gulf States, Washington, DC, Government Printing Office, 1977, 407 p.

Saudi Arabia, Washington, DC, Government Printing Office, 1977; xiv-389 p.

INDEX